PENGUIN B
THE RETURN OF A NATIVE REPORTER

Robert Chesshyre was born during the war. He has a degree in English from Oxford, where he was editor of the university newspaper, *Cherwell*. After short periods on the *Morning Telegraph*, Sheffield, and the *Sunday Citizen* (both now no longer published), he joined the *Observer* in 1967 and was with the newspaper for over twenty years. During the 1970s he was news editor and home editor. Apart from his posting to Washington, DC, he has also been Northern Irish correspondent and 'Notebook' and Pendennis columnist. He is now a freelance writer.

ROBERT CHESSHYRE

THE RETURN OF
A NATIVE REPORTER

PENGUIN BOOKS

For Christine, Thomas, Edward and Kate

PENGUIN BOOKS

Published by the Penguin Group
27 Wrights Lane, London w8 5TZ, England
Viking Penguin Inc., 40 West 23rd Street, New York, New York 10010, USA
Penguin Books Australia Ltd, Ringwood, Victoria, Australia
Penguin Books Canada Ltd, 2801 John Street, Markham, Ontario, Canada L3R 1B4
Penguin Books (NZ) Ltd, 182–190 Wairau Road, Auckland 10, New Zealand
Penguin Books Ltd, Registered Offices: Harmondsworth, Middlesex, England

First published by Viking 1987
Published in Penguin Books, with a new Afterword, 1988

Copyright © Robert Chesshyre, 1987, 1988
All rights reserved

Made and printed in Great Britain by
Richard Clay Ltd, Bungay, Suffolk
Filmset in Monophoto Sabon

CONTENTS

Acknowledgements
6

1. 'The Poverty of Their Own Desires'
9

2. 'My Wife Would Never Leave Surrey'
34

3. 'On Yer Bike'
61

4. It's No Go the Milkman
89

5. Serious Money
117

6. By the Sweat of Our Brows
141

7. Boom and Gloom
166

8. The 'New Jerusalem'
190

9. A Little Learning
219

10. 'A Plastic Lollipop'
245

11. 'We Are Here to Protect Our Own'
267

12. Damn Yanks
292

Afterword:
Moaning Minnies and Montrachet
321

ACKNOWLEDGEMENTS

A large number of people not only helped me with this book, but also spared me a great deal of their time. Most of them will recognize their contributions even when – usually by their own request – they and their quotations appear anonymously. (Only one person put such obstacles in my way that I failed to see him, and only one other suggested she should be paid for her trouble.) The major pleasure of being a journalist is that the vast majority of people are not only prepared to talk to a wandering reporter, but are often generous with their hospitality and with their views. I have enjoyed enormously rediscovering Britain largely through the eyes and minds of the people I interviewed, and, although I have covered some of the world's great happenings, I remain convinced there is nothing of such interest and compulsive fascination as the affairs that touch our daily lives and shape the country we live in. I thank, therefore, everyone I spoke with for their stimulating assistance and good company.

I would like also to thank the *Observer*, my benign employer for many years past. If the paper had not sent me to the United States, I could not have returned, and there would, therefore, have been no book. I am grateful to the editor, Donald Trelford, for giving me the opportunity to go to Washington DC, and for allowing me the time to research and write the book when I came back.

Finally, I would like to thank Tony Lacey, my editor at Viking, for support and enthusiasm far beyond the call of duty, and my agent Gill Coleridge, of Anthony Sheil Associates, for her encouragement, optimism and advice.

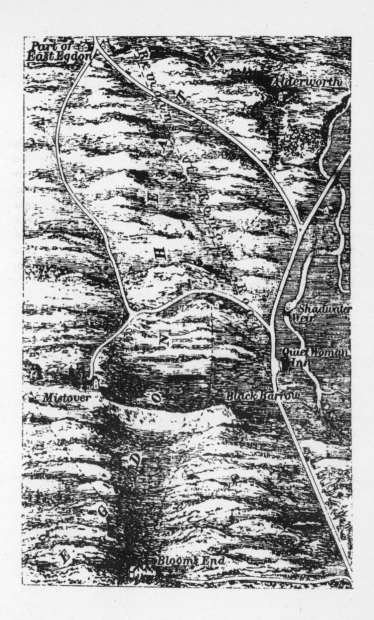

❧(1)❧

'THE POVERTY OF THEIR
OWN DESIRES'

It was 7.00 a.m., not a good hour when one has just flown the Atlantic economy class. I was stiff from spending eight hours in a seat like a straightjacket, shivery from lack of sleep, and vaguely queasy from inhaling the stale air that gathers in a Jumbo towards the end of a long flight. Half the lavatories, as ever, had been out of action, and somnambulant passengers had lined the aisles from the Irish coast till the seatbelt sign went on. Our sense of slumming it had been rubbed in by the occupation of the first-class cabin by mail bags and their escort of two security men slumbering in the wide luxury of their seats. That put *us* in our places. But if there is one thing worse than travelling through the night, it is the chaos of arriving before dawn.

'BRITISH RAIL WELCOMES YOU TO GATWICK' read a big sign; 'London Victoria, trains depart every 15 minutes'. It was still dark, and a cutting wind drove along the buried platforms as if propelled by icy bellows. Someone – vandals? British Rail itself? – had skilfully removed the seats: the holes where the bolts had been showed mockingly in the tarmac. A loudspeaker barked: 'British Rail regrets . . .' It was one of those deliberately articulated third-person announcements that make the inefficiencies of public transport appear like acts of God. Not one but three Victoria express trains had been cancelled.

I had always enjoyed coming home. I recalled – as our train, filling with unknown yet familiar people, pursued its slow way towards London – the contentment I had felt as a small boy more than thirty years earlier when flying into Northolt Airport aboard a *DC-3* of British European Airways. Then, as the plane made its approach, I had peered with high excitement to catch sight of the red-tiled roofs

of Middlesex suburbia, which – drear though they might have been –
to me were like a lighthouse to the returning sailor, the first glimpse
of an anxiously sought land. My parents lived then in France, and it
was a journey I had made three times a year for three years to return
to school in England, and I had never been disappointed. My last,
very much more recent, return had also been great pleasure – a sun-
filled August holiday in a borrowed house on Richmond Hill. But this
was my first journey to Britain for two years, and shortly I was to
resume living at home again after an absence of nearly four years.

Nothing could have tested my nerve more than arriving on a commuter train at the height of the rush-hour on a bleak, cold February
morning. Commuting everywhere depresses the spirit; passengers
exist in limbo, their personalities temporarily on hold. Once the
obviously resented disruption of the air travellers – several of them
over-apologetic Americans whose tartan bags blocked the gangway –
and their luggage had been absorbed, that morning's London-bound
workers resumed their quotidian routine. The elderly dozed, the
young listened to headphones, from which the 'boom-de-boom'
rhythm of percussion leaked, and those of in-between years read
newspapers suitable to their station in life.

Looking round, I realized with a shock that, although I had been
living in the United States for over three years, I could none the less
make a shrewd guess at the circumstances of most of my fellow travellers – their education, their income, their prejudices, their place in
the pecking order, even perhaps where they took their holidays. It
was not something I had been able to do in the States – neither,
several friends told me later, could Americans – and I had grown
accustomed to being amongst people less easy to read. George
Orwell, in his study of *The English People* written after the Second
World War, had reached a similar conclusion: 'The great majority of
the people can still be "placed" in an instant by their manners,
clothes and general appearance.' The reminder that so little had
changed was both comforting and alarming. I had been stimulated by
living in an unpredictable and – by me at least – still largely unex-
plored society, but I had missed deeply the sense of belonging, of
being amongst familiar, small-scale landscapes and buildings, of
being with people whose outlook had been shaped by the same
influences as mine had been, and of being wrapped in history and
traditions that stretched in the mind's eye back almost to the
beginning of recorded time. I had, I confess, briefly considered

staying in the States and seeking a further job there, but it had been a whim rather than a serious exploration of the idea. The United States had been an adventure, but Britain was home.

That Gatwick arrival was in fact the start of a preliminary visit, rather than my eventual return. I had gone ahead to scout out the territory for myself and my family; inspect our house; warn local head teachers to expect our children; dip a toe into office politics. We were due to return permanently six months later from Washington DC, where I had been the *Observer*'s correspondent. But this for me was the psychological moment of re-entry. From now on the questions for which there had been little time for thought for three and a half years would become incessant. What kind of a country was I returning to? What was the future for my children – at school and after? Had the British found cohesion and direction under Mrs Thatcher's leadership? Were we a more open society? Were we less class-ridden? Were we still compassionate and tolerant? And, for me personally, how long would it take for the momentum of the United States to slow? Spies who had gone ahead, other Britons returning either to live or on holiday, deeply imbued with the expatriate outlook, had sent back dismal dispatches of overcrowding, filth, sour attitudes, inefficient shops and services, vandalism. (Twelve months later it took Mrs Thatcher a mere week in Israel to be sufficiently struck on her return by the physical squalor of the country she had then ruled for seven years to summon Richard Branson and order a national clean-up. Nearly twelve months after that, as I write this, the place is just as filthy.)

However, there was another national characteristic which I feared more than the physical squalor that I knew awaited: if anything dampened my enthusiasm for home, it was, without doubt, British insularity. Watching the commuters that morning; eavesdropping on conversations about late trains – 'I went for the five-oh-seven last night, but they'd cancelled it'; the perils of winter holidays abroad – 'the change in temperature's too great. You come back and within a few days get a stinking cold'; I felt a degree of panic. A study of the news-stand at Gatwick Airport had brought to mind Ernest Bevin's observation of forty years earlier that 'the working class had been crucified on the poverty of their own desires'. The papers carried front-page headlines about Princess Michael; stories on football thugs; pictures of royal children; hue and cry over 'sex fiends'; stories about 'Dirty Den', a television character rather than a sex fiend; one tabloid led its front page with a 'he deceived me' story about a professional footballer. A hurried perusal of the shelves turned up six magazines with front-page pictures of Princess Diana. Little had changed, certainly not the names. Little had changed either, so I was to discover, at the 'serious' end of public affairs. I woke on my first morning to a sycophantic radio interview with a complacent junior minister, bound to his interlocutor by a cosy conspiracy of first-name terms. Apart from Mrs Thatcher herself, there appeared then to be only three figures in British public life whose opinions were worth airing – Roy Hattersley, Norman Tebbit and (most over-exposed of all) David Owen – who were interviewed on every topic that arose, appeared, often together, on every discussion show, wrote leader-page articles, and between them set the national agenda. There was only one man of greater national consequence, Terry Wogan, the apotheosis of the prevailing national infatuation with glitz. (I am writing this eighteen months later, and the national appetite for inconsequential distraction remains insatiable. The *Star*, the most woeful of all our papers, yesterday 'splashed' with a massive picture of Princess Diana meeting the cast of 'EastEnders' – the ultimate 'pop paper' story.)

These were the symbolic irritations of coming from a capital city where events of real significance to the world took place, to one that had lost its power, but not all its delusions. In its obsession over the royal family, the nation seemed to have taken leave of its senses: 'What's it all in aid of?' a character in John Osborne's *The Entertainer* had asked nearly thirty years earlier. 'Is it really just for the sake of a gloved hand waving at you from a golden coach?' The answer, it appeared, was an emphatic 'Yes'.

The other, countervailing, national obsession was, without doubt, 'yobbism'. Inner city districts had become 'no go' areas for milkmen, council workers, postmen, social workers, and (though they denied it) the police. The respectable poor trapped in these horrific zones lived nightmare lives, locked indoors after dark, mugged on their way to buy food, with drug addicts on their landings, and human excrement on their stairways. The yobs themselves emerged into public view when they travelled from one ghetto to another to support soccer teams. They were vicious, ignorant, cruel, unemployable, drunk, criminal, uncaring, anti-social, beyond the pale.

The questions, as Britain struggled to come to terms with this monstrous alienation, were who was responsible and what had gone wrong? The denim-clad yobbo, with his narrow horizons and anti-

social activities, was the ugly symbol of a society that had failed to fulfil its benign aspirations. The right-wing, led by Tebbit, blamed the
permissive sixties: the left-wing blamed the hopelessness of the yobs'
stunted lives under Thatcherism. The middle classes had begun to
build American-style ghettos: a friend had just bought a flat in a 'safe'
area behind electronic gates – symbolically within view of the Chelsea Football Club 'shed', a yob citadel. The only native industry with
boom potential, said one wit, was burglar alarms. Surprising though
it seemed to friends reared on stories of American crime and violence,
where we had lived in Washington we had seldom locked our car
doors at night; and neighbours went on short holidays leaving their
front door unlocked.

A wise temporary expatriate might take the precaution of living
with the implications of pending return to his native land throughout
his years abroad, taking them out of mental storage occasionally, and
pondering upon them. I didn't. The new life in the United States
drove out the old. I had had time for only the occasional glance over
my shoulder at Britain. Of course, I missed family and friends, and
the easy familiarity of being with people with whom one can take up
after years as if one had simply left the room to put on the kettle. But
the regret I anticipated at the loss of small pleasures – cricket, English
beer, the countryside – faded swiftly before the impact of new preoccupations. (I never dreamed that baseball could take the place of
cricket, but eventually it did.) Living abroad, even in an English-
speaking country, was akin to plunging into a foreign language and
allowing one's own, perforce, to grow rusty. Coming home, one had
to learn again the native idiom.

I knew the aspects of American life I was going to miss – the optimism, the classlessness. It is a canard, put about by apologists for the
British class system, that the United States is a class-ridden society,
with snobberies undreamed of even by the English. There are small
pockets of virulent class, money and 'who-do-you-know?' con-
sciousness, but they mean nothing to most Americans – the wide
variety of the country, the feeling renewed almost every morning that
anything is possible means that for 70 per cent of Americans equality
of opportunity is a reality: they are launched into life with enormously positive impulses. Virtually every child stays in school until
he is eighteen: to leave sooner is to be branded a 'drop-out'. An
English schoolteacher, who had worked for many years in the States,
wrote to me that in American schools one factor was common, 'that

was a desire to learn, to get ahead (not always perhaps in a manner of which you and I might approve), but the drive was there. And of course class distinction – still nauseously rife throughout Britain – was non-existent.' In our Washington neighbourhood, packed with successful migrants from every corner of the States, educational and 'class' differences not only did not matter, but also were all but invisible.

Michael Davie, an *Observer* colleague, researching his book on the *Titanic*, interviewed descendants of the survivors of the two working-class groups on board the liner – the steerage emigrants from Italy, Russia and Ireland and the British crew. Seventy years on, the grandchildren of the first group were to be found in law practices, corporate management, doctors' offices across the United States; the stokers' grandchildren were still living in terraced houses on the back streets of Southampton and Liverpool – only now there are no ships left to stoke. Britain was still a nation of village Hampdens and mute inglorious Miltons.

I was, of course, aware of the harsh realities at the bottom of American society. Under Ronald Reagan, as under Mrs Thatcher, poverty and genuine destitution have grown sharply. As a child I had often wondered what it would have been like to be a Victorian, when the gap between rich and poor was so great. By the time I left America, in some part at least I knew. Other American 'immigrants' – those brought in slave ships from Africa – had not fared as well as the *Titanic* survivors. Inner city and rural black people are not among the 70 per cent of equal citizens. A 'southern' city like Washington is still effectively segregated in many ways. Fellow workers go home at six o'clock to different parts of the town. A study carried out shortly before I left found that a distinctive black argot was becoming more common in urban ghettos. Many black children have not spoken with a white person by the time they go to school. Homeless kids go hungry, and grimy vagrants roam the streets of major cities, cheek by jowl with some of the most affluent people in the world. Many black people are wealthy, but the majority – except those blessed with supreme sporting talents – are still locked out of the American Dream.

In Washington, I had toyed with the idea of starting a business, which in retrospect was little more than a *jeu d'esprit*. However, I mentioned it to my accountant while he was doing my dreary (and to him piffling) tax returns. Immediately he came alive, thrusting the tax bumph to one side. Where were the premises? What was the pedestrian 'traffic'? 'How much capital could I raise?' I said I had a modest London suburban home. 'Good, sell it.' He called another client in the same line of business to organize a meeting. My problem, he was telling me within twenty minutes, was going to be keeping my eye on the ball once the business was up and running. One had to be careful of managers. That night, at a party, I told the story to a man I knew slightly – mainly through having children at the same school. He was in the head-hunting business, but apparently also had access to venture capital. How much would I need to get launched? My best guess was $100,000. 'I could raise you $200,000 within seven days.' 'On what basis?' 'Because I know you.' If I had told my English accountant that I was thinking of starting a business, he would probably have called for men in white coats. But, at the very least, like a detective warning me of my rights, he would have pointed out that I had no experience of that or of any other sort of business; that four out of five new businesses go bust within two years; that by selling my home, I would ensure not only that I would be bankrupt, but that my family would be homeless.

The American bond is the pursuit of success. Reagan could state without being howled down: 'What I want to see above all else is that this country remains a country where someone can always get rich. That's the thing we have, and that must be preserved.' What he meant was not just the log-cabin-to-mansion American Dream of writers such as Horatio Alger, but something like the pioneer concept of the right to bear arms. Individual wealth in the American mind is a defence against tyranny. Reagan would probably replace 'the pursuit of happiness' in the American Constitution with 'the pursuit of riches'.

I knew that whatever Thatcherism might have achieved in bringing greater efficiency to British industry, it could not in so short a time have changed the fundamental nature of a deeply cautious and anti-entrepreneurial people. In simple terms, an American, watching a Cadillac drive by, is likely to say to himself, 'In ten years I'll have one of those'; a Briton, seeing a Rolls-Royce, will spit and say, 'Bloody capitalist'. (He'd probably be wrong: it was no doubt bought with inherited money, still the largest source of wealth in a country in which, when it was last counted, 1 per cent owned 21 per cent of the wealth, and 50 per cent owned 93 per cent of the national goodies, which doesn't leave a great deal for the rest.) A Washingtonian in a full-time job – on Capitol Hill, in an attorney's office, as a journalist – may well have a part-time commercial interest, a share perhaps in a restaurant, or be expanding his options, like one White House reporter I knew who was taking a business course. A British middle-manager will sit tight in his job, and carry on commuting, unlikely to do anything bold unless his hand is forced, as it increasingly has been, by impending redundancy. 'Sit on your arse for fifty years and hang your hat on a pension,' wrote Louis MacNeice, and it is ever so.

I knew all this, and the Gatwick journey had reminded me, if I needed it, that I was returning to an overcrowded, dirty, sluggish corner of Europe. 'Isn't everything small?' my children said when they returned. The road at the bottom of our street is designated the 'South Circular', and bears all the through traffic from south London to the west (and back again): it is an ordinary shopping street, two carriageways wide, narrower than one of the suburban roads we had lived on in Washington. The London 'supermarket' seemed Lilliputian, with inadequate space between the aisles, and a pathetic square foot on which to heap intended purchases. Washington garages were bigger than London living rooms.

Britain had obviously been changed by the often dramatic events of the previous four years. One assumption that I had been raised on – that no Government would long survive if unemployment rose above one million – was dead and buried. Weren't you surprised, several leftish acquaintances asked, not to find Britain in flames? No, I could answer in all honesty. We may have begun to hate with a frightening intensity those with whom we disagree, but we will endure real privations with bovine patience. Orwell had watched the poor coping with the Great Depression: 'Instead of raging against their destiny, they have made things tolerable by lowering their standards.'

But what I was not ready for was the deterioration in the daily quality of life, in people's tolerance for each other. The national cohesion that had been built so painstakingly in the post-war years was fragmenting fast. People were harder, more selfish, less caring, less 'wet'. The hard right had captured not just the political high ground, but also the 'intellectual' and moral high ground. Whatever the economic gains of Thatcherism, they appeared to carry a high human price tag. To be poor was to have failed: pensioners and the unemployed, drawing their money from the Post Office, were a legitimate object of scorn, even hatred, to the stamp-buying classes who read Auberon Waugh. Comfortable Britain did not wish to know of the privations of these failures. Waugh himself wrote that 'those of us who live in happier circumstances would prefer to forget, or at any rate shelve [society's backwaters], just as we tend to forget or shelve the daily horrors of life in Chile or the Soviet Union'.

There had been stirring events while we were gone. The Falklands war had been fought and won – an enterprise for which I had little stomach but for which I none the less found myself congratulated in America. (I was also congratulated, even less logically, on the birth of Prince William. Strangers in lifts, hearing my English accent, would grip me by the hand or slap my shoulder. It seemed churlish to say that I had nothing to do with either triumph.) Mrs Thatcher, who did enter my life from time to time when she came to lecture Ronnie (on one occasion at Camp David it was reliably reported that she spoke for forty minutes without the Great Communicator getting a word in), had been re-elected with a wondrous majority. Miners had staged their futile strike against the forces of history, bringing the worst out of themselves and out of Mrs Thatcher. Teachers, reflecting the sour spirit of the times, had withdrawn their enthusiasm, which, in many cases, appeared likely to remain withdrawn. And the political leaders of Liverpool and certain London boroughs had retracted their consent to be governed, plunging their communities into anarchy and destitution.

All this I had seen through foreign eyes, taking my news from the American papers, which had treated the Falklands like a Gilbert and Sullivan revival. The American superpower cheered itself hoarse at the sight of British fighting men sailing halfway round the world to defend the sovereignty of inhospitable rocks. (Not for them the cynicism of Jorge Luis Borges: 'It's like two bald men fighting over a comb.') Lord Carrington – much admired in the States for his aristocratic sang-froid – actually resigned, an acceptance of responsibility almost unknown in Washington. Maggie's war was like a clarion call from another age.

American journalists headed for the British pub, where they found all manner of wondrous British dramatis personae who knew what was wanted of them. 'When I was a lad, England was a large, powerful country,' analysed a factory inspector, 'now we're not.' The report continued: 'He spoke, caressing a pint of beer. Then he looked up sharply, "If Churchill was still in the Government, there'd have been some trouble," he said with conviction.' There had been a certain amount of trouble even without Churchill. A reporter on *The New York Times* travelled to Cornwall, where he found Heather Crosbie: 'white-haired and pink-cheeked, who put down her glasses and said she was "shattered." Sitting in her little whitewashed Cornish inn, with a swan floating silently past on the creek outside, she told a visitor that she and her friends had "never thought it would come to this, in our day, over something so very far away."' Little old ladies, lovable cockneys, who chided the Yanks for being late once again, stout-hearted yeomen who wouldn't take an Argie invasion lying down: this was the Britain of Pinewood Studios, of the tourist posters. An expatriate would have to be abroad for a lifetime to swallow that lot.

But once the bunting had been taken down, and the United States had staged its own little island triumph with the invasion of Grenada, the American media returned to another image. 'BRITAIN IN THE 1980s: PORTRAIT OF A SOCIETY IN DECLINE' ran the headline over a long analysis in *The New York Times*. I began to notice that the word 'decline' was seldom far from the word 'Britain' in headlines. The articles were built with common materials – union bloody-mindedness, wooden-headed management, idle, unmotivated workers, antiquated technology, loss of empire, loss of pride, ridiculous class barriers. The aristocracy were no longer quaint: Britain had become impoverished and backward, the industrialized community's first candidate for Third World status. Mrs Thatcher was depicted as right-minded and tough, but overwhelmed or betrayed by the frailties and intransigence of her people.

By the time I returned, the focus had become sharper. 'A DIVIDED SOCIETY' had become the new headline over stories which drew comparisons between north and south, between private and public, between rich and poor. 'The contrasts', wrote one journalist, beneath the headline 'LUXURY AND BLEAKNESS IN BRITAIN', 'are stark in Britain today ... wealth pouring into central London fuels a real estate boom to rival anything in New York or Boston. Estate agents talk of family houses, nothing special, going for the pound equivalent of $1 million and up. The shops have never seemed so full of luxuries. But in the North of England, only 150 miles from London, the unemployed loiter in bleak streets.'

Britain was being painted as a country that had not just lost its way, but had also lost its charms. Transatlantic television audiences were horrified by the nightly violence and hatred of the miners' strike. Institutions that liberal Americans admired, like the health service and universities, were reported to be cracking up. This decline, said the writer quoted above, 'has led middle-class people increasingly to seek private substitutes'. The Heysel Stadium disaster, when Liverpool football fans ran amok and dozens were killed, added a further unpalatable dimension. British youth had become violent and antisocial. Dan Rather, the anchorman for CBS News, argued in an emotional (and self-righteous) broadcast that Americans should no longer look to Britain for leadership in civilized values.

Only seven years earlier, another American journalist, Bud Nossiter, had concluded a posting to London with a book with the title of *Britain: A Future That Works*. In 1978 Nossiter thought we had it right – first into the industrial revolution and first out. Such priorities had seemed sane then: better to fish on a Saturday morning than to bust a gut earning overtime payments. That was the theory that had been cosily adopted since the discovery that the inefficient manufacturing industries of Britain could not compete internationally. Perhaps we would not have as many television sets as the Japanese, cars as the Germans, or such fine homes as the Americans, but we would muddle through, feeling superior to those regimented foreign workers. Services – they were the answer – pop music, fashion and banking. Something would come along.

My generation – I was born during the Second World War – had subscribed to the Nossiter thesis. It did seem possible to live well without unseemly effort. There was a further assumption: Britain was moving, even though more slowly than most would have wished, towards certain shared goals. An unparalleled spirit of common purpose had been created by war and austerity – we, the British people, were, at last, all in it together. This time, unlike the twenties – 'homes fit for heroes', and all that – we would not squander our chances. The welfare state and the mixed economy underpinned fundamental expectations. Everything was going to get better. The 'something' that Edward VIII when Prince of Wales had so quixotically wanted was at last being done: slum dwellers were moved to live amongst green fields; children were liberated from satanic secondary-modern schools; working-class families swopped Blackpool for the Costa del Sol; cars all but replaced trains and buses. Full employment for those who wished to work and the abolition of poverty were taken for granted. We may, as the historian Corelli Barnett has argued, have been putting the cart before the horse, creating Utopia before we had created the means to pay for it, but we had a great deal of collective sin to expiate – child labour, sweat shops, slums, the Great Depression – and we wished to get on with it.

People would become healthier, better educated, more cultured; class divisions would erode, creating a modern, technocratic, meritocratic society, softened by retaining the best of our traditions. It was unwise to take it too far – unwise to take anything too far: look at the Swedes with their high suicide rate – but forty years after the war there would be in Britain a new society as close to an earthly paradise as flawed humanity could achieve. As people became healthier, the cost of the National Health Service (the NHS) would diminish; as schools improved, there would cease to be a market for fee-paying education. Owning the means of production would instil diligence and pride into the working man. Britain would never again be a world power, but we could show the rest of the world the middle way between the materialism of the United States and the dismal, totalitarian equality of the Soviet Union. Equality of opportunity would be a reality – scholarship boys like playwright Dennis Potter and television presenter Brian Walden had broken from their under-privileged redoubts to the commanding heights; now every girl and boy of ability would pour through the breach.

It was taken on trust that British institutions, the British political system and the consensus that underpinned them could deliver the society desired by British people. But the fractured, disagreeable seventies disabused people. Consensus was buried; the British people had lost their way and lived in a Britain without maps. Mrs Thatcher was elected in the hope that a determined woman who knew her mind could restore the certainties we, the British people, had mislaid. With varying degrees of enthusiasm we came to terms with a new realism. Managing directors could no longer seal chronically unproductive agreements with their workforces before lunch, and then head for the golf course. Workers could no longer expect a measurable rise in living standards each year, and start washing an hour before the bell rang. Fishing on Saturday mornings after all bore a heavy price tag. While I was in Washington DC, Britain for the first time began to import more manufactured goods than she exported. In the autumn of 1985, a House of Lords committee forecast the collapse of manufacturing, which, it said, would be followed – once North Sea oil is exhausted – by virtual national bankruptcy, bringing with it social and political turmoil.

However, although by the time I returned very little was any longer being manufactured in Britain that you could eat off, sit on, drive, watch or listen to, money was being made in some mysterious way. Nightly, in between the City scandals, financial reporters told of fresh Stock Exchange records. The old folk who used to live on our street had mainly been replaced by yuppies. There were Mercedes, BMWs, Audis outside many homes (most of them are company perks); it was hard to park at night; neighbourhood car pools swept children away to fee-paying academies; quite modest homes changed hands for sums that a decade earlier would have made someone very rich. Such wealth seemed unreal: what was being done to justify it? Had Britain become overnight a nation of risk-takers and wealth creators? Was I surrounded by entrepreneurs? It seemed unlikely. They did not seem men of the stamp I had known in the States: this had to be some form of North Sea Bubble. There had been a lack of financial reality about Washington DC, with lobbyists and lawyers creaming millions of dollars off the Federal Government and off their clients, but in 1981, when we went there, at least the country was rich and productive enough to afford them.

I presumed that it was this new ostentation that had provoked Roy Hattersley into threats to soak the stinking rich, of which I had read in America. The figure he chose at which to start the soaking was £25,000 a year, which was roughly what a city bus-driver in Washington earned at the prevailing exchange rates. The main problem seemed not that some were too rich – though with the continued concentration of Britain's wealth in so comparatively few hands, and the exorbitant salaries on offer in the City, some undoubtedly were – but that most were too poor. A decent income for all is the cornerstone of democracy. It emboldens the plumber to look the stockbroker in the eye and tell him what he thinks; it liberates citizens to demand the best and to refuse to be fobbed off with the tacky. It is certainly the foundation of the United States, where the term 'middle class' says what it means, and embraces the broad mass of the people, blue-collar and white-collar. In Britain the middle classes are as 'middle' as the public schools are 'public'.

These were some of my thoughts as we began the serious business of 're-entry'. An American academic has calculated that it takes the returning native one month of re-integration for each year spent abroad: a calculation I found to be impressively accurate. (She also said that if you are abroad more than nine years, complete reassimilation becomes impossible.) A few days after our return, riots broke out in Tottenham, north London, and Birmingham, in which several people, including a policeman, were killed. But these, as we unpacked and put up our pictures, were distant, background noises. What had most impact on me was a series of everyday encounters with social disorder.

The first was on the London Northern Line at six o'clock one workday evening. A gang of young people, dressed casually smart – at first glance I took them for art students – burst into our carriage. They were all drinking, gripping beer cans or bottles of wine, and most were smoking. They were noisy, drunk, obnoxious, threatening, and swiftly cleared one section of the carriage, while the rest of us, like New York subway riders, tried to look as if we weren't there or buried our heads in our newspapers. A man I took to be a senior civil servant boarded, carrying a black briefcase embossed with a coat of arms. Either unaware of what was going on, or braver than the rest of us, he challenged the rowdies to stop smoking. With an oath, one young man hurled a lager can towards the commuter's head: it crashed against the shatter-proof partition, and fell fizzing to the floor. The rest of us didn't stir, burying our heads yet more deeply behind our *Standards*. Shortly after, the gang swaggered out, disappearing noisily down the platform, and a collective sight of relief went round the carriage.

One incident no more makes a national mood than one swallow makes a summer, but to me, anxious as any foreigner to catch a clue about the sort of society I was rejoining, that brutish encounter was both an omen and part of a sad pattern. (Aggressive drinking in public appeared ubiquitous: the beer can in the fist was as much part of the macho image as the studded leather jacket had once been.) Two days earlier, my thirteen-year-old son and a friend were set upon by a group of girls in a park, who assaulted them and wrested Thomas's prized baseball bat from him. Later my second son was held up by some boys a couple of years older than him, who threatened to 'smash your face in' if he didn't surrender his American dirt-bike to them. Both these incidents were within a few hundred yards of our home in one of the leafier and gentler of London's suburbs.

I had taken the boys to a soccer match on their first Saturday home. They were in considerable trepidation, having watched the American coverage of the Heysel Stadium riot, awestruck at the picture it presented of the English sports fan. (Professional sports events in the States are family occasions: I do not remember one incident of sports hooliganism while we were there.) I told them not to worry: we were only going to Fulham, a gentle, eccentric club by the Thames supported if by anyone, I said, by spectators no more aggressive than a convention of bank clerks – most of them probably were bank clerks. Outside the underground station there was a detachment of mounted police and a police control van equipped with a television camera: there were police every few yards to the ground. By the time we reached the game, the boys were thoroughly intimidated, and too terrified to support either side in case they were set upon.

Essential services were deteriorating fast. Half the trains I went for were cancelled 'because of staff shortages'. The ticket office at our local station was often shut during the day, leading to time-consuming and ignominious queuing the other end at 'excess fare' windows. I accompanied a woman who was in considerable distress to the casualty department of a London teaching hospital: she carried a letter from her GP saying she should be dealt with as a matter of priority. After three hours, considerable fobbing off and a row with a doctor, she left untreated, and booked into a private hospital in the morning. Two other elderly women, who had been brought by ambulance that morning for routine treatment which in the event they hadn't had, had been waiting five hours for transport home. A woman whose husband had been admitted in a coma, but who could find out nothing about where or how he was, wept from time to time. An obviously very ill man, wrapped in a blanket, shivered for more than an hour while his wife battled with the bureaucracy.

I also was later referred to hospital. I went four times before abandoning the effort to get treatment. On the first occasion after the obligatory 45-minute wait beyond the appointed time, I was shown into an empty consulting room. A young doctor entered by a side door, walked round me without saying a word, sat down avoiding my eyes, and finally asked: 'How old are you?' Maybe that has become an obligatory NHS greeting in these days of harsh priorities to discover whether a patient is worth treating. I was told I would be summoned in due course for an in-patient examination. Sometime later I was again asked to attend out-patients – the lists, I was told, were being reviewed. After X-rays and a fourth appointment, I quit the process when I was kept waiting nearly two hours on a busy day. The patient may not have been cured, but the list had been shortened, which – in bureaucratic terms – comes to the same thing. (I read at that time of a woman who received a letter from her local hospital, asking her whether she wished to remain on the waiting list. She had died seven years earlier.)

Less essential services than the NHS and transport seemed in an equally dismal state: outwardly bright young shop assistants produced calculators to add simple sums – 'six plus six' in a chemist's shop on one occasion. The supermarket made me want to scream: there have been electronic check-outs in the States for ten years, but here in Britain we still depend on Doreen bellowing to Fred to check the price of baked beans from which the price tag has fallen. The American 'Have a nice day' may be a little glib, but it is better than being totally ignored, which is my common experience with British check-out assistants. But what is worse than the service is that we, the consumers, are so terribly deferential.

We positively cringe in the presence of professionals like doctors: we are not much braver with shop assistants or ticket collectors. People *apologize* when they return shoddy goods: they mutter inaudibly if the train is cancelled. In Hong Kong passengers rioted over what they considered to be an unjustified fare increase and sank a ferry. I have seen an American Parent–Teacher Association (PTA) march into a school and demand the dismissal of an inadequate teacher: she was out at the end of term. Try that here, and the local education authority – and possibly the national system – would be brought to a halt. It was said devastatingly of the British Army in the First World War that they were 'lions led by donkeys'. My fear was that I was returning to a nation of 'donkeys led by sharks'. When Ernest Bevin criticized the British for the 'poverty of their own desires', he was not, as a socialist in an unmaterialist age, advocating fridges or Spanish holidays for all, but rather that we should occasionally lift up our eyes from the pavement whereon we walk and focus on the distant hills. A Liverpool social worker, with years of experience of people at the receiving end, said to me: 'We are certainly brought up to know our place.'

When I reported my initial home-coming experiences and some of these reflections in the *Observer*, I received a great many letters from people who had not been away, but none the less perceived similar ills. Most rejected populist answers, such as those on offer from hangers and floggers and Norman Tebbit. They were troubled, as I was, by the depth and complexity of the national malaise. Trivial, daily, anti-social disorders were the short-change of the arson, looting and murder of inner city riots. A significant number of British people have such a small stake in society – usually because they lack a marketable skill that would give them minimal value or dignity – that they are restrained from riot or mayhem only by a very thin veneer of social control. F. F. Ridley, the Professor of Politics at Liverpool University, said to me: 'Our ruling classes fail to realize just how far outside the society they know many young people are. The potential for violence is enormous: it only needs the inhibiting factors removed for an instant. The idea that the mass of Scousers, for example, are loyal to the United Kingdom and law and order is very far-fetched.'

This it seems to me, writing eighteen months after returning to Britain, is where the real cleavage in British society lies: it is between the majority – identified by David Sheppard, the Bishop of Liverpool, as 'comfortable Britain', and an increasingly disconnected minority. Whatever Thatcherism has done to make British industry more efficient and competitive, its legacy may prove to be the creation of a permanent sub-class, trapped like the children of the Victorian destitute on the pavements outside, staring through the window at the goodies. A politician in a democracy can rule with a majority at the ballot box, but, without the necessary consent or participation of the minority, sooner or later some sort of compulsion will be needed to keep everyone 'in line'. The history of Northern Ireland makes that point starkly. The Unionists' 'majority' did not legitimize the systematic discrimination against the Nationalists: its abuse in the end has made the province essentially ungovernable.

The British 'ruling classes', as Professor Ridley describes them, have long been complacent. They create models, which, if everyone were reasonable and well motivated, ought to work. One, then, has only to isolate and deal with troublemakers – a task which will obviously be supported by the right-minded majority – and everything will fall into place. Such models of human behaviour are (or at least were) created in the public schools, which ultimately operate beneath a benign, but despotic, authority. The real world is messier, and by the time our rulers are old enough and have reached a position to make decisions that affect the rest of society, they are yet more isolated by their social and domestic experiences. Professor Peter Townsend, of Bristol University, pointed out that decision-makers increasingly live in a different environment, perhaps, in the case of Eurocrats, in a different country from the people they administer. They may know little of lives led on inner city streets a few miles from their comfortable suburban homes.

The motives of most members of these 'ruling classes' were entirely decent. They believed in the Beveridge Report, the 1944 Education Act, indoor lavatories, the NHS, and public libraries, which would inevitably lead to 'them' becoming more like 'us'. The corpus of reasonable, well-motivated, adequately educated citizens would grow. Decent middle-class virtues – tolerance, culture, 'taste', education – would trickle down like wealth under supply-side economics. These were expectations I shared as a child of the 'liberal' professional classes, though I had been appalled by the snobbery, ignorance and philistinism of many I had encountered at close quarters at a public school and at Oxford. However, nearly a quarter of a century later, Britons live in a society that is too frequently bitter and confrontational, which the optimists of my generation would have found hard to imagine. The 'bourgeois' middle-class traits are in the ascendancy, creating an enclosed, intolerant, selfish tier of privilege.

Expectations about working-class progress have been largely confounded. Without sufficient help from the other side, the gap in the end has been too wide for most to cross. Royce Logan, a lecturer at Warwick University, surveying his students in 1986, wrote in the *Guardian*: 'What is most striking is the inordinately different levels of wealth, and of opportunity; the inordinately different starting-points in life. It has never been clearer to me than now just how much some people have to struggle against all kinds of adversity – financial, social, against disrespect accorded to certain regional accents – while others are handed opportunities on a plate.' The consequence was that those 'trapped' on the wrong side of the divide either gave up or became alienated and embittered. (Snobbery, however, is a two-way street: the son of a friend was fired as a City messenger because he had two A levels. He had been acceptable, he was told, as a holiday relief, but the firm wanted the permanent position filled by a 'real' messenger.)

A character in a play by Ron Hutchinson, a Coventry playwright, said of 'Cov': 'It became a graceless town. It seemed that if you gave the working man one and a half times as much money as he had had before, all he would demand would be bigger pubs, brighter clubs, somewhere to shop on Saturday and somewhere to park his car.'

From this proletarian culture grew proletarian politics, in which social class, in a sterile Marxist sense, was all. It was narrow, introverted, hostile. Dennis Skinner, MP, could boast that he did not possess a passport: even a holiday in Torremolinos was suspect as a 'bourgeois' activity. Politics became vitriolic. A friend of Robert Kilroy-Silk, the former Labour MP who quit a Merseyside constituency after a running battle with supporters of Labour's Militant tendency, said: 'I don't think people actually realize what it is like under the "yobbocracy" of Militant in Liverpool. You find you are dealing with people who live by abuse and venom and by poison.' A union elected its general secretary on the grounds that he had never accepted promotion, and had therefore never 'sold out'; that he ate in pubs, while his rival for office favoured restaurants; that he refused a taxi in a downpour, a gesture that caused a supporter to enthuse: 'It's a return to grass roots; John is one of the lads.' An American worker is two and a half times better off than his British counterpart: his union leaders drive large Buicks.

Professor Townsend, a stalwart socialist, pinned the blame for the widening social gap firmly on Thatcherite policies. The Government, he said, had masterminded a blatant shift of resources from poor to rich, motivated by a belief that the poor have had it too good, and that working people need discipline. The Conservative vision, he argued, was a future resting with 'an elite bunch of computer-aware people', making do with fewer productive workers, and managing the rest as cheaply as possible. He bitterly regretted the passing of consensus, of Butskellism. 'Even patrician despots then extended at least minimal benevolence towards the poor. Today, there is a kind of vindictiveness towards the poor, on whom blame is fastened,' he said. The mood, he argued, had been caught by the previously generous-spirited middle classes. In thirty years 'there had been a divide of immense magnitude. It is hard to credit that attitudes could change so radically in one generation. Gone are the collective values, the fair shares and the queuing. The philosophy now is that we need in-equality to give incentives.'

Professor Townsend argued that 'we fooled ourselves as to the extent to which the welfare state has moderated inequalities'. The welfare state in Britain is now 'pitiful' compared to many others, but, because it was one of the first, we take great pride in it. George Orwell suggested during the Second World War that getting rid of the public schools and the House of Lords might be a better use of socialist ener-gies than nationalizing the railways. All the measurable indicators, such as disparities in health and wealth, show that the British class structure is still firmly in place. Professor Townsend claimed that his researches were beginning to show that deprived societies, like some in inner London, where unemployment among men was fifty per cent, were becoming so ravaged that the capacity to respond to each other's problems was being destroyed. People have, he said, sunk into abject depression. There has been 'a disintegration of social values and such a generalized impoverishment that people have been driven into themselves, like snails into shells. They close their doors, and don't go out, becoming isolated individuals no longer dependent on one another.' He broke off this grim catalogue of inner city depriva-tion with a sudden outburst. He remembered that a friend had phoned him from Haslemere in Surrey to say she was starting to teach adult literacy classes – 'Illiteracy! in Haslemere! for God's sake!'

A man of very different political stamp to Professor Townsend, Sir John Hoskyns, director-general of the Institute of Directors and once head of Mrs Thatcher's Downing Street 'think tank' (though he had fallen out with the good lady subsequently), told me that if a man from outer space had wanted to fix British society to ensure that nothing fundamental would change, and that there would be no dynamic, he could not have made a better job of it than had been done by the British people themselves. Britain had had an admirable sys-tem for the rich to hold on to what they had, and an almost useless one for enabling new people to become rich. When we met over a splendid lunch in Sir John's Pall Mall office, another Britain was out-side in force. It was the day of the Wembley football match between England and Scotland, and thousands of Scots were swarming over London, singing, climbing statues, waving flags and throwing up. Attentive retainers served us melon, salmon and fresh fruit salad. 'We are not,' said Sir John, 'a homogeneous population genetically programmed for failure. We may all be equal in the sight of God, but it is intellectually dishonest to suggest that special people don't make things happen. If they don't perform, we die. The best way for capitalism to care is for it to succeed.' Sir John dished it out with equal fervour to Whitehall, Westminster, Oxbridge – elites who have never taken a greater risk than crossing the street – and to the trade unions. 'When I get an abusive letter from a left-wing activist, I write back that I created a company that now has a turnover of sixty million pounds and employs 1,600 people; that the taxes it generates help keep the hospitals going; and ask, what have you done except moan and groan that the capitalist system is a disaster?'

I was converted to the virtues of what has become known as 'an enterprise culture', not by Mrs Thatcher's hectoring, but by the example of what I had seen in the United States. Nine million new jobs were created while I was there, almost entirely by small enterprises. In retrospect, it was shocking that my generation in Britain had been brought up with the sole presumption that we would work for someone else, no matter whether we left school virtually illiterate or emerged from university with a first-class degree. The only people who thought in business terms were those whose families had been in business, and the cultural pressures were on many of them to 'improve' themselves by joining the professional classes.

One of the first people I interviewed after my return was Robin Cole, to outward appearances a thoroughly English 'chap', wartime commission, Cambridge degree and all. He is also the kind of engineer and entrepreneur one encounters frequently in America – on domestic flights, in hotels – but here in Britain is a rare bird. In 1947, instead of hanging his hat on a pension, he and a partner rented a blacksmith's forge near Winchester for twelve shillings and sixpence a week. When I met him, his company, the Conder Group, a worldwide construction company, had 1,300 employees and an annual turnover of £125 million. 'We took on anything that came our way. All we had to do was keep our eyes open to opportunities.' At one stage he was so strapped for cash that he had to sell a shepherd's hut on wheels, which served as his office, for twenty-five pounds to raise capital. Forty years later a reproduction hut stood beside the Queen Anne house from which Mr Cole worked. In the entrance hall of each subsidiary company, there is the bust of a somewhat quizzical man – a Greek philosopher? – which bears the legend 'The satisfied customer: the most important man in our business.'

Mr Cole accepted that it was perfectly valid to wish for a less competitive society, provided the corollary of less materialism was also accepted. 'Most people,' he said, 'insist on TVs, cars *and* long holidays. It's inconsistent.' He said that 'no-tariff barriers' – the resistance to buying foreign products – were lower in Britain than anywhere else. 'More than half the people who shout about compassion drive a foreign car, never take a pay curb or buy British. They don't actually give a damn.'

It is the upper middle classes who buy most foreign cars and consumer goods. I suspect it is because few of them actually earn their livings making things. To them the connection between buying British and their own livelihoods is tenuous. Corelli Barnett is right to argue that much of our industrial inefficiency can be blamed on the public schools (and on the aspirations of those who send their sons there). Boys sent to public schools learn the habits and style of 'gentlemen', and 'gentlemen' naturally have nothing to do with wealth creation. So the chief educational resources in Britain have gone into generations of district officers, dons, civil servants, clergymen, school teachers (of the public school variety), service officers, and 'real gentlemen' (on whom the investment was more wasted than on all the others put together).

But there is a yet more baleful inheritance from these schools: an assumption that all human beings will abide by the rules of the Eton wall game or are, at least, amenable to benign coercion. The schools are tightly controlled structures, which, through selection, exclude poorly motivated pupils and virtually all those who are not brought up with certain common assumptions. In such an environment social engineering is quite feasible. The pressures to play according to the rules are enormous: the coercive force of the school, peer group conformity, and potentially furious, fee-paying parents. A dissenter could be (and is) expelled. This may be a workable method of controlling a closed society, but – at least since Australia stopped taking convicts – it is not a practical way to run the real world.

After five formative years in that system, it appears to most pupils to be an accurate microcosm of the real world. Ex-public school boys boast that after that they can survive anything – by which they mean prison or the armed forces. But survival in a hostile, tough environment is not the same as understanding the forces at work in an open society. My sons go to an open school, 'public' in the literal sense, where the education is imperfect and where they sit alongside children who are totally anti-social, have no stake in the school or wider society, who are desperate to shake free of whatever limited authority the school can impose, and create mayhem on a wider stage. My children suffer disadvantages they would not have suffered in a private fee-paying school, but they are under few illusions about the range and nature of human behaviour.

The cosiness of an elite, segregated education reinforces the natural instinct of movers and shakers to club together. 'Them' and 'us' becomes a natural frame of mind. 'Us' seldom see 'them': 'us' rely on tiny scraps of first-hand information which travel from club to bar to office to dining-table. Most of our decision-makers and commentators lurk far from the front line in the safety of Whitehall or 'Fleet Street', safely out of shelling distance, like First World War generals. Promotion inevitably means further distancing from the grass roots. The political correspondent dares not leave Westminster in case he is scooped; the education correspondent seldom gets inside a school, or the industrial correspondent inside a factory. Their beat is news, and 'news' is what the decision-makers, equally trapped inside this magic circle, create.

A serious newspaper will clear its feature pages (as it should) to bring a blow-by-blow account of the machinations behind the Westland affair or the Zircon spy satellite revelation – what the Attorney-General had for breakfast, and at what hour. It will be less enthusiastic about reporting the condition of Britain. People do like to know who's in, who's out, in London, and what policies are being fed into the machine, but what really concerns them is that they have a job, a decent school for their children, the right climate if they wish to start a business. It would be salutary for our leaders to remember from time to time that there are those who have no interest in what goes on in London: I once took regular holidays in isolated parts of Devon where locals scarcely knew the name of the prime minister.

Democracy in Britain is very remote: a few crosses against names for local and national office every four or five years does not leave much fine-tuning in the hands of the people. In the United States, tiny communities elect dog catchers, judges and school boards; the House of Representatives is returned every two years. In Britain there is limited faith in the responsiveness of Government – national or local. I was frequently told, as I researched this book, that it does not matter 'which lot get in'. Whenever I write about a situation with which readers can personally identify, I receive not only a great number of letters, but also letters from people who have something to say and want to join in. They are tired of having the likes of Owen, Tebbit and Hattersley rammed down their throats; tired of slippery answers. They know more than their masters do of what it is like to have a child in a comprehensive school, or to be unemployed, to try to start a business. They are the reliable witnesses.

The British system produces elitist leadership. It is such a full-time task to reach the top that only professional politicians make it. By the time they get there, they are sincerely convinced they know best, and therefore have a duty to tell the rest of us how to manage our affairs. The American system produces 'representative' rather than 'elitist' leadership: members of the House of Representatives are cut from the same cloth as their constituents. The president is the people's choice.

I went on a pulse-taking mission to an industrial area of Pennsylvania. In Britain such a region, with its redundant heavy industry, its high unemployment, its working-class or blue-collar culture (pool halls, ethnic clubs, determinedly masculine bars: *Deerhunter* country), would have returned a Labour MP regardless of the economic climate. This Pennsylvania district was represented by a young Republican congressman, and supported Reagan. 'Why?' I asked. 'Because,' answered a redundant steel-worker, 'he's a regular guy; he could be on the town bowling team.' For all Reagan's imperfections, he is the common man, trusted to understand the fears and aspirations of other common men. If you had said to those blue-collar workers that Reagan would be coming to supper, they would have been delighted, anticipating a memorable evening of baseball and Hollywood anecdotes. If you said to a British working-class family that Mrs Thatcher was coming to tea, they'd bolt the front door and flee over the garden fence for asylum elsewhere until the all-clear was sounded.

A Government headed by a 'regular guy' is more likely to be trusted than one headed by someone who has clawed his way through a deeply partisan system. (This is a general rule, I hasten to add, frequently breached in the past twenty years by dishonest or incompetent US presidents.) The result is an acceptance, which appears to have been lost in Britain, of the general direction in which society is moving. In the United States, I encountered virulent public antagonism on only two subjects. One was abortion, about which moral and religious passions run deep; and the other was Northern Ireland, 'imported' whenever Mrs Thatcher or Prince Charles visited the country. In Britain, polarization intensified while I was away.

People seem to hate those with whom they disagree, as evidenced by the miners' strike and Wapping. I have had virulent letters from *Observer* readers who disagreed with something I wrote or someone I quoted. One person, on reading the comments of a wartime bomber pilot on the city of Winchester, its cathedral and mellow medieval buildings – 'This is what people fought for, why they flew aeroplanes during the war. If it was worth flying, it was for this – the England worth preserving' – wrote that he wished that Hitler's bombs had flattened Winchester.

After an article about an unemployed man in the Midlands, who dared to confess that he had twice voted Conservative, I received a shoal of hostile letters, as well, it is fair to add, as highly supportive ones, some offering the family help. I had described the man as 'one of the bulldog breed'. One correspondent wrote: 'They've had it too good for too long, and it's about time the bulldog suffered. Then maybe he'll have more sympathy with the so-called underdogs who have never had a slice of the cake and never will.' A second said: 'What right have they to come whingeing to the British public over their troubles, when in my opinion they deserved everything they got.' So much for our common humanity.

This declining tolerance has spilled over into everyday life. The British even drive more aggressively than they did. The once common British saw of 'giving credit where credit's due' no longer seems to have any validity. The chief executive of a northern new town said: 'A lot of people do want to get things back to where they ought to be. However, a lot don't unless they get the kudos, so they set themselves against it. Some actually don't want to see things improve: their role in life is to keep things festering. We are retreating into tribal divisions.' That seemed a fair, if horrifying, summary of the Britain I found on my return.

⚛(2)⚛

'MY WIFE WOULD NEVER
LEAVE SURREY'

I had been in Easington Colliery in the Durham coalfield only a few hours, talking to officials of the National Union of Mineworkers (NUM) in their snug, creosoted hut at the pit gates. On one wall was a series of blown-up black and white pictures of the village. One of these showed tiny figures stooped on the beach scrabbling for coal. Slightly surprised, I asked whether much of this coal-gathering still went on. 'Take a walk under the railway when you leave here,' said a miner. So I did, past a gaggle of garages and allotment huts that looked like a squatters' town, and past piles of filth and household rubbish. A second low, cavernous bridge was guarded by a barred steel barricade, which would have stopped a small tank: it was, I learned, to prevent the coal-gatherers taking vehicles on to the beach, although they could drive on to it some miles to the south and make their way back to Easington Colliery at low tide. A squad of cleaners with high-pressure hoses and detergents was removing crude daubings from beneath this second tunnel. One way, a muddied track, led towards an overhead colliery conveyor belt, and the other, a well-made path, nursed the cliff-top.

From the edge I could see dozens of men bent on the task of retrieving the seacoal: a fire, around which those drying out their sodden clothes had gathered, burned beneath the conveyor, and, immediately below where I stood, two ancient lorries were backed into the waves, each surrounded by men armed with shovels, who dug energetically in the shallow water. Further out the fierce wind whipped up venomous, coal-stained waves, and a small fishing boat was pitching and tossing some distance from the shore. The beach was as black as a coal tip, which is literally what it was. Later I was amazed to see men angling in the murky waters: one would have imagined that such a spoiled sea would have destroyed all living creatures.

A middle-aged miner appeared at my shoulder, and was obviously amused by the impact upon a visitor of a daily routine which the village took for granted. He had with him a fine collie, which barked with frustration at his master's stopping to talk to this stranger until silenced by being put on a lead. (Dogs and men are inseparable in the Durham coalfield, but few miners have such handsome pedigree animals as this collie: more typical is the tiny mutt I had seen peeping from beneath the denim jacket of a young miner waiting at a bus stop.) 'You should see the lads in the summer when they strip down,' said my companion, watching two young coal-gatherers crest the cliff-top pushing a brakeless bike between them, 'they've bodies like prize-fighters, lovely builds on them.' He added, as if I might dispute it: 'Work like a horse at two pounds a bag: they didn't get that coal for nowt. Their lungs are bursting by the time they get back to the top of the cliff. A lot of the lads still owe money off the strike.'

The workforce, he said, was demoralized; had the stuffing knocked out of it by the strike, which had then been over for eighteen months. Men in their forties were selling out their jobs for £1,000 per year of service. What were they going to do now? 'Nothing: there's nothing to go to in the north-east. It's like Germany after the war. We've got to start again. The Government has got to pump money in to open a few factories. There's no work for the youngsters: it's bloody awful for them.' And he laughed harshly at the memory of a Conservative MP who had recently attracted publicity by living on the dole for a week. 'He ought to try it for a bloody year.'

As the miner left, his collie finally liberated to joust against the wind, two more men appeared pushing a bikeload of coal. They were deeply wary. 'How much do you get for it?' 'We wouldn't know: we bunk it.' One, an ex-miner with one gold earring, heaved the bike towards the shanty town of huts, and the other loosened up, though he said fiercely, 'I don't want my name in your book,' as if there was some way I could divine his name from his sooty face. They would return to the beach, he said, for another bikeload: although it was so cold I could scarcely write a note, to them it was a 'good day'. It depended on the wind. Sometimes there wasn't a nut of coal on the beach: at other times you could get thirty bags in a day, no problem. Later a friend would bring a three-wheeler truck, and they would hawk the coal round a housing estate.

Easington Colliery is where any film-maker who wants to capture the raw authenticity of a northern pit village should take his cameras. The air is pungent with the sooty fumes from a hundred coal fires. The pit itself, opened in 1910 when German freezing technology first enabled drilling through water-bearing limestone, lies between the black beach and the bottom of the steep main street, named Byron Street, and (further up the hill) Seaside Lane, a designation which mocks the concept of the seaside having anything to do with pleasure. The colliery spews its waste along an overhead conveyor, dumping it on to the margins of the sea. With every hundred tonnes of rock and stone are intermingled six tonnes of coal, trapped in the washing process which winnows the valuable black carbon from the rocky dross.

When I first saw 'Coals', his bicycle was propped against a graffiti-stained bus shelter, and he was sitting on the kerb, his back bowed with obvious fatigue against a wind that howled down the hill, driving high clouds towards the slate-grey North Sea. He wore an orange wool hat and an elderly donkey jacket above jeans, which were black with damp coal dust, and muddy Wellington boots, and he gazed at the world asquint, half through and half over a pair of thick spectacles that rested partway down his nose. He was fifty-four and thick-set; his awkward, square body that of a man who had laboured hard but was none the less – perversely and unfairly – unhealthy, exhausted rather than fit. His skin was red and veined and flaky, and he showed at least two days' growth of beard. His wife, he said, had left him many years ago, and he lived with a 26-year-old son who had been unemployed for nine years, all the young man's 'working' life; their diet was bread and butter, fish 'n' chips and strong northern beer. His resting bike was carefully stacked with four large plastic bags of coal, three blue and one bright orange, flattening its worn tyres nearly to the rim. Was I, he asked with deep suspicion, looking at my relatively couth attire of blue windcheater and grey flannels, from the 'Nash'? If I were, he said, he was 'finished'.

Without having heard the term before, I could guess what he meant. The 'Nash' – short for National Insurance and otherwise known as the 'dolies' – are, I learned later, dreaded investigators from the Department of Health and Social Security (DHSS), who lie in wait for the likes of Coals, the men who eke out a meagre supplement to their state benefits by trawling the black beaches for nuggets of coal. If the dolies can prove this seacoal is being sold – it fetched then between two and three pounds a bag when sold door-to-door

– they can stop those benefits (in Coals' case fifty-six pounds a fort-night) and haul the beachcombers into court. A triumph for the hard-working taxpayer over the shiftless, workshy scrounger. Christmas was coming and the investigators, an official at a local unemployment centre told me, had been 'having a beanfeast down there on the beach'.

'Coals' – it was the only name he was prepared to give, though he did allow me to load his bike and his precious bags into the back of my estate car and drive at least close to his home – was nowhere near as organized as these two men. He spoke about getting a van for £250, but I sensed it was a romantic notion indulged in to while away the agonizing hours of his daily haul. He could certainly have done with a vehicle. When I had discovered him, he was only one mile into a six-mile push to his home, much of it uphill. He had left at seven o'clock, well before light on a northern December morning, and, now that I had given him a lift, he would be able to make a second trip. He found companionship on the beach – 'we bike lads stick together' – and a community round the fire with which his home life obviously could not compete.

He told me that, after working in the Hartlepool docks, he had become a miner in his forties. He quit after seeing his best friend killed 'straight out' by a rockfall ten yards away from him. He had tried farm labouring for a time, but reckoned he was exploited. The last I saw of his stumpy figure was pushing his bike up yet another hill in the incongruous modern surroundings of Peterlee, a new town a few miles from Easington. The veracity of much of what he had to say was hard to judge. But what was undoubtedly true was that, in middle-age and poor physical shape, he was desperate enough to undertake a Herculean task, seven days a week if the coal were there – sometimes twice daily, to make a weekly sum that would scarcely buy him a pair of trousers in a central London store. What was also true was that no industry would have been allowed to despoil the beaches of Sussex as the coal industry has been allowed to despoil these Durham beaches, and that if several hundred residents of Brighton were forced to spend twelve hours a day bent double in the surf, garnering what amounts to waste, in order to make enough money to keep their families in decent rather than indecent poverty, the scandal would not be tolerated by either parliament or press. Those who equate unemployment with being workshy should try pushing one of those bikes up the rutted path from the beach, and those who shake their heads over the 'black' economy should try living on the dole, and contemplate finding a job in an area where it is not unknown for seven hundred people to go after one vacancy.

By chance, a few days after I returned from Durham, Mrs Thatcher made one of her rare, and clearly distasteful, forays north of the Trent. A year earlier, on a visit to Newcastle, she described northerners as 'moaning minnies'. Like other spineless, disadvantaged groups in Britain, they had, according to the harsh tenets of new Conservatism, only themselves to blame for whatever misfortunes they might suffer. Responding on this occasion to a complaint from the Manchester Chamber of Commerce (presumably not a body comprised of Militant supporters) that the Government was doing nothing to narrow the widening north–south gap – 'We search in vain,' said the Chamber's president, 'for some indication that the Government is adapting its policies to take account of the problem' – she described the divide as a 'myth'. There were, she added, 'areas of difficulty' throughout the country. Which is true, but it so happens that a vast majority of those areas, where the difficulties are particularly profound, are north of a line from the Wash to the Bristol Channel.

Newcastle University's Centre for Urban and Regional Development Studies (CURDS) produced in 1985 a league table of 280 communities in Britain, judged by such yardsticks as the change in numbers employed over a ten-year period and by car ownership, which revealed that forty of the wealthiest fifty towns are in the south – those outside included Aberdeen, then still enjoying the oil boom, and such special towns as Harrogate in the Yorkshire Dales and Kendal in the Lake District. It also found that only five of the poorest fifty were south of the Midlands. The most prosperous town in the northeast was Hexham – at number ninety-eight on the scale! Consett, a few miles to the north of Easington, was at the bottom of the league, a poverty ranking confirmed a year later by a building society survey of house prices. The people of this former steel town were, I was told, sick to death of the continuous trail of sociologists, journalists and European television teams that this unwanted distinction brought them. The Department of Employment's own job census, published early in 1987, showed that 94 per cent of the jobs during the first seven years of the Thatcher Government were in the north, Scotland, the Midlands, Wales and Northern Ireland. In the same period the south-east had lost only 1 per cent of employment, and East Anglia had actually gained 3 per cent. The census revealed a 28 per cent national drop in manufacturing and construction jobs between 1979 and 1986 – a loss of two million jobs – the brunt of which had been born in the regions. (Japan increased employment in those categories by 4·9 per cent over the same period.) More than two-thirds of the new service jobs created during the Thatcher years were in the south-east.

Devastating evidence of the harmful effects of the north–south gap was produced in the autumn of 1986 by Professor Peter Townsend of Bristol University. His report, on behalf of the Northern Regional Health Authority, made the overwhelming connection between social inequality, suffered in such places as Easington, and life-threatening ill-health. He published mortality figures – linked to joblessness, poor housing, low birth rates, and overcrowding – which showed that 1,500 people a year die prematurely in the northern region from deprivation, and 13,800 suffer from permanent sickness or disability who would be healthy if they lived in more favoured areas of the country. Townsend compared the health records of the populations of 678 local government wards: six of the unhealthiest twenty-five were in the district of Easington, including the winner and/or loser, the village of Wheatley Hill, a community devastated by the closure of its pit. The report itself attracted a certain amount of attention, but was propelled into the national limelight by Edwina Currie, who had just been appointed a junior health minister by Mrs Thatcher (with whom she shares a birthday and much else). Mrs Currie pooh-poohed the connection between poverty and ill-health, blaming the mortality figures on northern ignorance, and a penchant for chips, booze and fags. 'My family grew up in Liverpool, and they didn't have two beans' – presumably she was speaking figuratively – 'but as a result of good food, good family and good rest, they grew up fit and well. The problem very often for people is, I think, just ignorance.'

I went to Easington to give a local habitation and a name to the nebulous concept of the north–south divide. Easington district council, fifteen miles south of Sunderland, includes most of Durham's remaining coalfield in scattered villages along and near the North Sea coast, together with the new town of Peterlee, which was built after the war to provide better housing for miners and factory work for their wives. I chose it specifically because it was the home area of a group of ten school-leavers, all bright boys with O Levels and CSEs, who were about to head south for two years to the Thames Valley town of Slough to train as engineers on the Government's Youth

Training Scheme (Y T S). No local employer was able to offer them both training and the high probability of a job thereafter, while in Slough firms were crying out for trainees, 90 per cent of whom secured permanent work when their time was up. I visited both Easington and Slough to see at first-hand the mismatch between two communities, both of about 100,000 people, which illustrated much about Britain's chronic economic imbalances. In Easington, the Y T S 'Job Link' was a controversial scheme. 'Bloody disgraceful,' said John Cummings, miner, leader of the council and elected a few months later as Labour MP for a constituency once held most improbably by Manny Shinwell. He interpreted it as a victory for the hated Tebbitite 'on yer bike' philosophy. Jobs, say Labour stalwarts, should be brought to the people, not people to the jobs. 'I was told of one trade unionist who argued that the offshore oil industry ought to be moved to the coast of Durham rather than local people being compelled to travel to Aberdeen!)

The north–south divide had widened substantially while I was in America. Property price differences had accelerated crazily in the south, up to 20 per cent annually, while they remained static in the north, virtually cutting the country in half – 'there's an exclusion zone south of Watford', said one frustrated Slough employer. He interpreted it as a victory. Jobs were going begging in the Thames Valley, where firms were compelled to turn down orders because of labour shortages, and people were going begging in the north.

Inequalities in Britain are reported in dramatic terms in the United States. It is one of the few subjects that gets London-based American journalists off their bottoms. 'THE TWO BRITAINS: the gap between stagnant north and prosperous south is wider than ever' proclaimed a headline in *Newsweek* a few days before I travelled to Durham. It contrasted pictures of Etonians disporting themselves in fancy dress on the Thames with the children of the unemployed playing amidst the dereliction of a shattered housing estate. 'Some housing projects in Manchester seem straight out of the Third World', read one caption. Kids hanging out on a northern council estate – 'For the country's underclass, few prospects of a better life' – were set against young people in evening dress at a party at St Paul's public school – 'Laps of luxury'. Crude stuff, perhaps, but the persistence of such reporting creates exactly the image of Britain as a class-ridden, inefficient society that Mrs Thatcher's whole premiership has been dedicated to eliminating, and in the country that Mrs Thatcher admired above all others and wished Britain to emulate. American reporters quote Disraeli with relish: 'Two nations; between whom there is no intercourse and no sympathy; who are as ignorant of each other's habits, thoughts, and feelings, as if they were dwellers in different zones, or inhabitants of different planets; who are being formed by a different breeding, are fed by a different food, are ordered by different manners, and are not governed by the same laws.' 'You speak of . . .' said Egremont, the hero of Disraeli's novel, hesitatingly, 'the rich and the poor.'

Gordon Chopping, manager of the Easington unemployment centre, brought Disraeli up to date: 'We will never provide jobs again on a sufficient scale. There is a new proletariat. It doesn't wear suits; it doesn't *have* suits; it doesn't use credit cards or banks; it doesn't pay taxes; it doesn't buy consumer durables. Any work it does is on the black economy. Its members are a million miles away from people who watch ads on TV and can say "Oh yes, we'll go and get one of those." The trend is that if your father doesn't work, you won't. There is a permanent underclass, a dual society; whole streets where scarcely anyone works.' Mr Chopping, grey-haired and bearded, wearing a venerable dark pin-striped suit, was the modern, benign equivalent of the workhouse master. His centre ran 102 'community programme' jobs for the unemployed – which lasted for a year, and for which each worker was paid about fifty-five pounds a week – and it was his job to maintain morale, firmly chiding his flock with an avuncular authority when they invariably became negative. 'We have to believe the pessimistic view is wrong. We cannot allow two societies to develop if we can do anything about it. We have got to continue on the assumption that everyone trains for work.' This is a difficult assumption to make in the east Durham coalfield in the declining years of the twentieth century.

In late 1986 unemployment in Easington stood at 18·7 per cent, of whom 38 per cent were under twenty-five and 41 per cent had been jobless for over a year. In seven years nearly four thousand jobs had been lost in coal mining, taking with them an estimated two thousand jobs in linked industries and services. Six thousand new jobs would have been needed within five years to reduce unemployment to the national average of 13·6 per cent.

Mr Chopping is a former journalist and businessman, with a

sardonic realism about his charges. He angered his superiors by suggesting that one-third of young people who seek help had sub-standard literacy. 'That was based on asking them to write down their names and addresses, and the number who hadn't got a pen, and didn't care to use mine, and would rather bring the forms back in the morning.' The centre offered such work as decorating, draught-excluding, gardening, visiting the old and handicapped as 'good neighbours', constructing a B M X park for the village youngsters, and working in the office itself. Women were far more likely to land permanent jobs at the end of their year than were men – especially if they had a skill that could be used in an office or in caring for the sick or elderly. For young men the outlook was as bleak as the cold December North Sea that pounded their despoiled beach. 'Half the kids leaving school in this area will never have a proper job; for the lads there is really nothing,' according to Mr Chopping.

His centre was once the Co-op department store – a shabby supermarket still exists, but the store went the way of most other amenities, like cinemas, in such areas. 'Even the fish 'n' chip shop,' someone joked wryly, 'closes for lunch.' In one room, the 'good neighbours' – eleven women and one young man – were waiting for their weekly pay. The man was aged twenty, substantially overweight, had a round, pudgy face behind his glasses. He had left school two years earlier with one A and nine O Levels, which would have guaranteed him a job in the south: yet more than seventy job applications to offices and banks had not secured him a single interview. (Several of his friends, despairing of their civilian chances, had gone into the armed forces.) Very few seated round that table were prepared to move to find work. 'I don't see why we should: it's the Government who should provide jobs for everyone. Young people from this area have got to stay here and keep this place going, haven't they?' said one. Each had a dismal story to tell: the fat woman who couldn't keep pace with piecework in a garment factory – she made thirty pounds a week against the norm of eighty pounds; the girl who was going to marry in six months' time, even though the coal haulage firm for which her fiancé worked looked likely to lose its only contract, and he would be sacked. She spoke of her father, a miner, redundant at forty-eight – 'he's no ties, he's not bothered now, he goes up to the garden and that.' Another young woman had been out of school for eight years, of which she had only worked for one year; an older woman said she saw no hope for her own son.

A heavy silence fell regularly. Gordon Chopping, who had been listening to this catalogue of despair, told them: 'People who put themselves out most get a job.' He was rounded on by a middle-aged woman in a blue pullover: 'Pack it in, Gordon – we know we're going back on the dole. There are thousands of young 'uns competing for the jobs. When you go for one, there's someone from a Government scheme doing the job already.'

Upstairs, the decorators were sheltering from a sea 'fret', a heavy drizzle that reduced visibility to the width of the street. Allan Parrish, a thin man of thirty-two with a wispy ginger beard and spectacles held together with Sellotape, had left school in 1970, trained as a lab technician, and worked at a comprehensive school for ten years. As a result of Government cuts, teachers had taken over lab work, and, after a year on the dole, he got a similar job with a sixth-form college in Middlesbrough. Science teaching was centralized, and once again the lab jobs went. That was three years before I met him, during which he had tried 'a couple of hundred jobs' and been granted five or six interviews. Mr Parrish, unlike those downstairs, would have moved anywhere – he had tried London and Leeds. His father and grandfather had been miners, and what he found bitterly ironic was that his siblings, who had never trained and did manual jobs, were all better off than himself. Two nineteen-year-olds, Peter Sugden and Arthur Bannister, had had their names down for the pit, but it ceased recruiting a few months before they left school. They felt cheated of their heritage. Neither had worked since, apart from Government schemes. 'I've a pile of regrets that high,' said one, indicating a couple of inches with his finger and thumb.

'The difference,' said Mr Chopping, 'between the twenties and thirties and today is hope. Vandalism didn't occur then as now; kids are disassociating themselves from a society that has failed them. Their parents grew up in stages, through school into a job. Now it comes to a halt at sixteen: everyone knows that YTS here is not a proper job. There's no hope.' Often I was struck by a local sense of fatalism about the bad times, as if they, like the weather, were beyond human control. Mr Chopping said: 'You need an income to be politically active, a lift if you are going to a meeting, money for a drink afterwards. It's easy to understand why people give up: they might write between thirty and two hundred applications without getting a reply. You can't keep your phone up. You can't go on spending three pounds a week on stamps. You stop getting up particularly early, and concentrate on getting your cabbages in, so the days get shorter.'

Outside in the rain a youth on another Government scheme was gathering litter into a blue plastic bag from a seemingly endless supply on waste ground behind the bus stop. When he had finished the litter remained so abundant one could not tell that he had been. His futility was a pathetic microcosm of the region's futility. Across the road from the Co-op, and past the gaunt miners' welfare hall, a notice on an iron gate announces the 'Easington Colly Parish Council Welfare Park', a memorial to a tragedy that struck the pit and community a generation ago. Fifty yards from the gate, past another posse of 'make-work' men, scrabbling at the dead, grey grass in desultory fashion, was a bronze plaque.

On the 29th May 1951 81 men died together in Easington Colliery following an explosion and in the rescue bid two men gave their lives. The trees hereabout were planted. The memorial avenue was made and this tablet placed on a stone from the scene of the accident.
TO HONOUR THE MEMORY OF THOSE WHO LOST THEIR LIVES.
Let passers-by do likewise, get understanding and promote goodwill in all things.

Roses still bloomed in drab December around this shrine, on which were scribbled in large letters 'the Parky Stinks of Fuck Head'. From the brow of the hill beyond the memorial, I looked towards the sea, across an unlovely cluster of houses known as 'East', most of which were boarded up awaiting the outcome of a dispute between the ground landlords, the Church Commissioners, and a housing trust for miners. Each was designed with a tiny yard, where washing turns grey in the smoke-filled air. The last tin bath wasn't thrown out until 1968.

Redundant men in the north contrast the poverty of their environment with the wealth that has been drawn from it and taken elsewhere. J. B. Priestley on his *English Journey* in 1933 remarked that there was 'easily more comfort and luxury on one deck of the *Mauretania*' than there had ever been in the drab Tyne towns where the ship-builders lived. He speculated on all the fine things that had been conjured out of one Durham mine – 'the country houses and town houses, the drawing rooms and dining rooms, the carriages and pairs, the trips to Paris, the silks and the jewels, the peaches and iced puddings, the cigars and old brandies'.

Today the connection is less glaringly obvious, but the people of the Durham coalfield, tucked away in grimy villages where no stock-broker has ever visited, did help lay the foundation of Britain as a prosperous society. And some, like the eighty-three men commemor-ated in the parish park, gave a great deal more than just forty-five years of back-breaking toil one thousand feet below the sunlight. Every £100,000-a-year City whizz kid, as he switches off his computer terminal, climbs into his BMW and heads for dinner in a Chelsea restaurant, ought to say a little prayer of gratitude to the people of Durham and such regions and to those people's forefathers. The miners' legacy is back-to-back colliery houses, a closed Co-op store and the worst health in Britain. The brass went elsewhere and the muck remained behind. Would today's Gstaad skiing, Concorde flips to New York, Porsches on sale in central London for £83,000, cash-mere dresses and Italian boots, weekend cottages in Gloucestershire, fine art auctions, booming wine sales have been possible without the generations of riveters, miners, steelmen, platers, whose children are now spied upon for collecting lumps of coal from the beach?

The new Conservatives, with their homilies on dietary ignorance and bikes, are as harsh in their attitudes as Dickens's Gradgrinds and Bounderbys. Perhaps the compassion that went with the paternalism of Harold Macmillan and Alec Douglas-Home was not fully appre-ciated at the time, but it is greatly missed now it has been replaced by hard-nosed Conservatism. Alan Cummings, the Easington NUM representative, said: 'It's the Tory philosophy that you should move to work. This area has built this country's wealth. The Government owes it to us to attract employment. Money has never been ploughed back here. We're down to the bare bones, most of the flesh has gone.' Northern Conservatives, with their roots in the soil and the commun-ity, know it. Sir Michael Straker, chairman of the Peterlee Develop-ment Corporation, is every inch a Conservative of the old school – Eton and Coldstream Guards. When we met he had been 'farming', and wore an elderly tweed jacket and grey trousers above brown shoes. From time to time he looked over his half-moon glasses as if to a better past somewhere in the middle distance. He had just learned of a friend's son who was leaving the army to go, guess where? 'That's right. Into a merchant bank. It's a tragedy. His father was a nuts and bolts man.' 'Politicians,' he said, 'get it wrong. You've got to have a feeling for coal, probably for another decade, and what coal has meant. Neglect that at your peril.' He spoke, in a way that no doubt sounds romantic nonsense to new Conservatives, of the companionship and loyalty created underground – 'tunnelling, naked to the waist, sweating shoulder-to-shoulder. If one man fails, he lets the team down, possibly costing them their lives.'

It is an irony that a community that has sworn for generations that its children would not go down the pit now will take to the streets in defence of those pits and the rights of their children to descend a hole in the ground. A miner in the Colliery Arms at Murton, a few miles inland from Easington – one of those bleak mining pubs where the only cheer is in the heaped coal fires and the beer, and where women, by indelible custom, are rigorously segregated – said: 'My dad used to threaten me with the pit if I didn't work at school. Now I can't even promise my kid that.' Recruiting from school, which used to run at one hundred a year at Easington Colliery, stopped in 1983: older men are tempted out by redundancy payments, and the vacancies are filled by men from closed pits inland who are bussed to the colliery. Some travel twenty-five miles, unheard of commuting distances in such an area. Alan Cummings, of the NUM, said: 'In the sixties there was always a job in mining for young people – you left school on Friday and started at the pit on Monday. We've always said the next generation won't go down, but it's in people's blood, like deep-sea fishing. It's a stark prospect now – from cradle to the grave on the State. You have to get married, raise a family, and try to live on that kind of income. It's frightening.' In 1947 there were 201 collieries in Durham; by 1986 there were only six. 'We have our backs to the sea, there's nowhere else to go,' said one miner. (The coalfaces at Easington stretch seven miles under the sea. 'Five more miles and we'll be able to serve duty free and declare UDI,' said one miner.) I had visited a miner's house in a Yorkshire village a year before. A large lout of a lad was slumped in front of a vast television, roasting his bare feet before the fire. His 42-year-old father, redundant through injury, was bemoaning his son's lack of prospects: the only available work was stacking boxes in a supermarket and, heaven forbid, cutting cheeses. The father screwed up his face: 'That's not reet for a lad; that's not man's work.' It was more manly, it seemed, for the still-growing youth to vegetate at home until no one would want him even for cutting cheeses.

The engineering trainees who were to go to Slough were enormously excited by their prospects, particularly of leaving home and spreading

their wings. No lack of 'on yer bike' spirit there. But many northerners still look upon the south as morally polluted, and, as it was
caricatured by Orwell, as 'one enormous Brighton inhabited by
lounge-lizards'. Those of us who live south of the Trent are not all
rentiers, but there is no doubt that the majority of us —even if we are
not making millions by whistling Eurobonds round the world – produce none of life's necessities, nothing as tangible as a chair you can
sit in, coal you can burn, a car you can drive, a steel beam with which
you can open up the ground floor of your bijou Victorian cottage.
'Real' men and 'real' work in those senses exist almost exclusively in
the north. With that gritty reality go other 'northern' qualities: friend-
liness and bluntness. (Within a few hours of arriving in Durham, I
was not only made welcome, but had also been asked my age, wage
and what I had paid for an indifferent second-hand car. For fear of
being thought soft or 'nesh', I lied about the latter.) A northern
bishop, who had had the misfortune, as he saw it, earlier in his career
to be assigned to a London parish, told me that his spirit always lifted
when he arrived at King's Cross on his way home, and he found himself surrounded once more by Yorkshiremen. A conversation with a
total stranger, he said, can leave you feeling you are related by the
time you've finished. Even though he now wore a bishop's purple,
northerners were not intimidated by him. I scarcely met anyone in Durham who had not stories, recounted with horror, of
friends or relatives who had gone south, and, after many years, still
scarcely knew their next-door neighbours. One miner said: 'I've got a
sixteen-year-old son. I would chain him by the ankles and nail him to
the floor before I'd let him go south. Not into that exploitation. Lads
who go to London for jobs fall into vice and everything else – homosexuality and rentaboy. A boy down there would become a servant to
the people with money and high qualifications.'

Much of what northerners say about themselves as people with different qualities from southerners is true. I moved to the West Riding
when I left university and was rapidly made to feel at home by almost
everyone, spending one Christmas when I couldn't get home in a
miner's terraced house. I could never imagine a young man going in
the opposite direction to start his working life as being anything but
very lonely, at least for some time. The north is no longer as ugly as it
was when Orwell castigated it, or even as it was twenty-odd years
ago when I used to write stories about roofs collapsing under the
weight of industrial pollution; but that is because most of the indus-

try has gone and taken the ugliness with it. The Don Valley between Sheffield and Rotherham, which once contained more smoke than Hades, is a desert, like Hiroshima after the firestorm had subsided and the mushroom cloud had drifted away. Looking around the wasted area, I needed the map to tell me I was in the place I once knew with its rows of terraced housing, its fuming chimneys, red furnaces lighting up the night and its cacophony of industrial noises.

But there is still a northern quality, evident in the chirpiness of the people, and the dour landscape. On a wet Sunday night, at an hour when all sensible people were abed, I stopped for petrol somewhere near Scotch Corner on the A1. A lorry driver from Manchester was bantering with the cashier – it was unoriginal stuff: 'What time did you come on, luv?' 'One o'clock.' 'It's time for me to take you away.' 'How much are twenty fags? ... I want to smoke them, not frame them.' It lifted the spirit; someone was trying, giving it a go, and his good humour stayed with me as I drove on north. By the morning a ferocious wind was blowing; it rattled at the hotel windows, trying to worry them from their hinges. Outside a black clump of pines rolled with the wind in the morning darkness. Beowulf and the monster Grendel might have been out there somewhere, fighting their legendary battles for mastery of bog and moor. On the way to breakfast, I picked up a local weekly newspaper from the hotel hall to be met with the headline: 'SO WHAT IS THE MYSTERY BEAST? – "Something's out there," says PC.' The story began: 'A mystery beast lurking in east Durham could be of an unknown breed which has lived undiscovered in Britain for thousands of years ... this is not just a myth, according to the policeman who is on its trail.' I could not visualize such a splash story in a Sussex weekly. The north is another country. History is alive; the past is a companion in every conversation, and the thirties – generally seen as 'good' times, despite the Depression – are as vivid in older people's minds as if they had happened yesterday. 'There was not so much stress in those days. We accepted things on an even keel,' said one retired miner.

One night I met the Revd Tony Hodgson, vicar of Easington Colliery, who, during the miners' strike had become virtually an honorary miner. Born in Leicester, he had committed his life to the north-east after studying at Durham University. He is a vast man, his midriff sprouting out between a shabby black pullover and his trousers: he likes his pint, and, although he has already had one heart attack, smokes like a chimney. He is learned and eccentric, his name bringing a benign smile to the faces of those who know him. A university Conservative, he became a socialist through exposure to need and deprivation. In his first parish in a slum area of Gateshead in the early sixties he was called to the home of a blind man, who was trying to raise a child in a house by the River Tyne that was so damp there was mud rather than dust on the floor. 'He wanted to top himself. My politics came out of my Christian belief. I was burying babies.' Reflecting on the apparent 'politicization' of the Church of England, with its critical report on inner city conditions and its outspoken prelates like David Sheppard of Liverpool and David Jenkins of Durham, Mr Hodgson argued that the church had, in modern times, been consistent in its social policies. Archbishop William Temple and others had been among the architects of the post-war 'new deal'. It was, he said, the modern Conservative Party that had moved. 'Maggie rolled back the carpet and rejected our values.'

John Cummings, the leader of the council, whose constant companion is a little Jack Russell he had found abandoned and lousy, said: 'We've got to get back to the old values – make good use of history. The Durham coalfield invented the "welfare state" before the war: it was paid for out of your wages. You had your doctor and your medicines free. No prescription charges *then* if you were ill. In the thirties everyone was the same – no TV, no fitted carpets, no jealousies, no break-ins. You left your door wide open because there was nowt to be pinched. We must reflect back on why it is important to have what we have now like the Health Service. Why we got rid of the Poor Law. History is important.' A man called Joe, with a corncrake voice that must have been useful if the pit telephone ever broke, spoke of the 1926 soup kitchens. Another ex-miner recalled 'police station' shoes, handed out to the indigent, but specially marked so that they couldn't be pawned. Southern remoteness is raised time and again. One of the Slough-bound trainees suggested the north–south imbalance could be cured by moving the House of Commons to Sunderland. Mr Cummings said: 'We're administered by proxy, by civil servants three hundred miles away. If a minister comes up, it's for all of six hours.'

Northerners are deeply frustrated by the control exercised over their lives and businesses by bureaucrats and financiers whose experiences and ways of life appear wholly alien. Such people are not even provincial satraps or colonial governors, who at least lived in the territories they ran. A group of miners told me how they had driven through the Thames Valley, Sussex and Kent during the miners' strike. Rubber-necking at the large houses along the banks of the Thames, they felt in another world, as far from their steep streets and red-brick back-to-backs as if they had been transported to the set of 'Dynasty' or 'Dallas'. 'You cannot compare the wealth: we're not living, man,' said one in awe. Another had a friend who lived in Taplow, near both the Thames and 'where Terry Wogan lives'. (Television stars, so close to everyone's lives and yet so far, are now the definitive success symbols.) This friend held midnight barbecues, which people attended dressed in shorts. No Roman orgy could have seemed more sybaritic or exotic.

People who led such different lives had to be at best ignorant of, at worst indifferent and callous towards, the industrial north. F. F. Ridley, Professor of Politics at Liverpool University, put the northern perspective in a *Guardian* article:

The government is London-based and shares with many southerners a peculiar view of the provinces. The north ... is not only a different world, but inhabited by a troublesome people who cost it money and irritate it politically. There is something almost racist about this view: all the people ... are tarred with the same brush, all are somehow responsible for the crisis and all can be left to stew in their own juice. We are supposed to be a United Kingdom. In such a kingdom, the troubles of one area should be the troubles of all, its welfare the responsibility of all. But we are not a united kingdom. We are deeply divided. Not by language as Belgium, not by religion and national identity as Northern Ireland, but by class ... A nation cannot survive without a national government committed – and seen to be committed – to the security of all its citizens, their education, their social services, their jobs. It cannot survive with a government that appears foreign to large parts of the country.

When visitors, like the 'six-hour' ministers, did make flying visits, Easington miners felt patronized. My companions still complained years later of a national newspaper article that had painted Easington as all whippets, tatty second-hand shops, and leeks. The writer, they claimed, had deceived them by wearing shabby clothes – an old mac and hat – and by talking to people who didn't realize they were being interviewed. 'He should have gone the whole bloody way, and worn a pit helmet and carried a ferret under his arm,' said one. The Revd Tony Hodgson, who on such occasions is the village spokesman, had written a letter of complaint. Durham miners are aware of their own problems, but don't like them advertised by outsiders, which creates in them an ambivalent attitude. The Townsend report, with its swingeing indictment of the health and living conditions in the area, was welcomed in that it was evidence of the battle scars suffered through the years, proof there was something special about being a miner, travelling in a crouched run five miles daily to the coalface, shovelling coal over your shoulder, and breathing a fine black dust that ate at your lungs. But woe betide the outsider who suggested that Wheatley Hill or Horden or Wingate or Shotton were not fine places to live. 'We have everything here,' a miner said to me, surveying Easington Colliery village with pride, 'allotments – see there and there, and right there up on the hill – recreation, a close community.' At that moment, I felt, he wouldn't have swopped his colliery home for a Florida beach house.

The northern resentment at being run like an overseas colony by a complacent establishment of Sir Humphreys and Sir Roberts and by hard-faced politicians, with braying didactic voices, has been heightened by the decline in the past twenty-five years of the north's own regional importance. When I lived in the West Riding, Manchester just over the Pennines was still a subsidiary capital. The speed of communications, the drift of the ambitious to the south, the removal of even some of London's powers to Brussels, Luxemburg and elsewhere, have eroded the north's limited independence. Banks, building societies, breweries, have been gobbled up into national conglomerates with headquarters in London. The north has been left with the branch offices and the branch factories, the first to be closed in recession. If you want a loan to start a business, the chances are the ultimate decision will be taken elsewhere by people who don't understand about manufacturing, and who see their professional skill in terms of eliminating risk and maximizing profit. The coal owners, the steel masters, the ship-building magnates lived in the north: the colliery manager was a substitute village squire. It was a sign of the times, said John Cummings, leader of the council, that he had recently been invited to become president of a village cricket club: in the past such honorary leadership of the community had always been undertaken by the pit manager. British Coal might 'belong' to the people, but its headquarters at Hobart House, London SW1, is a long way from Easington. The coal owners may have been hated – there was a notorious nineteenth-century Lord Londonderry, who was said to have raised rents on his Irish estates to drive his tenants off the land and into his British mines. 'They buried the bastard face-down,' said John Cummings, 'so he couldn't scrabble his way out' – but they were known individuals. All the major northern cities have lost something of their dignity and independence, and it hurts.

Westminster and Whitehall have been fitful in their attention to the region. In the early sixties, Lord Hailsham donned his cloth cap and took a brief interest. The first Wilson Government appeared to offer some hope: it provided a moment of local optimism. Wilson himself came to open the Labour Club in Peterlee. T. Dan Smith was 'Mr Newcastle'; John Poulson was designing civic buildings suitable for a newly affluent proletariat. Regional incentive schemes came and went. Peterlee discovered to its cost that its houses were more suitable for a Mediterranean climate than for the bitter north. (They had been built with flat roofs, which held the water and had to be replaced.) Peterlee Development Corporation did a sound, if unspectacular, job. Employment grew steadily. In late 1986 there were seven thousand jobs on the corporation's estates – half male and half female. But the corporation – described by Ed Henderson, its chief executive, as the 'most successful job creating agency in the sub-region' – was philosophically offensive to the Conservative Government, which was pledged to dismantle it. (One reprieve was granted and another was being sought when I was there.) 'They didn't analyse what we were doing, thirty guys getting on with the job in hand,' said Mr Henderson. Without it, job prospects would have been worse.

Private capitalists, then falling over themselves to get a piece of the 'Big Bang', would not finance a site in Peterlee even for such a risk-free enterprise as a new factory for a national food conglomerate. Mr Henderson complained that the Government believed that the only public help that private enterprise needed was roads, as if the north-east was as desirable to venture capital as is London's docklands. If the dismantling of Government 'Quangos' contributes to equality and efficiency, I'm for it. The 'great and the good' should be sent packing. But the north-east clearly needs special treatment, and in Peterlee the Development Corporation was well spoken of by both the guy with the spanner, one hundred pounds and a bright idea, and by multinationals like NSK of Japan. Mr Henderson said: 'I get a tremendous kick out of bringing companies to our area. You cannot enjoy seeing your own people without work.' The north needs people who care: market forces are not enough.

The Development Corporation's advertising budget is spent in London to overcome widespread board-room prejudice against the region. One television commercial showed a board meeting at which the chairman trotted out a series of misconceptions about the north-east, while his nose grew longer and longer, like Pinocchio's. The corporation produces a booklet, containing pictures of executive-style housing, wild, unspoiled country, new shopping centres and historic buildings. A four-bedroomed house, with four acres of land, on the outskirts of a pretty village was available for £65,000. Managers and professionals who are sent north often fall in love with the life, and resist when their time comes to return to London. But the prejudice remains. 'What we are up against,' a Yorkshire planning officer said to me, 'is the attitude of a businessman I was trying to persuade north. "My wife," he told me, "would never leave Surrey."' Mr Henderson claimed that old-fashioned work practices are not a problem in the new industrial environment of Peterlee, though they might have been a few years earlier along the Tyne and the Tees, where the attitude was, 'You were shop steward last time, Tommy, you'd better do it again.'

I had been in South Shields, a few miles from Easington, in the early months of Mrs Thatcher's first Government, when the 'on yer bike' philosophy first hit the headlines. The people I was seeing were middle-aged ship-builders, men past fifty, a Rubicon age for the unemployed, recently made redundant by the collapse of their industry. They had as much control over their fate as Bangladeshis trapped by a surging delta flood. These were hard-working, decent men, of an age to have served in the armed forces – some of them had fought in the Second World War. They had risen before dawn for thirty-five years and gone to work in cramped, noisy and dangerous conditions, which I found hard to tolerate even for thirty minutes as a mere spectator. By Tebbitite standards, they may have lacked foresight, living complacently in their council houses, taking little thought for the morrow, which, they were led to believe at successive elections, would take care of itself. They came – like miners – from a dependent tradition, working, when there was any, for large employers, who often also provided housing. ('Six generations of my family have been "nurtured" by Murton Colliery,' one miner told me, a choice of word that summed up the umbilical relationship.) They may have been too easily led into demarcation disputes and wildcat strikes, so contributing to the decline of their industry, but when ship-building collapsed, it collapsed worldwide. They were washed up at fifty: they would never work again. 'The new leisured class,' said one bitterly, 'are people on the scrapheap. Geordies could end up like Red Indians – as extras in films about the north-east.' Their skills were redundant, they were too old to be considered for retraining, they were anchored to council houses which could not be exchanged for hovels elsewhere in the country. Proud men wept as they talked of the collapse of their lives; their derisible redundancy – men had been bought out of a life-time's work for four or five thousand pounds – had already gone on carpets and sofas, and, yes, even colour televisions. Then on those very televisions appeared this gimlet-eyed man, with his thin slicked-down hair and his flat, south-eastern accent, telling these men to get on their bikes, as if tiny, overcrowded Britain, with its clapped-out industries, was a land of milk and honey, of limitless pioneer possi-bilities like the United States. 'We were already in the gutter,' one ex-shipyard worker said to me, 'now we are being kicked in the groin.' It wasn't elegantly stated, but it was language Norman Tebbit at least would have understood.

The northern tradition bred a collective identity, rather than an entrepreneurial, property-owning society. Property, almost by defini-tion, was owned by someone else. The northern working class lived on the margin, the loss of one week's pay packet was an economic disaster, which involved getting the weekend food 'on tick', to be repaid at the rate of ten bob each Friday over the following months. I calculated in 1964, when I lived in the West Riding, that the average family's possessions in the south Yorkshire coalfield were probably not worth more than three hundred pounds, an amount that even then an upper middle-class family might have spent on a holiday. Today a miner in work is much better off than he was then – 'we were bought out of the class struggle in 1974,' one grumbled only partly in jest, pointing to the irony that they finally achieved a decent wage just as much of the coal industry was being wound up. In pit car parks new vehicles have replaced the old bangers held together with the resin used to stop minor underground rockfalls. I met smartly dressed wives, who were stylish in a way that would have been inconceivable in the pit villages of their mothers' time. The homes I visited were well-carpeted, contained comfortable modern furniture; children played on com-puters, and two video stores in Easington Colliery village thrived.

But the attitude of mind from those years of dependency has

changed little. One couple – a sophisticated pair: he had been on a scholarship to the United States, and she, in new boots, jeans and sweater, was snappy and bright – had moved some years previously the unimaginable distance of five miles to a new house in Peterlee. They hated it, feeling isolated from the womblike community to which they were accustomed. The wife only slept there two nights a week, when she could have her sister with her, and, after eighteen months, they were once more in a colliery back-to-back, two minutes from the pit gate. A few streets away I met another miner, now retired – he had been on the NUM executive throughout the miners' strike. This man's son had trained as a chef, and, after a spell at a colliery canteen, had got a job at the Princess Hotel in Bermuda. He was back – 'don't laugh,' said his mother – within a week, saying that everyone he met in Bermuda had been on drugs. He was now twenty-four and had been out of work for three years since that brief trans-atlantic adventure. The young man was 'under the doctor' for de-pression. I sensed that his parents subconsciously preferred to have him at home, even if that meant being out of work, than gainfully employed an ocean away.

Ed Henderson's father was a miner, who always swore that his son would not follow him underground. Mr Henderson, now chief executive of Peterlee Development Corporation, fulfilled his father's expectations, pursuing a career in new towns and local government. Eventually the time came to move for promotion. 'I said, "Mam, dad, I'm leaving." "Why, you've got a good job here, why do you want to move? Can't you develop your career in the north-east?" They had three other children living almost on top of them, and I was only going to the Midlands, yet if they could have locked me in a room, and not allowed me to go, they would have done so.'

Many Durham people's ancestors had been economic refugees at least once – from Ireland, from the Highland clearances, from the Cornish tin mines. Moving is linked in the subconscious to defeat at the hands of harsh landlords or uncaring capitalists: moving in the eighties would mean another defeat, inflicted by a hated prime minis-ter. That gut reaction lies at the root of much of the opposition to Tebbitism. 'A crying shame really, lads going down south, dividing us still further,' said the retired miner whose son had fled Bermuda so precipitously, when I told him about the scheme to send the engineer-ing apprentices to Slough. This, naturally, is not the way the man who devised the Slough scheme, college lecturer Alan Dixon, sees it.

He argued that individual young people ought not to be sacrificed for a dubious principle or local pride. He had no problem with them leaving the region in pursuit of opportunities. The only thing he regretted was that he could not offer the trainees at least the choice of a worthwhile alternative nearer home. 'Young people do not improve with time. They are not the same after two or three years unemployed.' As for 'on yer bike' being an answer to regional unemployment, Mr Dixon laughed. 'It must be apparent even to a fool that that is nonsense. Jobs in other areas are not of the same magnitude as people here in need of work.' Bright kids in depressed areas, he suggested, face two particular disadvantages. Children perform less well at school than elsewhere in the country, lacking motivation because they feel there will be no jobs for them at the end. (While I was in Easington, Government figures were published showing that local O Level results had been considerably below the national average for the previous three years.) They also accept jobs for which they are more than adequately qualified.

The ten youths who were going to Slough were mainly from working-class backgrounds. They had been attracted by the prospect of an almost certain job at the end of their training, something for which they didn't hold out much hope in the north-east. One said that only one boy out of four hundred in his year at school had secured an apprenticeship. They had been impressed when they went south on a preliminary visit by how fast some young engineers had been promoted. They were going on a YTS scheme, but didn't feel it would exploit them as such schemes did in the north – 'here we'd be just like a slave sweeping up,' said one. They weren't very analytical. There was work in the south, they said, because London, the capital, was there, and because, with better opportunities, southern children could become 'doctors and so on', leaving humbler vacancies to be filled by the likes of them. They were not political: one said he had 'nearly fallen asleep' listening to students at Peterlee College – where they do their theoretical work – discussing the Government. Politicians promised a great deal, but essentially they are 'in it for the money, trying to make themselves richer,' said one. Although most of them thought they might stay in the south, or even go abroad, they valued what they perceived to be homely northern virtues. 'Southerners,' said one, 'are snobbier. The only snobs we have up here came from somewhere else. In the south they keep up with the Joneses; here we say "to hell with the Joneses".' To prepare them for the realities of living away from home, they had been instructed in such basic information as how to register with a doctor and what clothes not to mix together in the washer.

Self-reliance is also being promoted among young people on northern YTS schemes, many of whom have never been away from home. Trips are arranged to London and Brussels, and children are taken sailing. On one initiative test children were taken thirty miles from Cleveland and dropped in Newcastle, with enough money for lunch and a bus home. Some parents were outraged even by that. 'They did what? Dropped Tommy in the middle of Newcastle. How dare they?' one parent complained. An organizer said: 'If kids do move away, we'll get the blame. We'll be told "if you hadn't shown them, they wouldn't have gone".' There are some new local jobs – like the four hundred at the much ballyhooed Nissan car plant just north of Easington. The Japanese ball-bearing firm, NSK, was about to double the size of its plant in Peterlee. When news of the expansion leaked out through the planning application – like many Japanese firms, NSK do not publicize their achievements, much to the despair of the Peterlee Development Corporation who want all the good news broadcast – lads came running to the company gate in the hope of being taken on. The Japanese want malleable young people straight from school, untainted by the industrial practices for which the north-east was notorious. NSK has 'single status' – everyone has the same terms and conditions – and a single union agreement. Employees are expected to do (within reason) whatever needs doing regardless of their job titles. A maintenance engineer might be handed a paint brush. A company official told me that with his previous firm he had spent his whole time 'fire-fighting' industrial relations problems, often aggravated by the existence of seven unions at the plant. Now he was free to make a more positive contribution to the company. After ten years of operation in Peterlee, the average age of NSK employees was only twenty-five.

One dark afternoon, when the wind chased clouds of every shade of grey across what seemed to a city dweller an impossibly large sky, I drove to Bishop Auckland. The cold had cleared the streets, and I felt I was leaving the modern world as I turned under the clock tower and through the Gothic arch into the grounds of the Castle, official home of the Bishop of Durham. The Rt Revd David Jenkins is affectionately known in his diocese as 'Bishop David', and is much approved of by socialists like John Cummings, leader of Easington district council. He is less affectionately known and less approved of elsewhere for his supposed heresies on the literal truth of the New Testament, and his identification with the Labour cause. Bishop David's mobile face beneath a shock of white hair might have been created for 'Spitting Image': his hands, as he emphasized points from within a deep arm-chair in his study, were seldom still. He has, said a vicar's wife later, the 'air of a precocious schoolboy'.

Why, he wondered aloud, had the nation again become obsessed with the north–south divide? After all, it had long been with us, Disraeli and all that, and in hardship terms the people of Sunderland and Jarrow experienced nothing today like the deprivations of the twenties and thirties. (Although he added the caution that further cuts in supplementary benefits might yet reduce the poor to the dire straits of the past.) Was the renewed fascination, he suggested, because – despite the brave new world apparently emerging from the 'Big Bang' in the City of London – the more probable future for most of us lay here in the north where the post-industrial age had already dawned? Two Swiss television teams had recently been in the region pursuing just this thesis. It seemed unlikely to the bishop that money could perpetually breed money in the way it appeared to in the City of London. (In this the bishop is in tune with his flock: an Easington miner said: 'We can't all live on services like tourism, like those buggers in Spain.' The bishop himself had just heard of what he considered the ultimately unproductive service industry – a company set up in London to deliver takeaway food from restaurants to diners too idle to go themselves.) Sooner rather than later we were all going to be forced to tighten our belts, said the bishop. The sort of economic policies thrust on the country – and he cited deregulated buses – were 'a sick or nasty joke up here'. Seen from the midst of a shattered region, the remedies of neither Militants nor monetarists held much appeal. Politics, he said, had become self-indulgent – moral and theoretical: the tests ahead would return them to the pragmatic and prudential. In the nineteenth century, belief in progress was tempered by a realization that it would take time and require hard work. Now both extremes promise instant solutions. When people with whom we disagree fail, we feel we are entitled to hate them. He saw ahead a 'leaner, more communal Britain. The north is leading the way.' In the meantime he fears that the widening gap between the haves and have-nots may cause violence and unrest.

John Cummings said the region had suffered a stroke rather than a heart attack – just as potentially fatal, but less dramatic, and therefore easier to ignore. Miners I talked with spoke of a feeling that they were close to 'the last kick of the match.' These men saw the bishop's class war coming, with the police being equipped for the front line. 'There's a boom now, but when the spending stops, what then? The Government's answer is to have a highly trained, paramilitary police force,' said one miner. 'All we want is a decent job, a decent standard of living, a decent education for our children, and a holiday once a year.' Those modest requirements are already out of the reach of many British people. When you work in hard and dangerous conditions, it is difficult to accept that your activity might not be economic. I had recently visited a mine in South Africa where the coal is scooped out by the bulldozer load, with no one going underground. Each man – black and white – was something like sixty times as productive as his British counterpart. The manager told me – with only slight exaggeration – that they could wrap each lump in gold foil and still deliver coal to the British market more cheaply than it can be produced by British miners. We live in a global economy – as the people who once made cars and television sets in this country know to their cost. Britain still produces industrial cannon fodder rather than the technicians needed for the international trade war which is now fought from computer terminals.

Before I left Easington District I drove to Shotton. In 1933 this small mining village shocked J. B. Priestley more than all the other horrors and poverties of the industrial north. He described it as a village beneath 'an active volcano'. 'The atmosphere,' he wrote, 'was thickened with ashes and sulphuric acid; like that of Pompeii, as we are told, on the eve of its destruction . . . the whole village and everybody in it was buried in this thick reek.' Priestley hastened away, wishing that the volcano would 'always be there, not as a smoking "tip", but as a monument to remind happier and healthier men of England's old industrial greatness and the brave days of Queen Victoria'.

I don't know whether Priestley returned before he died in 1984, but his monument is now a gentle grassy hill, grazed by sheep. A parachute club, made homeless when Nissan took its previous site for its Sunderland factory, is to create a small airfield on what was once its summit. The village air is clear enough today, and many of the poor houses Priestley saw have been pulled down. There remain some back-to-backs, with cobbled streets, but the environment is now no worse than rather drab. A village store sells everything from gaudy wreaths to clothes, and the assembly hall is boarded up. I suspect there was a great deal more village activity and community life in the days of the volcano. The fire and the sulphur have been replaced by a bleakness; and a visitor still leaves thanking God that he lives elsewhere. Unlike the unfortunate people of the inner cities, whose riots are clear-enough statements of utter frustration, the human survivors of the industrial north-east have no voice. The population of Easington District has declined by fourteen thousand in the past twenty-five years: industrial workers are no longer needed for the battle, and, like old soldiers when the war is over, they are fading away.

⍟〔 3 〕⍟

'ON YER BIKE'

Charlie led the way across the frosted ground, limping at a fast gait.
His feet slipped erratically inside his battered, oversized sneakers. He
wore a soiled dark blue overcoat and on his head a filthy trilby. He
was tall and thin and angular, and his shoulders were slightly
stooped: from behind, under the occasional street light, he looked
like an animated scarecrow, escaped from the Berkshire fields. His
companions were equally bizarre to the eye. One, Nigel, was arrayed
in an old mac, flapping jeans and heavy boots, his dirty face was
punctured with small scars. We crossed the railway footbridge above
Newbury station, an echoing metal structure, refrigerated by a cold
wind slicing through smashed window panes. 'I've slept here,' said
Nigel, 'a railwayman woke me in the morning, gave me 10p for a cup
of coffee and told me to move.' It was a matter-of-fact statement,
without rancour.

Late commuters travelling the fifty miles from London pulled their
collars up and moved aside. The ice was already thick on the wind-
screens of the few cars left in the station car park. 'Hello, darling,'
Charlie shouted to a lone policewoman in a small panda car. She
ignored him. Past the still-lit council offices, round a corner and
through a hole in a high wire fence that was just the size of a man
bent low. Sharp right into the back of an abandoned do-it-yourself
shop, where once timber, steel and glass were stored for improving
the homes of high-tech yuppies who have colonized the Thames Valley. A faint light shone through the shop window. We stopped in
what once must have been an office: abandoned files and papers
strewed the floor. 'This is where we sleep,' said Charlie defiantly.
One could just see some filthy bedding. Something stirred heavily upstairs – cats? winos? Charlie shrugged.

'It's warmer than you might think,' I said encouragingly. 'Not at
2.00 a.m.,' replied Charlie, 'it's fucking cold then.' 'I can imagine.'

'No you can't,' he said fiercely. 'You can't start to imagine that cold unless you've tried to sleep in it.' He was right, of course I couldn't, heading back eventually to a centrally heated home. We were in another world, yet only a few yards from estate agents, restaurants, boutiques, as removed from comfortable society as if we had been in Fagin's kitchen. Charlie and his companions were like rats: by day an eyesore that affronted decent citizens as they scavenged and begged and got drunk in public. By night invisible in holes. When I left them, a young, well-dressed couple, hand-in-hand, on their way for a night out, looked strangely out of place: visiting that squat, and meeting those poor, bare people had worked a subtle change on reality.

Four and a half years ago, when he was nineteen, Charlie had 'got on his bike', headed south from Merseyside, where his parents had been destitute and his several siblings jobless. The only work he had ever had was on Youth Opportunity Projects. He had not had Dick Whittington expectations, and he found a job, as a care assistant to handicapped people at Aldermaston – £127 a month plus food and lodging. 'I thought I'd make a go of it,' he said. It lasted sixteen months. That gone, for a while he had a bedsit in Reading.

Had he worked since? He drew in his breath. 'Not since 84, not since then. No,' he said. The slide had been rapid. Once he had lost his bedsit, he could no longer present himself in respectable enough clothes to expect the most menial of jobs. Why didn't he go back to Liverpool? 'I've made my mates down here, like. There's nothing up there for me.' The future? 'For me?' he stroked the fluff on his chin, surprised that anyone might think he had one.

Nigel, who had been brought up in Stafford, walked out on his parents because they were always arguing. Like Charlie, he was to be twenty-four a few days later. He had never worked. What would he like to do? 'Work in a record shop.' The way he is now, it would make as much sense to wish to be a brain surgeon. He reflected: 'I hope to get a bedsit in the end. I can't go on living like this for the rest of my life.'

The contrast between their destitute lives and their Thames Valley neighbours' affluence did not escape them. Everything Charlie owned, he wore. A rag merchant would have burned his clothes. 'Most people here have got a lot of money, so they have the attitude we should dress properly. We're isolated because we're out of work and everyone else's in it – leading normal lives, with cars, houses and families,' said Charlie.

I met Charlie, Nigel and their companion, a local man, in Newbury in the Royal County of Berkshire. An hour later, in Reading, in an overnight refuge for homeless men, an unemployed man called Martin told me how he had boarded a bus in Peterlee, Durham, at midnight on Sunday. He had had five pounds in his pocket, and in his head an idea from mates who had gone south that there would be building work in Reading. Martin was lucky: the refuge in a castellated former army barracks – known as 'The Keep', and, in the frozen mist, the perfect backdrop to a Gothic horror film – had had to turn several men away into the inhospitable night. It is only allowed to take thirteen.

Like Charlie and Nigel, Martin was twenty-three and the only work he had had since school was also on Government schemes. He had never had a proper job, only occasional 'fiddle work' on the black economy. His mother had said: 'What are you going to do? Spend the rest of your life sitting waiting for the dole cheque to come through the post?' So here he was, respectably dressed in blue windcheater, check trousers, and light grey loafers, but penniless, hope oozing out of him like a falling tide. In the outer room, his twelve companions for the night, having finished their soup, watched television. Most, like Martin, were tidily dressed: the 'tramp' types kept to the back. Three days searching by Martin had failed to turn up either his mates or work. Three consecutive nights is the limit in The Keep. If his luck hadn't changed by the morrow, when he was hoping to find a bedsit and get it financed by the DHSS, he said he would hitch home, and perhaps try again in the spring or summer, when there might be seaside work. There was no point looking for work if you were sleeping rough.

Martin, Nigel and Charlie were the ultimate victims of the accelerating unemployment gap between north and south. Their varying plights served as bleak and unhappy human evidence that more people than we may care to consider have fallen off the last rung of the ladder. Their problems were not purely geographic: they were none of them stupid, but they were uneducated, without skills and poorly motivated. As such they would probably have been unemployed even if they had been born in the affluent Thames Valley. The two Englands are increasingly divided between those who have a relevant skill for the late twentieth century, and those with a broad back, a pair of hands and a limited degree of commitment. But in coming from the north, the young men suffered further disadvantages, which, in at least two of their cases, had nearly crushed them. Their tragedy is our tragedy. As they rot on the margins of society, Britain's national capacity to compete is being eroded by a shortage of skills, and by a critically undereducated population. But, even if Charlie and his companions had had marketable talents, their chances of establishing themselves in the south would have been very remote. The odds are overwhelmingly stacked against a northern working man moving south, however skilled, and however strong his motivation. If he has a council home, with whom can he exchange it? If he owns a house, how can he sell it for anything like the value of a home in the south?

Before I met Charlie and Nigel, I had spent two weeks in Slough, looking at the community and economy to which the ten Peterlee YTS trainees were to come for their engineering apprenticeships. It had been dark for an hour as I stood on my first evening on Buckingham Avenue in the heart of the Slough industrial estate. Lights shone from the office windows, and from the factories came the sound of men at work. Lathes were turning; computer terminals were flickering busily; forklift trucks were carrying finished goods to waiting lorries; other lorries were delivering steel sheeting; machines, of impossible complexity to the lay eye, were turning out parts to make other machines. In the reception areas of mostly small and medium-sized firms, there was a regular ebb and flow of visitors – buyers, salesmen, engineers. In one, a grey-suited, bespectacled team of Chinese – themselves, in their earnest similarity, the human embodiment of component parts – were checking in with elaborate courtesy, having just arrived for training on machinery their company was to import. A production engineer, talking specifications with a visitor, was paged twice in three minutes. Outside on the street, men sat in Ford Escorts and BMWs talking on car phones.

The buzz of a highly charged atmosphere was apparent everywhere. This is how it had once been in Coventry, on Merseyside, along the banks of the Tyne. Making things can be just as exciting as making money. Hours later, long after conventional going home time, lights were still burning that December night in many of these factories, as workers on shifts or overtime bent to their machines to meet deadlines. Those who went home promptly joined a line of cars that took thirty minutes to edge its way one mile from the industrial estate to the M4. If anyone doubts that some people at least are gainfully employed in Britain, let him come to Slough. It is the cockpit of the Thames Valley, and therefore of modern industrial England, itself unfashionable and disregarded – as travellers on the M4 strain to catch a glimpse of Windsor Castle in the opposite direction – but a town at work in a manner that is only a memory across vast tracts of Britain.

I had just left the down-to-earth production manager of a typical Slough firm, which employed 140 people – sixty to seventy of them on manual production jobs. The company was between ten and fifteen people below strength, despite conducting recruiting drives across the country, and, if they could have found them, could have employed next morning fabricators, electricians, machinists, designers and people to quote prices. The labour shortage was so acute that they took unsatisfactory, highly priced agency workers by the week, who travelled up to sixty miles daily.

'It is iniquitous,' said the boss, 'people are crying out for work, and we can't get any staff here. Something is wrong entirely.' That something is, of course, housing. It was a theme I was to return to in every conversation I had in Slough. In a town of drear estates and uninspiring architecture, the top floor of a pebble dash, thirties terraced house, 'converted' into a maisonette – and described as a 'starter home' by the estate agents who proliferate in this climate like frogs in a pond – commands, at £45,000, a substantially higher price than a four-bedroomed detached house in the industrial north. Even presuming that a northern working man owns a marketable home, he cannot – on the most lavish or slavish of overtime – bridge that gap. In late 1986 the average price of a semi-detached house in Greater London was £76,215, in Yorkshire and Humberside a similar house was priced at £26,317; the average flat in Greater London fetched £52,720, in Yorkshire it was priced at £16,699. Slough, I was told by the relative of one valuer, has the worst pound for pound bricks and mortar values in Britain, and I could well believe it.

When the production manager goes north on a recruiting drive, he takes with him Slough newspapers to show not only the property prices, but also that there is both plenty of employment to which the worker can switch if the first job proves unsatisfactory, and that there is stacks of part-time office work for women. But such marginal blandishments are seldom sufficient for people who are not only faced with gigantic mortgages, but also with the emotional shock of leaving the close-knit support of their home towns. 'It may take three to five years for a northerner to get back on his feet,' said the manager; a daunting prospect even for desperate, long-term unemployed who sincerely want to get a job. It helps, naturally, if the northern job-seeker does not have children: with few exceptions, the people I did meet who had transplanted themselves were childless. Several said they were 'fortunate' to be so, a sad and amazing assertion forty years after the foundation of the welfare state, and a generation after we were told that we had never had it so good.

I asked the manager if he had thought of moving his firm north. Yes, he said, but by so doing they would lose their most highly skilled people, some of whom reached their full value to the company only after three or four years of employment. Such people could easily find alternative work in Slough. He estimated that only half a dozen of his present workers would be prepared to make such a move. The dilemma, as he put it, was that if the firm stayed it couldn't get sufficient basic workers; if it moved it lost essential staff. (To mitigate the labour shortage, he was 'de-skilling' jobs, using computers to enable unskilled men to carry out skilled functions.)

He bore also a prejudice, which I was to find to be common in Slough, against northern working practices. He had seen them firsthand, when, as a young engineer, he travelled the region maintaining machinery. 'Our northern cousins,' he said, 'don't do themselves any favours.' He recalled spending two days on a job he estimated should have taken an hour and a half because a different 'craftsman' was required at each stage to perform such sophisticated tasks as unplugging the electrical supply. He spoke of 'torrid' times, adding, 'I wouldn't relish putting a manufacturing plant into one of those areas.' (His company no longer recognizes trade unions, ending its agreement after its workers had been forced into a national strike, although the firm was already paying more than the amount for which the strike was called.) A partial remedy to the critical labour imbalance, he said, was for the Government to spend some of the money now going on dole on resettling skilled men where they are needed – say £20,000 a man – before their skills waste away or changes to their industry make them redundant.

At the same factory, I met a 48-year-old engineer who had moved from Manchester six years earlier; there he had owned a substantial house which was worth enough to enable him to buy a much smaller one at Bracknell, a few miles from Slough. He had received £3,500 in Government relocation grants, which are available to lower paid people. He added that although he didn't regret coming south – skilled men who had been made redundant with him six years earlier were still out of work – he had found southerners unfriendly. 'Luckily,' he said, 'the next-door people are from Leeds.' Other neighbours, even after six years, avert their eyes when they meet on the street: his wife had been ignored the day after a Tupperware party by a woman she had sat next to and with whom she had had a long, friendly conversation. She had been deeply hurt. (Other transplanted northerners I met clung together: in the face of home counties indifference, Bolton teams up with Newcastle, and Stockport with Sheffield.)

Slough, the second leg of my inquiry into the north–south divide, is best known outside the town for lines penned by John Betjeman:

> Come, friendly bombs, and fall on Slough
> It isn't fit for humans now,

It had been the fastest growing British town between the two World Wars (and has virtually doubled in size again since), and clearly offended Betjeman, the high priest of Victoriana, by its rapid industrialization and determined functionalism. Slough is still far from being a beautiful place – though it has a parks department that carries off gold medals at the Chelsea flower show – with its power station and its pylons, its sewage works beside the M4 (an area of town known as 'Pong City', the smell of which even a liberal use of deodorant has failed to curb), its former LCC (London County Council) overspill housing estates, its factories and sprawling industrial area hugging the Bath Road. Close to tourist attractions and beauty spots like Eton, Windsor, Burnham Beeches, and the Thames itself, it is crammed within a tight boundary, a ghetto of worker bees amongst the butterflies of Taplow, Marlow and Maidenhead, prevented from expanding by surrounding green belt, in which the butterflies enjoy fine and spacious living. In the midst of ancient privilege and plenty, it is a determinedly working-class town.

A visitor who knew nothing of Slough's unusual prosperity would be surprised not just by the number of estate agents – I counted nine, together with eight building societies and a money-lender, in a two-hundred-yard stretch of the High Street – but also by the money being spent. 'Like there's no tomorrow,' said the town's public relations officer happily, adding that it was routine to see 'nice new middle-class cars' like BMWs and Porsches' outside the town's fast-food restaurants. Slough is at the heart of the national consumer boom, fuelled by the explosion of high street credit: a man in work in 1987 could borrow until not another electronic gadget could be squeezed past his mock-Victorian front door into his starter home. But, while Slough's shopping and its thriving, largely union-free industry is the epitome of Thatcherism, its municipal politics in recent years have been left-wing, marked by rhetoric and gestures worthy of Liverpool Militant Derek Hatton. A sign outside the town hall proclaims 'Welcome to Slough, an anti-nuclear town.'

Despite the sleek, glass and steel, architect-designed factories – there are parts of the industrial estate where you could fancy yourself in a booming Massachusetts town – Slough is not a 'silicon' town like its neighbours Bracknell and Reading: much of what goes on behind both the art-deco factory fronts and the tatty corrugated iron shacks is an updated version of good old metal bashing, and its worker population still reflects that – at least when electing a council. (The town returned a Conservative MP in 1983 and in 1987, but is a marginal constituency. Joan Lestor represented it for Labour for many years.) Slough is not therefore the pampered south. Orwell wrote in 1936: 'There can hardly be a town in the south of England where you could throw a brick without hitting the niece of a bishop.' Not many bishops' nieces are to be found in Slough.

Local history has not shaped attitudes here as it has in Easington: few people's roots go back to the days of royal excursions from Windsor. The only relevant history was practical – the building of the Great Western Railway in 1835. It was naturally opposed by the Establishment of the day in the shape of nearby Eton College, whose provost feared that, if his boys could be 'carried a distance of five miles in fifteen minutes', they could easily remove themselves from the authority of the school. The college's influence was sufficient to have a clause inserted in an Act of Parliament that there should be no railway station within three miles of the school, which ruled out Slough. However, even without a station, the trains stopped in the tiny town, and tickets were sold at the Crown Inn. Eton College protested, but at the same time ordered a train to carry boys to London for Queen Victoria's coronation.

Slough was an appropriate place in which to test the reality and practicality of the 'on yer bike' philosophy. The Peterlee trainees, who were to be placed with a number of different Slough companies, were following a seventy-year tradition of labour migration into the town. In 1917 the Government turned a six-hundred-acre site on the outskirts of what was still a small country community into a repair depot for army vehicles damaged in the First World War. After the war and a loss-making attempt to run what was known locally as 'the dump' or 'timbertown' as a nationalized industry, the Government 'privatized' the depot, selling it to a business syndicate for seven million pounds. A magazine called *Motor News* commented: 'It will be something of a miracle if they succeed in converting Slough into a money-earning concern... If private enterprise is successful with an establishment which drove officialdom almost to despair, it will be a telling argument against bureaucratic methods.' A telling argument it proved: the syndicate did succeed, and, as the repaired vehicles were sold off, let out the redundant space as factory units. So was created the Slough Estates company, now a worldwide enterprise, around which the town itself prospered. In 1987, there were 25,000 workers on the estate in 320 companies – though that figure is lower than its sixties peak of 33,000, whittled away by the introduction of new technology.

Between the wars, it was the Welsh who left the valleys and headed east along the A4 to the town rising from 'the dump': recent newcomers have been Asians ('it's the first town they come to after leaving Heathrow' is the local joke), and nearly a quarter of the population has origins in the Indian sub-continent, a proportion projected to rise substantially by the end of the twentieth century. Between these two mass migrations came Cockneys, Irish and Poles. The mobility continues, and one-fifth of all owner-occupier houses change hands each year. Because of its solid industrial base – and despite the extortionate house prices – Slough remains a community without frills. Shortly before my visit, the mayor, a former Londoner with a rough diamond reputation, had crossed swords with, of all people, the Queen Mother – a skirmish that said much about both the town and how its grand neighbours see it. She was quoted as saying that Windsor had been much nicer before the development of Slough. He was then said to have called her a 'nasty old woman'. It ended with the mayor inviting the Queen Mother to a cup of tea – which she didn't accept.

Slough, in short, with its factories and its immigrants, its right-wing entrepreneurs, its left-wing Labour council and its working-class ethos, is an unlikely town to find on the Queen's doorstep on the banks of the 'sweete Thames'. But, with the planes from Heathrow trundling across the skyline, the M4 on its doorstep, the M25 girdling London a few miles to the east, Slough symbolizes the prosperous energy of the south. If all Britain was as hard and as profitably at work, the nation would be enjoying a prosperity that would put it alongside Japan in the world industrial league table.

I pondered several questions during my visit. Is there a magic to be found there that could transform a northern town like Peterlee into a similarly thriving community? Are there Government policies that could spread the wealth more evenly and create opportunities that would keep the travelling trainees at home? Why would most industrialists, faced with a choice between a green field site in the northeast, backed with development grants and other incentives, and an overcrowded, urban site, still, one suspects, plump for Slough – despite the town's housing shortages, the labour difficulties and the high rents and rates?

Of all the people I met in search of some answers, Matt Sobol most embodied the spirit of the place. His parents had moved the twenty miles from London when he was a child. According to his own account, he had been a deadbeat in school and lucky to get an engineering apprenticeship. He was in his mid-thirties and looked like a younger version of the football manager, Brian Clough. He was manufacturing director of another small engineering firm, Production Machines, which employed 110 people and manufactured special purpose machine tools. He loved complex, infinitely precise, steel component parts, as a Russian aristocrat might have loved Fabergé eggs, handling them with delicate care. 'Components are living things. We don't do mass production. We don't want automatons pushing a button: we want thinking men. You're turning a block of metal into a work of art. One tiny mistake can wipe out a component worth ten thousand pounds. One-thousandth of an inch out and you have to chuck it in the bin.' Feeling like that about his firm's products, he valued with an equal intensity the men who were skilled and dedicated enough to make such mechanical wonders. He said: 'We don't want a labour turnover. We want to think we can keep them, that they'll buy a house, settle down, become an integral part of the company. I get so annoyed when engineers are maligned, caricatured like "Wack", the cartoon character. We've got the best workforce in the world. We don't manage them properly. The attitude is "you work for us, and do what you're bloody well told". They need to be cultivated. There's no point in driving people.'

The company had been taken over thirteen years earlier by a management buy-out, and, in a recent production reorganization, had been shrewd enough, enthusiastically supported by the bank, to make Mr Sobol a director. He was often in at seven in the morning, and was usually still there twelve hours later. So acute was the firm's labour shortage that he spent 60 per cent of his time on recruiting, despite a vast range of other responsibilities. Orders were met only through 'excessive' overtime – the factory worked between sixty and seventy hours each week – and even so business was occasionally turned away. 'We'd like to expand, the business is there,' said Mr Sobol. The crux of the problem is that in recent years, as British manufacturing industry has collapsed like a cliff battered by a relentless sea, almost no young people have done apprenticeships.

Mr Sobol found to his regret – and to the firm's cost – that unemployed people trained at Government skill centres were not good enough. (They are known unkindly in the trade as 'dilutees'.) He said: 'With the best will in the world they couldn't make it. You can only learn so much in six to nine months. You need total immersion in engineering. The might be able to operate a machine, but they don't have a feel for the job.' Boys who do come are often reluctant volunteers, sent by parents who think they ought to have a trade 'Ask them what they want to be doing in five years, and they'll say "drive a lorry". People don't want to get their hands dirty.'

So, when the Production Machines' business picked up in the mid-eighties, Matt Sobol recruited in the north. Two things struck him immediately – the despair of the unemployed and the complacent inertia of Government bureaucracies. 'They like,' said Mr Sobol, 'to keep their benefits secret.' One DHSS office was furious when he told a job applicant that the man was entitled to his train fare south. 'What bloody right had you to tell him?' he was asked. He squeezed a council flat out of Slough Council under the national mobility scheme – an almost unheard of achievement – by threatening to publicize his employee's difficulties in local newspapers. But his deepest concern was with the anguish suffered by the unemployed victims of this official indifference. He said: 'I wouldn't wish to be in their shoes. They may have been made redundant three or four times in a couple of years, and used up all their savings. All they are left with are their wives and families. They have to leave them to come down here for a job and live in a cheap bedsit. All the people I know from the north have undergone some form of personal trauma. They're shell-shocked when you pick them up at the station: sometimes it's nearly brought tears to my eyes.'

Like the first manager I spoke to in Slough, he is not, however, enamoured of northern work practices, though he understands the history that created them. 'They have always had to fight for their rights. Employer/employee relationships are abysmal. Workforces are wary and unco-operative. Everything the guv'nor wants must have something behind it. Management in the north is based on the big stick, going back to the days of sweatshops in the textile mills. It's a diabolical way to get production. You don't get the flexibility we get. Here you can say to a guy, "Do me a favour, jump on a lathe or a mill or a forklift truck".' Production Machines and six other Slough firms did open subsidiaries, not in the north, but in south Wales. All of them, faced with union inflexibility, had pulled out within two and a half years, Production Machines being the last to go. Mr Sobol, then a foreman, was sent down by his boss, who thought it was time he was exposed to industrial 'reality'. 'When we told them that in Slough we had working foremen, the shop steward said, "Well, you're not going to have the first working foreman in south Wales."'

Bernie Beeston is one of the people Matt Sobol had in mind when he talked of the traumatized unemployed. A universal miller by trade, he had been out of work living in north Wales for four and a half years – 'I can tell you exactly when I was made redundant: 4.10 on Friday, the 10th of September 1980. I was given twenty minutes to pack all my kit and sling my hook' – when he read an article about job opportunities in the south. He rushed to his local Job Centre, and demanded to know why he hadn't been told of the national vacancies computer, mentioned in the feature. 'They said I was too old at thirty-eight,' he said incredulously. 'If I hadn't seen that article, I'd still be sat there drawing my dole money now.' The computer threw up nine or ten suitable jobs, one of them at Production Machines, which had been vacant for nine months. While Mr Sobol had been scouring the country for just such a man, Mr Beeston had been eating his heart out for just such an opportunity. So much for the efficiency and co-ordination of the national system.

Mr Beeston was rusty after his years on the dole, but Mr Sobol stuck by him. However, his troubles continued. After a few months in a furnished room, he raised a mortgage so that his family could come south. But, after years of living on 'Maggie's money', the Beestons plunged into debt. 'As soon as I was working again, I was handed credit by the bucketful. It was easy to go mad on carpets, fridges, microwaves.' Those debts and, more crucially, the mortgage broke him. The bank repossessed the house. His family had to return to north Wales and Mr Beeston to a bedsit. The story had a happy ending for the Beestons: the family found another house, this time in south Wales for £16,500 – 'it would have been £70,000 in Slough' – and, after some months commuting from Slough at weekends, Mr Beeston landed a job near his new home. Mr Sobol had given a good man a fresh start, but was himself again left with a vacancy. Mr Beeston said: 'The biggest bugbear in the south is housing. If anything is going to break your back it will be that. No working wage is enough. If they chop your overtime, you've had it. People who say "on yer bike" don't know the half of it.'

Tony Whitworth, an articulate man in his early thirties, with curly, prematurely greying hair, is another Sobol success story. He was working in Oldham, but was unhappy, living on a derelict estate – '"rough" wasn't the half of it' – in a lousy house that shifted on its foundations so the doors wouldn't close. He felt in a rut, and found management–worker relations poor. 'Loyalty was a one-way street. If you had problems, tough luck. If they had problems, they made you bend to them. Gave me the hump.' He said that the northern companies he had worked for had been concerned only with getting the goods out of the door. Workers, consequently, had been less flexible. They downed tools on the stroke of time – 'on the nose, straight into the washroom. They timed it to the minute. Here you might spend ten or fifteen minutes handing over to the next shift.'

The divide between 'them' and 'us', said Mr Whitworth, was much greater in the north – a view that would surprise the Durham miners who contended that class distinctions chiefly existed south of the Trent and that southern employers were more likely than northern ones to exploit their workers. The Oldham working class, according to Mr Whitworth, are stuck away on their big council estates. As a man in work, he was a freak where he lived. He estimated that 80 per cent of the estate were unemployed – 'they looked at you as if you were a monster when you came home.' Vandalism, burglary, foul language on the street, even glue-sniffing were a constant menace: the Whitworths didn't allow their children out to play. One set of neigh-bours, he said, summed up the estate: 'the man in his late twenties had been out of work for six or seven years. He had no intention of working; three months was the longest he had ever held a job. He sat on his backside and did nowt. He told me they had more children to get more money. They had four and one on the way when we left. They had a seventy-foot back garden. They threw their bottles out there. You'd hear them shout to the kids: "Don't play in that back garden, there's broken glass out there." The only people who bothered with gardens were those in work.'

Before Mr Whitworth took the Slough job, he had considered emigrating to Canada, but his wife didn't want to go that far from home. 'When I see the Mounties on television, I still get a little touch here,' he said, tapping his chest. It was for the Whitworth family that Matt Sobol pressurized a council flat out of Slough Council. Until Mr Whitworth gets to know a long-term Sloughite properly, he is cagey about this stroke of good fortune. 'They don't take kindly. The first question is "How did you get it? My brother's been on the list six years".' The flat was in poor condition, but Mr Whitworth has been improving it. In late 1986, he was earning, with overtime, £15,000 a year, and planning to buy the flat, which – with the discount to sitting tenants and the years of 'credit' he had accumulated on his council home in Oldham – he would be getting for little more than half its market value. Had he owned his own house in Oldham, he could never have afforded to come south. In his case property-owning would, ironically, have been a bar to mobility.

His wife was learning word-processing skills at Slough College: a local agency told her she could have her pick of fifty jobs to suit whatever hours she wished to work. 'Fifty! The *Oldham Chronicle* wouldn't have had fifty across every category of employment,' said Mr Whitworth. He was intending to vote Conservative: '85 per cent of people are in work, and a Government has got to look after them. It's no good biting the hand that feeds you. Labour would be restrictive on people.' (He told me that in November 1986, and from that moment I was convinced Mrs Thatcher would win the impending election comfortably.)

We had been having this conversation in a barren roadhouse where the waitresses wore Beefeater dresses which, far from creating the cheerful effect presumably desired by the management, accentuated their sullen attitudes. When I ordered food, one waitress, with a pinched face and peroxide hair, looked furtively at her watch, clearly hoping I was too late. There was not an ounce of generosity in her whole frame. The drinkers looked morose or lonely, men who'd spent too much of their unfulfilled lives in such bars: one in an unclean, shapeless jacket and trousers was vaguely in control of a mongrel that scavenged round the jukeboxes and fruit machines for scraps. The decor was oak beams and counterfeit loaves of bread gathering dust behind the food counter. Why do we British tolerate such cheerless places? On the way back to Production Machines, in a steady downpour that washed away what colour there was on the back roads of the industrial estate, Mr Whitworth suddenly burst out: 'Look at all these people at work.' It was a spontaneous cry from the refugee from the Oldham council estate, a man who has lived in both halves of divided Britain, revealing a fundamental happiness at being in work, having a home he was about to buy, and being amongst other citizens equally gainfully employed, than any number of depressing bars or wet days couldn't suppress.

Mr Whitworth, with his council flat, is a lucky man in the context of the 'on yer bike' debate. Many others, just as well motivated, have been driven back north to unemployment by their failure to find anywhere to live. In late 1986, there were an estimated 250,000 unfilled jobs in the south-east, as a direct result of the housing shortage. British Rail alone had seven thousand vacancies, which makes more explicable, if no more tolerable, those persistently cancelled commuter trains. A Conservative MP initiated a job link scheme between Cleveland in the north-east and High Wycombe in Buckinghamshire, but after a few months only twenty-four of the original 100 remained in the south. One who went back to the dole had found a £140 a week job as a caretaker. He left his wife and two small children in the north, lived in lodgings, and spent every evening for seven months searching for a house he could afford. His own house on Teesside was worth £15,000, and anything large enough for his family in Buckinghamshire started at £35,000. A fifty-year-old electrician persevered for a year, hoping for a council house.

Employers have tried bringing workers from Birmingham and south Wales into the Thames Valley on Sunday nights, putting them up in local digs, and shipping them home again after work on Fridays. Such schemes, born of desperation, seldom survive long, as the transported workers tire of the weekly commute, and are always looking for jobs nearer home. Other would-be migrants simply can't get jobs despite their eagerness – although there are vacancies for skilled men, there are not enough semi-skilled jobs to go round. A Maidstone garage received one thousand inquiries from the north-east for twelve vacancies after its managing director had written a letter to a Geordie paper complaining that he could not fill the jobs with Kent labour: he had to carry out the interviews at a secret location for fear of starting a minor riot. (This company solved the accommodation problem by buying property to let to its northern workers.) A Sussex hotel manager wrote a letter to a national newspaper reporting that, despite a six-month advertising campaign, she had been unable to fill ten jobs. She was instantly swamped with four hundred applications, and three young Liverpudlians hitched nearly three hundred miles in the speculative hope they could land jobs. The ten Peterlee trainees, housed in a Y M C A hostel and protected by a 'moral tutor', were cosseted by sponsors who naturally wished the experiment to succeed. The lone job-seeker must do without such organized support. Damien Wolmar, a Slough careers officer, suggested there should be tuition in the schools careers programme on coping on one's own. 'On yer bike' assumes all sorts of skills to survive away from family and community which few teenagers have.

Despite the transatlantic parallels favoured by Mrs Thatcher and her colleagues, the British context is totally different from the American. While I was reporting from Washington D C in the early eighties, a devastating recession swept the north-eastern 'rust belt' in the United States. Ohio steel-works shut down, throwing up to ten thousand out of work in one blow; redundancy figures of an order of which we have, fortunately, no experience. Most of those who lost their jobs faced ruin unless they rapidly shifted for themselves: their unemployment pay expired after six months, welfare payments only started when they were virtually destitute. So they packed their belongings into camper vans and headed south and west in the tracks of generations of pioneers. Often they stopped at the first town that offered a job. The smart ones spotted a need in their new communities and started catering for it: soon they might be employing one or two others. In four years, as six million jobs were wiped out by recession, nine million new ones were created. It was a staggering achievement, which on a smaller scale we have managed in the past. The Scottish 'Mac' or 'Mc' is the most common prefix in the London telephone directory: tens of thousands of northerners and Welsh came to the south-east and the Midlands between the wars. Midlands towns like Coventry grew on labour from elsewhere. But such migrations will never again be emulated in our cramped and cold islands: slashing the dole, American-style, would simply convert the unfortunate into the destitute. Even in the States, as times began to get harder in 'sunbelt' states like Texas, there were limits to opportunity and tolerance: local communities attacked camper van migrants, much as their grandfathers had turned on the Okies who struggled west from the dust bowl of the Great Depression years.

In Britain it is easier for the middle than for the working classes to migrate. Their removal is often subsidized by employers, and they are more likely to have worthwhile property to sell. But even they end up with gigantic mortgages and living in houses far inferior to the ones they left. A Newcastle academic, occupying a spacious home, laughed when he told me how he invariably had to sleep on a sofa when visiting colleagues who had taken posts in the south. It was rare for them to afford homes large enough to have spare rooms. Norman Stone, Professor of Modern History at Oxford University, wrote in late 1986 that the rise in housing values in the south-east encouraged not the enterprise culture, but 'parasitism'. 'There is something very wrong with a country that rewards people lavishly for doing literally nothing but sit in a property, while depriving them of almost two-thirds of their income when they start to do something useful.' He concluded: 'If the discrepancy in house prices grows, there really will be two nations in this country. The northern unemployed will continue to include skilled, middle-class people who could easily find a market for their abilities in the south, but who would not have the capital to set up house there ... the gap between London and Liverpool could all too easily resemble that between Milan and Naples in the old days.'

The gap is surely already that wide, which should be sobering news for people on both sides of the divide. Those who smugly boast of the continuously rising value of their London homes forget that it is a worthless value unless they intend to make themselves homeless by selling and blowing the cash on holidays; that if they were to move north, they could never break back into the south-eastern property market; and that one day their children will need homes, which – on beginners' salaries – they will no more be able to afford than will migrating northerners. When small houses in a working-class town like Slough cost what they do, the value of money has been distorted to a point that threatens economic stability. Professor Stone calculated that in two years a man could make more profit on buying and selling a large middle-class house in Oxfordshire than a doctor could earn in eight years.

A Slough training officer told me that he had come south from

Manchester because he felt that he owed it to his children to launch them on the world in an economically buoyant environment. He said: 'I was comfortable: I could have stayed where I was. But friends said. "You've had your go. Your son deserves his now." He's nineteen, and the comparison with opportunities in the north is so great that I sometimes feel it is immoral. He thinks he can change his job at any time. In many ways there are too many opportunities.' This man's mortgage payments had rocketed from £27 a month to over £300, and he was punch-drunk at the altered value of money, laughing slightly manically at the figures. Like several recent arrivals to the south-east, he said he was overwhelmed by the pace of life. He had just been back north to visit friends and found the gentle tempo unnerving. 'We were all sat down and relaxing, and kept on talking. At six o'clock my friend said we'd better get changed because we were having a party. We sat a whole day, and didn't do anything.' When his family came south, his wife had had to change her car for a more powerful one, so that she could break into rush-hour traffic at the bottom of their road. *That* appeared to be the ultimate distinction between north and south: if even the cars have to be slicker and faster, there must be two Britains!

Others move south for the sake of their children. A Northumberland vicar left his living in the Tyne Valley after his family had taken a battering in the north. One 22-year-old son was made redundant from what had appeared to be a secure laboratory job, and hadn't worked for two years, and two daughters failed to get employment at the end of YTS programmes. They had been working part-time in Woolworth's. The vicar moved to a tied house, for which he was thankful, comparing his own situation with those 'whose husbands and fathers have got to go down south for work, and then find they can't afford the property.' The Church of England was finding difficulty in persuading clergy to go in the opposite direction, mainly because wives with jobs feared they would never be able to replace them in the north.

The obvious economic lesson to be drawn from Slough is that success breeds success. Much as it makes more sense to open an antique shop next to a row of already thriving rivals than in a street full of grocery stores, so it makes sense to start a manufacturing business in an environment like the Slough industrial estate. It oxygenates people to be in the midst of economic activity. Mr Wolmar, the careers officer, had recently exchanged a four-bedroomed detached house overlooking Dartmoor for a three-bedroomed semi above the railway line in Slough. 'In the south-west,' he said, 'you know you're not going to do any more with your life after thirty-five. Here the character is "go, go, go," and you feel the spirit of success. It's cramped, living on top of one another, not nearly as nice as Dartmoor, but we wanted to move to an area orientated towards achievement. It is more stimulating to be here, and to be part of the success that other people are creating.' I remembered as he spoke the Durham miners, who sold out their jobs in their early forties, and passed the rest of their lives pottering between allotment and pub.

Slough's best known manufacturer is Mars. I was told that the sweet, chocolate smell of success frequently pervaded the town's air, though I never detected it myself. Mars is an authentic product for the proletarian town, the favourite chocolate bar of the British people manufactured daily by the millions. (More chocolate is produced in Slough than in any other European town.) It would have been out of character for Slough to produce a confection even as loosely associated with frivolity or aristocratic pleasures as an after-dinner mint. Today, with the 'single status' workforces of Japanese companies in Britain, industrial democracy does not seem such a novel idea, but Forrest Mars, a Yale-educated American, pioneered the status-free factory in Slough in 1932, when many British workers were still touching their caps to the bosses. He was then twenty-eight, the son of Frank Mars, who had founded the original business in Chicago, and who sent his son forth with the recipe for what was known in the United States as 'Milky Way' to seek his fortune outside America. Forrest first looked at continental Europe, but was frightened away by the impending rise of fascism.

A visitor entering the Mars factory passes a big clocking-on desk where all 2,400 employees, including the managing director, must punch a card; every employee is on first-name terms with every other employee – again including the managing director; there are no reserved car parking spaces for senior staff; in a vast open-plan office even the directors sit out on the floor at desks indistinguishable from those of secretaries; there is naturally only one cafeteria, in which everyone helps himself and then clears away his own place. When I was there, a committee was investigating whether there were any previously undetected differentials, apart from pay, that could be eradicated. I suspect they had their work cut out.

There are no unions, but even a local union organizer, who had been complaining to me that Thatcherism had unleashed a ruthless attitude amongst employers, found no fault with this company. His own wife had been kept on full pay by Mars throughout a serious illness, and had been encouraged to take her time before returning to work. Pay rises and bonuses are triggered by a formula which everyone understands: pension and insurance are non-contributory. Workers even get a bonus for clocking-on on time. The factory is in continuous operation, yet in fifty-five years has never lost an hour's production through an industrial dispute. Mars has always been good to Slough, in recent years replacing the mayoral mace when the town was moved from Buckinghamshire to Berkshire, and rebuilding the Slough College lecture theatre. In 1987 Forrest Mars was still alive, living in Las Vegas, where he had occupied his retirement by founding yet another candy manufacturing company.

Paternalism is part of the ethos of Slough and the industrial estate. Between the wars the employers joined forces to found a social centre and an occupational health scheme. Both thrive today, though the social centre is now run by the council. The catalyst for these amenities was the Slough Estate company, whose chairman is Sir Nigel Mobbs, grandson of Sir Noel Mobbs, one of the men who bought the vehicle depot after the First World War. Sir Nigel is a tall, bulky man, who, when I met him, was just back from a trip to America, where he must epitomize the upper-class Englishman. If Slough has a non-resident grandee, it is Sir Nigel: Marlborough and Christ Church, Oxford, married to a peer's daughter, chairman or president at some stage of every institution with clout in town, whose leisure time is spent riding, hunting, travelling, skiing. He wore a check suit, and at his feet lay a large rectangular, American attorney's briefcase. He was well organized, keeps his own files – he found me an eight-year-old article in thirty seconds flat – and courteous. We drank coffee made in one of those ubiquitous machines that have liberated secretaries in even chairmen's offices at the cost of producing a sour, grey sludge: democracy and automation have combined to produce a close to undrinkable liquid. Sir Nigel had known Slough professionally for twenty-five years, and, through his family, had an institutional memory of its development. The complaint that house prices are too high goes back, he said, at least to the sixties, when managers coming to the town from the north were shocked by what they had to pay for homes. There have also always been skill shortages, though both prices and shortages are more extreme now than they have ever been.

'Why,' I asked, 'does Slough prosper, while much of the industrial north languishes without work or much hope?' 'Some of the reasons,' replied Sir Nigel, 'are subjective and have little to do with rigorous cost analysis.' Executives like living in the Thames Valley or Buckinghamshire. But the main reasons are practical: the town has always had first- or second-generation, upbeat industries – even in the thirties the St Helen's Rubber Company moved its operation, including its workforce, south, to get away from Merseyside and to be near the expanding radio business which required rubber cables. There has been little union influence and few demarcation rules, which has allowed enterprise to flourish. Shortages of labour encouraged its efficient use. Competition for workers meant high wages, eliminating 'the bloody-mindedness generated by low pay.' Workers feel secure, because usually they 'can go round the corner and pick up an equivalent job.' Junior and middle management are confident of finding promotion without having to move house. (Sir Nigel told of one firm that decided it would be attractive to move from Slough to north Devon. They made two mistakes. They did not realize that summer seasonal employment would strip away their workforce; and they did not foresee that their managers would find the professional isolation intolerable. The managers resigned almost en bloc to return to Slough where they would once again be surrounded by opportunity.)

Even before Heathrow and the M4 were built, communications out of London were best to the west. Americans, looking for industrial sites before the Second World War, found the north cheerless and inhospitable, with few decent hotels and without what they would think of as 'executive housing' for managers who came to Britain to work. 'American company presidents wanted a degree of comfort. There were few northern hotels with bathrooms,' said Sir Nigel. (The poor quality of northern hotels in the early thirties is confirmed by J. B. Priestley's continuous grousing in his *English Journey*. To my own cost, I know most of them are not much better today.)

Sir Nigel said that northern employers often have themselves to blame for poor labour relations. One of the few Slough firms that had severe labour difficulties was managed from the north, and, quite exceptionally, did not enrol its workers in the occupational health scheme. 'A small thing,' said Sir Nigel, 'but possibly an indication that they did not cherish their workers.' What about the town's left-wing politics? 'Did they not frighten capitalist business people?' I asked. If anything, Sir Nigel appeared to favour a Labour council.

The extreme left, he said, tended to be more vociferous than effective, and were mainly not involved in planning or other areas where they might be harmful to business. There were also good council officers. 'Why, given such a rosy picture of Slough's economy, should anyone be out of work?' I asked Sir Nigel. 'There are not many seriously looking for work who could hold a job down,' replied the chairman, a view widely endorsed by other Slough businessmen, who state with great assurance that the town has a thriving black economy.

To be a trade unionist in such an environment is to farm stony ground. In the ten years that Dixie Dean has been district secretary of the Amalgamated Union of Engineering Workers (AUEW), local membership has collapsed from nine thousand to six thousand. Mr Dean is one of the old school. He served twice in the RAF, first in the war and then he re-enlisted; he had been a miner in Nottinghamshire for a short period. During our conversation he rose to produce his campaign medals from a filing cabinet. He is the sort of man with whom Harold Wilson used to have beer and sandwiches at Number 10. But he was truly indignant about what he considered to be a new industrial callousness. 'In the wonderful world of Thatcher things shock me to the core.' One well-known multinational, he said, had sent a routine warning letter to a woman suffering from cancer, telling her she would be sacked if she didn't improve her attendance. Another company gave a man an hour's notice of redundancy, after he had worked for them for nearly thirty-two years. A girl who suffered a nervous breakdown was sacked because her speeds had slowed. 'If this lot,' he said, referring to the Conservative Government shortly before it was re-elected in 1987, 'go on another five years, no doubt we'll survive, but employers' attitudes are so ruthless that I don't know what will happen.' I wasn't sure that he spoke with much heart. With his malapropisms and his bons mots – on privatization, 'if we all become bloody millionaires, who's going to deliver the post?' – Mr Dean is among the last of an endangered species. When Britain still had its post-war map, men like him were as familiar and reassuring as signposts at country crossroads.

Ironically, Mr Dean's image of the affluent society without postal deliveries is a real enough threat in Slough. So acute is the shortage of postal staff that in winter second-class mail is sometimes taken to south coast resort towns, where it is sorted by seasonally unemployed people, and then returned for delivery; and letters have been put on trains to south Wales for Welsh workers to sort as the train shuttles back and forth. In 1986 – when officially there were 4,500 people out of work in a town with a population of 97,000, 313 postal workers had quit by the end of October out of a complement of 1050. Nearby, Maidenhead is always fifteen or sixteen workers short out of a total establishment of one hundred. It is not unusual for five or six workers to resign in a week. Postal staff get paid according to national wage scales – special payments are restricted to London – which are uncompetitive and inadequate in Slough. It is possible to earn a decent living as an 'overtime baron', but only with extraordinary hours on a split-shift basis that leave no time for social or family life. An Indian supervisor told me that he used to get up at 4.00 a.m. six days a week, work till noon, and then go back from 4.30 till 8.00 in the evening when the heavy sorting was done. 'You never go out for a blooming drink or anything. It gets a bit monotonous. The first couple of years are bad.' He sounded like a lifer discussing how to get through his sentence. The Post Office locally spends more on advertising vacancies than would be needed to match the London weighting allowance, but efforts by successive postmasters have failed to budge the powers that be. 'We are told,' said the supervisor, 'that the line has got to be drawn somewhere.' Postmen who leave Slough for another part of the country, expecting an immediate job, are shocked to find a waiting list.

Sharon Richmond, an Oxford graduate, wanted to be a journalist, but couldn't find a job. She had been running the Slough unemployment centre for eighteen months when I met her. She was a thin, articulate girl, with a flowing shirt outside her jeans, and a scarf tied through her short brown hair. The centre was founded in 1982, after unemployment had tripled in three years to the then unheard of figure of four thousand. (Unemployment had been 0·8 per cent in 1973, 2 per cent in 1979, and by 1986 was between 8 and 9 per cent.) The rise was caused by recession in certain industries – like car manufacturing – for which components were made in Slough, and by new technology. Mars, for example, was producing more chocolate than ever in 1986, yet employed 1,500 fewer workers than fifteen years previously. Less skilled people inevitably lose their jobs to machines, and each year Slough's corpus of employed semi-skilled dwindles, throwing people with marginal abilities or resolution on the dole. Very few of them will get back. New firms will be yet more automated than existing ones, requiring highly skilled workers, whom they'll either have to poach locally or recruit from outside the town, bringing more highly paid people to Slough and forcing house prices yet higher.

The outlook for those who fall off the bottom is just as bleak in the south as in the north – and often more lonely. Miss Richmond told me of middle-aged men who had been job-hunting for years in vain: a 45-year-old electrician with a twenty-year work record who had been filling out applications for a year; a 'progress chaser' in his late thirties who had been out of work since 1980. She estimated there were almost six people out of work for each vacancy. But the unemployed were, of course, the wrong people for the jobs. 'The ads in the papers are aimed at those already in work,' she said.

The consequence of this process is that the two Britains of the haves and have-nots increasingly live side-by-side. It isn't just the north and the inner cities that cannot provide work for the unskilled or the less well motivated, but towns like Slough and Winchester – discovered by a team from Newcastle University to be the most affluent community in Britain – where half a generation ago everyone with a pair of hands had a job. As the majority become more affluent, the poor become relatively more deprived. A simple illustration is that bus services will inevitably decline once most people have cars: the poor and the old are left almost immobile, while roads we can no longer afford to maintain become chronically overcrowded. A Slough journalist said some of the housing conditions on Slough council estates were sordid and unhealthy, reflecting both the poverty and the demoralization of the tenants.

There is no point in getting 'on yer bike' unless you have something to offer when you arrive, as illustrated by teenagers from the provinces who are workless and homeless in central London. In Winchester I met people, not much more than a literal stone's throw from the cathedral and college, who were as isolated from the affluent existence of their neighbours as if they had lived in a derelict pit village. I went one sunny spring afternoon with a young and radical local clergyman, Rick Thomas, to the Highcliffe estate. There we met Charlie Bicknell, a 25-year-old married man with two small children. It was an effort for him to remember when he had last worked, finally settling for 'three or four years ago.' Brought up as a farm labourer, his last job had been as a cleaner. His supplementary benefit, he said, was inadequate, and had it not been for the Church, his family would not even have had a cooker. Indoor lavatories and baths had only been installed on this estate two years before, progress that was nearly twenty years behind the colliery houses of Easington. Nearby, a child played outside a house with broken, boarded windows. Mr Bicknell's children rampaged behind drawn curtains. 'It's not easy bringing a family up on the "social",' said Mr Bicknell, adding that he couldn't see anyone starting a business in town that would òffer him a job. 'All those antique shops, they're only making things better for themselves.' Across the River Itchen, outside the Bishop's Palace, prep-school boys were climbing out of a minibus ready for a game of hockey and, in a bookshop next to the house in which Jane Austen died, a tweedy schoolmaster was ordering Latin texts. Here, indeed, one might hit several bishops' nieces by hurling a brick. Rick Thomas commented: 'It is hard for those who haven't experienced poverty to imagine the numbing powerlessness of the very poor.' His stories of hardship had shocked local councillors.

An unemployment centre had just been closed, and its organizer sacked because of lack of funds. It was a battered and barren place compared to those I have seen in the north, with such graffiti on the walls as 'Smash the State' and a drawing of Mrs Thatcher with horns. But a Conservative councillor lamented its passing: 'It was pretty horrifying that we couldn't get across to intelligent people what good was being done by comparatively small sums. One person was saved from suicide. *That* was enough to justify the money.' Those in humbler jobs are not much better off than the unemployed: I met a male nurse in a geriatric hospital who took home sixty pounds a week. At the Job Centre I heard that, when some employers are told they are offering impossibly low rates, they reply: 'But we've been paying that for the past ten years.'

The pressures that keep northerners out of the south-east also drive native sons and daughters away. Bernard Goodyear, chief executive of the South Bucks and East Berks Chamber of Commerce – the organization that is sponsoring the Peterlee trainees – spoke of educated, first-rate, ambitious young people leaving Slough when they get married because they cannot afford even the 'starter homes'. 'Our seedcorn is drying up,' he said. School rolls are falling fast, and the over-65 population growing by 10 per cent a year. Vacant building land within the town boundary can be listed on a mere three sheets of paper. 'We are,' said Councillor Denis James, chairman of the planning committee, 'a walled city'. Mr Goodyear's remedy would be to expand the town into the green belt between Slough and Uxbridge; land which he said was of no agricultural or recreational use, blighted and desolate, occupied only by didicoys. He is a cheerful cynic, putting good race relations in the town down to the fact that most people work too hard to make mischief: 'The trick is for everyone to have two cars in the drive, preferably not paid for, and a huge mortgage.' Mr Goodyear believes the local unemployment figures are highly misleading. He told of one local 'Restart' course that was attended by only eleven people. At the coffee break someone asked if it were true that they would lose their benefits if they weren't there. He was told no, and when the course resumed there were only three people left – all married women seeking to get back into jobs after bringing up children. 'The others were all back on their window-cleaning rounds,' said Mr Goodyear. 'It was a farce. There's plenty of work. It's impossible to get things done.'

But Mr Goodyear is deadly serious about the lack of suitably skilled people, not just in Slough but throughout Britain. In Japan, he said, an engineer doesn't start work until he's twenty-one, here it's sixteen: young people should not be chasing a job at any price, but getting their A Levels and training. He estimated that six companies in the Thames Valley could employ three-quarters of the national graduate output of electronic engineers for each of the next five years. When there is a recession, no one invests in training for the future: when work picks up, shortages are so great that firms won't release people. He concluded: 'If we don't get a trained and educated workforce, we'll be in the third league of banana republics. It will take twenty years even if we start now.' Outside the City of London that has become an increasingly familiar cry.

Every Slough employer looking for staff to do more than twist pieces of wire was desperate: an architect couldn't find another to join his small practice and was also in the market for two technicians (the existing partners were working every weekend to keep clients happy). Arden Bhattacharya, the town clerk and first Indian chief executive of a British town, reported great difficulty in filling some major posts – even though the council offered six months' temporary accommodation to allow time to look for a house.

An executive with a specialist engineering firm reported 'mega, mega problems' in recruiting and holding technical sales staff: he told of one man in his mid-twenties whom they had been paying £12,500 a year plus a car, who left to join another company for £15,000 and a better car, but was snapped up by a third company as he was about to move, with an offer of £17,500, plus a yet better car. Even to get YTS youngsters, such firms have to pay bonuses above the Government rate. The Chamber of Commerce, as a YTS managing agent, could have filled another hundred vacancies in 1986 if they had had the young people, which is why they were so eager to co-operate with placing the Peterlee ten. Nearby Heathrow is an employment honeypot – Slough managers grumble that between them they have trained much of Heathrow's workforce – when Terminal Four was being built, the town suffered more acutely than normal. 'It's very frustrating: young people are chasing money,' complained the executive. His firm has thirty-five salespeople instead of the forty-two it needs. They brought four young people to Slough to be trained, found them accommodation and gave them transport, but none of them stayed. 'Missed mother's cooking, that sort of thing. The attitude is that you have a birthright to a job on the doorstep,' said a foreign-born colleague somewhat sourly.

A major engineering company said it took from two weeks to nine months to fill vacancies. National recruiting drives had proved fruitless. Advertisements in the *Sun* had produced just one worker from Manchester, while an intensive drive in Sheffield, where twenty-two were interviewed, failed to lure a single person south. 'Maybe we jump to the conclusion that people desperate for jobs will naturally take them. But we're not able to offer sufficient financial incentives to offset the cost of uprooting, and leaving friends and family.' The lack of skilled sales staff and labour shortages had cost the firm dearly in lost orders and delayed deliveries.

No one could argue that it is sensible to crowd our productive industry increasingly into one corner of the country. Yet Government direction to compel it elsewhere has seldom worked. The car industry was inefficiently dispersed from its home in the Midlands to places like Linwood in Scotland and Halewood on Merseyside. Foreign investors will not come to Britain if they are directed to parts of the country where they do not wish to be. Mrs Thatcher's Government hoped that continuous growth would force companies to break out of the southern industrial redoubt. But 'overspill' factories are always the first to be closed when times get tough. The argument against moving north tends to be circular. What is the point of training people – largely inadequately on Government schemes – for work that doesn't exist? Yet who will open a major plant where at best the workers are rusty and demoralized?

The answer lies in restoring confidence in the north, and creating in towns like Peterlee the energetic atmosphere of Slough. When potential investors feel the buzz on the Peterlee industrial estates that I felt that night in Slough, then they will start renting factory space. But, like confidence in comprehensive schools, it requires a few people to take the plunge. When you tell northerners that southern company bosses distrust the northern industrial environment and believe that the militant stance of Derek Hatton and Arthur Scargill are representative of political and trade union attitudes north of the Trent, they get very angry. They point to the Japanese firms that have chosen the north. But the Japanese build from the bottom up, employing almost exclusively school-leavers and graduates. There is, I believe, promise in small-scale enterprise, but in terms of numbers, relying on the Japanese and one-man enterprises is like trying to drain the North Sea with a bucket. It is hard to escape some pretty bleak conclusions.

Denis James, Slough's planning committee chairman, told me that people from Coventry had recently arrived in town to sell pictures made from silver paper door-to-door. From Coventry! The symbol of Britain's post-war resurgence, with its modern shopping precincts, its cathedral rising next to the ruins of the one that Hitler's bombers gutted, its once invincible car industry. That's where the unemployed of Durham moved in the thirties, the generation of the grandfathers of the boys who were now coming to Slough. Councillor James is just old enough to remember the pre-war unemployed, bringing their baked bean tins, threaded with a piece of wire to serve as a handle, to the backdoor of his childhood home to beg for a cup of tea. The Coventrians with their silver paper pictures had transported him back to his childhood. The have-nots are once again at the backdoors of the haves. Harold Macmillan said very shortly before he died in December 1986 that when he was MP for Stockton in the twenties the unemployment rate was 29 per cent; when he returned as a nonagenarian in the mid-eighties for a reunion, the figure stood at 28 per cent. It made him, he said, 'very sad'.

≋ 4 ≋

IT'S NO GO THE MILKMAN

Mrs 'Smith' hadn't been out after dark for five years unless accompanied by her son – and that only rarely, since he was almost as frightened as she of the long walkways with their dark hiding places and of the lounging teenagers. Five years ago, returning with four other women at ten o'clock at night from 'a little bingo', Mrs Smith had been set upon a few yards from her front door by three 'muggers'. The youths snatched their handbags and kicked the one woman who had hung on and resisted, severely injuring her wrist. Mrs Smith, then sixty-two, who had already twice been burgled, became a hermit, scuttling out when necessary during daylight hours, but for the most part living a claustrophobic life of siege in her small maisonette – 'I have never been out at night since, never been to bingo,' she said. She gave up her work for the tenants' association, knocking on people's doors and delivering leaflets. 'I wouldn't do it now.'

Her home is in the heart of one of Britain's ill-famed inner city housing estates – those that have been dubbed 'no go' in the popular press – the North Peckham estate in the London borough of Southwark. The milkman has long since given up his milk round, the police move hesitantly in pairs, and, from time to time, doctors, postmen, social workers, deliverymen, repairmen and taxi drivers decline to venture inside. (When Mrs Smith's husband was dying from lung cancer, a taxi driver refused to bring them home from the hospital.) The estate was built in the mid-seventies, home to six thousand people, its flats linked by mile upon mile of asphalt walkway, and connected by bridges to other estates of equally formidable reputation. From one office, staff administer eleven thousand of the least desirable homes in the country. Seven years after Mrs Thatcher had boosted the ideal of a property-owning democracy by compelling local authorities to offer council houses for sale, not a single one of those eleven thousand tenants had bought the roof over his head.

Between them the residents owed the borough five million pounds in rent arrears. Well over three-quarters of them fervently wanted to go elsewhere, a wish that will be fulfilled for only a tiny minority.

On the ground floor many windows are permanently boarded, the occupants preferring life in a half-light to the near certainty of being burgled when they go out. (There are people on the North Peckham estate who have been broken into a dozen times.) Other flats are gutted and/or blackened by fire, too derelict even for the squatters who often seize an empty property within half an hour of tenants moving out. In the mornings the caretakers find the abandoned syringes, and the matches and tinfoil – the paraphernalia of 'chasing the dragon' – which betray the widespread drug habit on the estate. Graffiti are ubiquitous, even some front doors are totally covered in daubings: there is dog mess every few yards. The council had recently contributed five thousand pounds for development work on a fortified milk float – which will look like a cross between an armoured personnel carrier and a bullion lorry. However, because of the faulty design of the estates, milk still cannot be delivered right to the door, and residents like Mrs Smith will have to pluck up enough courage to leave their homes and descend to the roads beneath. To most Britons, North Peckham would be a glimpse of hell, one of those places that confirms the deep fissure in our society between 'comfortable' Britain and the increasingly abandoned and feared world beyond. Even the none too scrupulous avoid the estate assiduously. In an Old Kent Road pub a man with a string of criminal convictions stated emphatically: 'I wouldn't go near the place; it's like a foreign land.'

Mrs Smith was not a frail 'little old lady' of popular imagination. She was still robust, keeping house for two people, and, when I called, was wearing a smart blue dress and had clearly just had her grey hair crisply permed. She lived with a series of comparisons in her head: life before North Peckham, life at the beginning of North Peckham, and life away from North Peckham. She had been brought up in Worcester, but had spent most of her married life in the intimate terraced streets of Bermondsey, 'Cockney' territory, where many of the men made their then good living in the Surrey docks. For most elderly people in the inner city, life thirty years ago, whatever the privations and the reality, had become the 'good old days'. Mrs Smith said: 'We never seemed to get that sort of thing [meaning burglary or mugging] then. It was a friendly atmosphere.' Her forty-year-old divorced son, who had moved back with his twelve-year-old daughter to live with mum, as much because he was frightened of living alone as to protect her, added: 'It was your own community. If you went away for the weekend, everyone kept an eye.' He had, he said, drunk coffee and listened to the jukebox with another Bermondsey lad, Tommy Steele, a memory which – since he must have been considerably younger than Mr Steele – may have been part of the myth.

But the early days in their new home had matched the Smiths' optimistic expectations. 'We really liked it. It was more like a holiday camp. It was very, very good,' said Mrs Smith. And certainly the interiors of the North Peckham homes, with central heating and hot water and spacious kitchens, were, as residents said frequently, 'little palaces' compared to the ancient terraced houses they had replaced. After a few years, said Mrs Smith and others, North Peckham 'deteriorated', when 'we got the class of person we have now' – a description which is in part, though not entirely, a code for 'Afro-Caribbeans'. 'I have,' she added hastily, although the subject had not been explicitly broached, 'good coloured neighbours, who said to tell them if the music is too loud.' But the good years on the estate ended nearly a decade ago, and the comparison Mrs Smith now cherishes is the life led by her daughter in a small Sussex village near Brighton. Although Mrs Smith is fearful to go away in case her home is burgled, once with her daughter she is transported to near paradise. 'It was amazing,' she said of a recent visit, 'we went out for dinner on Saturday night with no fear or thought of anything. It seemed as if we were in a different world. There's no fear there at all. My daughter can go down to the village and not even lock her door.'

Back home, at least two of her friends no longer visit, refusing to enter an estate with a 'no go' reputation. Her deceased husband's one surviving brother, now in his seventies, will visit only at Sunday lunchtime. 'He likes to keep in touch, but he makes sure he leaves his wallet behind,' said Mrs Smith, who walks her grand-daughter across the footbridge where a man had been murdered recently and through the neighbouring Camden estate each morning to put her on a bus for school, and waits anxiously at the bus stop each afternoon for her return. The girl was not allowed (nor wished) to go outside her front door alone. Mrs Smith is on sleeping tablets, and her son sleeps fitfully, conscious of the noises on the walkways. Twice in his own flat he had been surprised by intruders on his balcony in the middle of the night. On other nights there is worse noise from the all-night parties. The weekend before, it had gone on until a quarter to seven in the morning. Mrs Smith did not dare do anything about it – even call the council – for fear of reprisals. It was dangerous, she said, to draw attention to oneself, which is why she remains anonymous here. 'The police say "don't be afraid to call us," but they are short-winded in coming round,' she said. After her 'mugging', the police did not bother to interview her. Her son discovered 'bullet holes' in his bed-room window, but the police never came. They both thought the police had grown soft: her son remembered being frequently stopped and checked when he was a teenager roaming the streets with his friends. Now, he suggested, the police were too frightened, particu-larly of black youths.

Mrs Smith bitterly resented the squatters, and the non-payers of rent: 'I pay half my pension in rent. I'm very proud of the fact that I have always held a clear rent book. A very small percentage round here can say that. I was brought up that even if you hadn't got a meal on the table, you always paid for the roof over your head.' Rents were about to go up, which simply meant, said Mrs Smith matter-of-factly, that arrears would go up. She blamed the general deterioration of the estate on 'ignorance', people who didn't know how to keep themselves or their homes clean, didn't use the chutes for rubbish, and allowed their children to spray-paint the walls. On her walkway, the kids had been back within days of a major repainting operation – 'Daryl wos 'ere' mocking the 'wet paint' sign left by the contractors.

It was almost dark as I left Mrs Smith, and the walkways were deserted. At the next corner, a few yards from her front door, a beer can rattled into sight – kicked? thrown? blown? Who was lurking there? I nearly turned and walked the other way, but at the corner there was no one. I was crazily relieved, and glad that I hadn't made a fool of myself to myself by retreating. The fear locked behind the doors had seeped its way on to the empty passages. Why else would a rolling beer can make the heart race? I also left my wallet at home when visiting North Peckham.

'Pattie' until recently had lived alone on the neighbouring Camden estate, a few yards across the footbridge from Mrs Smith. She was a schoolteacher, a rare case for these parts of someone who had 'made good'. Walking in broad daylight with a friend, she had been grabbed from behind by a man, who appeared, she said, 'to want a grope'. The friend seized a broom that was lying by and drove the man away. Each night when Pattie came home, she parked her car in the dark labyrinth beneath the flats, and waited to see if any shadowy figures lurked amongst the cars or on the steps she had to climb to her flat. Then she ran, phoning her mother as soon as she got through the door. Her mother would call her at 8.00 a.m. before Pattie left for work to make sure her daughter had survived the night. 'At twenty-eight it was a bit off, wasn't it?' she said. She carried a mental map of where her friends' homes were, so she would know where to bolt if attacked. In the end it was the squatters who drove her away: one night a television came crashing on to her balcony at 3.00 a.m. They would knock in the early hours asking for a loaf of bread: the evidence of drug-taking was all around – 'you knew what was going on, but you didn't ask any questions,' she said. 'You just learn as a female that it's frightening.' After a while, she said, you even stop commiserating with people who have been burgled. Normality is changed when crime is so prevalent.

That had certainly been my experience in the United States. I had been surprised by how quickly I came to accept the American valuation of crimes that the British would consider to be quite horrific. Murders which, if committed in London, would have dominated the evening papers for days, were tucked away in the *Washington Post* 'Metro' section. One summer when I visited Detroit, murders in the city were running at four or five a night, and all teenagers had been curfewed. The first time that I wrote about handgun laws, I took a figure for the annual number of murders in America from a newspaper cutting – it was something like 24,000. I woke in the middle of the night, and did some mental arithmetic. That came out at 460 a week, which was more than the annual total in Britain. I called the FBI in the morning to say I was sure I had it wrong and could they check for me. 'You sure have,' came the reply. 'That figure's a year out of date. It's up a thousand since then.'

Such violence – much of it almost as casual as illegal parking – is justifiably held against American society. I could never get over the cheapness of human life – it took a really exceptional murder to raise public concern – nor the easy way in which politicians were bought off by the gun lobby from enacting gun controls that would have gone some way towards disarming hoodlums and disturbed citizens alike. But while I was away, Britain's crime figures rose inexorably, numbing the public with meaningless statistics of the 'serious crime every nine seconds' variety that eventually make any subject as incomprehensible as economics. More concretely, the head of Brixton CID announced: 'We are now dealing with more serious crimes than the busiest precinct in New York.' Individual criminals were showing a wanton contempt for their victims that could scarcely have been matched in Los Angeles.

In the few days I was in North Peckham, an attacker elsewhere in London threw a two-year-old girl strapped in a pushchair into a canal, having first knocked out and robbed her mother; a few miles away in Deptford burglars tortured a sixty-year-old man for forty minutes, repeatedly hitting him in the face with a hammer, driving a nail file into his eye and eardrum, and slashing his body with a knife. In the months after my return there had been some reported story of violence to file every day, ranging from 'Bored boys tortured gerbils to death' to 'Rugby match P C "bit off ear of opponent"'. Stabbings, attacks on transport staff, sexual assaults, even the 'bombing' of punters on the River Cam rolled on day by day. I had once almost been a 'mugging' victim myself, when I was attacked by two youths after I had inadvertently stopped them robbing from a woman's handbag on the Underground, so I knew a little of the fear and the impotence felt by people on the receiving end. My attackers ran off when another man – by great good fortune – appeared round the corner.

The use of knives in south London was beginning to rival the American use of guns. Dr Robert Ware, head of the intensive care unit at King's College Hospital, Denmark Hill, which lies between Brixton and Peckham, told me that the lives of cancer and heart patients were at risk because of the amount of operating theatre time occupied by the victims of stabbings. Even when lives were not at risk, patients awaiting operations frequently had to be sent home – often deeply distressed – for a further wait. 'It seems the macho thing to carry a knife, and the bigger the knife the more macho. They are going round now with eight-inch knives' – and he demonstrated their wicked length with his hands – 'and there are not many places in the body where you can push that without causing serious injury,' he said. He told me that when he had been a young casualty officer fifteen years ago, knife injuries were rather messy slashings by drunken Irishmen; now they were systematic through and through stabbings, mainly of and by people engaged in the drugs business. The hospital, he estimated, received seven stab victims a day, at least one of whom would require major surgery. One a week had to be admitted to intensive care where the mortality rate was almost one in three. The victims – sometimes brought to casualty in stolen cars – were fortunate in that King's College has a cardiac unit, which saved several lives that would have been lost in less well-supported accident hospitals.

By the late 1980s, this avidly reported violence had convinced politicians, commentators and the public that society had undergone a moral sea-change. The basic social contract, whereby citizens enjoy certain rights – including health care, decent education and housing, and a job – in return for which they observe the rule of law, was breaking down. As a consequence, an underclass was evolving – football hooligans, muggers, inner city rioters – somewhat more frightening than their Dickensian forebears because they were mobile and all too visible. The victims of poor schooling, poor upbringing, economic blight (you take your pick of explanations according to your prejudices) were beyond the pale, a danger to be feared at the best of times and contained at the worst.

The week in which I returned to Britain, the worst occurred. The country was suddenly pitched into a series of conflagrations, sparked by some maladroit policing, which illustrated just how stark the divide had become between these young people and the rest of society. Serious rioting broke out in several inner city areas – Handsworth in Birmingham, Brixton in south London, and the Broadwater Farm estate in north London, where a policeman was hacked to death by a mob. Petrol bombs were thrown at the police, and – for the first time in a civil disturbance – shots were fired. Two Asians were burned to death in a Birmingham Post Office. Coming only a few months after the Heysel Stadium carnage, these riots appeared to signal the disintegration of urban society. The alien hordes – football hooligans and rioters – were at the door. A few streets away from gentrified terraces, there was a world where the Queen's writ ran but fitfully. The disorders buried any misconceived notions that the suppressed anger and bleak despair of Britain's inner cities had somehow melted away in the four years since the petrol bombers and looters had last taken to the streets.

But to me, returning home, what was almost as terrifying as the glimpse of mayhem round the corner were the knee-jerk reactions of national and local political leaders. Each spoke sad volumes about how polarized Britain had become after six years of inner city recession and an essentially uncaring national government. The right picked on the consequences of permissive child-raising by parents who had been brought up in the free-wheeling sixties; while the left concentrated on economic devastation wrought by Thatcherism on already deprived communities. Neither side in the polarized political environment of Britain was prepared to concede that there was some justice on the other side: the riots became just another opportunity for political abuse.

Norman Tebbit blamed them on 'wickedness', a cosy notion that absolved the Government from doing much more than seeking to lock up the offenders. Bernie Grant, the black leader of Haringey Council and now a Labour MP, whose leadership then consisted of underscoring the prejudices of the most alienated of his constituents, suggested, 'Maybe it was a policeman who killed another policeman.' What was chilling and salutary about these two reactions was that both speakers were populist figures articulating the gut reactions of many Britons. Another of our post-war assumptions was finally buried – the hope and expectation that black Britons, the children and grandchildren of the motivated, hard-working and God-fearing West Indians, and the white children of what had been the slums would become fully integrated citizens sharing the opportunities of their fellow Britons. Here was another cleavage – and perhaps the starkest of all. The most alienated and locked-out section of British society – the black and white urban poor – lived just a short bus ride away from Westminster, Whitehall and the City of London: from the top of the Gloucester Grove estate, next to the North Peckham estate and just south of the Old Kent Road, one can see both the Houses of Parliament and the new tower blocks in the City. How to contain 'yobbism' had become the political question of the hour: the week in which I first visited North Peckham, Scotland Yard took delivery of twelve armoured vehicles. A doctor who saw something of senior police officers in between stitching victims of stabbings said: 'The police are predicting problems with North Peckham, and are all tooled up – water cannon, rubber bullets, CS gas, the lot.'

It is the middle classes who install burglar alarms, write letters to the newspapers and attend Conservative Party conferences to demand harsher sentences, but the real victims of a breakdown in law and order are the poor, cowering like Mrs Smith behind their flimsy front doors, fearful of going out, fearful of staying home, living in a medieval world where might makes right, and where the police are often of little more avail than a paper umbrella in a typhoon. June

Mortimer, a motherly Yorkshire woman who runs the Southwark
Victim Support Scheme, had just lost four of her volunteers. She said:
'They couldn't cope, they found they were powerless to help. What
the victims needed was money, the one thing they couldn't give. The
victims live in siege conditions. Yet if they go out, their homes might
be burgled and they might be attacked. It is a fearful state of affairs.
The quality of their lives is nil, there is nothing left to be burgled.'
Many of these people are on or below the poverty line already. Insurance is either unobtainable or so expensive as to be out of reach. One
woman on the North Peckham estate, whose home had been burgled,
told me she had been treated by the insurance assessor as if she herself
were the criminal. He challenged all her claims, even suggesting,
when she had receipts with her own name and address on them, she
might somehow have forged or borrowed them. In the end the company paid half her claim, and told her they would double her future
premium. She now takes her chance and has four locks on the front
door.

You won't find 'Broadwater Farm', 'North Peckham', or 'Gloucester
Grove' in the index of the A–Z, nor the names of the walkways on
which the residents live. Even if you drive past, unless you know what
you're looking for, you almost certainly will not realize that populations the size of small towns are shut away behind walls that look like
the outside of multi-storey car parks. Camden, North Peckham and
Gloucester Grove lie a half mile or so from Peckham Rye station,
where even at 9.00 a.m. human derelicts had taken up their positions
for the day on public benches. 'KICK AFRICANS OUT OF BRITAIN'
was neatly printed in large letters on a Barclays Bank hoarding; an ema-
ciated, elderly blind man in a filthy black mac tapped his lonely way
across the rutted pavement and past the black rubbish bags; 'Tories
Out' said a hopeful poster, and 'Strike Now Against YTS' said
another, though how the unemployed can 'strike' was not explained.
Old bangers were lined up in a car lot – nothing over £800. Outside
North Peckham estate someone was trying to sell an 'S-Reg' Ford
Escort: 'Good Runner – £120' read the scribbled sign. A man on a
Community Programme scheme was painting a fence, his radio blar-
ing out 'Lazing on a sunny afternoon . . . in the summer time, in the
summer time, in the summer time . . .' as if to mock the drab surroundings and the grey, chill April day. On a wall nearby there was
an incongruous touch: someone had retrieved from an earlier build-

ing and remounted two stone tablets, which read: 'To the lasting
honour of those who fell in the Great War.' Litter lay around the
bottom of the steps to the 'vicarage': squashed beer and coke cans, a
Lucozade bottle, Kit-Kat papers, paper plates.

A notice on the vicarage door, two flights up on a walkway
especially notorious for drug users, told callers to ring the bell – but the
bell had been ripped out leaving a small blackened hole, and the glass
replaced with shatterproof perspex. The reinforced glass on the
vicar's living-room balcony had been shattered by catapults and
airgun pellets. 'You can sit by the window,' laughed the Revd Graham
Derriman, six years into a ten-year stint, which, he said, was under-
mining his health. 'A leg infection blows up out of the blue and
immobilizes me. I assume it is the stress.' His home, he said, was one
of only three non-council properties in his parish of eight thousand
souls. He had come, he said, because he had not found a reason to say
'No', but, had he known then what he came to know later, he might
have been 'too frightened'. It helped that he was single; he could not
imagine a married vicar bringing up children on North Peckham
estate. He had set himself the task of persuading people to settle
down and make something of the estate; a necessary, if possibly
unachievable, objective. 'It may be wishful thinking, but I want to get
people to change their attitudes. This estate can be all right if we can
stabilize it,' he said. He had been burgled twice himself, and people
he had trusted had stolen from him when they visited. Someone had
even taken the bell out of his alarm. In the days when there had been
milk deliveries, his milk had been pinched more often than not before
he could bring it in: he had always meant to lie in wait to see who did
it, but never got round to the effort.

He did not, however, feel frightened or intimidated on the walkways, asserting his right to tread the 'streets' of his parish and the
Queen's 'highway', though he realized that if he ever were 'bashed on
the head' he might change his attitude. He was overwhelmed, like
Mrs Mortimer of the Southwark Victim Support Scheme, with the
crippling poverty that lapped round him. The night before a hungry
man had called at his door for food; a young father had come plead-
ing for shoes for a child, such a requirement being a 'disaster' for
some families; for many in his congregation – there had been nearly
seventy people in church on the previous Sunday, most of whom were
black – every penny counted. They could never enjoy the 'luxury' of a
40p bunch of flowers, never bought new clothes, making do with

jumble sales and Oxfam shops. 'They do not have the elemental free-dom to choose clothes to suit their personality or mood. It's quite a crippling thing,' he said. Some parishioners would not let him pene-trate past their kitchens, because they were ashamed of the shabby state of their homes. (Many were not very good at coping anyway – North Peckham is near the Maudsley psychiatric hospital, and houses a fair number of discharged patients. A breakdown is one way of ensuring that someone else will cope with unmanageable problems.) Mr Derriman had recently taken a group on an outing to the seaside. It had been a drizzling, grey day, and the trip mildly depressing. Sud-denly one old woman had burst out: 'Oh, isn't it lovely?' 'Isn't what lovely?' asked Mr Derriman in some perplexity. 'To see the grass,' she replied. She had not been out of London for two years, and spent most of her life staring at the drab, yellow-brick wall opposite her kitchen window.

The violence and fear of violence are ever-present in North Peck-ham like Muzak in a department store. Mr Derriman had got to know some of his congregation at first by shouting through letter-boxes to people too frightened to open their doors. He was sure that, if you removed all the existing tenants and replaced them with stable families, the newcomers would also suffer the same social problems within a few years – victims of the architecture of the estates, where privacy is at a premium and noise is endemic, and where there is nothing for young people to do except loiter on walkways and paint graffiti on walls. 'Life is just empty of everything; there is no pattern to it; there is nothing to do, no point to anything. There is lethargy and apathy. My heart bleeds for them,' said Mr Derriman. Crime, he suggested, was almost inevitable in this environment. 'Breaking in,' he said, 'is the kind of work that's seen to be viable. A youngster who might get forty or fifty pounds for a legitimate week's work, can pick up £200 in a night.' He believed the young criminals had little sense of guilt, and justified their crimes by pointing to upper-class criminality involving millions of pounds, like the Guinness affair and MPs making multiple applications for privatized shares – then much in the news. 'Everyone's out for themselves, that's the feeling. Some lads tell you they put a limit on mugging, but there's nothing wrong in steal-ing from shops because they can afford it,' he said. One of the few supermarkets on North Peckham had recently been attacked and burned out by a gang who complained that its prices were exorbitant. The fish 'n' chip shop next door had been closed by its proprietor, an ex-policeman, because he was tired of being robbed, usually by black teenagers. Many young people were totally unconcerned about the consequences of their criminal deeds. One young woman who stole to feed her drug habit asked Mr Derriman to lend her £250 for bail. 'Oh well,' she said when he refused, 'it was worth a try.' The sum was imposed because she had failed to attend court when her case was first called – she had been in Tenerife at the time.

Black people in such areas as North Peckham were, said Mr Derriman, denied real power because those in authority were frightened by what they might do with it – a local group had, for example, been refused the freehold of a building they wanted as a resource centre. One way of compensating was to seek power in other ways. 'Frightening people and creating fear of riots is one of those powers,' he said. The kids went around telling white people that there had to be a revolution, knowing full well the effect they created. One beefy, white lorry driver, with an ex-boxer's broken nose, was so terrified of black youths on the walkways that he made long detours to avoid them. A young man who had come from Cambridge to work at the adventure playground quit after six months because he could not take the pressure of being surrounded by people by whom he felt constantly threatened. In these circumstances there was virtually no cooperation with the police in detecting or stopping crime. People see cars and flats being broken into, and do nothing because they are frightened of reprisals. Crime, therefore, flourishes unhampered. A black youth worker told me that street thieves will now often simply stroll away after robbing a victim: chasing and apprehending muggers and burglars on North Peckham is virtually impossible. In six years Mr Derriman had come across only one case of someone acting the good citizen to promote law and order: a woman had called him anonymously to report children lighting fires in the playground. Children start fires, he said, because it gives them a sense of power to see the fire brigade called out.

To survive in such an environment – whether one is criminal or straight – it is necessary to be tough and street-wise. I met two middle-aged women into whose souls the iron had entered, and who, had it been within their physical power, would have taken the entire population of the estates by the collective scruff of the neck and shaken sense into them. Mary Ellery stands five foot nothing in her bare feet, which was how she was when I first met her. Her hair was scraggy, and she wore large red-rimmed glasses and a blue dress over purple trousers. She was a Southwark Labour councillor, smoked like a chimney – the air in the Blackwall tunnel could not have been fouler than the air in her cramped front room – and was much amused at having been described by a reporter from the *Daily Telegraph* 'with a plum in his mouth' as a 'salty character'. Recently, all her windows had been smashed in a mini-riot. With a council official at her side, she reeled off the statistics behind North Peckham's reputation: the highest rent arrears, the highest living density, the highest unemployment, the highest numbers of single parent families and of people on housing benefit – 25 per cent of this, 62 per cent of that. 'Anyone who went door to door asking people their problems would get a hell of a shock,' said Mrs Ellery. I didn't doubt it. The estates had started to decline, she said, when unemployment surged upwards at the beginning of the eighties – until then, she said, the estates had been 'brilliant'. 'Unemployment knocked six kinds of shit out of people. Careers officers came into schools with the bad news when kids were fourteen, and from then on they knew there was no bloody point. All you need to know now is how to write your name and how to go on the dole. If you're forty-plus, you're on the shitheap,' she said.

Factories had closed, hospitals had closed. At the same time millions of pounds had been stripped from the council's housing funds, so property deteriorated. On the older estates, balconies were flaking, window-frames rotting, asbestos was being left untreated. It would take ninety million pounds just to make good the shortfall since Mrs Thatcher came to power, according to Mrs Ellery. The one million pounds on offer from the Urban Task Force to put local people to work catering for local needs, which was much ballyhooed at the time, was like a 'piss in the ocean'. Her own young family was, she said, typical. Three of her four children were out of work – a 22-year-old son had never worked; the only one with a job was 'on the dust'; a bright seventeen-year-old with seven O Levels was at home. 'What does he do?' 'Walks around in his shorts and spends the day watching TV, I suppose,' said Mrs Ellery. This son had become discouraged because employers never 'let him know', Mrs Ellery said: 'If you give this address, you've had it. The employers have no respect; don't treat the kids as human beings.'

She had ambivalent views about the police. People who voted for her told her they wanted her to work with them, and she held regular surgeries with a policeman present. But for months during the Wapping printing dispute the estates, she said, had been largely unprotected. 'Every time someone was burgled, the police were at bloody Wapping or out of London at the mines. We have to take all this shit because it's more important to look after Mr Murdoch's factory,' she said. (Quite a few Murdoch printers had lived on the estate. A neighbour had worked in print for thirty years, and 'lost his pension, the bloody lot,' which had led to a nervous breakdown. What many commentators who were surprised by the sustained picketing of Wapping overlooked was that the east end and south London communities from which the printers came were in many ways as tight-knit as mining villages.) The day I met Mrs Ellery there were police everywhere. 'Ah,' she said, 'our MP is due here today. They always put on a show for her or if a wally comes from the Government.'

The other equally doughty woman was Sandy Cameron, who led the North Peckham tenants' association. 'Nothing will happen if we don't get together, if everyone just sits and moans and groans. People wanting to move away creates apathy. I have no intention of moving away. I like the people. There's nowhere else you'd get so many different nationalities, foods, languages, clothes as here. My kids are street kids. I'm not keeping them covered in cotton wool. They've got to equip themselves to face the world,' she said. As she talked, she breast-fed the youngest of her large family, and poured scorn on the nation's rulers. 'The people who have the power to make changes are so far away from the problems, they haven't a clue what it's all about. They get all their information from the hierarchy,' she said, describing the 'massive entourage' with which politicians and senior police are surrounded when they visit the North Peckham estate. Beat police, she said, understand the community, and have to deal fairly with residents in order to survive on the streets. It is the 'big boys' in the drugs and serious crimes squads who cause bad relations – 'anyone who lives on North Peckham is dirt as far as they are concerned. If you're an ambitious copper, you've got to be a shit to get up there.' She described raids in which the wrong doors had been kicked down, neighbours abused, and bystanders pulled in on suspicion. 'Erstwhile law-abiding people get fed up when they are maltreated,' she said, and accused the police of caring more about local shopping areas than about the safety of the residents of the estates. The police, she said, drive gangs on to the estates to disperse them, and care nothing for the consequences.

She described working for the tenants' association as 'having a finger in a dyke'. She said: 'People are so demoralized. They have no power, no hope, everything is too far out of their reach.' And she talked about the pressures on kids to conform, to wear the right brand-name shoes. 'They've got to have this expensive uniform or they are not accepted. They'd rather go out barefoot than in shoes with no name.' An unemployed teenager trying to keep up the style will almost inevitably turn to crime, she said. Had she been burgled herself? 'Oh yeah, quite a few times. You just take it. That's it.' She got a dog as a deterrent, but 'that just lumbered me with another problem.' Once dogs had frightened teenagers, but now most families have got their own dogs. 'For every deterrent, they build up a resistance,' she said fatalistically. Most of her neighbours wanted to blow the estate up, but Mrs Cameron looked on it as an old piece of furniture in need of renovation. 'We know what the problems are, so let's tackle them on a drastic level. If we built again, we wouldn't realize what the new problems were for a few years, and then we would have to start again.'

Ali Balli lives on the neighbouring Gloucester Grove estate, and, when I met him, had just resigned as a Labour councillor, disillusioned by what he said was his party's lack of commitment to improving housing. He had been fighting for the renovation of his estate ever since he returned from one holiday to find burglars had broken into his flat by the simple expedient of removing the one layer of plasterboard between the back of an outside pramshed and his bedroom. 'It couldn't be right,' he said, 'it was obviously a design fault. I was very aggrieved.' He took legal advice, but got nowhere, and threw his energies first into the tenants' association and then the council.

Gloucester Grove's most notorious feature is a series of towers on the end of each block, which house lifts, stairs and rubbish chutes. They stink, breed flies and vermin, and are more severely vandalized than the bleakest city centre underpass. 'How,' asked Mr Balli, 'would I like to invite a guest to my home up one of these stairways?' 'You wouldn't believe that human beings actually live in these appalling conditions,' he said, 'the parents inevitably give up, and the kids get out of control.' All the blocks on Gloucester Grove are named after Gloucestershire villages, and Mr Balli laughed at the idea of the villagers coming to live in them. They wouldn't, he said, know where to begin. (Which would apply equally to the residents of Gloucester

Grove, were they to be dumped in the middle of the country.) Gloucester Grove flats open on to long internal corridors – one I visited must have measured well over a hundred yards – which looked like the inside of cell blocks. 'Think of the old people, who have worked all their lives, and finish up stuck in here,' said Mr Balli mournfully. Gloucester Grove had been built like a snake, with a result that the noise was echoed and amplified. He showed me where Gloucester Grove's only shops had been – now gutted – and the burnt-out tenants' hall. 'Now,' he said simply, 'we've got nothing.' The nearest source of milk was half a mile away, and the nearest proper shop a mile. It wasn't yet quite dark, but no one passed us. A blue metal sculpture stood forlornly in the deserted piazza. On one wall there were tablets on which two verses of Lewis Carroll had being inscribed, and which Mr Balli apparently had not noticed:

> How doth the little crocodile
> Improve his shining tail
> And pour the waters of the Nile
> On every golden scale!
>
> How cheerfully he seems to grin,
> And neatly spread his claws,
> And welcome little fishes in
> With gently smiling jaws!

The block that housed the shops, built as a community amenity and focal point, was to be demolished. The original architects, said Mr Balli, had not taken account of the type of person who was going to live there; they expected them to have the outlook of their own class. He said: 'They should have been more down to earth, with community involvement from people like crime prevention officers. Local people should have been given a say in what was being built for their habitation.' According to Mr Balli, as it was presently designed, it would take thirty or forty policemen to police the estate.

However, some remodelling had begun: gardens were being added on the ground floor to keep passers-by from the bedroom windows; the stairs and the rubbish chutes were to be removed from the towers; and each block and corridor provided with entry phones. We peered through a door into one corridor, which seemed like another world from the smelly, urine-stained cell blocks. The corridor was immaculate, there were mats outside each flat, and brass knockers and numbers gleamed from the doors. The people, as Mr Balli pointed out, were the same, but the improved environment had revolutionized the way they lived.

A similar plan to the one being implemented at Gloucester Grove had been drawn up for the renovation of North Peckham, and had been costed at thirty-five million pounds. A pilot scheme was due to start on one corner of the estate in the summer of 1987. Predictably and ironically, the money is to be spent returning the estate as near as is now possible to a traditional housing development. A block is to be demolished so a road can be run through; the ground-floor apartments are to be converted into maisonettes with front and back gardens; the bridges connecting the walkways are to be demolished, thereby isolating each block, which will all have entry phones both at ground level and on each floor. Tenants will have their own 'defensible space'.

By 1987 Professor Alice Coleman of London University had demonstrated that environment was of far greater consequence than either Mr Tebbit's notion of innate wickedness or the left's belief that crime is a consequence of social inequality. She wrote: 'Research shows that crime levels vary with sixteen specific features of bad housing design. Blocks of flats without any of the sixteen did not report a single crime during our study years, while those with thirteen or more defects averaged one crime for every five dwellings. Juveniles are seven or eight times as likely to be arrested if they live in the worst blocks than in those with three or fewer defects . . . The effect of bad design is two-fold. First, it omits certain features now seen to be vital in socializing children, with the result that some of them grow up to be vandalistic and violent, with a "standing decision" to commit crimes. Second, this type of design is highly vulnerable to assault by criminals, both those who have been bred there and intruders from outside.' Then she added: 'Having said that, it seems that unemployment affords long idle periods, which help maximize the *number* of crimes committed by those who already have a pre-existing bent for it.' Her clinching evidence was the north-eastern town of Hartlepool, where 'a low crime rate co-exists with massive joblessness . . . Hartlepool, which has never built flats, has a lesson to teach.'

Dave Sutherland was an unlikely man to find in charge of the North Peckham housing office. With his careful haircut and immaculate white shirt, he looked as if he had strayed there from a west end estate agent's office. He was, he confessed, feeling 'burned out', his commitment to public housing sorely tested by the unequal odds against which he struggled. Southwark's authority to borrow capital sums for housing renovation had been slashed in real terms by 60 per cent during the Thatcher years, leaving thousands of crucial repairs undone; the sale of council houses had deprived the borough of better homes elsewhere into which to transfer people; half of the few available homes were earmarked for the growing numbers of homeless or for victims of racial harassment; squatting – encouraged by a politically sympathetic council – was growing apace, the number of properties squatted in Mr Sutherland's bailiwick had grown from three to 513 in three years; in the next three months Mr Sutherland would have 155 homes (not all of them very desirable) to offer 5,003 candidates who had been accepted on the waiting or transfer lists. He thought a third term of Thatcherism would reduce public housing to 'welfare' housing; that situation already was very close.

A few months earlier staff in his office had been attacked three times in as many weeks, once by an irate tenant armed with a hammer. One of the attackers – a discharged mental patient – actually thought he was in the neighbouring borough of Lambeth, and became angry when he discovered his mistake. The office had been closed so that a ceiling-to-floor shatterproof perspex screen could be erected between the staff and their customers, but it couldn't prevent intimidation. One caller, who was awaiting a flat, had threatened violence against an official. Mr Sutherland visited the man in his home and told him he was being struck off the waiting list and that, if he came to the office again, the police would be called. Because of such dangers all the officials were recruited from outside the estates. The previous summer Mr Sutherland had closed the office one afternoon and sent the staff home after gangs armed with clubs had taken to the streets of Peckham and begun looting shops. He feared there might be a serious concerted assault on the office, and that some tenants might try to settle old scores with staff. 'There were thirty or forty people running riot; there was nothing we could have done,' said Mr Sutherland, adding that there were days when the atmosphere is distinctly 'iffy'. On such days a 'fever' would build up, he said, and one could sense the excitement the teenagers – 'six-foot jobs' – derived from violence.

For most tenants, there was only one issue – security. Seven years earlier, when Mr Sutherland came to North Peckham, there was the occasional mugging. Now fear of burglary and attack was a constant preoccupation; most of the danger was perceived as coming from squatters within the estate. Some of the squatters, he said, were very violent, unpleasant people. 'Why,' I asked, 'didn't the council reassign tenancies fast, so that squatters didn't get the opportunity to move in?' He laughed. Many tenants, 70 per cent of whom receive some form of housing benefit, owe large arrears and do a midnight flit. Squatters can be in within half an hour; sometimes they pay the departing tenant for the key. Many councillors are sympathetic to the squatters – some were darkly suspected by officers of handing out addresses of vacant homes. The council itself has to go by the book, obtaining repossession orders through the courts. Two months is a minimum for that process. 'We can't just employ heavies to throw them out,' said Mr Sutherland.

The council has few sanctions against defaulting tenants, whose attitude often is that if they are evicted they can only go somewhere better: it has an obligation under the Homeless Persons Act to house most of those who are likely to be evicted. A family can be thrown out in the morning and in a new council property by the afternoon. It could perhaps be argued that some of them were intentionally home-less because they 'wilfully' refused to pay rent, but that might mean the break-up of a family and taking children into care, which – social considerations aside – would cost Southwark more than letting the family live rent-free.

Mr Sutherland did not entirely share the Alice Coleman thesis. North Peckham, he said, could be a pleasant place to live if you could hand-pick the tenants, but there were some families whose poor behaviour infected the rest. The theory was that you tried to put such a family amongst 'good' families, hoping that they would improve through the example of their neighbours. In reality, the 'good' fami-lies gave up. For a while they might tidy up the rubbish chutes and even sweep and wash the walkways, but battling against such odds eventually proved too much. The 'trendy' view, said Mr Sutherland, is that it is all down to the environment – 'some, I'm afraid, would not respond.'

But I did visit some homes in which after a few minutes I forgot the surrounding problems. Mrs Kemi Ogunleye from Nigeria had an immaculate home, decorated with artificial flowers and religious texts. Above the living-room door a gold-on-red notice proclaimed: 'Christ is the head of this house, the unseen guest at every meal, the silent listener to every conversation.' She had recently apprehended a gang of four- to six-year-olds who had burgled her home. They had been spotted on the walkways wearing stolen hairslides, but the money and more valuable jewellery they took was never recovered. It was her fourth burglary, and she now kept an Alsatian. Someone had been taking it for a walk when the children broke in, which, she said, was fortunate, 'because the dog might have killed them.' Mrs Ogunleye never allowed her two daughters out except to go somewhere specific like choir practice or the dramatic society. She blamed lack of parental discipline for the vandalism and crime – mum and dad at the pub while children roamed the walkways. 'Children will boast to you, "We're under age, they can't jail us,"' she said.

Mrs 'Jones' is a bus driver's wife. Sitting in her sunny kitchen, with its microwave oven, pine furniture and wine bottles on the side, one might have been in a private housing development in Wimbledon. She and her husband had brought up two children on the estate, one of whom is now a shipping clerk and the other a secretary. She believed that the reason why young people hadn't got jobs was because half of them didn't want them. (I met a man with a longish criminal record who is permanently in work, and has changed jobs frequently, proving they are available. However, it is certainly harder for black people to get employment.) At first, like Mrs 'Smith', Mrs Jones had considered herself to be extremely lucky to have a North Peckham home. But, by the time I met her, she would have moved if she could have found a suitable alternative. 'If we could pick this flat up and move it elsewhere, we would,' she said wistfully, 'as people move out, those who take their place are not half so nice. They don't care how they live, and they cause the noise and the dirt. Even the "problem" families are getting fussy and don't want to move here.' (There had been an attempt to encourage people like art students and schoolteachers to move into North Peckham. In one case I heard of, one of several young women sharing a flat was severely raped, and after psychiatric treatment was recuperating with her parents. Her flatmates had fled.) Mrs Jones had been burgled once and 'mugged' once. A well-dressed man had stopped her near her front door to ask directions. He had snatched her necklace, leaving a small bruise at the nape of her neck. Now when Mrs Jones goes out, she wears no jewellery and leaves her bag behind. When the flat is empty, the family hide their valuables, leaving a few pounds and some ornaments out in the hope that intruders will not ransack the flat.

Life had a permanently nostalgic quality for many people I met. Two middle-aged school cleaners looked back to before they were rehoused as if to a golden age. They remembered helping drive cattle to a local butcher's shop, and watching a blacksmith at work. 'I'm sorry now we didn't buy our houses. Only needed £100 for a deposit, but we hadn't got £100.' (Needless to say that if they had, they would now be sitting on small fortunes.) Out of twenty-five flats in their block, four had recently been burgled. Said one: 'I don't think a woman is safe on the streets at night. When I was a child, I never heard of anyone being attacked. I think we was more happy then. We used to go singing and skipping along the streets. The most crime was when a girl got in the family way. I have walked home from Piccadilly of a night time.' Children, they believed inevitably, no longer respect their parents. Both women, now in their late fifties, said they would still never answer their own mothers back. Punishments had lost their potency. When they were children, being sent to bed early was being sent to a room with a bed and a chair and nothing else. 'Now, it's like being sent to Curry's,' said one. Again, inevitably, they raised the question of race: 'I'm not against foreigners. Don't get me wrong. But when I was a child, the only coloured man you saw was an Indian selling ties door to door. You'd say "first luck" when you saw him,' said one. They added that they didn't think people of their age would ever get used to immigrants, and complained that 'we're not allowed to sing half our nursery rhymes now.' One said: 'I have two boys in the Navy. When they go to other people's countries, they have to abide by their rules.' (A probation officer told me that one reason why Liberals were doing well in places like Bermondsey was because locals believed Labour was too much on the side of black people, espousing unpopular schemes like the renaming of streets after African nationalists.)

That same day I was with another Southwark probation officer, Rod Gillespie, an ex-guardsman and ex-hotelier who was brought up in one of the streets demolished to make way for the North Peckham estate. He devoted much of his spare time to a boxing club off the Old Kent Road, and believed strongly that boxing can save kids from a life of crime. After fifteen years – eleven as a probation officer and four as a volunteer – on the front line, he argued that communities like North Peckham and Gloucester Grove were only kept stable by a class of people despised and dismissed on the political right as agents of the 'nanny state'. These are the housing officers, the inner city schoolteachers, the DHSS officials, the social workers, the beat policemen and the probation officers, who act as a 'buffer' between the anger and frustration of the jobless, the badly housed and the hopeless and the wider society. He said: 'Some argue "sack the lot, and it won't make a blind bit of difference," but these people soak up the frustration, and without them the anger would come spilling over.' He feared that as conditions in the inner city continue to deteriorate, more of the better 'buffers' will take themselves off to more congenial jobs. Eventually, the dispossessed will take it out on society more directly. Of all the theories as to why the present Government not only survives, but appears to thrive with three million unemployed, Mr Gillespie's seemed as plausible as any. The British are slow to complain; by the time someone goes to a housing office he is probably pretty angry. When he reaches for a hammer to smash the head of the official on the other side of a desk, he has reached a state of blind fury, not with the individual, but with all the impersonal forces the official appears to represent and against which he feels utterly impotent. A riot is a collective spilling of that cathartic anger.

Father Austin Smith, a Catholic priest who lives in the heart of Liverpool 8 and for ten years was a chaplain at Walton Prison, said: 'To the people a riot is ecstatic – mysticism on the margins of society. For the first time the "enemy" is in his sights, all lined up with its riot shields. They are no longer whispering about their frustrations.' Politicians pile into the riot zones in their limousines, telling the people, 'violence will get you nowhere', their very presence denying the truth of their words. Some very unpleasant people will get to the top during a riot – such as the ringleader convicted of murdering the Broadwater Farm policeman – but it is not they who cause the riot. As hopelessness increases, and the riots enhance the status of extremists, the 'buffer' – which includes parents – has progressively less with which to negotiate, and negotiation in any case becomes less relevant.

This translates for the youth into a lack of trust in and respect for anyone in authority. According to a Southwark youth worker, 'The youth have lost confidence both in the institutions and in themselves. They assume now that they are not going to get a job, and so don't try in the first place.' A young female colleague said she herself had 'lost all oomph' between mock exams and O Level. 'Everyone got rebellious, starting asking what they were staying on at school for,' she said. Both of them worked for the Southwark Unemployment Youth Project, an organization that presumed its customers would never work, so concentrated on the individual's personal development. Youth work, as the Inner London Education Authority which sponsors the Southwark project recognizes, is no longer a question of providing table tennis and snooker. 'The kids stay in bed all morning,' said one of the workers, 'getting up at about one o'clock, and the night is the focus of everything that happens.' Seen through these workers' eyes, the Tebbitite refusal to make the connection between unemployment and crime is simply wilful. 'Crime is going on everywhere,' they said, 'it is a question of economics. When you take someone's possessions, you're imposing a tax on them.' Others described this redistribution as a 'yuppie tax', which is somewhat romantic, since most of the victims of Peckham crime are at least as impoverished as the thieves.

Why, I asked them, had there been no uprising? It was like living in an earthquake zone, they replied, people get used to the shocks. Yet, they were bitter about gentrification and luxury new developments in docklands. (The words 'wine bar' when lobbed into such a conversation have about the same effect as a hand grenade.) Yuppies, they said, appeared to find it trendy to live on the fringes of working-class districts, so long as they did not have to suffer from working-class evils like crime. 'You hear them say, "Oh it's really not too bad, not too many black people and it's pretty well policed, and the houses are not too bad."' As jacuzzis are installed in working-class blocks of flats, extended families are broken up, and crammed on to the shoddy estates. The shops move out to places like Lewisham and Croydon.

Drug-taking, they agreed, was getting ever worse, and some youth organizations were frightened of opening their doors because it was almost impossible to keep the pushers out. Cocaine made people feel super-fit. (They added that 'many of the youth are now very physical, pumping iron and martial arts.') They said: 'Five pounds will get you out of your brain,' and they said the pushers were replacing soft drugs with hard drugs to increase their profits. What about the police? 'We treat them with acute suspicion,' said a white worker. 'It's outright war,' said a black colleague. They accused the police at best of being heavy-handed and insensitive; at worst, of being corrupt, taking backhanders to allow after-hours drinking, and even feeding confiscated drugs back on to the street. 'You know when there is going to be a bust,' according to one worker, 'because certain people are not on the street. They've been tipped off.'

*

A minority of residents on estates like North Peckham pose a twin threat to society – rampant crime on the one hand and potential civil disorder on the other – which leaves the police in a dilemma. Increasingly, concern with wider disorder is reducing the time, resources and attention given to crime. In some areas, 30 per cent of police training is dedicated to riot tactics and keeping the peace. A police chief's priority is to prevent riots on his territory, and the solving of routine crime is receiving less and less of his force's attention. In many areas the uniformed police will spend no more than ten minutes at the scene of a burglary, and even where there are substantial clues – a description of the thief by a neighbour or a footprint on a window sill – it is very unlikely that the CID will follow up. A householder's best chance of his burglary being 'solved' is if the thief is caught red-handed elsewhere, and asks for his earlier offences to be 'taken into consideration'. The police are far more likely to be seen in clusters outside football grounds, late at night in city centres or in shopping streets than singly or in pairs in residential areas. A senior policeman said: 'When it comes to a breakdown in society, we have got to worry first about public order.' The onus now is on the householders themselves to protect their property, just as it was before there was a police force.

Detective Chief Inspector Alec Ross, picked to run a pilot scheme in Southwark that will formalize the new policing priorities, said: 'We have tried everything except standing on our heads to get people to look after their property. The vast majority may not actually invite burglars in, but they don't take the slightest precaution – they have inadequate locks and leave their windows open. They might just as well have a revolving sign outside. It is the same with handbags; they leave them open on shop counters and walk away. Even now, people are just not sufficiently aware how prevalent crime is.' Several times since the Second World War the Metropolitan Police have reorganized their resources to cope with the reality of being able to tackle only a decreasing proportion of crime committed. When Mr Ross's pilot scheme is complete, effort will be devoted according to a points system based on each crime's solvability. The value of the crime will be far less important when deciding whether to follow it up than the chances of catching the perpetrator. The practice, said Mr Ross, is similar to that employed by doctors during the Vietnam war, when some seriously injured victims were simply injected with morphine and left to die. With fewer police hours being 'wasted' on hopeless cases, between six and seven hundred beat police will be freed to return to the streets, which accords with public priorities.

Mr Ross was cruelly blunt about policing areas like North Peckham where, he said, society had withdrawn its support for the police, inevitably abandoning the weak and innocent to the law of the jungle. 'The police on their own will never win. If people will not report the crimes they see and are not prepared to come forward as witnesses, the police are unable to do anything. Even if a policeman is witness to a crime himself, he often can do little without the victim's co-operation. It is a gradual slide downhill. If you back away and back away, you'll get trodden on. If you want the benefits and privileges of belonging to a society, you've got to be willing to stand up and be counted.'

Once co-operation has been withdrawn, said Mr Ross, there is little point even in having policemen on patrol. You might as well have cardboard cut-outs, he said. Like deadmen propped against the ramparts of the fort, they don't fool the people inside. Even policemen will eventually pick up their wages and look the other way; it is very difficult, said Mr Ross, to keep up the morale of officers when there is no public 'thank you'. If the public are not for them, it is the same as being against them. 'Once the police have lost consent, they have lost everything. The only other way is military-style policing, which is not acceptable in this country,' he added.

Non-co-operation takes two forms. There is the refusal of the criminals themselves and their associates to have anything to do with the police – Dr Ware, of the intensive care unit at King's College Hospital, said that even victims of internecine warfare who have been 'nigh unto death' will not help the police – and the fear that silences the vast majority like Mrs 'Smith'. I knew what Mr Ross was saying, and sympathize with the police predicament, but in the end society must have a responsibility to the Mrs Smiths which cannot be rationalized away. There is no neat divide between the control of crime and public order. Constant, unchecked criminality destabilizes communities like North Peckham, softening them up for riot and disorder. Mr Ross saw the inner cities in guerrilla terms; if left alone long enough, eventually the criminals have enough confidence to come out and fight in the open.

What, I asked him, had gone wrong? Was it Tebbit's 'wickedness'? Alice Coleman's architecture? Thatcherism? Mr Ross had quite a bit of time for Professor Coleman, and acknowledged that both left and right perceptions of the roots of crime were important. But he added: 'It is so much easier to destroy than to build. Politicians spend all their time tearing each other down; no one wants to build a blooming thing. People who should be leading are fighting one another. There's a terrible lack of someone standing up to say what has gone wrong.' He was scornful of the justice system. 'The authorities have an abject terror of punishing anyone. They say that the inevitability of detection is the deterrent, but that means very little to the class of individual who is regularly committing crime. The first five or six times he is arrested he may not even go to court. He may be thoroughly amazed when he is finally dealt with,' he said. However, he added, the prisons are full of the wrong people. It is scarcely a punishment for inadequates, for whom 'it is akin to heaven to have a warm, clean bed, clothing, three meals a day and be told what to do.' For many others, it is a relief to have their overwhelming responsibilities temporarily removed and everything looked after. A probation officer told me that most south London criminals he knew were quite prepared to spend one-third of their adult lives locked up, so long as they were 'someone' for the other two-thirds – a name, a face, with a thick roll of banknotes in their back pockets. 'You're not anyone,' he said, 'unless you're hard, a Jack the lad.'

Increasingly, inner city crime is committed to getting money to buy drugs. Paul Hayes, who heads a team of probation officers in the New Kent Road, said that when he came to London in the late seventies drug-taking had been confined to middle-class drop-outs – 'left over hippies and eternal students'. Now, he said, it was relatively usual for working-class kids to be using heroin. It was cheaper than it had been, and was smoked rather than injected. Unemployment, social dislocation and hopelessness made it an attractive option – 'those may be clichés, but just because someone has said something forty-three times doesn't make it untrue.' Crime, he argued, was deeply affected by the prevailing social conditions. In the thirties in poverty-stricken places like Jarrow – often cited by those of the Tebbit tendency who believe there is more innate evil today than there was then – nearly everyone was out of work, and those with a job were very poor also. Now, not only is there more to steal but it is more accessible. An affluent lifestyle is being lived in front of people who have nothing; it is not hidden fifty or a hundred miles away. Someone on £28 a week supplementary benefit may live next door to someone earning over £200. Even in Liverpool, from where Mr Hayes comes, there are 'flash' clubs and shops. If you're seventeen or eighteen and want 'to pull a few birds', you've got to buy the right drinks and wear the right shirts. Crime is really the only source for that kind of income. The majority of people with whom probation officers deal would prefer, said Mr Hayes, to be in work than out of it, and there was still semi-skilled or unskilled work available. (The black economy, he argued, was a subsidy for employers, rather than a fiddle for the workers, since in certain jobs an employer assumes workers are claiming benefit, and pays lower accordingly.)

Mr Hayes was thoroughly cynical about what he considered to be the Conservative manipulation of the law and order issue. The rhetoric might be quite tough, but the policy was liberal. The 'short sharp shock' introduced by William Whitelaw when he was Home Secretary, for example, had been meted out to young offenders since the war. Whitelaw had simply been pandering to the Conservative notion that life in Borstal was soft. Leon Brittan announced that parole for violent, sex and drug offenders would be restricted to the last few months of their sentences, thereby guaranteeing good 'tough' headlines. At the same time he was making arrangements to let virtually everyone else out on parole. There was permanent juggling, said Mr Hayes, between the rhetoric and the reality.

If the Government had the resources to build an airfield in the Falklands, it could easily run up a few more prisons, he said. If Conservatives genuinely believed that gaoling more people for longer would reduce crime, it would be their duty to lock them up to fulfil the Government's primary responsibility for the safety and well-being of society. 'In reality it isn't done because it wouldn't work, and they know it,' he said.

What then would work? The sixty-four-thousand-dollar question has almost an answer for each dollar. My time in and around North Peckham taught me that none of them is mutually exclusive. The walkways must come down; people must be given homes not prison blocks to live in; the police must be returned to the streets; teenagers must be instilled with purpose – there are jobs, at least in London; police chiefs must keep their itchy fingers away from their new military-style equipment. The danger lies in the 'no go' mentality. American cities that have refurbished their downtown areas have wrought minor miracles: the same is beginning to be true in Liverpool. The city has to be for all its people: crumbling council properties only streets away from gentrification schemes are a recipe for social disaster. Dave Sutherland's nightmare of 'welfare housing' would signal that Britain had abandoned the post-war drive towards equality of opportunity.

On my last day at North Peckham the sun was shining. As I left one front door to step on to a walkway, I ran into about ten kids playing on bicycles. 'Watch out, Alan,' said a child, 'you ran over the man's foot.' Two policemen were threading their way amiably between the children. It was a thoroughly reassuring scene. As in many other areas of life, we have, I suspect, a crucial last chance. In this case, getting it wrong means armoured cars, water cannon and tear gas increasingly deployed on the streets of our major cities, abandoning Mrs Smith to a world beyond the protection of law and order, and leaving tens of thousands of children to grow up in seriously impoverished communities.

∰ 5 ∰

SERIOUS MONEY

In an estate agent's temporary office in Shad Thames, a few yards from where Dickens put Bill Sykes to death, there was a scale model in a glass case. It showed the Anchor Brewhouse, a late Victorian brewery immediately south of Tower Bridge, which – in the early summer of 1987 – was being converted into thirty apartments which ranged in price from £270,000 to £2,500,000. The flats were being sold as fast as they could be constructed – negotiations had opened on the most expensive one, which was not due for occupation for another fifteen months – and a minority of buyers were simply making an investment, never intending to live there, owning the flat only until it was finished and then selling it for a yet greater price. They were dealing in luxury apartment 'futures'. Given that certain classes in London were flush with money, I could understand the prices. What did catch my attention was that the sales model itself had cost £12,000, which, in certain parts of the country I had lately been visiting, could have put an adequate (if small) roof over a family's head. The agent – I had declared myself as a scribbler rather than a purchaser – showed me a three-storey apartment at the top of what had been the brewery boilerhouse valued at one million pounds. It had three outside terraces, and from the top floor the Tower of London was exactly framed between the towers of Tower Bridge. A bed had been constructed on top of a head-high construction which housed the lift workings. You mounted it by means of a short ladder. Lying there, the future purchaser will have a panoramic view of some of the world's most celebrated buildings.

From a balcony on the other side, the near view was of feverish development beneath four giant red cranes. 'It's going to be another Mayfair,' said the estate agent happily. Dust-covered navvies – shortly to sink several lunchtime pints in the Anchor Inn on Horslydown Lane – were constructing a mock Georgian square, which will include more highly priced flats, the inevitable wine bars, and a 'grocery shop' to be run by Laura Blond, the small, dark-haired wife of publisher Anthony Blond. 'Mrs Blond,' enthused that month's *Tatler*, 'will prepare rillettes, terrines, quiches, odeons sculpted from ice and fascinia sculpted from root vegetables to sate local yuppies.' Husband and wife were pictured – he, modestly described by the *Tatler* as 'the novelist, publisher, bon viveur and thinker', in what looked like a white grocer's coat and a back to front Martini apron – clasping a basket loaded with sandwiches and wine bottles. In the background were the cranes, the brewhouse and Tower Bridge.

Looking up from the splendours to be, I saw on the skyline some familiar structures – long, low barracks, the outlines of which cut through the summer haze that lay across south London. They were, I realized – consulting the agent about which way the Old Kent Road ran – my stamping ground of the previous few weeks, North Peckham, Gloucester Grove and their linked estates, London's 'no go' territory. On long, hot summer evenings, sometime in the future, brewhouse tenants will be able to shift their sights from the Tower of London and watch the smoke rise over Peckham.

Even nearer to hand, perhaps taking a stroll before enjoying Mrs Blond's gourmet comestibles, our future tenants will find dozens of destitute people. Along the length of Tooley Street, which runs at right-angles to Tower Bridge Road, they lie every few yards, drunk on the steps of banks, on benches, on pavements – one youngish man with dark hair and a heavy stubble, looking weak and exhausted, like a cholera victim close to death. The favourite spot is a tiny park between Tooley Street and Queen Elizabeth Street, over which a bust of Ernest Bevin, in waistcoat and open jacket – black, heavily streaked with green – presides. 'The Dockers' K C' reads the plaque. 'A forceful and inspiring leader of democratic principles, he gained a place in men's hearts few could equal.' Beneath him a dozen or so down-and-outs drank cheap cider; one, a massive woman, whose gargantuan breasts spilled over the top of her filthy blue dress, had a hand on a pushchair in which sat a small child. The rubbish basket had long since been overwhelmed by beer cans, wine and cider bottles. Smashed glass shimmered underfoot, like the first fall of snow. There could have been no more ironic juxtaposition than between Bevin and his aspirations for the British poor, and the human flotsam beneath his bronze gaze.

Many who are not homeless live in fairly wretched conditions in the Tower Bridge area. Southwark Council had to abandon a scheme to modernize (and make more secure) several large blocks on Tooley Street for lack of money. Neighbouring Lambeth Council took action that week to deter 'yuppies' from buying converted flats in their borough. They passed a measure protecting large houses from conversion – one-bedroomed flats had been fetching £46,000; restricting the number of flats that could be carved out of one property; and requiring the provision of off-street parking if more than three flats were created. The divide between two Britains is far more clearly demarcated a few hundred yards from the Thames than it is by that notional boundary, the river Trent.

I asked the estate agent whether they had 'political' problems, creating luxury so close to squalor, and bearing in mind that Southwark had a left-wing administration. Had anyone come marching by, demanding 'Rich trash and yuppy scum out'? No, he replied. People understood they were creating homes out of what had been derelict industrial land – the brewery closed in 1968. We had moved to a flat on offer for £580,000 in a warehouse next to the brewhouse – two bedrooms, jacuzzi, balcony over the Thames, original brickwork and beams. He was anxious to know whether I thought the flats offered value for money. Bearing in mind the escalation of prices in my own suburban area, I answered truthfully 'Yes.' Since the world had been turned upside-down, such money for a luxury flat in a south London warehouse was certainly no crazier than £250,000 for a semi-detached in Richmond upon Thames or £45,000 for the top half of an LCC overspill house in Slough.

I found I had returned to a society that was flaunting wealth in a way the rich had considered unseemly in the post-war years. Greed (and with it peacock-like ostentation) had become acceptable. Before his disgrace, American arbitrageur Ivan Boesky told New York business students: 'Greed is all right, by the way. I want you to know that. You can be greedy and still feel good about yourself.' It was the saying of 1987. ('Boesky' is surely destined for the dictionary alongside 'Rachman' as eponymous words for the evils of the late twentieth century.) Such greed, however, had a philosophical/political underpinning in Reaganism and Thatcherism, dignified for public consumption as 'supply-side economics'. By making vast sums, the rich generated economic activity, which eventually helped everyone, therefore one was performing a public service by becoming (or, in most British cases, already being) very rich and was quite entitled to

feel good about it. (Those less enamoured with the theory call it
'trickle-down' economics, and are frequently cynical about how far
the trickle reaches. Supply-siders consider that 'trickle-downers'
suffer from a further condition – 'the politics of envy'.)

The consequence of the new philosophy appeared to be the
unabashed spending of money, and rewards for certain classes of
people that so distorted the value system that they threatened social
stability: while young nurses lived on 'peanuts', the City of London's
'Big Bang' had propelled a not particularly productive class of young
person towards six-figure salaries; while a civil engineer might
earn £15,000 a year, a foreign currency dealer, without any formal
qualifications, could earn ten times that much. These were not, as
some of the defenders of these high salaries argued, special people
like sports or pop stars, but people with quick wits and fairly readily
acquired trading skills. The ease with which they made their money
devalued it, not least in their own eyes, and commercial morality
therefore declined. If money could be come by so easily, it could be
no big deal, so cheating to obtain more was scarcely a crime, more
a little bending of the rules. The days of 'my word is my bond' –
suspicious as people outside the City may have been of them at the
time – now appeared as a lost age of high probity.

What seemed to have happened – rather as 'bad' tenants on 'no go'
estates had influenced the good with their anti-social habits – was
that the easy accumulation of wealth by the none too scrupulous had
lowered the standards of those who had always had serious money.
The children of people who once believed in *noblesse oblige* were
now happy to get rotten drunk daily on champagne, to indulge in
expensive drug abuse, and to flaunt their scorn of the less fortunate.

There were various straws in the wind shortly after I returned.
Four 'Hooray Henrys' exposed themselves as sybaritic, spoiled
drones in a hilarious television programme entitled 'The Fishing
Party'. They gorged themselves on oysters and champagne beneath
the chandeliers of an expensive London restaurant, and went aboard
a fishing boat from which they shot seagulls, while crudely expound-
ing their right-wing views of the world. One or two of them worked,
but one of the others said bluntly: 'Work and myself do not get
along.' There were two reasons to get married – to have children,
who would naturally be dispatched to boarding school as quickly as
possible, and to have a chauffeuse when you were drunk. One said:

'The loyalty of a dog is fantastic; no matter how many times you kick it, it will always be back. Dogs are more bloody useful than women.' They regarded the unemployed as a threat – 'to security, to stability, to law and order' – and suggested that the armed forces might be concerned if Labour won the next election. They were in favour of capital punishment, even if there was the odd mistake, and one at least was prepared to carry it out himself. They were crude, talking of 'stuffing hand grenades up arses', snobbish, boorish, and jingoistic – 'the English, the English, the English are the best, so up with the English and down with the rest'. And one, at least, earned his money in the City in the commodities futures market – 'selling something you haven't got in anticipation of buying it back cheaper. You never, of course, take delivery.'

At the same time, Rupert Deen, a man of similar ilk as the fishing party, was filmed by Yorkshire Television taking a bubble bath while his butler served him a Bloody Mary. He declared, 'workers should work for the likes of myself. You shouldn't give women and workers the vote. Voting should be limited to people like myself. I don't even pretend to work, though some of my friends do.' Mr Deen's life was contrasted with that of a Yorkshire miner, who, asserted Mr Deen, should pay the Government for the privilege of digging coal. Mr Deen guyed the part to some extent – he did work as an insurance underwriter – but the Russians, at least, took him at face value, and bought the programme to use as anti-British propaganda.

Olivia Channon, daughter of Cabinet minister Paul Channon and one of the many wealthy scions of the Guinness family, certainly wasn't hamming it up. In the summer of 1986 she was found dead from an overdose of heroin and alcohol in Christ Church, Oxford, on the night after Finals. Her death revealed the existence of a smallish group of well-connected and very rich undergraduates – centred on the bizarre figure of the German Count Gottfried von Bismarck – who appeared to have no sense of responsibility to themselves or anyone else. I went to Oxford the following day. I found that members of the set seldom took part at the Oxford Union, in drama or university journalism – activities that their fathers' generation of the well-connected and well-heeled pursued ambitiously. 'These are not,' said one activist undergraduate, 'the baby Cabinet ministers. They are people you don't know. Their credo is "we're rich, and we'll have what we want." They represent a backlash against what people

expect of students.' It was a male-dominated culture, centred on dining clubs, dedicated to drunkenness and upper-class yobbishness.
Election to one club was marked by the smashing up of the new members' college rooms. A woman undergraduate who had recently
attended a party on the fringes of the set, said: 'It's fairly hideous up-
market hooliganism. I was shocked, shocked. There was a lot of
cocaine on offer.' This set, said another student, revelled in illegality:
'Anything that is the opposite of their upbringing is singled out for
reverence. Their fascination with drugs is part and parcel of this. It is
a point of honour to show a cynical lack of concern for the proble-
matic aspects of contemporary life.' The *Sun* produced some fairly
plausible figures showing that a fully participating Horay Henry
would need a tax-free income of £48,000 to maintain the sort of life
led by the upper-class hooligans. The Dean of Christ Church, the
Very Revd Eric Heaton, rolled his eyes, gripped his sherry, and said:
'Brideshead! We're far too near London. Cambridge is jolly lucky to
be out in the blasted fens.'

In London a few months after Miss Channon's death two enterprising teenagers joined forces to make serious money out of the prevailing hedonism. Jeremy Taylor, whose family owns the house
featured in the television series 'To the Manor Born', and Eddie Davenport, described by a friend as 'dynamic social gatherings organizer
and man about town', hit on the idea of running balls for the *jeunesse
dorée* that were free of the oversight of the 'wrinklies'. They hired the
biggest venues in London, and publicized the balls through a magazine called the *Gatecrasher*, which was circulated in public schools –
to 'rich' young people, Mr Davenport emphasized when we met at
the Fulham house that serves as their office. Charging between twelve
and twenty pounds a ticket for up to two thousand teenagers a
time – one ball grew into three balls on consecutive nights, so great
was the demand – they grossed £500,000 in their first year of operation, of which £100,000 was profit. Their dances had such titles as the
'Terror Ball' and 'Chaos at Christmas', so no one could be under any
illusion that mummies would be watching from little gilt chairs. Mr
Taylor revealed the spirit of the enterprise in his *Gatecrasher* notes
on the social year 1986: 'All the Sloanes went on their yearly trip to
the Badminton Horse trials, many were disappointed when the bars
closed in the afternoon, and the competition seemed to be to see how
few horses you could see during the day, and how many pints of lager
or gin and tonics you could drink.' After the 'Midsummer Mayhem

Ball', he reported, 'most people flew off to their summer villas to tan themselves.'

The *Gatecrasher* had a photo feature on 'Le Snog!!' and a popular paper reported that the privileged teenagers enjoyed uninhibited sex beneath the dining-table cloths as the evening wore on. But Mr Taylor said that Aids was cramping the young people's style – 'they worry about it a lot.' 'Did they see themselves in the tradition of past eras of excess,' I asked, 'like those written about by Evelyn Waugh?' He looked rather blank. 'I don't do much reading unfortunately.' Mr Davenport had to leave, and there was a brief hunt for the car phone. A few minutes later a young woman with 'CHANEL' written across her T-shirt came in: '*Harpers and Queen* are on the phone for Eddie. Shall I give them the car phone number?' The *Daily Mirror* had contrasted the money spent by the ballgoers with the pittance paid to people on the dole. 'Did that worry Mr Taylor?' It was, he said, 'hard to think of that sort of thing' when you were surrounded by people in jobs. The ballgoers had lived 'quite secluded lives in private schools and their parents' nice homes in the country. Everything was good, and they were going to turn out rich like their parents.' It was hard to avoid *Gatecrasher*'s essential snobbery – one of their dances was called 'The Slough Comprehensive End of Term Ball'. Comprehensive school pupils – or, put another way, ninety-four per cent of secondary schoolchildren – were, I was told by one ballgoer, known as 'Kevins and Sharons'. Where, I asked Mr Taylor, would most of his revellers eventually earn their living if it came to that? In the City, Mr Taylor supposed. Were they spoiled, like the children of the American rich are increasingly being spoiled? Not usually, said Mr Taylor, though 'the nouveau crowd, who had just struck it rich, might give their son a Porsche for his eighteenth birthday.'

It appeared that it was no longer considered either desirable or prudent for the rich *not* to flaunt their wealth. Messrs Taylor and Davenport were falling in with the prevailing mores. In the months before 'Big Bang' some dealers in their twenties had their salaries more than trebled between lunch and pink champagne time, from £30,000 perhaps to £100,000. Seventy-three people at the 'lower end of the employee scale' at one City jobbing firm were paid between £35,000 and £120,000. The firm was reported to believe 'it right and necessary to ensure that remuneration is fully competitive in the new environment.' Glossy magazines like *Harpers and Queen* and *Tatler* revelled in the wealth and consumption of people about whom they wrote. The Earl of Lichfield edited *Courvoisier's Book of the Best*, which told us that the 'complete house' should have two swimming pools, jacuzzis in each bathroom, a helicopter pad, a gymnasium, and a 'perfect couple' of servants. The book's recommended champagne, Roederer Cristel, sold at £37.75 a bottle, and the best claret was said to be Château Petrus, a Pomerol costing £280 a bottle. Shrewd public relations operators began to exploit the desire of the new rich to be accepted on the unashamedly opulent London social scene by organizing parties for their clients at which no one could be quite sure who had paid to meet whom. In 1919 a confidential Government document, drawn up to assess the possibility of revolution in Britain, listed 'foolish and dangerous ostentation of the rich' as a prime cause of unrest. Presumably by 1987, despite three million unemployed, no such danger was feared by Mrs Thatcher's Government.

'Big Bang' – the wiping away on 27 October 1986 of restrictive practices and demarcations on the Stock Exchange – caught the public attention and the headlines, but the process of 'liberalizing' the City had begun more than a quarter of a century earlier when exchange controls were relaxed, stimulating foreign currency dealing. Parallel markets – in Eurodollars, for example – developed, creating a faster moving financial milieu than in the traditional centres like the Stock Exchange and Lloyd's. One banker said: 'Gilt and equity traders stayed on the floor, scarcely recognizing that the telephone had been invented.' The old institutions became anachronisms, stately galleons, their decks lined with beribboned admirals, while the water around them churned in the wakes of fast-moving frigates. The 'barrow boy' dealers – kids with minds like pocket calculators, but otherwise scarcely touched by education – had been around for years already making big money in the newer markets. A senior banker said: 'There began to appear a new class of trader/dealer/broker, who came from a fundamentally different background, and had an uninhibited approach to business opportunities. They were orientated towards income and excited by trading, and not clouded by much thought and analysis. They were quick-reacting and sensitive to clients' needs, and, by definition, had to come from a different educational and social background.' At first in the traditional areas they were under-recognized and underpaid, but, by their skills, kept the old-style City gentlemen in the manner to which such gentlemen had always been accustomed. But, as in all culture clashes, the new inevitably overwhelmed the old. The last bastion of the old snobberies was Lloyd's, where, ironically, many of the worst City scandals of recent years have broken. The frauds were few, but the consequences devastatingly large – one bunch siphoned off thirty-nine million pounds, and cost their clients £235 million in losses. A few 'nasties' – as my banker friend put it – 'manipulated their positions of power.'

The new traders had nothing but contempt for the old boy net and the fuddy-duddy ways of their seniors. They revelled in the perils and excitements of unsecured markets. If there was to be capitalism for the people – created on the back of giveaway privatization – these were the men and women for the new world. Big Bang signalled the beginning of the end for the solid, snobbish, traditional stockbroker classes, with their relaxed commuting habits and self-protective paternalism. To compete with the new dealers, the old gang found they had to leave their Hampshire homes at 5.30 a.m., and not return till 10.00 p.m. As the banker said, their way of life was 'no longer sustainable.'

As the walls tumbled down, and the old guard retreated, the City increasingly became like a bright light to moths for young people who wanted, above all else, to make money. While I was meeting people in the City, the Civil Service Commission reported that it was losing 'golden graduates', including those with 'exceptional skills', to the City – in 1986 a record number of such graduates, fifteen, had eventually turned the Civil Service down. (A man in the Bank of England told me that in the City a bright graduate might be offered a ten thousand pounds joining present, £20,000 a year and a car, while the Civil Service was still concerned whether a recruit ate peas from his knife.) Other crucial skilled people – accountants, scientists and surveyors – were being drained away from public service by Big Bang. The report concluded: 'Analysis shows that salary is one of the reasons for withdrawal given by half of all respondents in the specialist areas.' In simple English, the Civil Service no longer paid enough, and old-fashioned rewards, like the satisfaction derived from duty, failed to compensate as they once had for comparative poverty. But, as in any gold rush, alongside the admirable entrants, Big Bang drew in those whose avarice outstripped their judgment and morality. Oddly, perhaps, it was an up-market 'bookmaker' who first blew the whistle from inside the Square Mile of the City of London.

Christopher Hales, who – after a brief period as a professional golfer – had started in the City as a stock jobber and had been a commodity broker, ran an outfit called City Index, which offered odds on, among other things, the movement of the Financial Times and Wall Street indices. His business allowed brokers and others, who spent their working days 'speculating' with company money, to back their hunches with their own: it was attractive because winnings were tax-free. His clients on occasions ran up seven-figure debts, but, until Big Bang, although gaming debts are unenforceable at law, he had always been confident they would settle. Most of his 'sporting gentlemen' were brought up in the tradition that you paid the bookmaker before the milkman because betting losses were 'debts of honour'. But the new young men, said Mr Hales, suffered from intellectual arrogance. They were sure they would be right, and, if they were wrong, you were only a bookmaker, and they didn't have to pay you. They were 'spoiled' with money, but didn't know how to take their knocks – they weren't prepared to part with the Porsche or take out an extra mortgage to settle their debts.

When he discovered that a number of defaulters worked for Merrill Lynch, he called the firm, and four employees were disciplined. One of them, Justin Tate, was already well known in the Hooray Henry world as a former president of the Oxford University dining club, the Assassins, where he had been dubbed 'The Baron'. While he was president in 1982, the Assassins caused six hundred pounds' worth of damage to a restaurant in Thame, near Oxford. Mr Tate owed Mr Hales £57,053. Over a lunch in one of those subterranean wine bars with sawdust on the floor, which are so beloved by pin-striped City types, Mr Hales gave me a talk about City probity that would have done credit to a Department of Trade and Industry inspector. There were not enough good-quality yuppies to go round, he said, so young people were given more responsibility than they could handle. Their 'monstrous' salaries were paid because the out-of-touch City headmen 'didn't have the faintest idea what these young people were doing,' a suspicion I had cherished since first writing about Big Bang.

The yuppies, he said, 'haven't got the breeding for the City, to put it quite bluntly. "My word is my bond" has been replaced by "Dog eats dog." With the stakes getting bigger, they forget the ground rules and get carried away by greed. There are not many people who are capable of being moral when they start talking in millions. Big Bang has changed the profile of the City.' He mourned the passing of the 'straightforward, old-fashioned, doddering public schoolboy. He may have had a lot of drawbacks, but he had an honest simplicity. He might not make you a fortune, but he wouldn't lose you one either.' There would, however, soon be a shake-out of the young tyros, he forecast with satisfaction, bringing with it 'a weak market in second-hand Porsches.'

Six months after Big Bang, most people in and around the City agreed that the boom would be followed by at least a mini-bust. Anyone can make money during a Bull market, several people said, but when it turns to a Bear there'll be blood on the pavement. 'The yuppies are starting at the top,' said the international funds manager of the subsidiary of a smallish American bank, 'and there's only one way for them to go.' And he drew a large downwards arrow on the pad in front of him. He, unlike some, was not rejoicing in the fall that might lie ahead for the unlucky. He regretted that there was no longer time or inclination for paternalism, and that dealers joined banks to make a killing rather than a career. Exceptionally, he took young dealers in his own firm to lunch to advise them to be prudent with their money while the good times lasted. Highly salaried young people in most firms had no such avuncular counselling. 'It is inevitable there will be some pretty disgraceful conduct. The most incredible salaries are paid to the young and inexperienced. The yuppies are immature, and many come from backgrounds which lack a gentlemanly tradition. They were brought up in a void, live in a void and work in a void,' he said, blaming the poor parenting of the sixties for the lack of moral standards. His young dealers came from a wide range of backgrounds – the father of one was on the Ford production line; one was black; one was a graduate, who had started his career as a journalist and seen the error of his ways; a fourth had the classic 'barrow boy' background. He disliked, he said, the barrow boy cliché, but he had to recognize its validity. 'Yeah, I'm a posh barrow boy, in't I?' he said mockingly. Men of his generation had evolved as the City money markets had evolved. When he started, a foreign exchange dealer earned only a few pounds a week more than a bank clerk. Then, far from there being 'golden handshakes', which these days lure dealers from firm to firm, this man had had to resign one job before seeking another, such was the etiquette against 'poaching'.

He was sympathetic to people who were poorly paid in other parts of the economy, having himself three members of his immediate family who did responsible but under-rewarded jobs – a hospital radiographer, an engineer and a police constable. His 31-year-old daughter, the radiographer, was in charge of a bodyscan machine,

and was paid £12,000 a year. When she had recently wanted to improve her skills in order to cope with a new scanner, she had had to
take time off without pay to visit another hospital where one was in
use. However, he argued that there were two justifications for the
present inflated City rewards. One was simple economics. Good
people had been in short supply at a time of high demand. The other
was that they lived a crazily hyperactive life, yelling down phones all
day. If you put the average doctor in a dealing room, he said, he
would not understand how the dealers survived one day. In his own
bank four dealers with three assistants settled two hundred trans-
actions a day, worth five hundred million dollars. 'You get paid for
living the life that has that sort of pressure on you. Information technology increases the volatility of the markets. You live with continuous nervous pressure. We are throwing young kids into battle each
day,' he said. However, six months after Big Bang I found fewer
people prepared to defend telephone number salaries than I had six
months earlier. Then the only senior note of caution had been struck by
Sir Timothy Bevan, chairman of Barclays, who warned that the City
'was subject to a lot of political and social opprobrium for paying
what is perceived generally as too much.'

The argument for the new freebooters, put forcibly by a leading
headhunter, is that Britain's economic activity had been in the hands
of unadventurous and easy-going gentlemen for too long. 'It is extremely desirable that business is controlled by people who are rest-
less and greedy. Since business in international terms is somewhat
akin to war, it is best to have people who imitate the action of the
tiger controlling companies, rather than the lamblike people who
have been at the helm for many years past.' He pointed to Britain's
1987 growth rate, and argued that it was propelled by 'the optimism,
the aggression, the competitiveness' of the new tycoons. 'All of these
are functions of a new cultural mood, and they go hand in hand with
the success we are starting to see.'

Until I met 'Geoffrey Jones', I had taken the claim that people burned
themselves out in the City with a small pinch of salt. There were
other stressful lives that were not eased by BMWs and 1980 Henri
Boillet Volnay that would seem more likely to drive a person into an
early grave. But, at forty-six, Mr Jones, a foreign currency banker,
had just had a heart attack, and was a deeply worried man facing a
heart bypass operation and expecting he would never work again. 'If

it's a choice between extending life expectancy or showing the world in the City what hot stuff I am for another two years, I know which I'll choose,' he said. I later met a banker who had known six people younger than Mr Jones who had died of heart attacks.

Geoffrey Jones's father had been a working man, and he had gone into the City from school. He had loved the life. 'You joined the club by wearing the uniform; charcoal grey suit, gleaming shoes polished top and bottom, white shirt, sober tie, white handkerchief in your pocket and bowler hat. I was part of a disciplined and ordered life, where respect prevailed for wisdom and knowledge. The big decisions were made by elderly people living in Surrey – "Charles and Herbert" – hand on shoulder, whispering in each other's ears, doing their business in the City chop houses. It was all very much an old pals' situation, and I never questioned the ethics or morality of that style.' He learned the terminology: speculating became 'taking a view on the market – "speculate" did not smack well of responsible monetary activity,' he said. In those days foreign currency was actually traded to facilitate international trade: today, 99 per cent of currency movements are speculative.

Mr Jones rose rapidly and travelled, selling what the City had to offer. 'It was a wonderful opportunity to see the world, even though the days were long and the living hard, with lots of entertainment. I didn't suffer any discomfort. I was not conscious of the mental pain, which was probably a pity because I didn't realize what damage I was laying in store for myself,' he said. He considered himself very fortunate to be in the small minority of people he knew who had clung on to their marriages. 'There are very few of the people in the City who started with me to whom I can say "How's the wife and family?" and be confident that it's the same wife and family I first knew. Divorce is very much related to one's degree of success,' he said, adding that 'money causes them to lose perspective.'

The next banker I met hadn't, I judged, lost perspective, but he had lost a wife, causing a drain on his finances, which meant he lived in Chiswick rather than Belgravia. He also talked convincingly of the strains of a business deluged daily with new information and money-making instruments. High salaries and intense competition made for a highly pressurized life. A bright, original idea lasted no more than one phone-call. A deal might be re-priced five times in one morning, during which the variables – such as exchange rates – on which it was based were constantly moving. He knew dealers who would walk all over you if you got in the way of a profit, even if you were marrying their sister. I said I had once been in a life assurance sales office where photographs were put on the walls of everyone who had sold a million pounds' worth of business – a kind of capitalist league table. 'We do not have time,' said the banker, 'to put pictures on the wall.' He slept only five hours a night, and even trips to Paris were really 'pure hell'. By contrast, when he started in the early seventies, the only people in before 9.00 a.m. had caught an early train by mistake. He was in charge of a dealing room, and much of his job was to keep his young dealers' feet on the ground – they oscillated between peaks of elation and troughs of despair. 'My family thinks I am completely bonkers,' he said. 'Eventually the City will disappear up its own rear end. It takes itself far too seriously.'

Though many City types claimed that dealers had to be at their screens twelve hours a day, leaving them no time or energy for the high life, my own experience and observation suggest something different. A Bank of England official once told me that an essential attribute for City success was 'the ability to operate when tanked up,' and for many that hasn't changed. In bars like Coates's in London Wall, decked out in neon, and the Altruist Champagne Bar in Bow Lane, the young dealers in their pin-striped suits, their white or striped shirts, and with their expensively coiffed hair, down Vollereaux pink champagne at £16.50 a bottle before heading off for a night's gaming. The notion that many of these yuppies – although most of them dislike the term it now has its own self-fulfilling accuracy – earn over £100,000 a year must disturb anyone who believes rewards ought to be in proportion to effort and contribution to society. Liberated from that essential connection between what they do and its value, it is little wonder that some of them welch on their bookies, and throw plates at Roy Hattersley. If you can make six hundred pounds a day when you're still in your early twenties, it is easy to consider yourself above tedious and petty rules by which others must live. Once the boorishness of the rich yob was a private phenomenon: now all the world is their stage. (Nothing could have been more revealing of the prevailing class attitude than the comments of the manager of the hotel in Birmingham at which yuppies threw a plate like a frisbee at Mr Hattersley's table, cutting deeply the face of a senior Labour Party man who was with him. He said: 'These people were nothing like your conventional football thug. Otherwise they would never have got into here in the first place. They were respectably spoken – more like City gents – the kind of customers we expect to see on a Saturday lunchtime. There was nothing to suggest they were going to behave in this dreadful way.') What price morality anyway, when yuppies see their elders at Guinness – and certain MPs, who bought into privatized industries with the zeal of a junkie after a fix – carving the rules up like so many pork bellies? Insider dealing was acknowledged to be rampant – after all, the City's stock-in-trade is 'information'. A word had even been coined for its practitioners – 'corrupies'.

A close observer of the City said: 'In any other walk of life, you get rich, if at all, through sustained hard work. The amorality of the quick killing soon leads to amorality in the wider world. City conduct is a kind of promiscuity. If you can't immediately get what you want, you have the perfect right to go somewhere else to get it.' He argued that the pressures on 'good' men were intolerable; with their huge salaries and the money invested in their golden handshakes and golden handcuffs and in the new City technology, they had to 'perform'. He said: 'Good people in the middle don't know which way to turn, and are being carried along on the tide. They dare not stop and look at the whole situation, the consequences are too damn frightening. They daren't face the crucial question: "Is what we are doing any longer serving a purpose except self-enrichment?" If you are making a profit, no more needs to be asked. That is the justification. The tendency has been a downward ratchet, with people sinking their standards to survive. There is no countervailing force, no moral breakwater – only bamboos in the sand which the sea runs through at will.'

City solicitor Andrew Phillips, a member of the Institute of Business Ethics, campaigns in the *Observer* and on radio against 'untrammelled capitalism'. He said: 'We have made greed, envy and avarice respectable; they are almost glorified by some people. It is about the biggest self-inflicted injury that this society could suffer. There are two hundred people in the City earning a million pounds a year and five hundred earning half a million pounds. That sort of money by any traditional standards is quite astonishing. It is a mark of just how far down the road of materialism we have gone that there are people in London who not merely justify what's happening, but say "Let's have more." They want their heads examining. Economic activity must be within a moral framework or it will ultimately destroy you.'

What was going wrong, so I gathered, was not the lack of rules – the Securities and Investment Board, which has the ultimate responsibility for licensing and regulating fifteen thousand investment businesses, has, a Bank of England official told me, a rule book thick and heavy enough to serve as the foundation stone for a substantial building. 'Big Bang' de-restricted rather than de-regulated the City. But the rules are now approached in the American manner. In the words of one senior banker, 'you obey the rules, but try to find a loophole. In the past the rules represented an intention. You stood by the intention, and didn't need the rules.' The Bank's official said: 'The American financial giants that now dominate the City are used to being told in great detail what they can't do. If it is not forbidden, you can do it.' That was certainly the case in my limited experience with American financial regulations. Income tax was a game played entirely to the letter of the rules, without any consideration of the intention. The rich bought yachts as tax write-offs and, when that was disallowed, they redesignated their boats as 'second homes', which was allowed.

City salaries do have consequences beyond the dealing rooms and the narrow streets of the Square Mile. An estate agent explained how property prices rose like a wave beneath the NatWest tower in the heart of the City and swept westwards sixty miles through London and the home counties. A choice Knightsbridge flat might have jumped £200,000 in price, releasing its former owner to bid higher for property in Wimbledon, who then enters the market further out of town flush with funds. The consequences include the £4·6 million an acre price tag in the docklands, the celebrated £36,500 for a 'broom cupboard' opposite Harrods and £10,000 for a Kensington car parking space, and – crucially for many people – such inflated prices in the outer suburbs that essential people like teachers and hospital staff can no longer afford to live and work in many parts of London and the south-east. My son returned from school to report that he was about to be taught by a third geography teacher in one year because, so he gathered, her predecessors had been forced out of the area in search of homes. A major local hospital has permanently closed wards because of lack of staff. None of this concerns the 'Big Bangers' who live locally, because they educate their children privately and belong to Bupa (the private health insurance scheme).

The madness (and some of the amorality) of 'Big Bang' was exuberantly captured in Caryl Churchill's play *Serious Money*, presented at

London's Royal Court Theatre in Sloane Square in the spring of 1987. A host of avaricious financiers and dealers on each side of the Atlantic cream what millions they can from predatory takeover bids with no thought for the consequences beyond their own wealth. Productive firms are closed down and their workers made redundant to suit the strategy of the moment. The play was bang up to date, with references to the many current scandals. Zackerman, an American banker, caught the prevailing philosophy:

> There is no question there are thin lines
> and this is definitely a grey area.
> And since Guinness it's a whole lot scarier.
> You can't play ball if you keep off the grass.
> So promise whenever you have to. Peddle your ass.
> Let's give it all we've got and worry later.

The action was set after a prophesied future Conservative election victory, and Zackerman commented that the return of the Conservatives had been 'handy though not essential because it would take far more than Labour to stop us,' and the whole cast concludes:

> Five more glorious years, five more glorious years.
> We're crossing forbidden frontiers
> for five more glorious years
> pissed and promiscuous, the money's ridiculous
> send her victorious for five fucking morious
> five more glorious years.

When it was over, the yuppies in the audience clapped their hands raw and spilled out chortling into the Sloane Square night. 'Pretty damn accurate,' they told each other heading off for a glass of 'poo'. 'Usually,' said the Royal Court's director, 'it's bicycles; now it's Porsches parked in Sloane Square.'

I asked all the bankers, the dealers, the brokers I met what it was that the City did for the rest of us. I had in mind the despair of manufacturers I had met in the provinces (the offstage victims, as it were, of Ms Churchill's play), who could have revolutionized their businesses – often creating exports and replacing imports – sometimes with as little as four months' earnings of a successful City yuppie. Mere mention of the City made conservative manufacturers angry and resentful. Its iniquities, as they saw them, were closely allied to the wider issues of class and accent, and even occasionally to the royal family, which, from the manufacturing outback, appeared to be the foundation of a structure that was snobby and ignorant about industry. (City men tended to respond to this question with, 'Ah yes, your average manufacturer of widgets,' thereby confirming the small industrialists' perceptions.)

The first line of City defence is always that most of the truly unimaginable sums of which we hear have nothing to do with the British economy. By trading in foreign currencies and securities, the City earns six billion pounds a year. 'It keeps a hell of a lot of people employed,' said one banker. High street banks, the *bêtes noires* of most small manufacturers, he argued, were businesses, owned by shareholders who would take them to task if they made rash loans. They could not be doing everything wrong if they made a billion pounds a year, an argument that missed my point. However, the banker had been bruised himself when a bank turned him down for a bridging loan to buy a new house – although he offered them the deeds as security – so he could sympathize with the point of view of my provincial friends.

But, in general, the City was no nicer about industry than industry was about the City. Another banker said that, instead of sitting around complaining about the City, industry should be quicker to put its own house in order. It was far too slow to innovate markets and produce new products. British industry had, until recently, been in a dismal spiral, with lack of success leading to lack of money for investment, and lack of investment leading to lack of success. Although performance was improving quite markedly, industry had its poor reputation to overcome, which 'unfortunately will take a hell of a lot more time than the improvement in the product.' 'Had industry had the money, would it in any case have invested it wisely?' asked my interlocutor. Thinking of the record of my own newspaper industry in the pre-Wapping era, I had to answer 'No.' Change, he said, was inevitably painful, which is why it comes so slowly. The London docks – now the back yard for 'Big Bang' – were one hundred years out of date before they closed. The problem for the well-run individual company, such as I had in mind, was often lack of financial knowledge, he said.

An official at the Bank of England put it more bluntly. He said: 'Industry has a mind-boggling ignorance of what the City is capable of doing if asked. The assumption is always that the answer will be

"No,"' The Bank published a booklet, *Money for Business*, the sort of publication that sat in the lobby of Department of Trade and Industry offices unread by all but 1 or 2 per cent of businessmen. He said he resisted the notion that the City had an obligation to the rest of society, like some branch of welfare. People don't ask in the same manner, he said, what the chemical industry does for the rest of the economy. The City was a sector of the economy making big profits in free competition. Tongue in cheek, he added: 'Perhaps in some future recession, the City will be a depressed zone, qualifying for regional assistance from Tony Benn as it collapses under the impact of Japanese competition.' However, he agreed that the policies of the clearing banks often don't percolate through to the branch officers, where the attitude remains that loans are based on your assets and securities. I had found that companies are certainly often ignorant; however, a small outfit, which may require an injection of capital only once every twenty years, can scarcely be blamed for not having up-to-the-minute knowledge of the capital markets.

The rest of us also remain woefully ignorant about capitalism. Of those who have bought shares in one of the privatized industries, many are likely to have put the certificate in a drawer along with family photos. Banks have been slow to offer financial services in the high street – I suspect there might be a killing for the first bank to make it as easy to buy shares as it is to buy foreign currency. We may not be natural capitalists any more, but we are natural gamblers, and banks are often conveniently close to bookmakers. Geoffrey Jones, the banker who had had the heart attack, said: 'In Britain selling a new concept is bound to be a slow and laborious process. Unless the British can relate to something they are familiar with, they are loath to give it serious consideration, let alone cough up any money. We're fifteen to twenty years behind the Americans in terms of familiarity with financial markets. Only in the last two years have the British been allowed to become more enlightened. The attitude is "Let's get involved, but not too involved."' My feeling is that as long as a rising market persists, and capitalism appears to be about something for nothing, a piece of a safe monopoly, John Bull will continue to shell out for new issues of privatized shares. But once the first disaster occurs, there will be a swift change of mood. There may even be demands for Government compensation for people who have lost money!

The people's capitalism will, I suspect, be one of Mrs Thatcher's legacies that, when it has genuinely worked its way into the national psyche, will be seen to be as significant as the sale of council houses. My sadness is that the concept is being marketed as a get rich quick formula. Owing to the undervaluing of the initial privatized stock, it has indeed been risk-free, which explains why voracious yuppies like the former Conservative M P, Keith Best, put their careers in jeopardy to get their paws on more than their fair shares. The *Daily Mail* in a profile described the curly-haired, baby-faced Mr Best as the 'archetypal yuppy – never afraid of hard work if it was essential to get him where he wanted, never short of ambition, always with an eye for the main chance'. He is, in short, the perfect Thatcherite, and it is an indication of the temper of the times that neither his fall nor the City scandals that by early 1987 had become part of the national wall-paper appeared to touch the electoral popularity of the woman in whose name all this striving after 'serious money' took place. (In the United States it was reported that it had become socially chic to have as a dinner guest someone of dubious financial morality.) However, the average punter, having taken his money out of the building society and stuck it into British Gas – thereby buying a piece of something he had previously owned as a taxpayer – was still light years away from investing in new of developing industry.

In the week I was in the City, a survey revealed that the directors of a private company in Scotland were being paid an average of £783,600 each. Increases for all British directors were running at more than twice the rate for the rest of the workforce. That same week nurses received a pay rise bringing the salary for a newly qualified staff nurse to £7,300. The most recent Inland Revenue statistics showed that the post-war trend towards greater equality in wealth had been halted – and in some cases reversed – since Mrs Thatcher came to power. The wealthiest 1 per cent of Britons still own 21 per cent of the national marketable wealth (up 1 per cent since the election of Mrs Thatcher); 5 per cent own 39 per cent; and the richest 50 per cent own 93 per cent. The figures for the Thatcher years contrasted with the experi-ence of the previous half century, during which the richest groups lost about 4 per cent of their total wealth each decade.

Money, class and work are inextricably mixed and linked in the British mind. Most Britons, even though they recognize intellectually that the rewards are handed out on an uneven and not very logical basis, emotionally accept as inescapable the divisions and inequalities that can trap them into a narrow corner of life. 'It's not for the likes of us' in its many guises is still a familiar cry. It is newspapers read by the less wealthy that have the most juicy news about the doings of the rich. (I had once thought that a serious revolutionary party in this country should dispense with its mind-numbing meetings and its dreary slogans, and load the industrial poor into buses and drive them round Mayfair, pointing out the contrasts between what they could see and their own lives. However, I now suspect they would return to Merseyside, or wherever, agog with what they had seen – especially if they had caught sight of the hem of a royal skirt – encouraged to buy yet more magazines with 'Fergie' or 'Princess Di' on the cover.)

Nesting luxuriously at the apex of the pyramid of national privilege is the royal family. It was a blessed relief to live in a republic for four years, to escape the incessant rubbish that is peddled about the British royals. (There may be too much chit-chat about Nancy Reagan, or, in Jimmy Carter's day, his brother Billy, but American presidents do not create dynasties.) Even Anglophile foreigners are sometimes driven from Britain by the mindless drivel we read and talk about royalty. 'When I've had it up to here with people telling me that . . . the royal family are overworked and underpaid . . . then I figure it's high time I took myself away on a good vacation,' wrote the American Paul Theroux. He's lucky; he had Cape Cod to which to escape. The rest of us are stuck with the Charles and Di show.

I am a believer in a constitutional monarchy. I do not wish to be presided over by 'President' Harold Wilson or 'President' Margaret Thatcher, nor by some deadbeat compromise from the House of Lords cross benches. (There are admirable constitutional presidents like Richard von Weizsäcker of West Germany, but the odds against finding and electing such a person in a politically polarized society like Britain seem to be regrettably long.) But the flummery that surrounds the royal family underpins the claustrophobic snobbery and divisions that mar society in Britain. Brian Walden, the television presenter, scarcely a radical these days, wrote: 'Instead of all the magnificent contributions Britain has made to the world, holding centre stage, we are characterized by our snobbery, patronage, resentment, envy and social distinctions.' Auberon Waugh, arguing in favour of the present arrangements, commented: 'By her existence [the Queen] reassures us that we need not be guilty about such privilege as may attach to our separate conditions, since this is but a tiny reflection of the quasi-divine privilege which reposes in the monarchy. Far more effectively than Mrs Thatcher, she convinces us that there is nothing wrong in inequality, that even wealth itself is not necessarily evil (or "obscene", as left-wing MPs may put it).' The Waugh thesis is pure sophistry. What the present opulent and privileged monarchy 'legitimizes' is not man's right to be unequal – that can be enshrined in such words as 'life, liberty and the pursuit of happiness' – but an unequal society that has insufficient social, educational and economic mobility effectively to thrive either as the pleasant, evolving country it might be, or as a successful international trading power.

The adulation we offer the royal family conditions us for passive acceptance of things we should rise up against, such as the inequalities in education and the brainwashing diet of soap operas like 'EastEnders' on television. We live in the wings of a permanent, live, glossy soap opera, which is about as relevant to our lives as the weekly shots of 'Dallas' or 'Dynasty'. We accept bromides, like the one that Theroux was walking out on, without challenge. Another canard is that the Queen, owing to her long service, is the accumulation of statecraft, political wisdom and constitutional knowledge. This may or may not be so – we are not so ready in other walks of life to equate long service with exceptional capacities – but there is simply no way its assertion can be justified by the known facts. Certainly the proliferation of her younger relatives, most of them – like the Princess of Wales – glorifying in their undereducated Sloane dizziness, is a significant encouragement to the Hooray Henry world of polo, *Gatecrasher* balls and indolent ostentation at Ascot and Henley. The British social structure of titles and gradations, our conditioned instinct that one person is 'better' than another by reason of birth or class, our bobbing and curtseying – all of which look faintly ridiculous from outside the country – take their justification from a privileged and remote royal family. Prince Charles may look like an 'ordinary bloke' when he hobnobs with inner city youths, but his genuine friends – as opposed to advisers like the architect Rod Hackney – are drawn from as narrow a circle as his mother's. The proximity of a 'royal' personage like 'Fergie' sends most Britons weak at the knees, and turns their brains to cotton wool. Television interviewers like Sir Alastair Burnet, of twice the age and achievement of the royal princes they are questioning, call them 'sir'. The royals are, people say in their Pavlovian way, national 'symbols'. But of what? They go to exclusive schools, join the armed forces, mix with a limited and unrepresentative group of people, travel by limousine and helicopter.

Thirty years after Malcolm Muggeridge and Lord Altrincham (as he then was) seriously risked lynching by parading republican tendencies in public, the royal family is still seldom criticized. For one thing, most editors calculate, it would be bad for circulation, and might even cost them a knighthood down the road. After a fire at Hampton Court smoked out the existence of grace and favour residences, the *Sunday Mirror*, under the ironic headline 'AMAZING GRACE (AND FAVOUR) OF OUR CARING QUEEN', attacked the privilege involved and its cost to the taxpayer. After quoting an elderly brigadier who lived rent-free in a four-storeyed house within Windsor Castle walls, the reporter commented: 'Snobbery, need I add, flourishes in its most virulent form at these best addresses in the world.' It was a rare tilt at a royal windmill in the popular press.

Most papers, given a choice between a picture of a 'real' news story and Princess Michael of Kent, will plump for the princess. One of the few ways a scribbler can become seriously rich – like Robert Lacey, author of *Majesty* – is by writing about the royal family. Thereafter they are licensed to make a fat living churning out all sorts of guff. On the morning of Prince Andrew's marriage to 'Fergie', one royal biographer informed readers of *Today* that the Queen would not confer the title of 'Duke of York' on the prince. Within a few hours of readers getting their paper, she had done precisely that, yet the royal 'expert' thrives, his 'insider' knowledge of the royals and the workings of the Queen's mind as much in demand as ever. Since no one knows the 'truth' about the royals, anything goes. It's like writing about the Kremlin. It is scarcely surprising that canny politicians like Harold Wilson and James Callaghan, whose Garter knighthood has just been announced, wrap themselves as nearly as they can in the royal standard. One of the few weak spots in Mrs Thatcher's political armour is the public suspicion that HM cannot abide her, fuelled as it was in the summer of 1986 by a 'leak' that cast the Queen as a 'one nation' 'wet' anxious about the divisive road down which the new Conservatism was taking her kingdom.

The fuss raised by these apparent conflicts between sovereign and premier showed just how fallacious is another piece of Pavlovian wisdom about the royal family – that they are above politics. Prince Philip has never hidden his saloon bar views – from his exhortation a quarter of a century ago to workers to pull their fingers out, to his recent indiscretions about 'slitty-eyed' Chinese. Now there is interest and anxiety about his strange son, who is popularly believed to talk to plants and be an all but paid-up member of the SDP or 'car-

ing' classes. He chafes, we are told, at the limitations placed upon him
when his contemporaries are well launched on satisfying and reward-
ing careers. Most of those contemporaries would probably swap their
careers for his – there is no shortage of young women prepared to
marry into the royal family – but this popular wisdom about the
prince is another example of the universality of unverifiable presump-
tions about the royals. Ah yes, we say, poor Charles, trapped in such
an unenviable position.

One of the few full-blooded assaults of recent times on the royal
family was an article in *Encounter* by the then *Daily Telegraph*
journalist Edward Pearce. He described the royal circus as a 'dream
factory [that] tends to keep people in a state of sottish content'.
Commenting on the extensive reporting of such a trivial happening as
Prince Charles cutting his finger, Mr Pearce wrote: 'The coverage
afforded to royal doings of the most quotidian sort is the kind reserved
for heads of state in highly undemocratic states . . . It isn't grown up. We
are supposed to be free men, yet we are skilfully crafted and conditioned into behaving like spaniels.' He pointed out that the British
don't even derive stability or orderliness from the royal family. 'The
things which are wrong with contemporary Britain – vandalism, violence, the collapse in the functioning of our schools, diminished literacy and incremental street-nastiness – are quantitatively worse than
anything to be found in West Germany or France, two republican
countries which sustain themselves on a combination of material
competence, success, and (especially in the case of France) a huge
sense of national identity . . . the flag flies at the castle mast and great
parts of our cities are moonscapes of secondary dereliction.'

Would it make a difference if the British royal family pedalled
around on bicycles, went to State schools, took 'ordinary' jobs in industry, education or the Civil Service? I suspect such a switch would
have a profound impact on the national psyche, encouraging us to
look at ourselves as free and equal citizens rather than as 'subjects' or
walk-on extras at the fringe of a national pageant. The supposed
necessity of the pomp and the extravagance is another of those royal
clichés. Mr Pearce wrote: '[The royal family] will do us all a favour by
adapting in a way that takes them out of the Big Top . . . there can be no
merit in any head of State acting as the alibi for the privileged and the
inspiration of the socially aspiring.' *We* Britons wouldn't like bicycling
royals, we tell ourselves, in much the same way as *we* didn't like foreign
food or holidays until we had tried them.

6

BY THE SWEAT OF OUR BROWS

The Monday after John Philpott left school he went to work at the village colliery. It was the natural order of things, and his birthright. Generations of Philpotts had been travelling to work in a plunging cage a thousand feet beneath the Durham sunlight. He was a clever boy, and, as such, learned a trade as a fitter. In his circumstances, that was the ultimate aspiration: tradesmen were a cut above the face workers, aristocrats in the narrow world of a pit village. For seven years he worked shifts in the waterlogged mine, sometimes up to his waist in the black water. 'It was like working in a shower.' When he emerged, it could be pitch dark, or perhaps he would trudge the few hundred yards home to bed as the glimmer of a new day began to lighten the sky. He got married, naturally to a miner's daughter, and the future stretched away in eight-hour shifts and Saturday nights in the club. His father-in-law's time to retire came, aged sixty, after forty-five years measured out in yards of black carbon hewed from the hard rock. 'He got,' said Mr Philpott, 'a medal. That was it. A little brass medal, more a token really. I was twenty-three. Forty years later I would end up like that.'

So he quit, joined a construction firm, had an accident in which he damaged a hand, tried to rejoin the pit, and was rejected on medical grounds. He became a service engineer, going wherever the work took him, including the middle of the North Sea on oil platforms. There he met a self-employed contractor who lived near Mr Philpott. 'I had never known anyone before with a Mercedes-Benz or a big house like he had, and he was just an ordinary lad.' Nearly twenty years after leaving school, Mr Philpott made a connection between his skill and value and the possibility of a way of life which, without considering it very carefully, he had assumed was as far beyond his aspirations as being an airline pilot. The final push came when his new friend told him of the sizeable gap between Mr Philpott's pay and the money his employers were getting for the hire of his talents. 'I was the one in the middle of the North Sea, and they were getting the profit. I said to myself, if I went on like that, I could be working for years and years, and what would I have to show for it? A couple of pints on a Saturday night. If someone else could make money out of me, I had to have something to offer.'

He had noticed when going about his job that firms were increasingly shedding their own service departments, and contracting the work to independent companies. 'Over the years you could see the decline.' He calculated: 'If I could have a little factory of my own, and hire myself out, I could make a go of fetching in engineering equipment, overhauling and repairing it.' He left his job, and sought advice. 'There's that many hotlines you can phone to be told how you can start in business.' He negotiated a ten thousand pounds loan from British Coal Enterprise, who put money into the creation of jobs in coal-mining areas; the local authority found him a new factory, rent- and rates-free for two years (it was within view of the by-then abandoned pit where he had passed his youthful working days); the bank loaned him five thousand pounds; through one of the small business advisory agencies he met a man with redundant machinery to dispose of; by the time he was ready to start he had been unemployed for eight weeks and qualified for the twelve-month forty pounds a week enterprise allowance. 'There are,' Mr Philpott said, 'all sorts of incentives here to set yourself up in business.'

His wife, whose only working experience was a short time spent operating a sewing machine, taught herself to be a secretary and much else besides. She also qualified for the enterprise allowance. 'She may be at a business lunch, and then cleaning out the toilets a few hours later. It's hard to believe it's the same woman. She hadn't a clue how to do bookwork, and now everyone who looks at her books says they are a model.' She has, when needs must, drilled holes all day.

Not only had his calculation about the amount of servicing work available proved correct – a year after he had started the business it was, he said, 'touch wood, rolling in' – but Mr Philpott, then in his mid-thirties, also turned out to be an inspired ideas man. Reading a motoring magazine, he had seen a small item reporting that the Department of Transport was to require all garages that issued

MOT test certificates to keep them in a secure place. The department specified the minimum acceptable strongbox – a small rectangular steel container protected by a seven-lever slam lock. Mr Philpott invested seven hundred pounds of his limited capital in such locks, and obtained a list of all authorized testing stations in the north-east. Using the one thousand free letters that the Post Office allows a new business, he circularized the testing stations, pointing out the impending law, and offering to provide the required strongbox. The department suddenly brought the date forward, there was a mini-panic amongst garage owners, and Mr Philpott pulled off a minor business coup.

His next idea had considerably more potential. His foreman went on holiday in a MGB sports car, complaining on his return – as all sports car drivers must do – about the lack of luggage space. Mr Philpott designed a rigid rack that could be attached to a towbar. A marketing entrepreneur saw it, signed a national franchise and ordered two hundred immediately. Mr Philpott had advertised his rack on local radio, and received a phone call from the husband of a young woman who had been crippled. The woman had an electric wheelchair, but it was impossible for her to go anywhere because they could not get the chair into a car, and it was too heavy to lift into a van. With ramps, the husband suggested, the Philpott luggage rack could be adapted to carry the wheelchair. The chair's manufacturer was enthusiastic, and, after trials with various materials, Mr Philpott was ready to develop the rack using aluminium for the ramps.

Mr Philpott already employed nine people, and shortly afterwards had to take extra factory space. His slogan was, 'If you can draw it, we can make it.' He still, he said, didn't see himself as a 'boss', but his perspectives had changed. While regretting the damage to communities that pit closures cause, he appreciated the rationale. 'If I had three shops, and one wasn't making money, I'd close it. That's fair enough. I'm looking at it now from the other side of the fence.' He understood also the sterility of some of his youthful habits. 'I'm not knocking the place, but it's a way of life. Friday, Saturday nights, in the pubs and clubs, you'll go in and know exactly who's sitting where.' It wasn't, he said, his ambition to be a millionaire. 'I'd like a few bob in the bank, and my children to come into the business when they leave school. I want to prepare a future for them.' His current ambitions were to buy his wife a car, upgrade his own six-year-old

Porsche, and be able to buy whatever the family 'fancied'.

He was ambivalent about the large number of unemployed people in the area. A local paper, writing about his company, erroneously reported that he had vacancies. He received three hundred letters. 'Some,' said Mr Philpott, 'were heart-breaking, from people who hadn't worked for three years, who wrote that any wages were better than dole money. Made me want to take them on.' For others, including people who had disliked him at school but now wanted his help and some who demanded three hundred pounds a week minimum, he had no sympathy. There was, he suggested, always work if you really wanted it – driving a taxi or working in a bar. As we stepped out of the small factory, Mr Philpott looked across the open fields to the silent pit. He had been back to poke around, he said. Papers had been blowing round the abandoned medical room, and he pointed out a white building to me. 'I remember people being carried in there who never walked out.' The flooded pit, the dangers, the night shifts were now another world.

A few days later I met two young men, Roger Hine and Ken Eagle, who had recently started a printing business. Mr Hine had been with the Gas Board for ten years, growing fidgety at the restrictions placed on his enterprise. 'You never really have any power at the Gas Board – even as a depot manager you're controlled from above, confined by a set of rules,' he said. Mr Eagle, a neighbour and drinking friend, was already in the print business, but at risk of being made redundant – 'the prospect of being on the dole didn't excite me.' The friends started a part-time business collecting waste paper, but trade was poor, and they decided to capitalize on Mr Eagle's experience. 'I had seen from the inside where printers went wrong, and decided we could make a better shot at it. Some weeks ten to fifteen mistakes would go out.' The two men also got premises rent- and rates-free for two years from Peterlee Development Corporation in Durham, raised a British Coal Enterprise loan, claimed the enterprise allowance, and six months later were already employing six people, and expanding their company, Advance Printing and Design, faster than they had forecast. Mr Eagle said: 'I didn't want to be working up to sixty-five. We get more satisfaction from the success than from making money. When we got our first job in, we were like two kids at Christmas. Each new order and client is a challenge, getting it just right. We go out of our way to make sure we satisfy the customer.'

*

When I returned from America, one of the national preoccupations was 'Can Britain create an enterprise culture!' It was a tenet of Thatcherish that, as increased efficiency shook out surplus labour, so the natural ingenuity and latent drive of the British people would begin to regenerate the economy from the grass roots. Prince Charles made a whistle-stop tour of the United States, returning to lament that his inheritance might be a fourth-rate nation unless his fellow countrymen could emulate some of the get-up-and-go vim he had detected between banquets in Dallas and Washington. 'The trouble is,' he said, 'how to kindle a spirit of enterprise . . . because one of the difficulties, it seems to me, is that we are so often struggling against a completely different culture in this country . . . the problem is how to change attitudes so [people] realize they can make a contribution themselves towards the creation of jobs.'

Britain was also on the eve of 'Industry Year', an eleventh-hour attempt by manufacturers to persuade the nation that man could not live by services alone. Unless there was to continue to be something concrete at the foundation of the economy, it would in the end, they said, collapse, like a house of cards before a puff of wind. A House of Lords Committee, deeply influenced by blue-chip industrialists like Lord Weinstock and Sir John Harvey-Jones, argued that Thatcherism was not enough. The decline of manufacturing, it said, posed 'a grave threat to the standard of living and to the economic and political stability of the nation'. Services, contended the Lords, are in the end dependent on manufacturing. Mr Leon Brittan, still at that time Industry Secretary, but about to be engulfed by the Westlands affair, piped up that the Lords' report gave 'a totally biased and misleading view of the economy'. We were once again embarked on a 'wets' versus 'dries' confrontation.

The Lords appeared to be speaking self-evident truth. Britain had invented the television, the commercial computer, the jet engine, the video recorder – but now imported millions of pounds' worth of these items each week. We needed jobs – even window-cleaning and carwashing generate economic activity and hope – but we essentially needed to start making things again. We still had sediments of the creativity of the first industrial revolution, most visible perhaps in the innovative street styles of London – striking after the conformity of American youth. But post-punk bravado was scarcely the structured basis for a national industrial revival: we were not going to fashion an economic miracle out of purple coxcombs.

It did not seem to me that the doctrine that went by Mrs Thatcher's name was a solid enough foundation for the necessary economic regeneration. Nor did she appear to have a sufficient grasp of the odds against both social mobility and enterprise in Britain. Her own rise from 'corner shop' to Downing Street is largely a political myth. Her father had been mayor of Grantham, chairman of the governors of the local grammar school, and host to Conservative Government ministers when they came to town. Margaret Roberts studied upstairs for Oxford, while fifteen-year-old shop girls served at the counter. The spoon in her mouth had been at the very least silver-plated. Her anti-Establishment populism, rooted in this myth, was therefore itself somewhat of a fraud. She sent her son to Harrow, and re-created hereditary peerages. The conservative in her nature was often at odds with the radical, and often emerged triumphant – as her Government's wielding of Section Two of the Official Secrets Act had betrayed. Her brittle, antagonistic personality – perfect for the Falklands war, if such a war were necessary – alienated so many whom she should have been winning to her cause that her legacy threatened to be a harshly divided society, rather than one harmoniously adapting to new ways. The shake-up she desired for Britain's ossified industrial habits was long overdue, but her flint-like certainty her lack of patience, were, by the beginning of her third term, alienating even enthusiasts for her cause. 'She's so bloody arrogant,' I kept hearing from businessmen.

It became a cliché to describe Mrs Thatcher as a schoolmarm, but the image is unfair to teachers. Yes, there are those who stand at the front of the class, ruler in one hand, chalk in the other, and woe betide the child who chatters. But they are not the teachers whose influence stays with a child throughout his lifetime. In part, economic Thatcherism has been essential, but it has been preached by a flawed apostle. Workers may have been cowed by the miners' strike and Wapping, but industrial antagonisms, 'them' and 'us', seemed to me on my return to be barely suppressed. Mrs Thatcher has often been compared to Ronald Reagan, but their political strengths are poles apart. Reagan was elected, not because – even at his finest hour – anyone thought he was competent to run anything, but because people liked him. If Mrs Thatcher had depended on that sort of popularity, she would not have become even the mayor of Grantham. If our new-found 'enterprise culture' is to survive, it needs a more fundamental underpinning than hard times and hectoring leadership.

My visits to Messrs Philpott, Hine and Eagle were part of an eigh-
teen-month inquiry to attempt to find out whether that underpinning
did exist.

I had known Brian Bottomley since before my American assignment.
Shortly before going to America I had spent some time in Coventry,
reporting from that city at the geographic heart of England, as a
metaphor for Britain's post-war rise and fall. First, the regeneration –
hope, Basil Spence's cathedral, pioneering comprehensive schools,
shopping precincts, the ring road, the municipal theatre, car factories
– for two decades Coventry had been the future. Then the disillusion-
ment – shoddy materialism, the vandalized and violent walkways,
unemployment, hopelessness. The day I met Mr Bottomley proved to
be the worst day of his life. He was the managing director of a large
machine-tool company, the subsidiary of a national giant. Or rather
he had been. A few hours before I called, he – and several hundred of
his workforce – had been made redundant. At first he was too hurt to
tell me what had happened. Suddenly, he rose, closed the door to his
outer office, and – on the strict condition that I revealed neither his
name nor his industry – told me his story. It was a microcosm of the
accelerating disaster that was overwhelming British industry. Here
was a man, then aged fifty-three, of immense enterprise and ability,
who had worked his way from the shop-floor via night school – he
had left school at fourteen – gaining an incomparable knowledge of
his business, from the smallest technical detail, to design, production
and a first-hand knowledge of foreign markets. 'I have tried very
hard, and feel that it has been a waste of time,' he said. He accused
Mrs Thatcher of killing the national golden goose.

We went our separate ways, and, as the unemployment figures rose
and British manufacturing crumbled, occasionally I thought of Mr
Bottomley, and what a national defeat his personal disaster symbolized, regretting that I was unlikely ever to learn what happened to
him. However, a few months after my return from America, he tele-
phoned. This time he had a story of remarkable success to tell. He
was still in machine tools, running his own business, and taking on
new workers proportionately faster than almost any employer in
Britain. He was back where he started, in Atlantic Street, Broad-
heath, near Manchester, a few yards from where he served his
apprenticeship. With his son, Nigel, the firm's financial director, at
his side, he brought me up to date. Back in 1981, after ten weeks out

of work, he had been taken on as managing director of a firm called Kearns-Richards, another machine-tool subsidiary of a large conglomerate. As soon as he arrived, the bottom fell out of the business. He was charged with the unpleasant task of laying off three hundred people and trying to sell the company. The more he looked at the figures he had prepared, the more confident he was that he himself could save and run the company, pulling off what is known as a management 'buy-out'. The parent company was sceptical and protective, worried that Mr Bottomley might ruin himself in the attempt.

They were not the only ones with cold feet. The Bottomleys rapidly discovered the large gap between the theory and reality of Britain's supposed 'enterprise culture'. Although Mr Bottomley had adapted his proposals to the realism of the market, supporting a machine-tool company was considered to be as desirable as cuddling up to a gorilla. Eventually, one bank had faith: the Bottomleys had their deal. When I met him again, he had increased the workforce of thirty-seven by one hundred people, and profits were handsomely exceeding forecasts. Twice during my visit Mr Bottomley had led me with pride to the cavernous works, where huge machine tools, worth upwards of £200,000, awaited shipment to all parts of the world. Asking him why he had risked so much so late in his career was almost a superfluous question. 'The alternative was to sell my house, buy a smaller one and hibernate. I love work and the industry, and have always wanted to do something on my own,' he said. There were still frustrations: the Ministry of Defence had been three weeks late paying a bill; while the Bottomleys waited, the Inland Revenue gave them a mere three hours to pay a much smaller amount, threatening to send in the bailiffs; the bank had pressured them when a storm in the Bay of Biscay held up an export order – although the bank knew the money was on its way and that the firm had security in buildings, plant and machinery far exceeding its overdraft. The Bottomleys were convinced also that foreign governments unfairly subsidized their overseas competitors. But these problems seemed like small clouds in a blue sky.

Nine months later Mr Bottomley phoned again. The roller coaster had taken another dip. The bank was bouncing cheques although profits were good and the firm was still secure: subsidies to Spanish and East German companies by their governments had cost him four orders in the home market – the foreign companies were quoting finished prices below the cost of materials and labour. The Bottomleys were embroiled with the bank and the Government, losing business while they battled for survival. They had incurred £55,000 in fees to financial consultants. I returned. Once again the Bottomleys were struggling back to their feet. A deal was about to be struck with venture capitalists, which would free them from the bank's clutches; orders were picking up; profit forecasts, despite the time wasted fighting unnecessary financial battles, looked healthy. As the Bottomleys told me the history of the past year; I began to understand what unusual resilience is required to run a manufacturing business. There were battles with the bank, dealing sometimes with faceless people, sometimes with ignorant ones – the Bottomleys had one horrific encounter with a man with the power to break them, who had outlined the history of *their* company to *them* getting virtually every fact wrong. There were battles with civil servants – Brian said: 'I vented my spleen on them. I told them that in other countries civil servants are aware that their salaries are paid by enterprise.' We were again touring the works, when he suddenly burst out: 'I cannot honestly believe that a country of our size can live by service industry. The City seems geared up to shipping money out of the UK rather than investing it here.' It was an anguished cry from a man in the front line of British manufacturing.

The Bottomleys' perspective has made them exceedingly patriotic: Nigel wears a union flag badge in his lapel, and the company's logo is based on the same motif. They buy everything British they can, though they have to go to West Germany for the computer controls and electronics they need for their machines. From Atlantic Street, where warehouses employing one hundred people handling foreign goods have replaced factories employing one thousand people manufacturing British goods, even the notion of protectionism looks attractive. Why is it, asked Brian, that the British will buy anyone else's goods except their own! He told of a recent Kearns-Richards triumph, when they were the only company to meet the deadline to equip an aircraft engine factory in Singapore. Japanese and German firms, supplying other machinery, were both late. The Bottomleys released a press notice, which was almost disregarded. 'If it had been the other way round, you can bet the press would have made a great song and dance,' said Brian. When I first met Nigel, he had, much to his dismay, just been forced to buy a foreign camera because there were no British ones left. Once, they even made cameras on Atlantic Street.

Frank Smith, like the Bottomleys, had exports and banks engraved on his heart. He had given up working as a manager for others because he was tired of being instructed to sack people. 'No way am I in business to put blokes on the street,' he said. With a British Coal Enterprise loan, like Mr Philpott's, he had started Yorkshire Reproduction Furniture in a Wakefield mill, part of which had been converted into twenty-three units for small enterprises. He was fifty-nine, an age when most men are thinking of taking it easy. Three years later, by then employing nine people, he was a deeply frustrated man. He had products that British and foreign retailers wanted, he had the know-how and the workforce: all he lacked was £50,000 to re-equip. 'We could have seven-day working till kingdom come. I could double my staff,' he said. The business, he said, was on his mind twenty-four hours a day. 'I go to church on Sundays praying, "For God's sake get me through next week." It's daft that, but that's how it gets you.'

His anger was aimed at the high street banks and the Government. The high street banks for their pusillanimity, and the Government for failing to provide alternative sources of capital for small business. A natural Conservative, he was none the less thinking of voting Labour because the Labour Party promised an enterprise bank. I frequently encountered businessmen who made the same basic complaint against banks – that they are not in the business of taking risks, simply of underwriting success – but few people gave rein to their feelings with such picturesque enthusiasm as Mr Smith: 'I've not a good word for any bank manager walking: they're a load of washouts. There's one or two I'd gladly strangle.'

A company with a national chain of furniture superstores wanted to place a large order with Mr Smith, but, without further plant to machine the parts, he could not get the work through his small factory quickly enough. 'I could go out of business just dealing with that one order,' he said. He knew there were export markets for his furniture – he had been invited to exhibit in Dallas – but without seed money, for demonstration furniture, an agent, promotion, a visit, he could not even explore the possibilities. A retailer fifteen miles away was importing £300,000 worth of chairs annually from Cyprus and Malta: Mr Smith knew also that, with new plant, he could match the order for price. His lack of £50,000 was, therefore, costing the country lost exports and creating sizeable markets in Britain for foreign goods. He had approached the Government through his MP, and had been told to go back to the high street banks.

'It's criminal, bloody criminal,' he said, 'the banks simply look at last year's balance sheet. Unless they understand the industry, they have no idea. If there's a risk, they don't want to know. They're not looking at the future of the industry or the commitment of the company. Nothing is going to happen until the banks start taking a calculated risk. There must be lots of firms like mine. We're importing more than we're making. It's all wrong. I'll keep going, but it's not the firm I envisaged.' Why, I asked him, as I had asked Brian Bottomley, at his age did he struggle on? 'There's no way I can stop. The work's out there. There's a huge market for my stuff, and there are thirty or forty thousand Yorkshiremen out of work.'

Two floors below Mr Smith's small workshop, another tenacious Yorkshireman ran a business he had started against the odds. Derek Barville is crippled: his right arm is withered, and he lives in a wheelchair. He was made redundant at the age of forty-five after twenty years with one company, an educational publisher. The following morning he started his own enterprise from his dining-room and garage, using outworkers. What he does is known in the trade as 'print finishing', a grand way of describing activities like assembling board games, punching the printed tops of egg boxes out of sheets of cardboard, distributing calendars, and dispatching mailings. His workers, called 'table hands', sit at long trestle tables carrying out these repetitive tasks on piecework rates. Many are 'married ladies', who, during school holidays, are replaced by sixth-formers. 'It looks,' said someone who had seen this subterranean exercise, 'like a Victorian sweatshop.' But the atmosphere was friendly and the workers cheerful. There were up to sixty people on Mr Barville's books, with about forty working at any one time.

In a labour-intensive, low-tech business, capital had not been a problem, but, like other small entrepreneurs, Mr Barville complained about Government pressures – especially VAT (value-added tax). He had to pay his wages immediately, while bills might not be settled for two to three months, yet no leeway was allowed for VAT payments. He had recently asked for a delay until his customers settled, and received a curt letter back telling him to pay at once or face proceedings. He was, therefore, not only gathering taxes on behalf of the Government but having to borrow money from the bank to do so. 'I was paying for the privilege,' he said. The National Federation of Self-Employed and Small Businesses publishes two pieces of guidance for their members, one headed 'Taking On An Employee' and the other 'Starting Up In Business'. To the lay eye, they look like instructions to pass through a minefield, with headings and notes, arrows and alternatives: tax and VAT, insurance and health, fire safety requirements and planning licences, union regulations, and provisions covering race and disablement, and many arcane obligations besides.

Mr Smith's and Mr Barville's landlord was a 130-year-old textile firm, M. P. Stonehouse, whose red-brick mill is a short walk from Wakefield city centre. There a visitor could imagine himself in the nineteenth century: he waits in a tiny room overlooking the dark mill yard. A notice advises: 'Would visitors please note that suppliers of wool and tops cannot be seen on Thursdays.' The firm had a long waiting list for its enterprise units, and had had three inquiries in the week before I visited. Its managing director, James Sugden, said: 'By many laws we were the sort of business that should have been closed, a private textile concern that could have quietly faded away.' But they had invested in computer-aided spinning machinery, introduced shift working to justify the investment, and found new markets. Turnover had doubled in four years, and staff, inevitably, declined. But the firm still employed 180 people, and, with 250 working in the units, the premises were providing employment for almost as many workers as in the mill's heyday. Mr Sugden was convinced Thatcherism had worked, both in his own business – in which surviving firms were leaner and more efficient – and beyond. 'We live more excitingly, more dangerously. Ten years ago we would get orders twelve to eighteen months ahead. It made us complacent. Now we never know more than three months ahead, sometimes three weeks,' he said.

They had developed the units because, with high rates, the empty parts of the mill were proving to be 'very expensive fresh air'. What they were doing, he said, was nothing new: one tended to think of mills as having belonged to one person and having housed one business throughout their productive lives. However, even in the 1890s mill owners had split up big factories, letting out separate floors to emergent entrepreneurs, so regenerating the local economy. The problem I encountered when I last visited was that Mr Sugden's tenants were bursting at the seams – most of them having far exceeded expectations of how fast they would develop.

A few hundred yards from the mill, back under the railway viaduct that carries the main King's Cross line north, and past the Jaguar showrooms where cars are on sale for £26,800, two young men who had founded a glass-fibre moulding business in hutted premises were also running out of space and about to move. Only fifteen months earlier, when I first met them, they had still been converting the build-

ing, putting in a lavatory and a small office. Then Graham Wood and
Graham Durant had both been twenty-eight. They had met at weekends to do odd jobs in their garages. They discovered that the glass-
fibre wheel arches they bought were 'like tissue paper', and they knew
they could do better. Mr Durant already ran a picture-framing business, and Mr Wood was an unemployed car mechanic. They had
scraped together what grants they could find, and had started to
make cash desks for the Gas Board. They were working up to sixteen
hours a day, seven days a week, and had two youths to help them.
What, I had asked them then, motivated them? Mr Wood, seemingly
never out of his filthy overall coat and stained jeans, said: 'I just don't
want to go into work every day, and retire at sixty-five with a couple
of hundred quid in the bank, and think "that's my life over." When
you are skilled and hardworking, yet have experienced unemployment, an iron enters the soul. Whatever the odds, it is better to pilot
your own craft.'

When I returned, Mr Durant had given up the picture-framing
shop, Mr Wood had graduated to a stained bomber-jacket, and they
had far exceeded their aspirations. Their company, Durwood,
employed eight people, and they were about to leave premises they
had thought would last them at least five years. The gas showroom
business had expanded, they were working with a national shop-
fitter, they had a contract to supply cladding to hide flaking, stained
concrete on high-rise flats and sixties offices. Pet ideas, like developing
a glass-fibre tailgate for Range Rovers, had had to be put on one side.
Mr Wood had two gripes. The first was that, although there was
plenty of support for starting a new business, there was very little
once you were up and running. By employing as many as they had,
they had demonstrated a good return on the initial faith placed in
them. 'All we needed was a little bit more help on the side. But our
success meant that we were not entitled to it. We could have
expanded yet further, and employed more people. When you get
started, you get great encouragement, a good kick in the backside.
Then you're left in the world.'

His second complaint was more fundamental. It was hard, he said,
to find willing and competent staff. 'We want decent young lads with
some bottle, interested in learning. Attitudes have really baffled me.
They don't seem career-minded. You teach them something, and four
hours later it's forgotten. They don't think further than tomorrow or
the pub at the weekend.' He accused the Youth Training Scheme of

not discriminating enough before sending young people to them. The two Grahams wanted to give the school-leavers a proper training, but had had a series of poorly motivated youths. Mr Wood regularly asked one who stood stock-still in a corner most of the day: 'Are you on strike! He'd say "mebbe I am." The rest of the time he spent washing his hands.'

The day I visited Durwood, the Association of British Chambers of Commerce reported that the lack of skilled labour in Yorkshire and Humberside was inhibiting companies' expansion plans. Problems to which the south-east had become accustomed were spreading north. Britain's lack of training looked likely to ambush any recovery. Two-thirds of all Americans have a skills qualification when they look for their first job (there are also 1.3 million graduates each year): only forty thousand British school-leavers a year get the equivalent of an apprenticeship. The British employment crisis will increasingly be a mismatch between the skills available and the work that the modern world demands. The inadequacies of our hierarchical, rationed education system will haunt us.

That same day *Today* published a poll that showed that the majority of Britons – especially the better-off – would prefer surplus Government money to be spent on improving such things as education and the Health Service rather than 'given away' in tax cuts. The paper called it an 'astonishing' finding, but it was not so to me: most of the business people with whom I had been talking were distinctly 'wet' on the issue of public spending. Four directors of Kearns-Richards, with whom I had lunch, had agreed that some people 'do need looking after', and that no one they knew at any income level objected to public spending, so long as it was going to benefit people and not swell the ranks of bureaucrats. One had broken out vehemently: 'It's terrible that young people can't get jobs, the single worst thing that I can think of. Soul-destroying, and creating the two nations of the future.'

Rodney Walker, whom I had met on my first Wakefield visit, was the epitome of the self-made man, Rolls-Royce and all. After being thrown out of work in his twenties, he had vowed 'to put myself as quickly as possible into a position where I would never be vulnerable again.' Fifteen years later he ran a highly successful business, and had a finger in every pie in town from the local radio station to trying to save Wakefield Trinity rugby league side from bankruptcy. He was exhilarated by American dynamism. After a two-week visit there, he found it 'takes me a little time to settle back into the much slower pace of the UK.' He had recently flown to Hong Kong for a two-hour meeting, winning a contract that was going elsewhere. But he was deeply angered by what he saw as the squandering of North Sea oil, and wondered why it had not been spent on the national infrastructure. 'What the hell are we going to do when it runs out?' he asked. The gloomy answer he provided himself was that the unemployed may 'one day turn on us and destroy us all.' We had, he said, perhaps been purged enough by strong Thatcherite medicine.

Before I left Wakefield, I drove out to visit two young men, Ian Conniff and Steve Chapman, whom I had first met fifteen months earlier. They had been on the verge of going down the pit after nearly two years on the dole, and their families were delighted. It meant an end to the mooching, the despair, the boredom, the inevitable rows at home, the long, time-killing walks across the rolling Yorkshire hills. Their drab village, clustered about the pithead, was only four miles from Wakefield, but it might have been another planet. I asked one woman whether young people from the village ever went to work in Wakefield. She looked at me suspiciously for an instant. 'Not from here, they wouldn't,' she said. Any alternative to the pit was unthinkable. The collieries, said Ian's father, a short, broad-shouldered pit deputy, were built for the people. No one had a right to take them away. His mother had added: 'Ian wouldn't settle if he were to move away from home.' Steve's father, a union official, said: 'I've been down that pit twenty-nine years. It's my pit. I wouldn't move if it closed tomorrow.' The heritage for which Arthur Scargill had gone to war was still intact for two families at least. Neither family had any regrets about the boys going underground. 'We're not bothered so long as they're working,' said Ian's mother, and Ian showed me a tankard he (and all 1,100 miners) had been presented with to mark a colliery triumph in mining one million tonnes in a year. Theirs was a 'long-life' pit, but the coal would probably run out when they were still relatively young men. Had they, I wondered, got it in them to become John Philpotts? No one was thinking beyond the weekend.

Moss Moor and Rishworth Moor high on the Pennines on either side of the M62 were grey-green in the misty February light, and the sparse woods black and cold. Huddersfield, Rochdale, Oldham – the names on the signs were redolent of British industrial history – slipped by, deep in their valleys. The sharp corners of the dark red, rectangular mills rose above the still-terraced streets, and, although there was no smoke from the tall, dark chimneys, a heavy smog lay across the towns. Clogs and cobbles and 'trooble at t'mill', a slice of the past locked within the hills and largely forgotten: up on the motorway the heavy traffic sped between the white and red rose counties, past the reservoirs and the tall television transmission masts, a symbol of economic activity from another world. I drove round the margins of Manchester on what was supposed to be a motorway, single file at jogging pace between the roadworks, out beyond the south-western suburbs and the comfortable villas of the commuting classes.

Here there was another industrial landscape, more modern, with its gas holders, bulky power station building, cooling towers, complicated, twisting chemical plant, waste burning into the sky from a perpetual flame – a memorial, perhaps, to the unknown industrial worker. Incongruous cows chomped moodily at the crew-cut grass. Alongside the infant River Mersey, making its way to the Manchester ship canal, planners had dumped a Manchester overspill estate, an unlovely place of poverty, unemployment and deferred hope. A wayside pulpit proclaimed: 'AIDS PROBLEM: The wicked are snared in the work of their own hands. – Psalm 9.' An ambulance pulled up beyond a litter-filled front garden, and an old woman was wheeled out, her feet swathed in bandages. The ramp was retracted, and the ambulance departed, taking the woman to the highlight of her existence – a day at the general hospital. Where I was going was a place of genuine hope, a beacon to enterprise, knowledge, talent, hard work, skill and guts. But, because it was such a place, it had nothing but two labouring jobs to offer the Manchester overspillers.

The Carrington Business Park began as an act of conscience, financed by Shell in expiation for massive redundancies from their once-thriving six-hundred-acre chemical processing plant. A seventeen-acre corner of it, formerly the site of Shell's chemical research operation, had been set aside and entrusted to Job Creation Ltd, whose brief was to restore what life they could – like landscape gardeners on a bomb site – to the derelict plant. Job Creation Ltd, an offshoot from pioneering efforts by British Steel, was by then one of three hundred British companies – recession doctors – making their living out of economic regeneration. It had operations in fourteen countries. By being first into mass unemployment, the British had learned something of value to the rest of the world. The strategy was to attract small, up-market, emerging businesses at the first stage of expansion, which needed office space or studio workshops. In the larger buildings there was some fabrication; a 'craft centre' was planned for activities like toy-making and picture framing, and a car park was to be used for off-airport parking for Manchester Airport: but old-fashioned metal-bashing activities – like car-breaking – were strictly deterred.

Carrington offered a package – secretarial services, telex, 'faxing', heating, lighting, and the use of a coffee shop, to which clients and customers could be invited. When I was there, about a year after its launch, the existing space was occupied by computer firms, designers, a dressmaker, cabinet-makers, sign-makers, a dental ceramics engineer, a wine merchant, redeployment consultants, stationery suppliers and other similar businesses, a total of thirty-nine companies. The number of their employees had grown from seventy-two to 108 in three months, and the expectation was that eventually that first corner of the site would house four hundred workers, nearly as many as there had been in the days of Shell research.

The project manager, David O'Brien, was in his fifties with grey, bushy hair, and a monocle round his neck. He had been born firmly into the comfortable classes – his father was the managing director of an engineering firm; he was educated at Sedbergh public school and Cambridge – and his early professional life was conventional – the colonial service and Shell industrial relations. But he had been called on to diversify the ailing family business, and for some years was a highly successful exporting entrepreneur, equipping hospitals in the Middle East and Africa – he 'built' the Bahrain military hospital. But the family firm crashed, and his company went down in the ruins, leaving him with one foot still in the traditional world of his upbringing – he is a governor of Sedbergh – and one in the more hazardous, invigorating world of enterprise. He has known hard times – after the family firm had been closed, his wife, a nurse, took patients into their home to pay the bills – and his consequent scorn for bureaucratic middle-managers, nestling in the 'corporate womb', multiplying their empires, playing everything by the book, was total.

'Managers,' he said, 'are not risk-takers: they're keepers of the park.' That is a crucial distinction that our naturally conservative society misunderstands. The respectable way to be in business in Britain is to be a rising executive with a blue-chip company: to risk, to start from nothing is still to be a 'cowboy'. As a governor at an upper middle-class school, Mr O'Brien saw that the parents' aspirations for their sons to have security and status – as lawyers, as doctors, as ICI management trainees – were in conflict with both the country's economic need and often the boys' own instincts. It is the parents and teachers, not the boys, who need exhorting towards enterprise and risk-taking, according to Mr O'Brien.

Since many of those who control capital – like bankers – are 'respectable' and unenterprising, they curtail and frustrate the risk-takers, driving men like Brian Bottomley and Frank Smith to the paroxysms of anger I had encountered. Unable to raise capital, emerging entrepreneurs often succumb to takeovers. The larger firm imposes its bureaucratic straitjacket, creativity is suppressed, and the sort of inventive businessmen who ought to be the engine of our economy retreat to pilot floating gin palaces round Channel Island ports. The most valuable time for an entrepreneur, suggested Mr O'Brien, is the very beginning of his enterprise, when he has nothing to defend. As soon as he has structures in place, he closes his ears to criticism.

Sir John Hoskyns, director-general of the Institute of Directors, put the matter bluntly: 'Our attitudes to capitalism and enterprise have been shaped since the war by politicians, civil servants, university professors, trade union bosses and a few big business leaders. Their common experience has been *safety*. Few have had competitive business experience, almost none has taken personal high-risk decisions. Most of them have had effective security of tenure and have neither experienced nor risked unemployment or bankruptcy. Together they have helped to shape a culture which has led people to expect and demand a life devoid even of minor risks . . . It is a culture which is snobbish towards small business.'

The tenants of Carrington would warm Sir John's heart. I met one man who had been made redundant three times, another who had been bankrupt. Many had a trauma in their pasts. All those I talked with had concrete ambitions to expand. 'Deb' Parrington had travelled a long way to become boss of an insulating firm employing fourteen people including himself and his wife. One of twelve children – 'first up was best dressed: we didn't always get to school when we should' – he had begun his working life as an apprentice on the Carrington site in the early sixties. He had worked round the country on such construction schemes as Fylingdales early-warning system and power stations. He himself was a union convenor, but he hated what he saw of industrial relations – buses called to take workers home *before* the strike meeting was held; buckets of excreta thrown over fellow workers sent to Coventry; militant groups who shouted the loudest dictating what happened. He returned to Carrington to work for Shell as a 25-year-old foreman with his political attitudes fundamentally altered.

His career with Shell went well, and he rose towards management, never thinking of breaking loose and starting on his own. 'I had a good job and prospects. I was young and comfortable. My wife had a job. We had two children. I didn't see why I should take any risks.' he said. Then came the redundancies, and, although Shell wanted to keep Mr Parrington, it would not have been in the job he had trained for. He was asked to put work out to tender, decided he could form a company and do it himself. He won the contract, and, when I met him, two years later, had never looked back. He remained deeply suspicious of human nature, working from an office with windows overlooking the shop-floor so that he could check on his men. 'Never a day goes by without problems,' he said. 'The biggest is dealing with people. Basically I've got a good core, but once you start building up, it's difficult to get all the right people.' I asked Mr Parrington how he was doing financially. He laughed. He hadn't, he said, had time to spend. He had only had one week off in eighteen months. He had had to stop playing squash through lack of time. But orders were coming in regularly – 'we've met our targets, and haven't let anyone down' – and he had even turned down a big job in South Wales, in part because he did not want to expand too fast, and in part because it would have been hard to exercise control at that distance. Slow payers had caused cashflow problems – though Shell, his chief customer, had a policy of paying small companies immediately – and he favoured a proposal then before parliament that all bills should be settled within thirty days. 'We have to pay our suppliers within thirty days. My wife spends a lot of her time chasing people for money.'

Mr Parrington (the 'Deb' is short for Debroy when you're one of twelve your parents have to be inventive) was fair-haired with a strong, determined face. His political odyssey had taken him from the socialism of his roots to a belief that a future Labour Government would 'destroy the foundations of the last few years, and we'll end up in a bloody quagmire. It just frightens me. I'd hate to see it all lost.' What would be lost he felt was management's new-found confidence to manage – 'there's been a hell of a change in the past few years: everything is turned upside down' – and working people's realization

that 'the world doesn't owe them a living.' He said: 'I can't understand why people think that everything should be done for them, that
they're entitled to a job, and that once you're in business you're
making a bloody fortune and don't have any problems.' He brewed a
cup of tea for his workers in the morning, and used the contact to put
his views in a bantering manner. 'We are not,' he told them, 'in business to provide ourselves with jobs, but to perform for the customer.'
Looking round his small office, he said: 'the buck stops here.'

Mr Parrington was then the biggest employer in the Carrington
Business Park, but an equally unpassable buck lay behind each door
throughout the complex. It was the tenants' common badge: they
were the commandos of the British economy. John Poulson sat in the
'Top Table' coffee shop, with a portable phone at his elbow. He had
a beard, tinted glasses and, for public consumption at least, a 'devil
may care' attitude. He ran a company specializing in computer-aided
design, and did design work and sold equipment. CAD, he said, had
moved from being fun for the enthusiast to a practical tool. You
could throw away the drawing-board like swapping your pen for a
word processor. He had expanded his business cautiously, having
seen others come to grief by growing too fast. By the time I met
him, he was on the verge of a big leap forward. His original company
might be launched on the unlisted securities market (USM); he was
thinking of buying a sports shop and even a cheese manufacturer; he
was about to attend Manchester Business School – 'like taking a
personal health check: it might open up one or two areas where I have
been short-sighted.' Life, he said, should be 'an extended hobby.'
By making money, he could afford the time to indulge in his
actual hobby, shooting. He had just bought a fifth shotgun.

What made him an entrepreneur? Well, he laughed, he was no
good as a delegator, he had no experience in business or staff management or as a salesman. What he had, he said, was 'self-reliance
and ego. I got fed up with relying on other people to make decisions
for me. I was big-headed enough to think I could do it better than the
gaffer who'd been telling me.' When he had been employed by others,
he found he got on better with his bosses than his peers. 'It had been a
long-term aim to work for myself: I was on the pushy side.' Most
people, he had decided, 'actually like to be told what to do.' His greatest problem was getting his staff to get on with it.

Mike Smith and Brian Jarman were salesmen through and through
– the firm handshake, the easy familiarity, the knowing wink, the

sharp suits, the shiny briefcases. Betjeman's lines swam into mind:

> I am a young executive. No cuffs than mine are cleaner;
> I have a Slimline brief-case and I use the firm's Cortina.

They had both worked for the Control Data computer company, and, like John Philpott, had spotted that belt-tightening by large companies was creating opportunities for small enterprise. The computer giants had been slashing their sales forces, down to one man, perhaps, instead of six or seven. 'We were well paid, with company cars, expenses, all the usual perks. But when we saw that the big companies were no longer able to offer a personal service, we took a calculated risk. You tend to be sheltered with a big company, and it is one hell of a jump to give that all up, take a deep breath, and go on your own,' said Mr Jarman. However, they had exceeded their forecasts for each of their first six months, and they were already desperate to expand, get bigger offices, employ a secretary and a tele-sales girl. They were working harder than they ever had, including at least one day each weekend, but were stimulated by being their own masters, and excited by the potential. 'We have a better day-to-day existence. Our decisions affect the course of our lives. We avoid the frustration of being told what to do by some god almighty.' Mr Smith was only twenty-eight, but he had once run a pottery business that had gone bust. He had repaid all the debts, and didn't regret the experience. In this, he was more like an American, bouncing back from adversity, than a Briton who is often crushed by one failure.

Their joint plans included getting into property, and speculating on the Stock Exchange. Mr Smith dreamed of running a multiple of big business, while Mr Jarman, who was forty, talked of making enough to retire in his mid-fifties. They both hankered after the 'good' life – Mr Jarman for a villa in Spain and a Ferrari (he was having to 'make do' with a Mercedes), and Mr Smith for a large boat. They admired and sought to emulate people like Freddie Laker, Alan Sugar (they were Amstrad agents) and Richard Branson. 'It can be done,' they said, 'you've got to buck the system, grit your teeth and go for it.'

Philip Cook had gone for it straight out of Manchester Polytechnic, where he had gained a degree in industrial design. He clearly had a natural spirit of enterprise, having marketed some of his college projects. From what I saw of his work, he also had considerable talent. One college idea, a 'bit of fun' – a 'soft' ghetto blaster in a bag, with a busy colourful design, which he called a 'Jimmybean' – had been bought by Sony. Several British companies had shown no interest. Sony had flown a man over from their German-based European design centre, and he had concluded a deal on the spot. The British tradition of allowing others to exploit our best ideas appeared secure for another generation. Mr Cook had designed an electric vehicle for airport use, was working on disposable fountain pen designs for Berol, and had just completed a trendy gas fire for a company that had jettisoned the idea because a similar fire marketed by a rival had flopped. Mr Cook had not realized how many design ideas end up on the cutting-room floor. 'It's very frustrating,' he said, 'when you do something you think could be a world-beater.' It was also frustrating that so few British companies understood the value of design. That had proved a 'massive stumbling-block' when he was starting out, and was the reason why he was aiming his work at design-conscious companies like Sony.

Mr Cook enjoyed the amenities of Carrington Park – the coffee shop, the conference rooms, the busy atmosphere. He laughed: 'I can look out of the window, and see the people drive up in their Mercs and Porsches, and think: "That's the reason why I am here." His art-student-like air – the wire-framed glasses, the pullover, baggy trousers, white socks – hid a thorough-going ambition. He wanted to employ one other person almost immediately, and visualized one day having his own design studio. 'You need material aims to keep you going – too many designers regard profit as a dirty word,' he said. He got his pleasure half from the creativity of his work, and half from its profitability.

Mr Cook's frustrations with the lack of vision shown by many British manufacturers, who believe that churning out the same old product is all they need to do to keep their share of the market, was widely shared by his distinguished elders in London. Louis van Praag, founder and boss of Sabre International textiles, was con-ducting a missionary campaign on behalf of the future of young people like Mr Cook. He had headed a working party, which had fash-ioned a design curriculum for inclusion in management courses, alongside marketing, finance, labour relations and the rest. 'I would claim without hesitation that Britain enjoys the best de-sign education in the world. Design is not the problem, management is,' he said, reserving his finest disdain for the City of London – the last bastion of philistinism.' He had failed to attract one volun-teer for this working party from the City. 'Most merchant banks would rather finance an oilfield than a new product,' he said.'

As a mature consultant, Wally Olins, the founder of a major London design company, had an experience a few years ago that fore-shadowed Mr Cook's failure to sell his 'Jimmybean' to a British manufacturer. When he was working for both Renault and Volkswagen, British Leyland executives declined to travel a mile across Marylebone to see what his firm might have to offer them. The idea that the British are a species of Neanderthal man, which doesn't care for style is, of course, nonsense, as the sales of Volkswagen, Renault, Sony, and the rest show. Good design is not a fancy option, like chrome plating, but an integral part of any product that is going to work efficiently and give maximum aesthetic pleasure. British manufacturers have tended to think that 'design' was merely for the Habitat shopping classes. The cooking-stove industry was almost wiped out because manufacturers presumed that only the brie and wine set wanted anything better conceived than the free-standing models their mothers used. Mr Keith Grant, the director of the Design Council, pointed out that one had only to eavesdrop on a pub conversation about new cars or compact disc systems to realize how sophisticated the British are in at least some design areas. Manufacturers have worried themselves to death over issues like labour relations, interest rates, unfair foreign competition and wages, and have almost ignored the product. 'Civilizations,' said Stephen Bayley, who was charged with launching a national design museum in London's docklands, 'are remembered by their artefacts, not their bank rates.'

So careless are we with our talents that 'new' industries like computer software, which were to replace the old, are themselves collapsing with the speed at which ship-building and steel contracted. In 1986 a government advisory body, headed by the chairman of Rolls-Royce, warned that the software industry was in danger of being wiped out by foreign competition. It said bluntly: 'The man in the street currently sees the U K software industry now and in the future as a high growth, export revenue-generating industry contributing significantly to U K employment and the balance of payments. This view is wrong.' The share of the world market owned by British companies had already dwindled to 2 to 3 per cent, and by the early nineties, said the advisory body, our balance of payments deficit in software was predicted to have reached two billion pounds annually.

I thought of such squandered chances and the billions of wasted pounds they represented as I talked with grass roots entrepreneurs, who were usually desperate for pathetically small sums with which to turn their ideas into a reality that might revitalize their home districts and put at least some of Britain's unemployed back to work.

John Neil is a Scot who served ten years in the RAF as a caterer, and then ten years in civvy street –much of it as a surface worker for the Coal Board. He had been shocked by how little work was done at the collieries – 'sure they work flat out,' he said, 'I've tripped over a few of them in my time' – and by how pampered most working people were, like dustbin men who moaned when refuse was not in correct bags. He himself had been warned to slow down by his work-mates. He knew what hard work was. In his RAF days it had been nothing to work straight through a weekend. Once he had helped cook a meal for the Queen and Duke of Edinburgh, and an hour later had been on his hands and knees scrubbing drains.

He had wanted to start a takeaway food shop in a Durham town that had no such amenity. Despite the need, and despite Mr Neil's obvious diligence and his proven track record as a caterer – he had worked as chef in several hotels – the banks turned him down, and instead, with a £1,500 British Coal Enterprise loan, he had bought a mobile canteen, which he and his wife, Elizabeth, took out twice a day. His short-term ambition was to graduate to the preparation of 'home-cooked' food for pub microwave ovens. I had a feeling that Mr Neil's abilities and Scottish determination would see him through, but a little more help would have strengthened his chances.

Whatever the bureaucratic tendency of British industry, at least some leading industrialists have become enthusiasts for enterprise. The most vociferous was Sir John Harvey-Jones, the former chair-man of ICI. In 1986 he was invited to give the BBC television Richard Dimbleby lecture, and he took as his theme 'Industry Year', which the nation was ostensibly marking. 'If we think,' he warned us graphically, 'we can get by with a bunch of people in smocks showing tourists around medieval castles, we are quite frankly out of our tiny minds.' When I saw him, he was equally forthright. 'It's a sad commentary on our history and values that we should have to have an "Industry Year". I haven't noticed the Japanese having one: it's Industry Year every bloody year in Japan.' He added: 'There are still a lot of people in this country who believe and hope there's a way out . . . my problem is I cannot make the maths work.'

Sir John was an unlikely tycoon, with his unkempt appearance, taste in flamboyant ties and love of animals (he keeps donkeys). His first career was in the Royal Navy, largely as a submariner, which, he said, was 'the biggest single formative experience that set my values.' He knew that 'as an absolute oddball, there was no way I would have got to the top,' but his service exposed him first-hand to classes from whom his education had cut him off. He discovered that they were 'super chaps capable of anything.' He said: 'The Navy taught one to communicate and care about one's people, to put them before oneself, and it taught other basic principles of leadership which industry doesn't teach very well.' The British, he said, live in pockets. If you go to a party, you meet people all of one kind – academics, lawyers, industrialists. In Germany, he said (he speaks fluent German), 'a typical party would have an industrialist, a university professor, a judge, a banker maybe, a senior civil servant, a whole range of different people. Here we form ourselves into coteries.' This lack of cross-fertilization means that people with power in Britain have a poor understanding of the range of human experience. It has also meant that most people think of 'business' as something way beyond their ken. The reluctance of people of my age to go into it was not just the powerful cultural pressures, but a feeling that we would be hopelessly incompetent at anything more daring than life in the corporate womb. That, though well paid, would be boring and a sell-out. Sir John had not been bored. Almost his first task at ICI had been to study the feasibility of a new factory on Teesside. The plant went ahead, and a quarter of a century later, the day before I met him, Sir John had diverted his chairman's plane to fly over it. 'It's still working, still up to date, still employing people. I know that plant wouldn't exist were it not for my efforts as a 35-year-old,' he said with enormous satisfaction. He added: 'Starting from where we are, I can't see how this country survives without a greater degree of manufacturing success than we appear to be setting our stall out for at the moment.'

I had been searching for common threads that linked the entrepreneurs and business people I had been meeting. 'Was there a formula for success?' I asked Sir John. He answered: 'I see no correlation between business success and academic achievement. I take it for granted that a guy is intelligent and numerate. What makes for business success are rather esoteric characteristics, which are not uniformly spread – like courage, humour, balance and the ability to communicate and to listen. We have got to project business as being exciting. What I find most difficult is really persuading young people that I have a super life.'

✺〔 7 〕✺

BOOM AND GLOOM

By the time I got to Aberdeen, the 'oil capital' of Europe, the good times were over. 'Was the plane full?' asked the taxi driver, knowing the answer already since the London flight had not been full for many months. 'Times,' he said, 'are hard, business half what it has been.' He would head home after this fare: there was not much point in sticking about in the evenings any more. On a black Sunday night, as a sharp wind funnelled between the small cobbled streets off Union Street, the only signs of life were couples embracing in the shelter of doorways. Out at sea, lights twinkled as if someone had parked a promenade a few miles offshore: they came from the surplus oil exploration rigs, waiting, as dockers once had, for what demand for their labour there might be. In the harbour lights also shone from the supply vessels, which were moored in hope of a charter on the 'spot' market: a security man in a Land Rover stared vacantly at the dark water. Across the street a vast hoarding announced: 'TO LET Victoria Tower. 78,449 sq. feet, with 140 car parking spaces. Can Divide.' Seagulls wheeled and screeched overhead. A train arrived at the station, and a scattering of men in orange oilcloth jackets, jeans and boots, slung their bags over their shoulders, hunched into the wind, and fanned out towards their lodgings. A flapping newspaper poster proclaimed: 'City oil workers take pay cut.' Two of the men paused to absorb the message, laughed somewhat bitterly and moved on. At the hotel it was too late for supper.

I had come to Aberdeen for what seemed like a simple story. What happens, the British had asked themselves ever since the improbable discovery of oil deep beneath the hostile, cold North Sea, when the oil runs out? It had become a refrain in all national economic discussions. Was there, could there be, life after oil? The oil was seen as some form of providential gift, compensation perhaps for loss of empire. We, the British people, had done little to deserve it, but, with its blessing, we had a chance to transform Britain into an efficient modern economy, capable of competing with the French, the Germans, even the Japanese. However, it was more likely, we concluded in our pessimistic way, that, like pools winners unaccustomed to large windfalls, we would squander the cash and the opportunity. And, because the oil seemed a liquid form of fairy gold, we had a vision of it drying up as suddenly as it had come on stream, as if some giant tap would be turned off. We convinced ourselves that this fateful day was just around the corner. Aberdeen would then be another of our industrial museums like north of England smokestack towns and the Welsh valleys, a further landmark on the road to national bankruptcy. Aberdeen today, Britain tomorrow.

Articles in the London press appeared to confirm this simple storyline. 'Bubbles' were bursting all over the headlines; oil rigs were 'idle and forlorn'; Aberdeen's house market was a 'nightmare'; 'Lean times ahead', said the *Guardian*, 'for oil capital'. Stories told of divers, once plutocrats earning £35,000 a year, driven destitute, selling their homes, their BMWs, taking their children out of private schools. Americans were leaving with the speed they had once evacuated Saigon – some, unable to sell their homes, simply threw the keys back at their building societies. City-centre pubs were said to be going bust; ten thousand jobs had been wiped out in a few months; and many of the unemployed had headed back to the depressed regions they came from – like *gastarbeiter*, surplus to requirements. The crash had been sudden.

I found Establishment Aberdeen defensive almost to the point of paranoia. In the panelled board rooms of lawyers, accountants and public relations firms, men in dark suits regarded me suspiciously. Was I another of the 'doom and gloom' merchants, a 'dismal Johnnie' come north to dramatize what one solicitor called 'our wee hiccup'? A public relations official, representing much of blue-chip Aberdeen, said: 'When the novelty of "boom" city wore off, the media in the south began to look for cracks, and last year they found them.' Edinburgh and Glasgow were, I was told, as guilty as London of dancing on what the local professional classes claimed to be an empty grave. John Condliffe, north-eastern director for the Scottish Development Agency, said: 'Most of industrial Britain would like our problems, we're not in the basket case league. This is still Porsche town. I've worked in the Port of London, and know a dead industry when I see one.' The public relations official commented: 'Aberdeen

had a good fifteen years while other parts of the country were suffering, now it's Aberdeen's turn. The rest of Britain has been dying to
get the "ABERDEEN GOES BUST" story. The danger is that if people
think it is the end of the road, they will invest elsewhere. It is still a
strong and diverse economy, and we must start paying more attention to the traditional side of things.'

Such men argued that Aberdeen had been inaccurately characterized as a former one-horse town that had enjoyed a few mad oil-rush
years, and was about to revert to its primitive, dozy previous existence. In the early days of the boom, Americans would ask before they
arrived whether the streets were paved, and some newcomers had been
amazed to find a solid city, rather than a picturesque outpost of scattered crofts. 'We weren't going around in bare feet and kilts,' said one
businessman. An accountant delighted in taking visiting Americans to
the university and showing them an archway inscribed with the date
1494, which was only two years after Columbus discovered America.
The city is an historic administrative centre, a seat of learning and
medicine, and has a number of traditional industries, like fishing, textiles, paper-making, agriculture, all of which have boomed in their time.
'Unemployment was never a problem,' said the lawyer. The gaping,
worked-out granite quarry next to the ultra-modern offices of Britoil,
Marathon and Conoco reminded oil executives daily that the extrac-
tion of natural resources had once before played an important part in
Aberdeen's fortunes, and that Aberdeen had survived its demise.

The Klondike days were over, but oil production remained at near-
record levels, and would continue to make Britain self-sufficient in oil
for many years into the twenty-first century. The oil price, the dramatic slump of which had caused Aberdeen's problems, was back in
spring 1987 at seventeen to eighteen dollars a barrel from a low of
$8.50 in the summer of 1986, and eventually exploration would
resume in the remaining North Sea oilfields. An American oil chief
had forecast that Aberdeen would survive to celebrate its centenary
as an oil city in the year 2069. Even at the bottom of the slump
Aberdeen's unemployment level was under 10 per cent. 'Most of
the nation would give their eyeteeth to enjoy a "slump" like ours,'
said one company executive.

There were clearly two realities. The 'Granite City' was still firmly
built on rock, or rather oil, but a great many people had been grie-
vously hurt. Aberdonians with a stake in the solidity of the city
denied the extent of the hurt, terrified that their assets might be talked

down yet further: the city's losers, overwhelmed by a turn in fortune that had cast them capriciously from affluence to a struggling existence, were uninterested in the greater prosperity. What had happened over fifteen years was a microcosm of what had been happening to the nation as a whole since the Second World War. While Britain had been dragging parts of itself towards new technology and work practices that could stand up against the rest of the world, Aberdeen, through oil, had been suddenly exposed to the full force of international competition: at its simplest, a technological breakthrough by a rival could put a firm out of business overnight. A drop in revenue could throw thousands out of work, and millions of pounds could be wiped off the value of property. In Aberdeen there was no protection against economic reality, while in greater Britain the change had come slowly, nibbling its way through archaic industries, resisted by vested interest and by conservative instinct.

Aberdeen had become a laboratory for the processes of late twentieth-century economic fortune. Its relationship with the oil, pumping at a rate of 2.5 million barrels a day from the grey sea beyond the horizon, mirrored the larger national relationship. If Aberdeen, with its close proximity to the oil, had squandered its chances, what hope was there that the nation was being more prudent? If an 'enterprise culture' was going to exist anywhere, it was here on the remote north-eastern brow of Scotland. Here one might find winners and losers on an American scale. The dip in the city's fortunes was a good moment to take stock.

Aberdeen is not everyone's cup of tea. American travel writer Paul Theroux visited the city while researching his book *Kingdom By the Sea*, a tour of the British (and Ulster) coast undertaken during 1982. Travelling clockwise from London, he was in a jaundiced mood by the time he hit the eastern shore. He had soured perceptibly as he journeyed: Blackpool – 'perfectly reflected in the swollen guts and unhealthy fat of its beer-guzzling visitors' – had finally eroded what indulgence of British weaknesses he had begun with. In Aberdeen, a hotel gypped him, and two nightspots wouldn't allow him in: the 'average Aberdonian', he concluded, was 'a person who would gladly pick a halfpenny out of a dunghill with his teeth'. Nothing was to his liking, and his comments, remembered in some places word for word five years later, explained some of the prevailing suspicion towards visitors with ballpoint pens and notebooks.

Perhaps Theroux's words had been taken to heart. I stayed longer, and visited after the oil price slump, which no doubt had had a chastening effect, but I found the people hospitable and helpful beyond average. The only hint of what Theroux perceived came when I tried to interview 'Honey', a woman who provides such necessary oil town services as striptease and kissograms. She had apparently been featured in a 'Panorama' programme, reading the *Financial Times* to gauge the state of the oil industry before making her own business decisions, and was clearly the thinking man's stripper. On the phone she agreed readily to meet me, and we arranged to have lunch. Later there was a message to call her. She was sorry, her business manager was angry that she had arranged to see me. Why? Money, she supposed. Could I ring him? and she gave me a number. I didn't bother. Out of the several hundred interviews and conversations I conducted for this book, that was the only time anyone hinted that his (or her) wisdom was worth money.

John Condliffe, of the Scottish Development Agency, is an Englishman, as were many of those I met, including Dr Geoff Hadley, the politically independent convenor of the Grampian Regional Council, who led a minority ruling coalition which included the Scottish Nationalists! (Small towns grown suddenly big often boast of their cosmopolitan ways, and in Aberdeen I suspect this was true of the oil boom years. Apart from the Americans, who came in all shapes from Texans in stetsons to Harvard business graduates, there were French, Dutch, Germans, Norwegians. Aberdonians had enjoyed having foreign neighbours and foreign children in their schools.) Accustomed to the task of straightening out ignorant fellow Sassenachs, Mr Condliffe told me about the oil. Britain, he said, was the fifth biggest oil producer in the world, outproducing every member of Opec (Organization of Petroleum Exporting Countries) except Saudi Arabia. Britain consumed 1.6 million barrels a day itself, leaving 30 per cent of total production for export. 'You can fall,' he said, 'a very long way from there, and still be a substantial oil producer.' In addition to the thirty-six fields in production, another thirty to forty had already been discovered, and, subject to the world oil price, advances in technology and British fiscal policy – the Government gave the oil industry a handsome tax break in the 1987 Budget – would eventually all be exploited. Every field was finite and oil production is always a slope going down, but the North Sea is likely to last for at least another forty or fifty years, and very few industries could look forward with certainty to that kind of future.

Although British oil costs a great deal to extract by Middle Eastern standards, a world barrel price of twenty dollars or more would make further development worthwhile. When the Forties field was discovered – Britain's first major oil strike – the price had, after all, been a mere three dollars a barrel. What was true was that the Government's direct take from the North Sea had already declined dramatically, and would never rise again. Future development costs meant that the days of big profits, and therefore tax revenues, were over. But both Aberdeen and the nation could look forward to sizeable benefits for a generation to come.

For the moment, Aberdeen was suffering a 'development gap', but, with stability ahead, Aberdeen and Britain had an opportunity to create an oil service industry second only to the Americans, which might have an export potential long after the oil itself had finally run out. Most of the other oil producing nations in the 'free' world couldn't, according to Mr Condliffe, 'ride bicycles'. We had, he said, less than 3 per cent of the world oil service market, but it ought to be possible to raise that to 10 per cent. However, why Britain should do better next time round, when margins will be so much tighter, than it did in the first fifteen years, was never fully explained to me. A popular bumper sticker from the darkest days of 1986 read: 'Please God send us a second oil boom, and this time don't let us piss it up against a wall!'

If Aberdeen wasn't facing ruination, it had certainly come to the end of a spree. When oil fetched forty dollars a barrel, cost was immaterial. An American oilman told me: 'Five years ago no one asked the price. They wanted to know, was it on its way yesterday? You'd say "Yes, what would you like?" If they haggled over the price they might lose production, and that would cost millions. Now is the time to squeeze the vendors. They don't need it yesterday or even tomorrow. Logistics are less important than the money side.' Mr Condliffe said: 'They were talking telephone numbers. They didn't care what it cost; the urgency was to come on stream. All that's gone out of the window. Now they've got to be cost effective rather than time effective. They are no longer prepared to pay through the nose.'

The cost of chartering an oil exploration rig had dropped from £100,000 a day to £10,000, at which price the operator was making a loss. One of the few British companies in the business had gone bust two weeks before my visit. A joke was doing the rounds about a rig operator who called a company which had put a job out to tender and offered to do it for nothing. 'When do we start?' asked the operator. 'Not so fast,' said the contract manager, 'I've still got twenty-nine bids to open.' Supply ships on the spot market were similarly chartered below cost. One operator told me that the best he could hope for was £1,200 a day, while his operating costs were £1,600. The week I was in Aberdeen only eighty-two vessels out of 138 available were gainfully employed. Against that background the oil majors had thrown themselves into reverse with the enthusiasm with which they had once gone forward. 'An oil company saving money is a formidable sight,' said Mr Condliffe. 'Esso actually cancelled an outstanding six months' subscription to a magazine.'

But such madnesses were not, he said, a sign that the industry was finished, rather that it was getting its costs under control. This was a cycle in the life of a sunrise industry. 'We haven't squandered it yet; we have an opportunity to build up a world-winning technology and supply industry.' Given past 'pissing against the wall', this seemed unlikely. So I went to see Professor Alexander Kemp at Aberdeen University, the academic guru of the North Sea oil industry. He was an adviser to the House of Commons Select Committee on Energy, and the pundit most in demand locally. I have been in many offices, but few where the paper lay quite so deep on every surface, or where treasured documents were scattered and buried with such haphazard abandon. The professor, a small man with thick glasses and fast-receding hair, leapt energetically round his domain, triumphantly producing crumpled cuttings from battered briefcases with far more improbability than the conjuror producing the rabbits from a hat which a shrewd audience knows are there to begin with. He had moved recently, he said, from a smaller office, and the paper had just spread to fill the expanded space.

Britain's share of the domestic offshore industry had, he said, risen through the years to between 70 and 80 per cent. 'We have done relatively well at lower levels of technology, where international competition was not so intense anyway. But we could have done better. There have not been all that many successes on a large scale.' Like Mr Condliffe, he saw Aberdeen's (and Britain's) long-term benefit from the North Sea in becoming competitive in the overseas oil supply markets, now dominated – for obvious historical reasons – by the United States. Although the present recession would restrict research and development, there would be a 'second chance', when the forty newly discovered fields were opened up, but this would, without doubt, be the 'last opportunity'.

Britain had, he said, been too open, allowing in foreign competition in a way that no rival developed oil countries, such as Norway and Canada, did. We should have insisted – and presumably still could – on joint ventures with foreign firms and the transfer of technology. Starting from scratch, companies faced formidable barriers in the foreign ownership of patents and the massive capital required. Was he not advocating protectionism that would encourage inefficiency? 'Not,' he replied, 'if it were properly done, fostering the child so that it grew up to be a healthy, robust adult, itself competitive overseas.' Had we 'squandered' the oil? He pursed his lips at my inexactitude. 'The popular view is that we have "consumed" rather than invested. There is a lot in that, though it is not entirely true,' he said. Britain had invested some of the proceeds overseas, which brings an income; taxation was lower than it would have been without the oil, which theoretically stimulated investment, though he would argue that it principally stimulated consumption. The oil should have been regarded as an asset, which the prudent manager ought to replace rather than consume.

'However, that,' he pointed out, 'is nice and easy to say, and more difficult to execute.' He would have liked an agency, independent of Government, to which some of the tax revenues were consigned. It would have been entrusted with using the money to improve the infrastructure and provide capital for private enterprise. There were models for such an agency in both Alaska and Alberta. However, consuming the oil revenues was painless in political terms: to have set them on one side would have meant unpalatable higher taxes – at the height of the oil boom, the Government drew 10 per cent of its income from the North Sea – and restraint on consumer spending.

For fifteen years there had been little constraint on local consumers. Wages shot up when oil was discovered; the trend of outward migration of Aberdeen's brightest and best was arrested (an Aberdonian businessman said that only three of his fifties class of sixty-plus graduate engineers at the university had stayed in the town); sixty thousand new people moved in, raising the population to a quarter of a million; development status with its Government subsidies was taken away; yet unemployment went down. The shock of the 'big' money was enormous. A secretary who went for a job with one of the new oil companies was offered 'ten'. She hesitated. 'All

right, then, we'll make it £12,000,' said the personnel manager. She
had thought he had first meant ten *pounds* a week! A middle-ranking
press officer for a major oil company was paid substantially more
than a senior journalist on a London-based paper like the *Observer*.

Traditional industries inevitably struggled to hold such people as
engineers, who were in massive demand by the oil companies. Office
staff were lured away. The result in many areas was not ruin, but
rapid modernization. For example, managements of the city's paper
mills, terrified fifteen years ago that the industry might be wiped out,
computerized their operations. (The accountant to one firm, which
had invested twenty-five million pounds in the world's most advanced paper-making machine, said it was eerie to visit the mill: there
was not a soul in sight, not even in the computer control room.) Yet,
even after the oil price crash, Aberdeen's unemployment remained
half that of Scotland's. Without oil none of the industrial estates that
stud the periphery of the city, all of them built since the wage explosion, would exist. The higher wages had also helped refurbish much
of the city – in spring 1987 millions of pounds were still being poured
into shopping developments – and the countryside, where 'oilies' had
bought and restored crofts abandoned by the declining rural population.

It was hard after the crash to find an American oilman in Aberdeen. The American school, I was told, was filling its places with children bussed from a US Air Force base. However, when I was
lunching with John Condliffe, an American accent rose above the surrounding hubbub: there, at the next table, with a weather-beaten
face, in three-piece suit, wearing a diamond ring on one hand and a
heavy gold bracelet on the other, was the genuine article. The man
was Ted McDowell, who had come to Aberdeen in 1973, shed an
American family and acquired a Scottish one, and stayed. We met
two days later shortly after dawn at his baronial, turn of the century
mansion just outside Aberdeen – eleven bedrooms, seven acres of
formal garden, more than fifty acres of woodland, a lake, squash
court and all-weather tennis court. A log fire blazed in the hearth,
peacocks paraded outside the french windows, and a black labrador
whined from the porch. It was easy to understand why this particular
American laird had not joined the recent exodus.

Mr McDowell's personal story was a fine illustration of American
social mobility. Although brought up in a tiny community in the
middle of the Mojave Desert, he had gone to university; although he

had gone to university, he had become a deep sea diver; although he had been a diver, he had risen to become an international director of a worldwide subsea company; although his life had been in diving, when I met him he had just bought three small printing companies and was planning to diversify further. He had broken with his American firm over the severity of the cuts he felt were needed to weather the North Sea development gap: he had wanted swingeing savings to eliminate the fat, while they were attacking the problem more gently.

What had surprised him about Aberdeen was the sedate nature of the boom. Although Aberdeen had grown during the oil years by between three and five thousand people a year, an American town sitting on such opportunities would have exploded with thousands pouring in overnight. It was to him an illustration that the British are not mobile enough for their own economic good. They had failed to take full advantage of the biggest bonanza of the twentieth century, which was a major reason why foreigners had been able to get in on the act. He said: 'When I was an operations manager we would hire anyone. You passed your physical by coming through the door, and your psychological by wanting a job. I hired Americans, not because I was one, but because every morning they were the people banging on my door and sitting in reception. The British would send indecipherable, handwritten notes, and expect you to summon them for interview. The Americans would be just out of diving school, and had travelled halfway round the world on their own money. If you wanted enthusiasm and job performance, you knew where to look.' Any Britons with adventurous spirit, he suggested, went abroad. 'They either don't move at all, or go the whole hog.'

Industrially Britain had also missed the boat, and had not made sufficient financial investment: only a handful of the drilling rigs out of over a hundred had been owned by British companies. The Dutch, the Norwegians and others had taken the big stake risks and reaped the benefits. 'Brits were never willing to invest in the high capital side of it,' said Mr McDowell. A few who had, had made a fortune. He was sceptical that the second chance would provide the opportunities of the first. He himself was looking for ways back into the North Sea, and in the meantime was 'hanging around town to see what comes'. With inevitable bankruptcies, there would be opportunities to get into businesses and buy equipment cheaply, and so it had proved with his printing firms. 'I don't expect to become a printer, but I can

make the firms more efficient. When no one looks at the price, anyone
can make money. In tighter times so much of business is money-
management,' he said.

Mr McDowell's strictures about Britain's failure to obtain a decent
share of the market appeared, in general, to be well founded. Aberdeen and the rest of the country had been characteristically cautious
and conservative. Oil had two crucial disadvantages: it was new-
fangled and risky. The British penchant for investing in proven enterprises – demonstrated in recent times by the rush to buy shares
in privatized industries – prevented Britain from exploiting fully what
might prove to have been Fate's last kind roll of the dice. However,
there were notable exceptions. The Aberdeen company that capital-
ized most on the opportunities was, by local agreement, the John
Wood Group. Have you, asked everyone I met, fearful the visiting
writer might miss the town's prize exhibit, visited the John Wood
Group?

Before oil, the John Wood Group had been a relatively prosperous
fishing company which owned, built and serviced trawlers, processed
and sold fish. It owned or had a substantial interest in twenty fishing
boats and employed between five and six hundred people. When oil
was discovered, the company was controlled by the founder's
son, Ian Wood, then in his early thirties, who was by nature a risk
taker. He visited the United States where he saw the enormous possibilities for oil-related enterprise. Like Rupert Murdoch (though without, everyone assured me, Murdoch's abrasive ruthlessness), he had
grown an oak tree from an inherited acorn. In thirteen years the
group's income from oil activities exploded from £120,000 to £90
million, and it employed 2,500 people worldwide in engineering,
onshore support, drilling and production. To provide a foundation
for the future, when the logistical activities in the North Sea declined,
it had bought two American companies engaged in pioneering technology. Its fishing enterprises had been separated from the oil
divisions, and still employed the same number of people as in pre-oil
days. The group's expansion had been financed by profits it generated itself. Ian Wood no doubt would have had a large slice of the
local market whatever the competition, but why, I asked his brother-
in-law and fellow director, Hugh Duncan, had no other Aberdeen
company grown comparably? 'The bulk of local people,' he replied,

'carried on doing their own thing. We were lucky that what might have been rival companies didn't choose to be rivals.'

Once Mr Wood had grasped the potential of the North Sea, he moved fast. 'Unless we got going, folks from the south would start muscling in,' said Mr Duncan. They restructured the company and bucked everyone's ideas up. A yard that repaired fishing trawlers in a competent but leisurely manner was no good for the 24-hour, seven-day-a-week oil industry: existing technical standards in welding, for example, had to be sharpened up. (The same applied to service industries like hotels and builders: those who woke up in time to the altered nature of the market grabbed a lion's share of the new business.) 'The old parochial Aberdeen ways would not meet the needs. Adaptability was required. The offshore industry demanded new ways. It was no good sitting pretty with what you had done last year. If you did, you had the wrong mix,' said Mr Duncan. 'We kept the door half open, and it was amazing in the first five years what business opportunities evolved.' Breaking in to the high-tech market was tough. The industry was dominated by half a dozen world names, who were 'very, very big', and it was hard to ensure a steady return. 'Technology results tend to be mercurial, one dazzling year and then a couple when you lose money. Stability is in steady, everyday support activities,' said Mr Duncan.

Aberdeen also had to adapt to new styles. The first Americans were brash figures, men with open-necked shirts who stuck their boots on the desk. 'The only thing they understood,' said one British oilman, 'was drilling so many feet a day in the fastest way they knew.' A builder told me of one such man he took to a Burns Night dinner. When the haggis was served, his guest violently stabbed the strange object on his plate, and announced in a voice that rang round the hall: 'Christ, I wouldn't give that to my goddam dog.' No sooner had Aberdonians become accustomed to this breed than preppy Americans with business degrees began arriving. Somewhere in that international mix were the makings of a fine comedy, and I wondered why Aberdeen had never been exploited as soap opera. The possibilities for a home-grown 'Dallas' must once have been limitless. Perhaps the lack of such a series was another example of the British inability to exploit opportunities under its nose.

Just what those opportunities were, and just how dozy the British were in seizing them, was brutally exposed by the experience of Steve Remp, who in the early seventies was a young American recently out of post-graduate university. Encouraged by his father, who ran an international oil service company from a London base – 'he had pretty good foresight into what could happen here' – he came to Aberdeen, 'snooped around', and decided what was needed was superior hotel accommodation. For a year he roamed Britain seeking backing, in the City of London, in Edinburgh and Aberdeen itself. 'I went everywhere, but no one would touch the project. They were suspicious, concerned I was too young,' said Mr Remp. He went to Houston, found oilmen who thought Aberdeen was attractive, and built a Sheraton. In 1977 Holiday Inns bought a minority shareholding and the franchise, making a tidy sum for the backers, and setting Mr Remp up with the capital to launch his present company, Ramco, a publicly quoted oil service and technology company. Mr Remp admitted that he had missed opportunities himself in the early days, and that it was easy to be smart twelve years on, but he saw first hand how slow the British were on the uptake. 'Foreign companies made a beeline and got cracking,' he said. The fact that John Wood is a rare jewel in the British crown is evidence of how poorly the natives responded. 'And John Wood,' said Mr Remp, 'are minnows by comparison with American oil service companies.' (For good measure, while he was developing his first business, Mr Remp bought Harthill Castle at Oyne in Aberdeenshire, built in 1601 and lying derelict since a fire one hundred years later, which no one else had got around to restoring. He won awards for the restoration, and the house can now be viewed by private arrangement.)

An indigenous company that did succeed at the sharp technological end of the business – after an admittedly precarious start – was Osprey Electronics, who make underwater television cameras so successfully that they have driven some American rivals out of business. Started in 1975 by an enterprising character who wanted to bring work to the far north of Scotland – Osprey's factory is twelve miles from John o'Groats – after four years it was going nowhere in particular, casting around for what its technical director, Donald Stewart, called 'a serious product.' It started manufacturing underwater cameras on a 'me too' basis to get a share of the market. In 1981 more substantial backers came in, a bankrupt company was purchased whose product line complemented Osprey's, and within six years the company dominated the world market. The founder took himself off, and, according to Mr Stewart, after several false starts had hit on another idea of immense potential. The entrepreneurial spirit is frequently inimical to the gradual, less exciting commercial development of bright notions. The three directors who remained – in 1987 all still in their mid to late thirties – had a 10 per cent stake in the company.

Mr Stewart, an electronics engineer, had been with Osprey at the start. When the company was in the doldrums, he quit to go to the Middle East, where he wandered the desert with a couple of Arabs dropping highly expensive electronic tools down oil wells to measure what was going on below ground. In a year he saved enough to put down a deposit on an Aberdeen house. He returned to work for a British company that was trying to penetrate the oil business – they have since succeeded. However, he found them conservative, seedy, fuddy-duddy and unglamorous, tied around with rules and regulations, and he was lured back to Osprey. He and the founder, who was then still with the company, had both worked for an American firm and they injected American style into Osprey. 'We try to have a healthy attitude towards the staff, keeping them in the picture with what's going on. We practise leadership from the front, rather than pushing from behind. The oil industry has an aura about it that encourages an expansive approach; it does things with a certain style,' said Mr Stewart. To compete in a business in which appearances count for so much, Osprey spends a great deal on marketing.

The company opened offices in Houston and Amsterdam, bought a British electro-optics company, which manufactured night vision equipment near Brighton – 'in the deep south' – and went from strength to strength with its underwater cameras. The firm provided a 'one-stop shop', offering specialized packages used principally in the inspection of offshore installations for maintenance and insurance purposes. The equipment takes a beating, lasting only a couple of seasons even if well looked after, so the demand continues during recession. Several American competitors were 'taken to pieces. We broke in and caused ructions.' Mr Stewart said: 'We were already saturating our own market, and suspected there might be a downturn.' So Osprey sought, and won, Ministry of Defence contracts, and began building a market in oceanographic research – the main colour television camera on the Alvin vehicle which explored the *Titanic* was manufactured by Osprey. Even so, their 1986 profits were wiped out by the collapse of the oil price. There were some redundancies, and the 120-plus remaining staff were asked to take a pay cut. 'We are not unionized,' said Mr Stewart. 'We hope we can look after people well enough for there to be no need.' When I visited, Osprey was back on an even keel, and the directors aimed to double the five million pounds turnover within five years. 'We can't afford to grow arrogant or complacent; there are one or two very enterprising new companies in the United States,' said Mr Stewart.

Survival in Aberdeen required people to be fast on their feet. When oil was discovered, the Webster Tyre Company – founded in 1947 to manufacture and distribute remould tyres – had twenty-five sales and service depots and a retread manufacturing plant. It had grown to a three million pounds turnover, and employed three hundred people. Radial tyres were being introduced, and the retread business was dead. The company changed its name to Webco, and went aggressively after the North Sea market. Sticking with the rubber technology it understood, it developed seals, clamps, pipe coatings and insulations, securing an international leadership. (Pipes manufactured in Japan for use on a production platform being built in South Korea were shipped halfway round the world for coating by Webco, and then shipped back again.) After a short period of contraction, the company grew to a seven million pounds turnover by 1985. It was heading for its first one million pounds annual profit when oil prices collapsed, and, when I visited, was rebuilding painstakingly once again, like an optimist in an earthquake zone.

The boss was George Webster, the founder's son, a shy, plump young man in shirt sleeves. 'We couldn't,' he said, 'batten down the hatches, sell off the Jaguar and hope that it would all blow over. We had to act swiftly. Fortunately, the skills we had were applicable to industries other than oil.' Once again looking for ways to develop rubber technology, Webco diversified into the car component industry, in which they already had a presence, buying a major company in Wiltshire, and two small companies which they moved to Aberdeen. The Wiltshire enterprise gave them a southern presence: Aberdeen, over five hundred miles from London, had proved to be a remote base from which to operate – 'people thought this was the North Pole. It was difficult to make an impact,' said Mr Webster. As I understood it, they had underestimated the problems associated with their new acquisition, but were pulling through with the bank's support. Because of its diversification, Webco was then employing a record number of people.

Don Riggs knew about roller-coaster fortunes perhaps better than any man in Aberdeen. He had left school at fifteen and driven a horse and cart on a farm. He became an engineer through night school, and spent five years on the road as an engineering inspector before starting a valve company in his native Cleveland. Seven years later his principal customers – the steel and chemical industries – went into severe recession. His business, which had been worth £1·9 million a year, halved overnight, and he clung on by his fingertips like a man at the edge of a cliff. He had already done business in Aberdeen, and later moved north to take full advantage of oil opportunities. By late 1985 his business was thriving, with a turnover of £2·3 million. Money, he said, had been no object; if a company needed a valve, it wanted it at all costs. In late 1985 he sensed that a slump was on its way. He sold his house (above its valuation), laid off many of his employees, ran down his stocks. 'I'd seen it all once before. I took the bull by the horns, action based on what I didn't do in 1979,' he said. Much of Aberdeen refused to believe the worst. On Mr Riggs's office wall is a cutting from the Aberdeen *Press and Journal*, dated 18 March 1986 – three months after he had battened down his hatches. It read: 'City Beats Oil Drop: Cut-Backs Have Not Hit North-East.' Beneath it Mr Riggs had scrawled 'Quote of the Century'.

Mr Riggs had the face of an Old Testament prophet, long and fringed with a beard, and strong engineer's hands. Two of his competitors had gone under during the oil slump: they had overextended themselves to cope with the demand, he said. He himself, when I met him, was re-employing people. He had just bought a house – 'a better-class small bungalow' – for £47,000. It would, he said with clear pleasure, have cost £60,000 two years earlier. Business was seeping back. Valves have a limited life in the North Sea, and production companies, he forecast, were going to have to spend a lot of money in the years to come to sustain the oil. 'There's going to be one hell of a good market in my business over the next twenty or thirty years. It'll see me out,' he said.

If Aberdeen showed insufficient drive and enterprise fully to exploit the opportunities off its coast, the presence of oil did, however, stimulate considerably more economic activity than takes place in most of Britain. Even if the city fell short of becoming a boom town on an American scale, it did attract bright, well-educated and ambitious people and the oil stimulated many natives to launch themselves on risky endeavours. If the main chance had been let slip, many people took mini-chances. John Freebairn, on loan from Barclays Bank, ran the Aberdeen Enterprise Trust. When it was first mooted in 1984 at the height of the oil boom, some suggested the money would be better spent in depressed places like Tyneside. Mr Freebairn's argument was that business ought to be promoted where the markets lie. The Trust was, therefore, in existence when the oil price plummeted, when inquiries from embryo business people doubled overnight to 120 a month. By 1987, Aberdeen had become the fastest growing enterprise area in Britain, with the highest number of new businesses surviving infancy. Mr Freebairn showed me several large albums of press cuttings about people the Trust had helped, ranging from the manufacturers of obscure technical bits and pieces for the oil industry to the man who had left oil after twelve years to start a farm raising pheasants (for shooting and eating) and quails. Both enterprises looked set fair. 'Mad inventors, however,' said Mr Freebairn, 'are undoubtedly the most difficult to help. Britain does not take kindly to innovation.'

As a bank manager by training, Mr Freebairn knew the difficulties of raising risk capital from banks – essentially, since banks make loans and do not take part of the equity, they are risking a great deal in return for only modest interest. But he had hopes that rich people with ties to north-east Scotland might invest, perhaps with a view to retiring in the area and taking a part-time interest in an enterprise they had backed. 'A lot of money belongs here emotionally,' he said. Of the people he had advised (the trust had no access to material assistance), one-third were English and over half came from outside Aberdeen. However, the combined employment potential of the four hundred businesses helped by the Trust in its first two and a half years was puny. Average employment at the time of starting-up was 2·3 people per enterprise, and Mr Freebairn said he would have been surprised if more than twenty of the total had real employment potential. Success for a small business, he said, is survival.

Three of the Trust's alumni companies had been housed together at Number Three King Street, in the heart of old Aberdeen, close to the cathedral. Two had survived, but one had been swept away by the oil recession. The one that failed was Meridian, run by two young women graduates in psychology from Aberdeen University. Their idea had been to provide a recruitment service for middle-sized firms by offering personality assessments and IQ tests on job applicants. After attending a graduate enterprise programme at Stirling University, they launched in January 1986, on the eve of the oil crash. Within weeks hundreds of people were being laid off, and a sophisticated recruitment company had less chance than a sauna salesman in the Sahara. They folded ten months later owing five thousand pounds. With the collapse of the oil price, millions of pounds had been written off Aberdeen property values. Wages had come tumbling down; almost no one was untouched.

A joiner told me that his hourly rate had collapsed from nine to two pounds. A taxi driver was working evenings and weekends instead of nine to five, and was making less money – there were 750 cabs in town, which, according to most drivers, was two hundred more than the market could bear. A former professional footballer had had two salesmen's jobs fold under him; he was trained as a plumber, but couldn't find any work. The Aberdeen Citizens' Advice Bureau reported a 16 per cent increase in the numbers of those seeking help – especially with marital problems; figures which were, said the *Evening Express*, 'the legacy of the boom which turned to gloom'. A 24-year-old offshore production engineer, out of work for six months, was selling his Porsche. The Aberdeen Petroleum Club, an up-market country club, lost three hundred of its 1,100 members during 1986, and was forced to launch a membership drive. One of the city's senior business figures couldn't sell his eight-bedroomed 'pile', although he had knocked £10,000 off the price – 'Don't talk to me about houses,' he snorted.

Everyone had a property story: the reporter, ambitious to move to London, who had seen the value of his house dive by £20,000, effectively meaning he couldn't afford to move; the helicopter pilot who had been transferred to England, and had had to leave his family behind because they couldn't sell their house. (Even the city's Gordon Barracks stood forlorn and empty, waiting for a buyer.) Aberdeen was ringed with modern housing estates rushed up by national development companies during the boom. Villages which once had half a dozen houses, a church and a bog, had become communities with three or four thousand homes. Every inducement was offered to buyers, including 100 per cent mortgages that covered carpets, curtains and kitchen equipment; there had been, I was told, joy rides in helicopters and weekends at Aviemore. 'It was easier to buy a house than a car,' said a solicitor. Ten thousand redundancies later these estates were plastered with 'For Sale' signs. In one notorious street – Lee Crescent North, in the Bridge of Don to the north of the city – there were sixty-one houses for sale the week I was there. The carpets were worn, the fine washing machines chipped, and there were no helicopter rides on offer; houses were worth up to 20 per cent less than the value of the original full mortgage. The *Property Register*, put out by the Aberdeen Solicitors' Property Centre, swelled to more than twice its former size. Aberdonians had traditionally bought new houses on bridging loans before selling their own. Once the bottom fell out of the market, the system jammed solid. Solicitors, who act as agents for most property sales in Scotland, were widely blamed for lack of imagination: they didn't know, said the critics, how to build property 'chains'. They had had it, said the man who couldn't sell his pile, too easy for too long. But the solicitors in turn were not kind about the buyers, and were angry about a 'Panorama' programme that had interviewed people unable to sell. People who took out 100 per cent mortgages at prices above professional valuation had only themselves to blame, they said. It was mainly the English, I gathered, who had been caught: Aberdonians had been too canny to pay inflated prices and most Americans were shrewd.

Johnnie Patterson, like Ted McDowell a Californian, was still in town after the crash because he too had married a Scot. By early 1987 he was clinging to the wreckage. He had come to the North Sea near the beginning, in his case aboard a rig that had been pulled out of Trinidad, refurbished in Florida, and towed across the Atlantic. He had worked for the same company, Santa Fe, for nearly seventeen years, rising to 'senior tool-pusher', top man on the job. It was his rig that had discovered the sizeable Thistle field. He had earned five thousand dollars a month clear of tax, which was handled by his company, and been given airline tickets once a year equivalent to a return fare to Los Angeles. Life had been good, and he had been planning to move to a smallholding outside Aberdeen so that his wife could have a horse.

Eight months before I met him, he had been 'let go'. He sat in his split-level living room – pool table, two televisions, Alsatian puppy, parakeet – dressed in Texan boots, open-necked plaid shirt, and jeans, and listed his problems. His house, which had been valued two years previously at £95,000, had been on the market for six months, most recently at £75,000, and he had not had a single caller; his twin ten-year-old sons were in a boarding school, and would have to be pulled out at the end of the school year if he didn't get a job; he believed he now faced prejudice because he was an American, and companies were nervous that he would be looking for 'big bucks'. Twice he had been told that he was overqualified. Cost-cutting had led, he said, to labour agencies providing scratch drilling crews. 'They expect these people to go out and drill an oil well. All I can see is screw-ups.' However, he was an optimist after the American fashion, and believed something would come along by summer. If it didn't, he would probably take his Scottish family back to California where he had some property, and seek work in the construction industry. His American nationality gave him an option not available to British oil-men.

Where I did find a bleak sense of defeatism was in the offices of the trade unions. Since the boom days the unions had suffered two grievous blows – the drop in the oil price with the massive local redundancies that caused, and Mrs Thatcher's successful assault on their powers. Their greatly altered fortunes were another of Aberdeen's microcosms of national trends. Tommy Lafferty, of the construction section of the Amalgamated Engineering Union, sat alone in his offices, wearing a yellow sports shirt and chewing the end of a large cigar. His walls were decorated with photos of giant oil platforms and the Sullom Voe terminal on which he had worked; occasionally he left his desk to point one out with pride. He had started life as a steel erector, travelling the country on big jobs such as power stations, a 'gipsy' as he put it. His branch's heyday had been during the construction phase, when a man might earn comfortably over £20,000 as a rigger, steel erector or scaffolder. But there were no union agreements with the production companies, and a man doing identical work once a platform had come on stream might find his wages cut by half. It was a difficult industry to organize at the best of times; during a recession it was clearly a nightmare. An official would have to stay offshore for a continuous 28-day stretch to meet everyone employed on one structure.

Mr Lafferty was 'angry, annoyed, disappointed' by the turn in events. He said: 'Once they no longer needed us, we were thrown to the wind, all in the name of commercial enterprise.' All the perks had gone – the air fares, the paid waiting time, the generous notice, the taxis, the sick leave, the payments when the weather was too bad to put to sea. 'I thought we had problems then. I wish to hell we could go back to them. Problems then were connected with working: now they're all to do with *not* working,' he said sombrely. 'For every job that comes up, we've probably got twenty men chasing it. We get car loads, six at a time, travelling perhaps from Tyneside, sleeping rough.

It's pathetic.' As we talked, the phone rang. It was one of his members who had been put ashore from a production platform for challenging the allocation of overtime. Although the man was not
covered by an agreement, he was lucky in that Mr Lafferty knew
someone with the company, and had managed to get him reassigned
to another platform. 'Son, the protection I can offer you is nowt.
Watch it, and don't put your head above the parapet. Keep your trap
shut,' he said. It was not exactly fighting talk. To me he said sadly:
'It couldn't happen onshore. The shop steward would get the lads
together, explain what had happened, and stop it.'

Industrial tribunals heard almost daily claims of unfair dismissal.
In one case an engineer said that he had been promised a salary rise
after three months, which hadn't materialized. Instead he had been
asked to take cuts in allowances and bonuses, which meant that his
pay would be 27 per cent lower than when he started. The company
also froze all other wages, closed their sales department and made
some workers redundant. The engineer resigned, complaining of constructive unfair dismissal. The tribunal, however, ruled that the company had acted reasonably. 'We lose nine out of ten such cases,' a
union activist complained sadly.

Harry Bygate, who came to Aberdeen to organize the National
Union of Seamen in 1974, is another of the old school. His name was
scrawled in homely fashion in Biro on a block of wood at the front of
his desk. Through the good years, he had played to the old rules, and
had built up membership on the supply vessels and rigs, and established closed shops. In 1987 his members were either redundant or
accepting massive pay cuts. Contractors were bidding the market
down. They obtained a list of names and addresses from the company they had undercut, and then offered the same men their jobs
back at 20 to 30 per cent lower wages. 'They all tell you the same
story – they've dropped £100 a week,' Mr Bygate said gloomily.
Jimmy, a sailor made redundant from anchor-handling tugs, had
been paid £1,400 a month for two weeks on and two weeks off, with
thirty-six days' holiday, up to six months' sick pay guaranteed, and
private health insurance. The last offer he had was for £400 for two
weeks on, with nothing for the two weeks off. He had no children,
lived in a council house and his wife worked, so he told the agency to
'stuff' their job. Other men with commitments were doing the same
job for half the money. It was, he said, 'raw greed' by the operators.

Two further victims of the shake-out sat in the offices of the

Professional Divers' Association, and told stories of even greater financial falls. One, a Geordie, had dropped from £35,000 a year to £10,000: he was meeting his commitments because his wife was working. The other had suffered a compression-related injury – a 'bubble on the brain' – that had caused him to walk off the end of the rig, and he could never dive again. He had been paid £35,000 a year for twelve years. Divers, they told me, had always been regarded as difficult customers – 'awkward sods, expensive and unpredictable.' Now the boot was on the other foot. 'Offshore the diving super-intendent is god. If you show him any disloyalty, you've lost your job. If he said "jump!" you were supposed to say "How high, Sir?"' said one. Many divers, he added, came out of the services, and had a 'backward approach' to trade unions. 'We're only aristocrats now we're rescuing people, otherwise you must be joking,' said the other.

Two or three freshly qualified divers ring the association each week looking for work. The divers complained that the men were being lured to the training schools on false pretences. 'Training schools coerce people who have redundancy payments burning holes in their pockets. It could cost £6,500 for a gas diving course,' said one. 'They're told that there's oodles of work in the Middle East or America, but the recession is worldwide. Qualified men with experience get whatever work is going here.' They believed that the profit from the North Sea had been squandered. 'We've been flogging our guts away to support people on the dole,' said one, adding hastily that he was criticizing the Government, not the unemployed. 'The money should have been used to put more people to work,' he said. Like Pro-fessor Kemp, they also thought that Britain should have been more nationalistic. 'All possible work should have gone to our people,' said one.

Aberdeen's recession hit the local service industries hard. Oil com-panies used to take whole floors of hotels on the off-chance someone might need a room. Men like divers were put up overnight on their way to and from the oil fields: taxis were taken as a matter of course. A partner in a men's clothing business told a story that illustrated the change. He saw in the street a man who had already bought eight suits from him in the first ten months of 1986. He racked his brains to remember whether there were any new styles in stock, expecting that to be his customer's first question. Instead the man greeted him: 'Hello Mr D, you haven't got any jobs, have you?' This man had been eleven years with one company, and until the month before had been earning £2,100 a month. In the boom days the chief problem for the clothing stores was how to hold on to even the dimmest staff. 'Mr D' remembered an eighteen-year-old getting a job offshore – 'he was no Einstein, the kind of guy if you said "hello", he'd be stuck for an answer' – who came back at the end of his first fortnight at sea with £150 in his pocket, which he showed to the other assistants, who became very despondent about their own comparatively meagre wages. Later the boss heard that the young man had fallen from a rig and been taken to hospital with hypothermia. 'I cashed that in with the other lads as quick as I could,' he said. 'They weren't so disgruntled then.' The income from Mr D's shops had fallen by 25 per cent – from an annual turnover of £1.3 million to £1.0 million – and they had had to lay off ten of their twenty-eight staff. 'For the first time in our business lives we have moved back. When everyone's doing badly, you've got to sit it out. There's no point even in advertising,' he said philosophically.

One of Aberdeen's most discussed losers was publican Bob Paige. He also was philosophical: 'I'm skint,' he said simply, 'but the easiest thing would be to say the world's been unfair to me. Yes, one enterprise went wrong, but I have done some good things in my time.' Mr Paige bought a 'spit and sawdust' city-centre pub, tarted it up, concentrating on good quality food and wine, threw out the pool table, barred the old regulars and the kids he darkly suspected of drug-taking. Within a few months he was out of business with his £100,000 house on the market to pay off his debts. He had had a good track record, running a successful 'English-style' bar by the harbour, where he sold real ale in premises that had once been used for professional purposes by the town's whores. The boom ended exactly as his refurbished pub, Babbie Law's, opened. He said: 'Oil companies knocked all the expense accounts on the head and opened cheap canteens,' and the restaurant side of the business, on which he had pinned his hopes, collapsed. He admitted to miscalculations, but blamed the recession for his woes: other pubs had since gone bust, and he was convinced the 'trickle would become a flood'. His former customers argued that he killed Babbie Law's stone-dead with his changes.

Aberdeen Harbour celebrated its 850th anniversary in 1986; fish has been landed and sold in the town since medieval days. With the loss of fishing grounds like the Icelandic waters, the overfishing of those that remained, and high landing charges in Aberdeen (covered by the national dock labour scheme unlike Peterhead to the north, where charges were considerably lower), the industry had declined through the oil years. The large trawlers had been converted for use as standby rescue vessels, and many of the crews went to work in oil. Two-thirds of Aberdeen's fish market lay idle most mornings. Tommy Symmer, who had been showing people round the fish dock for seventeen years, looked through his rheumy eyes across the open water to the far side of the Albert Basin and said: 'One time you could have walked from bank to bank on fishing boats, no bother, no bother.' When I arrived shortly after dawn, there was one last boat, the *Hélène* from Peterhead, unloading. It had been a good morning, half a dozen others had been and gone. The previous day there had been just two boats.

Aberdeen's fish-handling techniques hadn't been affected by the industry's proximity to modern oil technology. The hundredweight boxes were winched ashore, and hauled a few yards on ancient metal trolleys to be spread out on the market floor. Solid men with big bellies and red faces, wearing yellow oilskin trousers and Wellington boots, strode across the boxes, prodding and poking, turning out haddock and cod with wide-awake, baleful black eyes, sole – fetching on that day £200 a box, the high-value turbot and halibut, giant skate and plaice with livid red spots. The only signs of the twentieth century were the walkie-talkies and the portable phones with which dealers kept in touch with prices from other markets. When the dealing was over, men with long metal hooks dragged the boxes across the floor towards the loading bays. There was not a forklift truck in sight.

The profit in fishing boats was returning. Boats were grossing over one million pounds a year – in 1986 one boat had achieved this by August. Oil exploration had first disturbed the fish, but now the cod were growing fat on T-bone steaks and black-eyed peas thrown from the platforms, said Mr Symmer. A notice in the market proclaimed: 'There's nothing new under the sun, but there's plenty new under the sea.' So the good years had proved for Aberdeen and the nation, but should we still be hauling fish by hand? And did we really, like a Third World country, have to allow others to pinch many of the lasting benefits of British oil from under our noses?

When I left, there was only a scattering of oilmen at the airport, where once there had been dozens; the cocktail lounge in the terminal closed at 6.30 p.m. just as passengers for the last London flight were beginning to assemble; the airport shop sold tawdry, predictable Scottish souvenirs; the plane, once again, was only half-full.

THE 'NEW JERUSALEM'

No one would stumble upon the new town of Skelmersdale by accident. It is a remote bantustan; 42,000 people – most of them uprooted Scousers – dumped on the Lancashire plain between the Pennines and the Irish Sea. The town's isolation was ensured by planners who fractured the ancient road that linked the market town of Ormskirk in the west with Wigan to the east. The traveller is compelled on to a looping ring road which leads – via innumerable roundabouts – from the rich, black farmland of west Lancashire, with its dark stone walls, smell of Brussels sprouts, and occasional scarecrow, to the red-brick ribbon that marks the outskirts of Wigan. The bypass is set in generous open space, so little can be seen of the town apart from factory roofs and the fringe of housing estates.

To get that near requires local purpose and knowledge. Thousands drive by Skelmersdale each hour, pounding north and south along the M6, intent on the Lake District or Scotland perhaps, or counting off the miles to Birmingham. Those travelling east and west pass over the 'town' boundary on the M58, an almost deserted motorway that disgorges vehicles north of Bootle's docks, close to the Grand National course. (A clergyman told me he had only once seen all three lanes ocupied by traffic, a bleak comment on economic activity at the margins of the motorway.) Passing motorists may notice the unusual Lancashire names – 'Pimbo', 'Up Holland' and 'Skelmersdale' itself – sturdy village names, telling of generations of yeoman farmers. Stop for a pub lunch in Parbold or Scarisbrick, and your companions will be large, square-faced, curly haired men in brown overalls, who will depart in new BMWs. The dark peak they farm is among the finest, and most profitable, agricultural land in England.

If the sun is shining as you return past Skelmersdale towards the M6, your attention might be caught by an improbable, almost Levantine sight – four-storey blocks of flats, white against the low hills.

Locals, with heavy irony, dubbed those flats 'New Jerusalem'. Twenty years ago, in the mid-sixties, Skelmersdale was indeed to have been the New Jerusalem. The 'homes fit for heroes', pledged since Armistice Day 1918, were at last to be built: the slums of Liverpool fifteen miles to the south were to be razed; model factories would arise in the green fields; children would breathe truly fresh air for the first time, and attend schools made of steel and glass set in wide playing fields. Freed from the exploitive past, the citizens of Skelmersdale were to become the new Britons. The second wave of post-war new towns was to be the apogee of Harold Wilson's 'white heat of the technological revolution'. Skelmersdale was only a brisk crow's flight from Wilson's own constituency of Huyton; and it would have been a fitting tribute to the spirit of 1966, when the first new house was occupied, to have named the new town 'Wilsonia'. (A play performed locally in 1978, *Love and Kisses from Kirby*, caught the *Zeitgeist*: in it 'new town' tenants were made to remove their shoes when they inspected their homes-to-be.)

With hindsight, 1966 was a fulcrum year between the expectations of post-war Britain and the realities of the late twentieth century. England won the football World Cup. Wilson's Government was handsomely re-elected, giving its supporters hope that the country was about to make a final surge towards prosperity, better education, better health, better housing for all. Harold Macmillan's 'never had it so good' boom had prepared the way, but now the people, freed of Supermac's Old Etonian cabal and his seedy Edwardianism, would, as in 1945, again truly be the masters. A few miles from where the foundations were being laid for a neo-Napoleonic road system for Skelmersdale, the Beatles had been asserting the new egalitarian age: the class system, it seemed, was finally tottering from the British stage. Led by a grammar-school boy with a Yorkshire accent, a reassuring pipe clasped between his teeth, and a Gannex mac on his back, a meritocratic nation of pop stars and footballers, fashion designers and iconoclastic media folk like David Frost, was ready for the future. Colour television was only a year away.

I had been within a few hundred yards of Skelmersdale many times during the years of its building. My mother-in-law lived a short distance away, and my family would drive past 'Skem' – as it is invariably known locally – speculating about life in this invisible, unvisited town. Lancashire folk, even in the optimistic years, steered well clear and pitied the six thousand inhabitants of the former mining village of Skelmersdale who were trapped within the new town. But those were the good years; employment was abundant, and people had gardens and decent schools for their children for the first time; the town's football team won the Amateur Cup. However, even then, to judge from local papers, Skem's citizens kept Ormskirk magistrates busy, and by the mid-seventies the bad news was more fundamental. The industries on which this brave new world was to be founded were collapsing like tents in a gale. Thorn, the makers of colour television tubes, departed (it must be the ultimate industrial disgrace that a nation of telly addicts cannot manufacture the sets that enslave it); Courtaulds closed the most advanced spinning shed in the world. Thousands were thrown out of work, while thousands more arrived to seek a new beginning. Within ten years 'Wilsonia' had become 'Doletown'.

The policies that had pitched 35,000 semi-skilled Scousers amongst people they derisively called 'woolly-backs' were hurriedly thrown into reverse. The target population for Skem was slashed from 80,000 to 60,000: Liverpool realized that losing 20,000 of its youngest, fittest citizens each year, as it then was, to Skem and other new towns, was a recipe for disaster, and began to rehabilitate the city centre and encourage people to stay. Skem's hospital was cancelled, the population would now be too small to justify a Marks & Spencer store – a touchstone amenity in the minds of many residents; the road system mocked the low ratio of car owners. Twenty years after Skem's foundation, the town was a totem for Britain's lost illusions. It was more impoverished, more socially disturbed, more hopeless than Wigan, George Orwell's symbol of political and economic failure of fifty years earlier. By 1987 the metaphorical road to Wigan Pier snaked out of Wigan across the M6, through the village of Orrell, dog-legged past Up Holland, and ended six miles further on in a battered row of shops in Digmoor, Skelmersdale's most squalid estate.

Mine was the only car in the parking area for those shops, behind which litter and refuse piled up, giving the appearance of a shoreline on which a rubbish barge had been wrecked. Much of Skem is like that. Tons of waste must be dropped daily: the casual coke and beer cans, the fish 'n' chip papers, the plastic bags, the more purposefully dumped black dustbin bags, their contents spilling kitchen waste through gashes made by dogs. The animals are kept in their thousands to guard homes against the house-breakers who haunt Skem.

Each morning the dogs are turned loose to foul every path and walk-way: my introduction to the town had been a huge dog turd slowly dissolving in the rain on the bottom step of a chipped and scabietic stairway up which shoppers passed. A small boy asked if he could 'mind' my car: feeling intimidated, and visualizing a mighty scratch if I said 'No', I agreed, and he was suddenly idiotically pleased. 'Oh, I love minding cars, mister,' he said grinning. I decided to give him 50p rather than the 30p I first had in mind, and was genuinely disap-pointed not to find him at his post when I returned. (The worst that happened to my car was that someone pinched an American football 'Superbowl' bumper sticker, fresh from New York. 'You were lucky,' said a Lancashire citizen later, 'that they didn't take your wheels.')

Bulldozers had just demolished a second row of Digmoor shops, and two other small boys were biking furiously in the dirt. I was going to the offices of 'Low Profile', a drug counselling centre, staffed – when I called – by a pair of indomitable women. Both were Scousers who had come from Liverpool when times were still vaguely good. The older woman, Margaret Scullion, was an indefatigable 'doer' – she chaired the community centre committee, ran a weekly disco for teenagers (for whom there is virtually no provision in the town), spent each afternoon at Low Profile, and was as poor as a church mouse. Her companion, Lee Evans, had come to Skem twenty years before at the age of eleven; she lived alone and had been out of work for ten years, although she was soon to draw a wage for her Low Profile work. Both women smoked continuously, creating a smog in the small room. They drew deeply on their cigarettes, forcing the noxious fumes into their lungs and bloodstreams, as hooked as any drug addict likely to walk through their door. Both women wrote songs about Skem's plight, one of which – 'Worra Life' – Lee sang through the smoke in a tuneful, folksy, mournful way. In part it went:

> Don't complain, smile in pain,
> Everyone must play de game;
> Life means copin' wid da little bit more.
> Lost ye file, sarky smile,
> Got no Giro for a while,
> Can't borrow money 'cos everybody's poor . . .

Mrs Scullion's forty-year-old son had been out of work for ten years; one daughter was seeking to emigrate; a second, unmarried, was bringing up two children on a little more than thirty pounds a week. Once, Mrs Scullion said, Digmoor had Gas and Electricity Board showrooms, a catalogue shop, shoe shop and restaurant. The area was now poverty-stricken. She said: 'Some families, by the time they come up to their "money day", they're a bit hungry. We're on our knees. People have lost hope; they're just hanging on to each other. I've got eight grandchildren, and I couldn't give one of them a Christmas present. We're in a lost community. It's a terrible thing to say, but I'm glad I'm coming to the end of my life, and am not at the beginning of it.' She added that people in Skem appeared defeated: they don't want to cause trouble in case their money is affected. 'Seem to have lost their spirit. In Liverpool a whole street would stand together and fight, not in Skem.' Nostalgia for the gutsy atmosphere of Liverpool is common in Skem, but most remember the bad things also, and few desire to go back.

Lee Evans compared the days when she left school – 'If I was unhappy in a job, I'd cop out and do something else' – with recent times – 'I can't think of one friend who's in work.' Many people, the two women said, 'were forced on to the fiddle' to clothe and feed their children, panic-stricken in case they got caught. The women had tried one summer's day to test how easy it might be to borrow money from friends and acquaintances in Digmoor. They accosted fifteen people outside the centre, and did not find a single person able to help. 'They said, "I've just borrowed meself," or "I'm on me way for a borrow," or "Me Giro's lost."' Miss Evans did have regular sources for small loans, and showed me her 'debt list' at the back of her diary. Current debts came to £29, which was exactly the amount of her weekly supplementary benefit. Professional loans were available from offices in town, she said, at the rate of 47 per cent over twenty weeks: many had taken such loans to finance Christmas. 'You feel guilty,' said Miss Evans, 'because you want a glass of lager to get you out of your situation. We're just ordinary people and we haven't got a voice. Know what I'm saying?' She had recently been to London for medical treatment – her journey paid by the DHSS – and had been 'gob-struck' by the money she saw being spent.

The women sat beside a well of human misery. They told of a woman – 'housewife' is too privileged a term to use in Skem with any accuracy – whose electricity had been cut off a week after her seventeen-year-old son had been killed by a milk float: the 'lecky' board wanted £200 before they would reconnect her home. They might, I gathered, as sensibly have asked for £20,000. Another woman, said Mrs Scullion, had lost a four-year-old son in a fire. The bereaved mother received a death grant for fourteen pounds and her bills have come to £1,000. She was, as so many in Skem are, 'a one-parent family' with two other children. The little lad, they said, had been hyperactive because of his poor diet – 'egg and chips, chips and eggs.' A lot of people, they added, were sitting without electricity or gas in Skem.

Mrs Scullion said: 'People shout when there's trouble in the streets, but what do they expect? Skem deserves a pat on the back for its restraint.' Someone had to be to blame, and that someone in the early months of 1987 was inevitably Margaret Thatcher. 'Does Mrs Thatcher live on this earth or in cuckoo land?' asked Mrs Scullion. 'She's no woman. We understand that it is a whole Government and not just her, but the hatred is directed at her. An old man told me he wished he had what it took to bump her off.' (A young, unemployed man, who wanted to buy his council house, and start a small business – and therefore, exeptionally for Skem, was pro-Thatcher – said: 'A friend of mine blames Mrs Thatcher every time he has toothache.')

Low Profile has drug counsellors on the premises twelve hours a day. The cases they see range from glue-sniffing to heroin addiction. They refer addicts, and help them with their other problems. There is a support programme for people hooked on prescribed drugs like Valium. Bad cases, said the women, became like 'zombies. It's pitiful. They get panic attacks, lack co-ordination, and cannot even shop on their own.' Miss Evans said: 'We're just ordinary, poor people, looking for a decent day's work for a decent day's pay.' That is their tragedy: such people will never be in demand in significant numbers again, certainly not on Merseyside or in Skem, which have cruel abundances of the semi-skilled.

A few nights later, in one of the town's labour clubs, I met three men typical of Skem's population. They were in their early forties, and each had come to Skem as a young married man, two from Liverpool and one – via homelessness in London – from Scotland. They had come because Skem had houses. 'All we could get in Liverpool,' said one, 'was a room. If we'd waited for a house, we'd be waiting still.' Despite the years of unemployment, Skem had not disappointed them as a place to live. 'The kids hadn't even seen grass till they came here,' said one. 'It's nice and quiet, there's space, and it's healthy. I'm a travelling man, but this is my home.' Everyone said the schools –

especially the primary ones – had been very good. The three men's grown-up sons had left Skem for good. One had a degree from London University and was working in the City, one was unemployed and was bumming somewhere in squats, another had joined the army. (A Labour councillor I met had one son in the army, one on a YTS scheme, one unemployed, and one still at school, which must have made his family the pollster's 'average' Skem household.) The only money any of the three fathers earned was on forays out of town for construction work – mainly in London. They would board the 'Tebbit Express', which took working men south from Liverpool's Lime Street Station late on Sunday night, or take a cheap coach. In London there was a network of contacts – various Shepherd's Bush pubs were good places to start – which led to work, forty-pounds-a-day cash and no questions asked. They often slept where the job was; one, most recently, in the basement of a £200,000 Chiswick house that was being renovated. But they resented the travelling: 'I don't want to be away from home two to three weeks at a time,' said one. But they were realistic: 'There's loads from Skem working down in London. It's called surviving.'

The two Scousers hankered for the lost city of their youths – 'Twenty years ago, whatever Liverpool did, the rest of the country followed. All the vitality, that's what I miss. Beatles and that. I used to go to the Cavern,' said one. 'Now if you go to Liverpool, everything's boarded up, a wasteland. All my friends have grown up and gone. It's a jungle. The kids have to be street-wise. The kids down there would leave the kids here standing.' (It's as hard to find a middle-aged Scouser who never went to the Cavern as once it was to find an Irish Nationalist who was not inside the O'Connell Street GPO during the Easter Rising.) Another said: 'I used to get off the bus or train in Liverpool and say: "Great, it's great to be back." Not now, I wouldn't.'

As we talked we drank beer solidly. The club's environment was thoroughly masculine: women were not allowed to be full members or to play snooker. 'I'd tear up my card if they were,' said one of my companions, and it was hard to tell if he were joking. A gutsy woman sitting nearby took him up. She had a job, she said, was buying her own house. Why shouldn't she be a full member of the club? She didn't get far. A man renowned because his father had once won the pools asked me whether I could drive him to London. He turned out his pockets to show he was broke. Whatever share he had had of the fortune, had long since gone. A young man, playing the slot machines, hit the jackpot, and £100 in one-pound coins came splashing out, a veritable cataract of money, echoing across the momentarily hushed room before he went berserk. For a few hours there was companionship, laughter, booze, and even an unsuspected romantic streak – 'Skem's a frontier town,' said one. But the connotation was one of survival in the middle of nowhere rather than of adventure and possibilities. The atmosphere was jokey – 'Give me your address in case I don't like your book.' Skem, they said, was a comfortable place, a friendly place, where a man need never lack for company.

Early next morning I visited 'Mary' and 'Doreen'. The two women were 'single parent' families. Mary was a pretty woman of twenty-four, tall, with blonded hair and painted red nails, who was unmarried. One child had died 'of a tumour on the lung' when he was a few weeks old, and Mary now had a lively two-and-a-half-year-old, who batted an orange balloon around as we talked. Mother and son lived in one of Digmoor's most depressing streets – rows of prefabricated, pebble-dash houses, set at right-angles to the road, which looked as if a decent wind from the Irish Sea would flatten them. An above-average ration of Skem rubbish disfigured the neighbourhood, and swirled about in a strong breeze. Mary's gas had been cut off three years before – and £16.50 was deducted at source each week from her supplementary benefit. She and her son lived on £33.50 a week. The gas debt had originally been £800, but was down to £300. 'The bills just mounted up,' she said fatalistically.

What did she buy to feed herself and her child? A chicken, you could get two meals out of that. Hearts, they were cheap – 70p a pound. 'I can't buy other meat, or little things for him, like cakes. I can't manage at all. By the weekend we're down to bread and milk. The money seems to have run out.' With no gas, she had kept three electric fires burning throughout the bitter weather of 1987, with inevitable large electric bills. Monday is 'money-day' when the Giro cheque comes. By then she usually owes about eight pounds at the local shop. Clothes? Her mother bought them for the child. 'Me? I have to make do with what I've got. I was used to having clothes before I had the baby. I get dead depressed all the time. I'm just bored stiff during the day.' Was there a garden? Yes, but they hadn't been out in years because she'd lost the key to the back door. When had she last had a holiday? She had to think. When she was ten, at

Butlin's at Pwllheli. She goes to a disco about once a month when the family allowance is paid.

Her friends faced a similar bleakness. A nineteen-year-old had just come home from hospital after a nervous breakdown. 'She smashed the house up, couldn't cope at all. Her little lad died in the house. She was in hospital three weeks, on tablets. There's a lot of it in Skem.' A 21-year-old friend had been on Valium for two years. 'The doctor is trying to break the habit; says she's too young to be on them.' She paused and added: 'My mum says there are people worse off than myself, but I can't think of anyone worse off than I am. There are loads of us, just like me.'

Doreen's husband had walked out five years before, owing, she said, 'a gas bill', as a result of which her gas had been disconnected. Three years later the council had installed gas central heating: radiators that had never been used were now rusting while carpets rotted with damp and walls went green. One child was so severely asthmatic – 'really bronichal' [sic] – that she was in a residential school in the Wirral, coming home at weekends. Doreen heated the child's bed with an electric blanket, and kept two fires burning round the clock. I visited her in the first week of February, and her meter had just been emptied – £253 since Christmas, all in 50p pieces. 'I've got to keep my fires going: all I'm bothered about is my heating.' The amount required to get the gas connected would have been about £100, the sum a businessman might spend on lunch or a middle-class woman on a new jacket. 'I went down to the Gas, and asked them to put it on for me. I told them I'm on the social and on my own. The doctor told me that even a note from him wouldn't do any good. I'd have to have one from the consultant.'

Doreen had come to Skem ten years previously from the Liverpool suburb of Speke. She had left her first Skelmersdale home because 'we got broke into that many times'; her husband's work 'went redundant'. One son lived with his father, and Doreen had two children and her asthmatic daughter at weekends. Her weekly income was ninety pounds, including family allowance, of which thirty pounds usually went on electricity. It cost one child six pounds a week to get to school by Skem's pricey and erratic bus system. Doreen put money aside each week – for her Christmas hamper, for her 'catalogue'. When I asked when she had last had a holiday, she laughed that anyone should consider such a possibility. 'I'd love to take the kids away; I just don't have enough money.' They had been to Blackpool on a day trip – £2.50 return for Doreen and half-price for her children. Had the day been expensive? 'In Blackpool? Oh God, yeah.'

She was ten years older than Mary, and more philosophic. 'I've always been used to not having anything, so it's not bothered me. We get by. I don't think I'm too bad off considering some people.' People had been happier when she was a child, she said, although they had less. Lack of money wasn't the essential problem. 'More money would only mean more debt. All I need is help with my heating really. I'm for ever putting up wallpaper. I had to throw a carpet out at Christmas.' Liverpool was firmly consigned to the past; she would never go back. 'All them muggings. I wouldn't like my kids to grow up to drugs and muggings.' Skem wouldn't be a bad place if there was something for the teenagers. 'My daughter's fourteen: all she does is babysit. I used to go ice-skating; you can't go ice-skating in Skem. Nothing for them to do. All you see is them walking round with their ghetto blasters: they're even frightened of that because they get took off them.' She'd given up on politics – 'whoever gets in, I don't think the state of the place will be any better' – and was pessimistic about Skem – 'promises, and it's just a big flop.'

The day I met the two women the *Skelmersdale Advertiser* ran a front-page story under the headline 'WE DON'T KNOW WHAT TO DO . . .' It told of two Skem householders whose lives were close to intolerable, and illustrated their plights with pictures of filth and dereliction. The home of the first victim, a divorced woman, had been broken into four times in as many months. She had to stay at home continuously to guard her property. 'I feel trapped. I am too afraid to leave the house in case it is broken into, but I don't feel safe when I am at home.' Vandals, she said, were making everyone's life on her 'square' a misery, and one couple had been driven from the area. Their empty house had been totally destroyed: the windows and doors had been ripped out and what wasn't worth stealing strewn around the street outside. The second victim's house was surrounded by a deep bed of rubbish that came spilling out of dustbin bags that other residents hurled from their flat balconies a few yards away. 'It's like living on a council rubbish tip,' the woman said, a statement that was no less than the truth. The contents of the shattered bags included used disposable nappies.

Virtually the whole front page of the previous week's *Advertiser* had been taken up with the destruction of a Roman Catholic junior school by an arsonist. All that remained were a few twisted metal spars, which a week later had been scooped up into giant dumper trucks, leaving a barren patch of scorched earth. The school doubled as a church, and was a central part of local community life. Two small fires were started at other schools in the next two days. The local reporter told me that there was at least one arson in Skem each week.

Skelmersdale is not a natural community with social and occupational gradations. Its inhabitants are totally removed from the experience of most of Britain. The professionals who service the town, with very few exceptions – some of those are 'missionaries' like clergymen – live elsewhere. Eighty per cent of council tenants – the vast majority of the town – receive some form of housing benefit. Some unmarried mothers are so socially incompetent that the idea of going to a community centre for a cup of tea – in the words of a social worker – 'freaks them out, they can't handle it'. Even the Scouser accent sets them apart. Unlike a Yorkshire or Lancashire accent, it is an entirely working-class accent. With rare exceptions, the minute a Scouser opens his mouth, fellow countrymen can accurately pin him down as a man likely to be without skills or higher education. Skem offers few of those toeholds towards advancement, such as the back-street garage where a man can do his own thing, by which the enterprising can often survive in a settled community. The town lacks human compost. The relative of one family that had fled Skem back to Liverpool after two and a half years said: 'It was rather like plastic surgery. Because you get a new nose you think it's a new you. Once the novelty of the house wore off, that was it. No one went to visit them. They felt marooned, completely isolated.' Back in Liverpool the family had to live with relations, but at least there was work for the kids in a fast-food joint.

Skelmersdale is blighted first and foremost by the lack of jobs. 'There's nothing,' people like to say, 'that a good dose of employment wouldn't cure.' I became dizzy writing down figures that looked more like individual cricket scores than unemployment percentages – on the Digmoor estate, the male unemployment rate is 43 per cent. The big factories will never come back. If the national economy did improve significantly, Skem's unemployment rate would probably benefit most from the export of prime males to other parts of the country. But the town suffers not just from unemployment, but also from the kind of planning that looks wonderful on the drawing-board but is hell to live with. Father Michael McKenna, who, when I met him, was working on Archbishop Worlock's staff in Liverpool, had been leader of the Catholic Team Ministry in Skem for fifteen years. 'Every time they built a new estate, some idiot had another bright idea. Planners should be put against the wall and shot: they have no concern for the people. The disaster of Skem was that it was built on an island: no one crossed its boundaries. It wasn't a town, but a group of villages.' A Labour councillor said: 'There was no democratic control: every crackpot had free range for every fashion and whim.'

Each of these 'villages' – of which Digmoor is one – is separated from the others and from Skem's 'centre' by the elaborate road network, designed in the grandiose days of 'Wilsonia' for car-owning citizens. The footpaths were not entirely ornamental, but they took the lazy, decorative, planners' route from A to B, with the result that the carless citizens of 'Doletown' walk almost everywhere on the roads. I was told before I had had a chance to see for myself that it was only the skill of local drivers that prevented wholesale slaughter, an observation I had put down to hyperbole. At dusk that evening I was amazed to find mothers pushing prams in the fast lanes of the town's dual carriageways, and gaggles of people marching straight across major roundabouts.

After a few hours in Skem I also drove with the presumption that the roads are as likely to be occupied by pedestrians as by motorists. It is perhaps a blessing that strangers seldom do find their way to Skem, or road fatalities would indeed be substantial. (There is on Merseyside a general and dangerous contempt for cars: Liverpudlians dart across streets with little regard for the traffic. I always drive through the city prepared to slam on the brakes at a second's notice. Careless pedestrians were noted by J. B. Priestley more than fifty years before: he reported that on his way from the city boundary to the Adelphi Hotel several 'had started up not three yards from our radiator and slithered about as if bent on suicide'. Perhaps the cavalier attitude towards the roads has to do with the seafaring traditions of the area.) Obviously, not everyone in Skem walks all the time, and, in the absence of private cars and a decent bus service, taxis do a roaring trade. There are more black cabs outside the Concourse, Skem's shopping centre, than one would find outside the Ritz. Mothers, shopping baskets on wheels, kids, push-chairs, fathers, grannies, are all loaded aboard for the journey home. The plain stupidity of the town's layout was summed up by a clergyman: it was, he said, 150 yards from the front to the back of the ecumenical centre, centre, but by road it was two and a half miles.

Another disastrous planning legacy was the design of many estates. Presumably believing that people raised in slums would only be happy in back-to-backs, the planners re-created something of the street structure of the industrial north, with the results that the view from one house is frequently the back of another, that people walk directly past each other's windows, that the houses open on to complex warrens rather than on to streets. Such a layout is bliss for vandals and almost impossible to police. Finding my way through the warrens became a game of skill. People living a few yards away with the same street address often cannot help the stranger. Even with a decent map I allowed five minutes between leaving my car and finding the front door I wanted: in the dark it was safer to make that ten.

Most of the houses are poorly built; some genius even thought that flat roofs were appropriate in a region of gales, rain and snow. A professional plumber and do-it-yourself enthusiast – he had been out of work for most of the previous four years, so had had plenty of 'doing-it-himself' time – showed me round his house. Where he had repapered five weeks previously, the black stain of damp was already showing through; there was no roof insulation, so he was putting in false ceilings to create some protection against outside temperatures, and the recently redecorated bathroom was green with mould – Don't worry,' he joked, 'the fungus won't get you.' Many homes were prefabricated in now discredited factory-built systems. I was told that twenty million pounds was to be spent curing basic design faults. Ashurst, the most popular estate – least vandalized and cleanest: it bears almost no physical resemblance to the rest of Skelmersdale – is the exception, comprising traditional, brick-built houses, laid out along residential streets.

When Skelmersdale was still the promised land, you had to be vetted and to have a job within a twelve-mile radius before you were allocated a house. 'You had to *earn* your place in Skem,' said a Labour councillor. One family told me that their previous home in Liverpool had been inspected for cleanliness, and their finances were checked to ensure they were not in debt. Local Skemmers, appalled at the prospect of people they regarded as Scouser riff-raff being dumped on their doorsteps, were reassured with these 'precautions' at public meetings. One original inhabitant remembered the slogan

'No Scum for Skem' from those days. But after the town's economic collapse in the mid-seventies, there were no jobs to come to: the Skelmersdale Development Corporation at that time had empty houses on its hands and no takers. So the rules were changed, people were allowed in who hadn't got jobs, and they were drawn from a wider area. Existing families complained that Skem became a dumping-ground for problem families and unmarried mothers. A former member of the Development Corporation told me they were caught 'between the devil and the deep blue sea', and decided that it was a greater social evil to have empty houses than it was to have problem families.

The do-it-yourself plumber's one moment of employment in the previous four years had been on the necessary task of whipping radiators and boilers out of houses the moment that tenants quit, and putting them back as the new tenants moved in. (All empty properties in Skem are heavily boarded, but even so vandals frequently smash their way in. It is the knowledge that there is nothing worth stealing inside rather than the boards that deters further breaking and entering.) That was in the winter of 1985–6, and he was able to observe that the tenants leaving were usually conventional families, while those coming in were often unmarried mothers. The plumber's own teenage daughter had unmarried friends who had become pregnant and been offered three-bedroomed houses. 'Good' families bettered themselves by coming to Skem, and then bettered themselves further, either by getting out or by moving from a run-down estate like Digmoor to an area like Ashurst. Turnover in Skem is high – a Digmoor doctor estimated that he lost half his panel every two years.

But if Skem's housing is poor, its social problems chronic and its layout idiotic, its amenities are wretched beyond compare. There is no hotel, nor so much as an ordinary café. The health authorities had closed a Chinese restaurant, and the premises had become an 'amusement' arcade. There were a few run-down fish 'n' chip shops. I met a Londoner who had come from a poor area south of the Thames, where he had been accustomed to having takeaway food shops on his doorstep. He was amazed in his new home to find that he couldn't slip out for a hamburger at nine o'clock at night. Skem's two outlying shopping centres were dismal: the busiest shops by far were the sub-post offices, where supplementary benefit Giros were exchanged; queues formed long before they opened. In one there was a rack of worn, cheap second-hand clothes in a corner. Jumble sales were advertised in nearly every window. Graffiti were everywhere, painted, scratched, etched into concrete, drawn, spray-gunned. Most of them were simple names, assertions that in this abandoned town in the middle of nowhere there were human beings who could define their existence on walls, doors, stairways. Sometimes there were plus signs between the names – 'Donna + Frankie + Cheryl' – as if together they could mean something, could make a difference. The competing graffiti were mainly concerned with football – Everton and Liverpool being as much a passion in Skem as they are in Walton or Anfield.

The centre of the town is the Concourse, a white hangar-like construction which houses the town's principal shops. It is connected by an overhead metal walkway to Whelmar House, the hub of 'Dole-town' in that it contains all the essentials – the Housing Department, the Job Centre, the DHSS benefits office. Teenagers with white, pinched faces, inadequately clothed against a biting wind, pushed babies across that clanking walkway, while below, the black taxis hooted and jostled. I sat in the Concourse, watching bored youths trying to set off bangers. Middle-aged women clutched plastic bags – 'You'll be impressed at Presto' and 'Buy British at Norweb' – and gossiped, ignoring both the youths and a tiny old man, with sunken cheeks, a cloth cap, a white tieless shirt buttoned at the collar, a filthy, cheap overcoat, worn black boots. He clutched a stick and stared into the middle distance, a survivor in a world not of his understanding.

The shops were paradoxically cheap, yet expensive. They were cheap in that they catered for poor people, so goods tended to be flimsy and second-rate: they were expensive because their customers comprised a captive market. 'You could boycott a shop in Liverpool that charged too much: you can't here,' one woman said. Even petrol cost more in Skem that it did in the neighbouring town of Ormskirk – only half Skem's size, but affluent enough to stimulate competition. Poverty emasculated Skem. There was no point in starting a small restaurant, marketing higher quality goods, or providing a new service. Ten per cent of nothing is nothing. In the depth of winter, Skem offered its citizens a choice between television at home or the pub – you couldn't even 'window-shop' in the evenings because the Concourse was sealed off, and all other shops heavily shuttered. The local cinema, the 'Première Film Centre', appeared to be closed.

The first pub I visited was a desolate barn, with Liverpool soccer pennants, faded and dirty, pinned above the bar. It was two o'clock in the afternoon, and a few youths were playing pool without much heart. The red, vinyl seats were split and slashed in several places. Someone had scribbled a list of 'coming attractions' on a board – 'Bobby Buzz, brilliant singer' and 'Randy King, brilliant vocalist'. A jukebox played 'Talking About My Generation', a song written for another generation than the one whose representatives leaned here upon their cues. 'They all try to put us down, Jus' because we get around.'

Two analogies were inescapable in Skem, the wartime evacuee and the new world emigrant. It must have seemed to many of the original 'woolly-backs' that they had been invaded not just by a few slum children with labels in their buttonholes, but by the entire alien population of the Mersey docklands. Pasty-faced young people still looked as if they had slum air in their lungs. Alongside ruddy, raw-boned Lancashire farmers, they seemed anaemic and weedy. They were the descendants of generations who had been overworked and underfed, and who lived in polluted, unhygienic environments. It will take further generations to breed inherited disadvantages out of them. I asked a health administrator whether, if you took a control sample of northern industrial workers to California and offered them everything they desired, their grandchildren would still be physically inferior to people with more favoured ancestors. He said he was sure they would be. Each generation of worker throughout the industrial revolution and well beyond, he said, was punier than the previous one. When we measured men for war, we found startling differences between classes. Edwina Currie's exhortations to cut back on chips, beer and cigarettes were aimed at people who, if they dined alternate nights on steak and salmon, never smoked and restricted themselves to one glass of decent claret daily, would still have a shorter life-expectancy than their distant Surrey cousins.

Many who came to Skem had the spirit of emigrants. They were getting out and they were getting on, creating a new life for themselves and their children: they went with some of the expectations and trepidations with which families leave for Australia. The plumber who fought the bathroom fungus, Barry Nolan, and his wife were such a pair. When the good life in Skem juddered to a halt in the mid-seventies, they actually did emigrate to Australia – twice! In the early days Skelmersdale had been all it had been cracked up to be. 'I had umpteen jobs, me. If I lost one, I'd get another the next day. That's how easy it was,' said Mr Nolan. In the early seventies he was earning £100 a week with an American-owned company, and bought a house outside Skem. He was later sacked by another firm, after a row over pay. He won his case at an industrial tribunal, but, he claimed, was blacked in the town. He'd get a job, only to have it withdrawn at the last minute. So the family departed for down under.

After an initial shock – the converted barracks in Adelaide where they were first housed were nothing like the 'come hither' brochures – they had a successful first stay. 'We expected another England, and found a country more like America. We had a ball. I had a job I would give the world for today,' said Mr Nolan. They returned on holiday to Skem, and Mr Nolan took a two-year job helping to build the last estate at Ashurst. His Sydney job was kept open for him, but, when he returned, a friend persuaded the family to go instead to Perth, and everything went wrong. Back in Skem, Mr Nolan had been unemployed for most of the four years since, though he was about to start on his own as a heating engineer.

Politically, the Nolans were torn. They were buying their house, and were sure that salvation for the litter-strewn, dog-fouled warren in which it was situated was more home-ownership, and the pride that created. Mr Nolan was a pillar of the residents' association, which was investigating ways of blocking off entrances into the warren, restricting entry to those who lived or had business there. But Mr Nolan was also convinced that under a Labour Government he would work again. His own house – apart from the persistent damp – was immaculate. His wife said: 'We have been very low, but there is always someone worse off than you. Barry has his hobbies, the garden, the garage. I live for the house. We're not ones to sit and watch TV.' It was a defiant little speech, but a sad epitaph on the lives of two determined people, still in their early forties, who had 'emigrated' three times.

The Nolans told me a story that could be taken as a parable. When Skem was in its infancy, a number of thorn bushes had been planted behind the row of houses in which they lived. The idea was to beautify the estate. However, in the fullness of time the bushes became a dumping-ground for all manner of rubbish, black bags spewing forth orange peel, detergent bottles, coke cans. The bushes grew and their thorns became fierce, deterring stout-hearted council workers from clearing up the mess. The authorities told the complaining residents that it would cost £500,000 annually to trim all the bushes across Skem to a size that would make them penetrable by rubbish men. The residents had a brain-wave – why not rip the bushes up, a once-for-all cure? So it was done, and now rubbish bags are easily retrievable from the waste ground where the bushes once stood. Mr Nolan was very proud of the residents' association's part in this – 'These people,' he said, meaning the council, 'are paid to think these things out, not us.'

The thought occurred to me that, since a great many members of the residents' association were able-bodied unemployed men, perhaps a more positive solution would have been to have organized a rota of bush trimmers amongst the residents, who might at the same time have cleared the rubbish. Michael Caine, the actor, returning to Britain in late 1985, made such a point. He castigated people who sit in council houses watching the wallpaper peel away while waiting for someone else to stick it back. 'It never occurs to them to buy a pot of paint and do it themselves.' He added: 'People say the most extra-ordinary things: "When are *they* going to get me a job?" Who are they talking about? God?'

Frank McKenna was twenty-four, a local young man charged with a task that might have daunted the great social reformers of the nine-teenth century. He was Skelmersdale's Community Development Officer. Previous generations of officials who bore such titles had got it wrong, he told me, which I was quite prepared to believe. 'Community work in the seventies was rubbish basically, professionals try-ing to impose their ideas. We're trying to do things the other way round, and see what they want, give people more say in how the town is run.' That also I was happy to accept: in the 'them and us' divide, the people of Skem were clearly 'them', vulnerable to the best inten-tions of 'us'. Mr McKenna's own family story illustrated how diffi-cult it is to build a community amongst people living in a workless new town.

His parents moved to Skem when Frank was seven, and the town was still 'Wilsonia': 'There was no vandalism. We had a three-bedroomed house, with a car port and a back garden, which was unheard of. There was a brand-new, excellent primary school.' However, his father, who had been 'on the buses', had patchy work experience, moving once to Devon, and once back to Liverpool. Eventually, tired of the vagaries and emotional strain of the Skem labour market – 'wherever he took a job, there was always talk of redundancies' – he left for good for Milton Keynes. He could not believe the dramatically better economic environment he found there: for the first time in his life he had a choice of jobs and could change when he wanted to. He has had, said Frank, 'four or five jobs through personal choice. In Skem you grab and hold on to a job.'

Frank spent eighteen months writing plays, and had two produced. He was married at nineteen, and realized there was more to life than the dole. A BBC series – 'The Boys from the Blackstuff' by Alan Bleasdale – influenced him enormously. 'They were real; said more in five plays than the Labour Party has said in five years.' Despite that, he joined the Labour Party, and took a job as a community worker in a Skem secondary school. 'What can you say about the youth of Skem? They have absolutely no hope. Apathy in schools is unbelievable: it's bred into the town to such a degree that you fear for the future. Kids see no incentive. They argue "What's the use of working? Towards YTS? That's slave labour, and after twelve months they kick you out." It sets in as early as the first and second years.' (Later I noticed a pamphlet displayed in the Skem public library: 'LEAVING SCHOOL? A Guide to Social Security.' A Labour councillor told me that teachers meet what amounts to a physical barrier when they try to persuade children that they must have qualifications for the distant day when things will pick up.)

Mr McKenna's strategy in Skem was to build residents' groups, make his presence felt through campaigns – one residents' association had just succeeded in getting gas connected to their estate, and, with central heating, at last had a hope of drying the damp from their houses. He sought eventually a federation of residents' groups, with whom the council could negotiate. 'People have been passive too long. Councillors seems to think that the people aren't interested. They are, but they need a way to get involved.' One of his main problems, he said, was building up the confidence of the unemployed. Mr McKenna, a tall, thin young man with a sharp, birdlike face, had the sardonic Scouser sense of humour. The local bus service had long been atrocious, he said, but was worse since de-regulation. 'Profiteers go where the profits are, and basically there are no great profits in Skem. If you could work out a route that went straight to the dole and back, you'd make a fortune.'

Belonging to Skem, he said, was bad news outside the town. People at conferences would say 'you poor bugger.' Local kids identified with Liverpool. Teenagers were turned away from Wigan discos when they gave a Skem address. 'Go for a job interview, and God help you if you are from Skem,' I was told. Mr Nolan, the plumber, was going to use an 'Ormskirk' telephone number for his heating business, rather than a 'Skelmersdale' one – the two towns have the same code – because people 'class Skem as cowboys.' The residents of Ashurst, the unvandalized estate, once tried to change their postal address. And I was told that the director of finance for the West Lancashire District Council, a man charged with handling millions of pounds of public money, had difficulty getting his cheques accepted because his house – although outside the new town – had a Skelmersdale postal address. Twenty years on, the Skemmers still bitterly resented the Scousers. A third-generation local GP told his retirement party: 'The main change has been the building of Skelmersdale new town, which has effectively ruined the area. I think it is a case of bad planning. It has brought with it a considerable number of undesirables, and spoilt the Lancashire nature of the area.' He was talking about his own patients.

Crime is a major problem. Burglary victims do not in the main live in middle-class suburbs but in places like Skelmersdale, where there were burglar alarms on the £10,000 homes of the unemployed. The police were not greatly respected. Mr McKenna had recently issued a press release reporting on a residents' meeting, which had been told that 'between 8.30 p.m. and 10.30 p.m. there were only four policemen on beat patrol throughout the town'. Residents reported that police cars drove off when stoned by youths, and that officers responding to a complaint did nothing when their own car was violently rocked by the troublemakers. 'What astonished one most was that none of the residents was at all surprised by these revelations. All the residents' associations seem disillusioned with the town's police force', Mr McKenna wrote.

A young man, who had once considered enrolling as a special constable, was walking home in the early hours of the morning a few hours after the birth of his first child. He had drunk lager with friends – less than a can each, he said – and in his hand he carried a plastic bag containing disposable nappies. He was two hundred yards from his front door, when a police van screeched ('American-movie style') to a halt beside him. He claimed he was pushed around – he felt in an effort to provoke him – and finally thrown in the van, charged with being drunk and disorderly, and locked in a cell. He was convicted –

his word against three policemen's – and has lost much of his former faith in the police.

A close observer of the town's police said: 'The police have given up on Skem, which festers like a bad boil – particularly vandalism. The force is under strength, and the easy way out is to drive around in a panda. People want to bring back the bobby on the beat: fifty yards into one of the housing estates is a difficult environment for the police. There is cynicism on both sides. The police have limited faith in the people of Skem as honest British citizens: they are conditioned to believe that vandalism and hatred of the police are the norm. The people then don't have much faith in the police.' While I was there, a senior policeman issued a statement to the local paper, complaining that the force received very little public co-operation. 'On many occasions people are witnesses to offences, but for one reason or another seem very loath to give information to the police. We have been told by people that they know who is involved, but will not tell us about it.'

I sought an interview with the town's superintendent, but after several calls was asked to submit my request in writing, together with a questionnaire, asking such things as 'Are there particular difficulties in policing a new town?' I could visualize the minimal return for the time involved, and desisted. The superintendent was the only person in either Liverpool or Skelmersdale who declined to see me.

The town's politics are complicated. As I have described, it is essentially a one-class community, of semi-skilled, Labour-voting Liverpudlians. The 'missionary' professionals live in the centre of the community, and a few other professionals – like some of the town's Indian doctors – live on a small estate of Californian-style housing. (A white-collar semi-professional, who bought a new town house when Mrs Thatcher's sale of council houses policy took effect, stayed only two years. 'It wasn't a place to come home to after a hard day's work. You could feel the depression and the poverty. There was nowhere to turn to.' He estimated that seven of the first fifty buyers had been white-collar workers, but that very few of them had stayed.) The town therefore always returns a fistful of Labour councillors, but they remain a minority on a Conservative district council which is largely elected by rural voters and Merseyside commuters who live in the surrounding countryside. If the town had grown to its projected 80,000 population, the people of Skem – and therefore Labour – would have become the majority, and the boot would have been firmly on the other foot.

It was a microcosm of the national political picture: a Conservative administration ruling over hard-core socialists. But in Skelmersdale there was mutual tolerance, respect and understanding of a quality that has been absent from the national dialogue for a generation. Even Frank McKenna, a committed Labour supporter, conceded that the town's Conservative masters – about whom he had previously heard nothing but ill – were prepared to listen. It was also refreshing that no one beat about the bush. Out of politeness and deference to residents' sensibilities, I had approached the town's problems somewhat crabwise, but very soon my interlocutors would be talking about 'unmitigated disaster' or 'the most unsuccessful new town in Britain.'

The council leader was an avuncular, white-haired, retired educationalist, named Robert Hodge, who had been a member of the Development Corporation. Skelmersdale was first thrust upon his council in 1974 – he felt largely because neighbouring authorities didn't want it. 'I'm not sure that the new town concept was ever achievable. I doubt it. I don't think you can just pick people up and dump them in a new environment and expect them to grow into a satisfactory community. It was probably doomed to failure,' he said. He sympathized with Labour's resentment at being controlled by people not only not of their party, but also not from the town. 'We accepted we had a duty to understand their problems, which encouraged us to listen to the councillors from Skelmersdale on issues like housing. They are the voice of the area. Our people listen with a degree of acceptance, more than would be usual. Skelmersdale has different problems from those we are used to.' I tried to run those sentiments through my head in Mrs Thatcher's voice, and failed.

He had to persuade his colleagues that Skelmersdale needed help over matters that people in settled communities took for granted. Village halls, for example, run themselves: Skem required a Frank McKenna to get community associations into being. Mr Hodge had been to bat for Skem against central government, arguing in vain that it should retain its urban priority status, worth an annual £250,000. The money had been spent on smartening up amenity areas and putting right some of the worst eyesores. 'It might sound peripheral, but I don't think it is. The Government argued that urban aid was being spread too thinly. Something that looks thinly spread from Whitehall or Westminster doesn't look so thinly spread from our end,' he said, adding that a community like Skelmersdale might not have as many projects or people in need of help as Bristol or Birmingham, but it could still have the same depth of problems. Mr Hodge told me that the council had refurbished one clapped-out estate, replacing factory-built walls with traditional brick, tearing down vandalized garages, and blocking up basement areas where rubbish was dumped. Problem families, who used to be concentrated in this one area, were spread around other estates. The result had been a considerable improvement in the morale and physical appearance of the estate. It was thoroughly 'wet' talk.

In the days when Skem was an urban authority in its own right, it had, I was told, pioneered the 'loony left'. A council leader had protested against a royal visit by sitting prominently on the town hall steps chewing a chip butty while the royal personage passed by. The current leadership of the group belonged, I was further told, to the 'cuddly or Kinnock' left. The four leaders I met were anxious to convince me that Skem's reputation for bolshy workers was a slander on the town. They handed me a report – 'Skem: The Broken Promise' – to which David Sheppard, the Bishop of Liverpool, had written a sombre introduction:

Once claiming to offer its people a new and better way of life, [Skelmersdale] now embodies the human results of the collapse of manufacturing employment, the regional and local concentration of economic decline, and the wholesale redundancy of manual and unskilled workers . . .

Skelmersdale is special in being in the travel-to-work area with the highest unemployment rate in the north-west and in having its own story of promises broken and hopes dashed.

The report refuted a national press claim in the seventies that 'the town's troubles were the result of militant trade unionism . . . and the mud of that campaign has apparently stuck'. It cited findings by the then Development Corporation that in Skelmersdale 'the loss of industrial working time was only one-third of the national average figure'.

Almost everyone in Skelmersdale contended that companies had abused the regional grant system that had lured them to the town. Incoming firms received 22 per cent of their capital costs. The allegation was that as soon as a company had been in the town long enough not to have to repay the money, it engineered a reason to get out and shipped its machinery elsewhere. I was told that plant removed from Skem factories was in full production not just in south-east England, but also in Sweden and Portugal. Councillors had grown cynical about businessmen riding into town with a fistful of promises. They told of one man who was going to employ 1,200 people manufacturing buses and lorries. 'What that company was going to do for Skem and the razzmatazz were nobody's business: everyone was talking in the pubs and clubs. The Job Centre was inundated with requests for job applications: in the event, the company didn't even put in a lightbulb,' said one of the councillors. (The vehicles were to have been for Nigeria, and the potential deal collapsed along with the oil price, after which the firm could no longer get an export credit guarantee.) 'It's wrong to lift people's hopes up. We take it now tongue-in-cheek. We tell them "We're with you buddy, let's go." Three weeks later they often have gone – straight down the M6 to London!'

The councillors, after some hesitation, did acknowledge that Skelmersdale's lack of skills was a problem. Entrepreneurs researching the town found that it lacked the necessary skill base. But, said the councillors, capitalists only have themselves to blame, because they 'refuse to take responsibility to train the kids up'. The result, as they admitted with the candour that I had come to recognize, was that Skelmersdale had a 'social security culture. A vast amount of the money that circulates in the town is from Giro cheques and pensions. We are not in a position where we can take off.' That speaker was Councillor Frank Riley, an unemployed librarian, who had been working on another of the reports on Skelmersdale – 'People in Need of a Future'. He said: 'The days of Thorn and Courtaulds have gone. Skem was the creature of central government: *they* owe Skem.'

The Revd Deryk Evans, superintendent Methodist minister, who wore a large silver cross over a blue smock, gave me some gritty figures about the sort of problems he encounters. Although Skelmersdale comprises only one-third of the West Lancashire district, it has 55 per cent of the mentally ill and half the referrals to child psychologists. We met in his comfortable, cluttered study – pipe racks, squash rackets against the wall, the *Guardian* on the floor. Mr Evans came into the ministry from industry, and had been three and a half years in Skem after thirteen years in Swindon. He found the contrast between the affluent, naturally expanding Thames Valley and the artificial north-western new town overwhelming. On a visit to Swindon a few days earlier he had 'broken down and cried' in a shopping centre that 'was bigger and wealthier than the whole of Skem put together.' He looked at the fine things and prosperous people, and remembered 'cheapy Skem shops with stuff that won't last three months.' He began our conversation with the usual dose of brutal honesty: 'Skem was badly conceived and badly planned; an inner city population dumped fifteen miles away on a community that did not want it, and have gone on not wanting it and hating it.' Even the existing churches rejected the newcomers, he said. 'The essential planning problem was aggravated because hardly had the town begun to grow when every kind of tragedy happened ... Soon we shall have a ghost town populated by ghost people.'

The phone rang. It was a parishioner in some anguish, and Mr Evans counselled in jocular, broad-brush terms – 'God does not promise pastures ever new. He says: "There's a stony path – get on up it" ... stop taking your spiritual temperature all the time.' The caller, he told me, had a dilemma. He was intellectually frustrated through lack of education. Now in middle age he had an opportunity to take a degree; but this would mean his family suffering yet more financial hardship. What should he do? If he gave up the degree he would not become the sort of person he ought to be. It was a question of 'wholeness'. 'In Skem,' said Mr Evans, 'there was very little chance of people being whole.'

He listed some of 'Doletown's' more obvious afflictions. The single parent family: 'no fun living in a terraced house with mum and dad out of work and rowing. "Sod this," they say, "I'm off." In Skem they can get a flat and £800 to furnish it – a small fortune to them.' The workforce, thirty thousand Scousers: 'semi-skilled, because that's the only thing Liverpool has offered in the past hundred years – stevedore work. Where in the technological, microchip world do they fit in?' Depression: 'Valium is part of the barter economy – six for a pound.' Unemployment: 'We do have a rush-hour – seven minutes at four o'clock.' He told of visiting a woman, who excused herself at the sound of a car engine outside and went to the window, peeping through the net curtains. When she returned, she explained that she liked to watch the only employed man in her street leaving for work. Mr Evans was preparing an 'I love Skem' campaign with leaflets and stickers. He professed to love it himself: 'I'm glad I'm here. I laugh all the time – I've never beaten a Scouser verbally yet; never put one over. And I've tried very hard.' But he added that if he had not got colleagues, he would face 'burn-out'. Trying to improve things is to beat your head against several brick walls at the same time. 'Only BFs come to work in Skem, and thank God for them.' He spent an hour every week watching people's faces in the Concourse. 'Resources are needed to enable them to become full human beings and not just highly frightened people.'

A young man, who had been unemployed virtually since he left school, told me his routine. 'If I got up at the normal time, I had everything done by 11.30. So I was getting up later and later, usually about lunchtime.' He went to the Job Centre, then to the library – 'a different four walls' – then bought the ingredients for the tea he would make his wife when she got home from work. The greeting in Skelmersdale, he said, was not 'How are you?' but 'Got a job yet?' He had married at twenty, which at first had given him a great boost, but he later had difficulty paying bills, and had nearly been evicted. Skem had thousands like him.

The town's public assets are the responsibility of the Commission for New Towns (CNT), and – unlikely though it might have seemed – 'Doletown' was being 'privatized', by selling factories and houses to tenants; 26 per cent of the houses had already been sold. What hope there was for the future lay in these developments, and people were beginning to assert pride in their properties. Some industrialists showed their faith by putting their money where their factories were, proving they had no intention of crating *their* machinery and flitting from town. The CNT, charged with disposing of the town as quickly as possible, was pouring money into the rehabilitation of the shopping areas in order to make them saleable.

There were other hopeful signs. A small number of people – some, in their own words, driven by 'necessity' – were starting businesses, though there was a shortage of suitable factory units for them to grow into. Mark Sheeran was twenty-five. He had trained as a welder, but had not worked since a brief first job, though he had earned seventy pounds a week for a year as a twice-weekly 'resident' disc jockey at a club – which was more than most of the available Job Centre vacancies paid. Two of his aunts had married Chinese men, and the family came together for Chinese banquets. With time on his hands, he himself began cooking, experimenting with spices. He would go into Liverpool to get his ingredients, and Skem friends started to give him orders – perhaps £200 worth on one trip.

'I thought, "Hello, hello, hello. There might be market for it," ' he said. That was two years before I met him, and he had spent the intervening time preparing himself to go into business; buying and selling Chinese ingredients. He had been on a course, caught up on a maths deficiency from his school days ('came maths Friday afternoons, I always had a headache,' he said), and prepared a business plan. Raising money had been difficult and time-consuming. Enterprise schemes would say, 'We'll give you "x" so long as you first get "y" elsewhere.' With no experience, and living in rented accommodation, he was starting from an unpropitious base. He had wanted a shop, hoping to be able to offer employment to others, but had been disappointed. 'Waiting for suitable premises, with no money coming in, I was beginning to feel it would never get off the ground,' he said. However, after market research and trial runs testing the market – he had put advertising leaflets through doors – he was convinced that Skem and the surrounding district could support a business operated out of his home. He would also sell equipment, such as woks.

One of the grants he did finally get was from a fund under the patronage of the Prince of Wales, and he had met Prince Charles and Princess Diana when they visited Skem. The day before I met him he had got his first chequebook, and was a few weeks away from his official launch. 'It's a great boost to be able to hold your head up. I had never a wink of sleep last night, I was so excited,' he said. He had bought an answerphone, and was about to get an estate car to make his deliveries. Skem might not have seemed a natural market for his 'Spice and Things', but his business plan had obviously been impressive, and a local enterprise trust had put its faith in him.

However, Skem was designed for the industrial workers, not as a nursery for future captains of commerce and manufacturing, or even for purveyors of spices and woks. It would in any case, as a Labour councillor pointed out, take about one thousand small businesses to mop up the town's unemployed. (Thorn and Courtaulds who had pulled out eleven years earlier had employed 1,600 each.) There were a few schemes to train school-leavers with marketable skills – an Information Technology Centre and 'Tomorrow's People Today' – but they could not help more than a minority of the better motivated teenagers.

My last day in Skelmersdale was a Saturday, and I arrived early, just as a wintry sun had broken through thin clouds of differing greys. There were very few people about: a boy cycled across a footbridge, silhouetted against the pale morning light, a man with a fishing rod and basket waited by the old town's war memorial for a lift, a young woman stood by a bus stop. Beyond the 'New Jerusalem' flats, the dark hills rose towards Ashurst Beacon, inviting a brisk morning walk. At the town's edge, birds chirruped and whistled – it was seven days to St Valentine's – and the first snowdrops had appeared in the gardens of the small professional enclave at Elmer's Green. For a moment, 'Doletown' was transmuted once again into 'Wilsonia'. I drove slowly back towards Digmoor, but the illusion was shattered even before I reached the estate's wretched row of shops: a large mongrel was defecating outside the Up Holland Labour Club – or, as the sign said, the 'UP HO LAND LAB U   CLU '. I turned east and took the road to Wigan Pier.

Warehouses around the Wigan canal basin have been renovated, and now house the 'Orwell Bar and Restaurant', a gift shop, and an exhibition showing life in the year 1900, 'The Way We Were'. A plaque said that the Queen had opened the refurbished quay. The work had been carefully, if a little preciously, performed – like Covent Garden in London or an American historical site. Some feel strongly that turning Britain into a museum merely emphasizes the country's decline, yet it seemed that morning that the Wigan waterfront was a preferable place to be than Skem. But it is easy to succumb to images.

Across the water from 'The Way We Were' stood a terraced row of houses, which appeared from their battered and boarded backs to be uninhabited. I walked across the bridge, and past a renovated mill, to have a closer look. The houses were all occupied, and from the front window of one an elderly woman stared hopelessly at the traffic that flooded past her door: the ground shook under the weight of lorries. Her living conditions could not have improved greatly in the fifty years since Orwell. 'The Way We Were' scarcely needed a museum.

Barry Nolan, the Skelmersdale plumber who had tried his luck in Australia, had said: 'The working man's biggest downfall was the finding of the oil. At one time they used to depend on the working man. Now, with this "Big Bang", they don't need him any more.' Those who are no longer wanted have been dumped in reservations like Skem, stacked in high-rise flats in the inner city, or left where their grandparents were, in shoddy terraces. The moral failure of Mrs Thatcher's Government is not that it tries to encourage wealth creation, but that it has abandoned its responsibility for those who lose out during a period of such fundamental change. Robert Hodge and his Conservative councillors understood their liability for a

community not of their making, nor of their liking. Mrs Thatcher
and her Conservative Cabinets – with honourable exceptions like
Peter Walker and Michael Heseltine – have applied the same competitive laws to the dispossessed as they have applied the BMW
brigade.

The door to the George Orwell Restaurant was open, so I went in
for a coffee. I was met by a short, toothless cleaning woman of about
sixty, polishing the new brass. 'Coffee's seasonal,' she said. 'There's
no call for it at this time of year, and the bar's not open till a quarter
to twelve.' 'Could I at least use the toilet?' 'Yes, nip in the ladies. I'll
keep watch. There's someone doing something to the urinals.' She
told me on my return how the cotton bales used to be loaded from
this building on to barges, and how the railway lines ran from the collieries to the waterfront. Each had had its own little pier.

Did she, I asked, know of anyone who remembered this George
Orwell, in whose honour she was polishing brass so faithfully? She
looked dubious 'George *Formby* now, "senior" that is. They liked
him. They've got his picture upstairs.' 'Wigan Pier' was Formby's
joke, not Orwell's. Formby was owed the last laugh.

⧽❨ 9 ❩⧼

A LITTLE LEARNING

Knutsford is an ancient and comfortable market town, twenty miles south of Manchester. Its name comes from 'Canute's (or Knut's) Ford' – water clearly had a compulsive attraction for the good king. The town was billeted by Prince Rupert's marauding army during the Civil War, and was the 'Cranford' of Mrs Gaskell's novel – the town centre, with its surviving cobbles and arches, and the heath facing the Georgian Gaskell home would still be recognizable to her mid-nineteenth-century neighbours. Its two narrow main streets – Princess and King, known locally as 'upper' and 'lower' and studded with classy clothes boutiques – indicate the affluence of many of its modern residents. A few miles away Jodrell Bank telescope tilts towards the heavens, and the town and surrounding villages provide, in country houses, up-market corporate head-quarters for several national companies. Other professional and business people commute to Manchester.

But to the east – past a green shed on which a freshly painted sign intriguingly offers 'clog-mending' – a Manchester overspill estate called Longridge borders the tamed Cheshire countryside. Its residents have been plucked from the dingier Manchester slums, and at night many congregate somewhat morosely at the Falcon Bearer pub, the estate's sole amenity. When news reached one drinker that his wife had been rushed eight miles to hospital after a fire at their home, he stoically held his ground at the bar – there was still half an hour's drinking time, and why waste good beer money on a taxi? – reasoned this transplanted Andy Capp. While I was there, a senior policeman announced that, after a local crime, they always searched first for culprits in Longridge, which may have been good policing practice, but was shocking PR. The estate was up in arms.

There is little to bind these disparate communities together. The overspill residents find the town's bijou charms alien and expensive;

while prosperous Knutsfordians seldom head their Volvos or
Porsches beyond the executive estates in which the town nestles,
unless perhaps to drive a cleaning lady home. Two Englands exist
cheek-by-jowl, yet – with the exception of a few people coming
together in one common institution – see or know as little of each
other as they did before the town planners ripped up the Manchester
terraces and exported the tenants. That binding institution is Knutsford County High School, the town's comprehensive and only
secondary school, which lies a few hundred yards beyond Mrs Gaskell's home on the opposite side of the town from Longridge. Across
the open fields one can just hear the distant hum of the M6; a more
severe blight, suffered by rich and poor alike, is the unholy din of
planes labouring into flight from Manchester Airport. It was to the
school that I had gone to investigate whether the comprehensive
ideal, so bitterly denigrated by so many, could – in circumstances
that gave it a sporting chance – stretch the bright child and fulfil
the dull.

The comprehensive conundrum lies at the centre of a web of
national anxieties. When my family was about to come home from
the United States one insistent question peppered the inquiries of
our relatives and friends. 'What,' they asked, 'are you going to
do with the children?' The question was swathed in layers of
unspoken thought, touching class, 'standards', political philosophy,
accent and aspirations. Nowhere has such a deep seismic fault opened
in Britain as that between State education, symbolized by the horren-
dous populist caricature of the comprehensive school, and private
fee-paying schools, which are building as fast as they can to cope
with swelling demand. More than forty years after the 1944 Education
Act had promised decent secondary education for all, British children each morning depart to thoroughly separate experiences,
so perpetuating differences between us which are no longer even
quaint.

Businessmen and industrialists, pragmatically concerned more
with the quality and abilities of school-leavers than with the nature of
the system, know there is a gathering emergency. The week I returned
from Knutsford, Sir Peter Parker, the former British Rail chairman,
called for a 'war cabinet' on education. 'Somehow we must see the
educational crisis in terms of a national emergency . . . disaster stares
us in the face for the 1990s,' he said, pointing to the critical shortage
of first-rate teachers, especially in maths, the early school-leaving age

in comparison to Britain's industrial rivals, and the failure to educate adequately the least bright forty per cent.

None of Mrs Thatcher's Cabinet educates their children in State schools. A teacher wrote to me: 'Those responsible for administering and financing the system have decided that it is not good enough for themselves ... would you buy a Ford car if you knew that *all* Ford managers bought Japanese cars?' The gulf isn't just in quality, but in kind, as if working- and lower middle-class children still do not require the critical intelligence and cast of mind that most professional people wish for their own children.

Although, by the time I began this inquiry, one son had completed a year in a comprehensive, I felt I was little wiser about whether these schools – to which more than nine out of ten British schoolchildren go – 'worked'. So much of the concept and the practice was alien to my own distant experience at a famous public school a quarter of a century ago. There and then the aim had been – in monastic isolation – to turn out people with an education which would prepare the best to be top civil servants or lawyers. Such an education takes a tight grip on the psyche, not as strong as the Jesuits' grip, but real enough. Surely, our prejudices tell us, one cannot be truly 'educated' without learning large chunks of Wordsworth or Shakespeare by heart: 'poetry' now means free-form composition without rhyme or scansion – my eleven-year-old son thought that if you put a capital letter at the start of each line, you were a poet; and an educated man is one with Latin tags at the tip of his tongue. But a comprehensive – taking children of every ability and origin – cannot be expected to provide the high flyer with the environment of Winchester or Manchester Grammar School, or to achieve on behalf of its pupils all a grammar school did and more. Comprehensives are new beasts, not yet fully fashioned, and certainly not yet fully understood. It does them a grave disservice to judge them for what they are not.

The casual evidence is startling in its contradictions. There was the sixteen-year-old girl at Woolworth's, eight months on the job, without the self-confidence to look a customer in the eye, monosyllabic, and inefficient to the point that I had to suppress a strong urge to shake her. She had an infuriating way of expecting the customer to know the procedure – perhaps because she was too inarticulate to make herself understood – then muddled her own part, so that minutes were wasted while a supervisor came to sort out the nonsense she had made of her till entry. She was, my son told me, a former pupil of his school. With such examples in mind, a British teacher, who had worked much of his life in the United States, wrote to me asserting: 'The neglect of education in England, except for a thin line of the truly privileged, is perhaps our supreme national disgrace.'

Yet at Oxford, where I had gone to report Olivia Channon's death from a heroin and alcohol overdose – not a good advertisement for schooling of a very different sort: her drug problems were said to have started at a public school – I met well-adjusted, bright former comprehensive students, who swore by the system that had educated them. Indeed, a radical chic had seized the university, and 'cred' points were gained for not going to the 'right' school. No one, I was told, was more determinedly proletarian that the Wykehamist leader of one of the university's main Marxist groups. It was bad form to embarrass public-school boys by quizzing them on their educational origins.

But the difficulty in seeking dispassionate information about comprehensive schools is that it is impossible to find a typical school, and hard to find a representative one. In inner cities I could have visited 'sink' schools – though these are seldom measured against the problems with which they must contend: some of the apparently crazier manifestations of anti-racism, for example, are sincere attempts to cope with schools where well over half the pupils are black or brown. In the depths of Surrey, on the other hand, there is no doubt a comprehensive school exclusively peopled by the children of accountants and stockbrokers. What I needed was a school that had enough advantages to give its pupils a fighting chance, while it was not so exceptional that it would instantly be dismissed by the agonized reader with the thought 'of course, if I lived there I'd have no problems with the local comprehensive.'

A friend had alerted me to potential comprehensive school disasters. His own two daughters had gone to a well-considered London comprehensive – ironically, he had pulled strings to get them in. He told me: 'Violence was endemic with middle-class kids – the "melons" – being picked on as individuals and attacked as groups.' One daughter got caught up in a murder case – a former pupil killed another – and was threatened by the killer's sister, who was in her class, when she had to give evidence. His second daughter 'joined a group of disaffected punk kids who didn't work, played truant, took drugs, went shoplifting, etc., and finally dropped out of school altogether.' Another parent wrote a moving article in the *Guardian* about her own son changing from 'a willing, enthusiastic child to a surly, unhappy individual, who didn't want to get up in the mornings.' She quoted a poem by her son:

> He is the outsider
> The one they all mock
> He is the one they can't accept
> Just because he is different
> Because he works hard
> Instead of talking
> Because he's interested
> In school work.
> He gave up in the end
> He just wanted to stay at home.
> I was that outsider
> I was the one they couldn't accept
> I was the one they mocked . . .

Knutsford was suggested by John Tomlinson, Professor of Education at Warwick University and a former Chief Education Officer for Cheshire. He is a passionate and committed man, who might do wonders for the image of State education if he got the sort of media platform offered to the glamorous heads of big public schools. (Even the *Observer* invites public school rather than State school headmasters to write on the problems of the State sytem.) Our collective anxiety over comprehensives, he pointed out, 'is that the ideal runs counter to our national tradition and philosophy. Society is hierarchical and divided, while the schools attempt to treat people of differing abilities according to their needs in a common community.'

Such is the tarnished standing of the media with many teachers, I knew I would have to persuade the school I chose that I did not have horns and would not be making a beeline for kids smoking on the playing field. The Knutsford head, Mike Valleley, was nervous: 'What "control" would he have?' he asked. Three of his senior colleagues wanted to veto my visit. They were fearful that reporting the continuing effects of the long teachers' dispute – at that time officially over at least for a while, but still causing the senior school to be locked at lunchtime because of lack of staff cover so that children wandered the town centre – or mentioning scarce resources would cost them students. Mr Valleley was terrified of litter being featured: 'It's the one thing the local press will seize on.' But he clearly saw that exposing his school to a writer was a test of self-confidence that he and the school ought to be brave enough to take.

My first (and later confirmed) view was that Knutsford could stand the scrutiny. It became a comprehensive in 1973 through the amalgamation of two secondary-modern schools, each standing in generous playing fields – Mr Valleley, like an eighteenth-century landowner, was master of all he surveyed – and linked by a path that runs between a field of clover and pleasant suburban gardens. The town never had a grammar school: eleven-plus scholars had had to travel. As well as drawing children from the town's divided communities, the school takes pupils from outlying villages, so the school's catchment area is socially mixed. Although a quarter of local parents pay for their children's secondary education, the school is 'comprehensive' in that it is the only State secondary school, takes both sexes, and educates pupils to A Level.

A sixth-form block and sports facilities (which include an indoor swimming pool and are shared with the community) were added to the former boys' school – now the upper school. The newer, former girls' school – now the lower school for eleven- and twelve-year-olds – has such thin floors that it frequently sounds as if indoor hockey is being played upstairs. Paint has been at a premium since the school's opening, and the litter – as in most schools – blights the grounds. But there are well-maintained lawns and shrub gardens. In the autumn sun, as teachers' voices drifted through open windows, it seemed a positive and congenial school in which to pass one's youth and learn. Children are well-mannered – no bowling strangers over in the long corridors – and usually wear smart school uniforms. (Sixth formers are allowed mufti – jeans, sneakers and T-shirts. Several of the staff are distinctly snappy dressers. One senior woman would have perished at the thought, but she would have looked in place on a Conservative platform.) Discipline, I sensed, was not a great problem. At one assembly I attended, five boys were singled out for having played hoaxes on parents, including one with a heart condition: the offence was being taken as seriously as it would have been at any school. Sanctions include detentions and suspensions, and I was told that the school would not hesitate to remove a child who was a disruptive influence.

Knutsford has just under 1,300 pupils, two hundred of them

'refugees' from a neighbouring authority that still has selection, a number of whom passed the eleven-plus. The mother of one such boy told me that, ironically, they had moved to the selective area because they once thought 'comprehensives were the bottom of the heap'. Now, having rejected the old-fashioned limitations of their local grammar school and the divisiveness of selection, they are 'terribly, terribly impressed' by Knutsford. The two hundred incomers have buttressed the school against the worst effects of falling rolls, which, in causing widespread school amalgamations and closures, add to the national crisis of morale.

Mr Valleley, who had been at the school since 1981, was the son of a Manchester printer. He is married to a senior county education official, and was a potter by training. He is a neat, fastidious man, who wears sharp suits and coloured shirts with contrasting white collars. Almost his first act on arriving at Knutsford was to refurbish his office – 'it had looked like a National Insurance office' – leading to staffroom jokes about the 'presidential suite'. Local public relations became a priority. 'What was presented in the classroom was sound and good, but the physical environment wasn't as attractive. The school didn't have status in the community. The public needed to be told "this is a damn good school. I am quite prepared for us to be compared to anyone,"' he said.

While Mr Valleley persuaded his governors and colleagues to accept me, I talked with pundits and friends, worrying the comprehensive question back and forth. In my mind I had a model of what ought to be achievable – the standards and character of the traditional American high school, for the United States has built an extraordinary democracy on schools that educate all the children in a community. A decent common education has been a central part of the American heritage. Yet the British, with our self-deluding superiority to most foreign things, sneer at American standards. ('I seldom find that American practice is relevant to what we do here, Mr Chesshyre,' a local authority administrator had said to me a few days after we returned.) Two American friends in London had taken their children away from British schools (one private, one State) and sent them to the American School because they found their children uncherished and British teachers unresponsive. One said: 'Mary had only been at the American School for a week when I heard her singing in the morning. I suddenly realized that she hadn't sung like that for a year.' The other, who had sent her daughter to an English school for five years, said she was at last able to conduct a proper and equal dialogue with teachers. The English school had kept her at arm's length.

American schools are more accessible to parents, and American children are maturer and more self-confident than their English contemporaries. In the States fourteen-year-old boys look one in the eye and speak up: here they shuffle and mumble, or remain silent despite being bowled slow conversational full tosses. One British child – recently returned from the States – was selected for an inter-school current affairs quiz. He had mugged up the newspapers, and his team had swanned through. His parents noticed that he was far more casual in preparing for the next round. Why? they asked. Because, he replied, we'll win if I just glance at the headlines. Within a few weeks of getting back to the Britain, the boy's desire to do his best had been blunted.

So what was going wrong? Society, through politicians and the press, was devaluing the system, which itself, in places, appeared bent on suicide. As a rule of thumb, private education was portrayed as good and State education as bad. 'Me first' had become an acceptable philosophy. In such a climate what could be more re-spectable than 'to do one's best for one's child'? Indeed, it was self-indulgent to do otherwise, and almost public-spirited to educate a child privately. Did not the nation need thoroughly educated citizens? By paying, parents could ensure it got them, and at the same time relieved the burden on the public purse. In education it was to be BMWs for those who could afford them, and a clapped-out, erratic public bus service for the rest. More fool he who waited at the draughty bus stop when he could afford a car.

Almost weekly some crazed teacher or administrator threw raw meat to the eager press. Certain education authorities appeared deter-mined to promote homosexuality, Marxism and a brand of anti-racism that replaced 'Baa baa black sheep' with 'Baa baa green sheep'. An enthusiastic headmistress at a primary school banned the egg and spoon race as too competitive, and sports fields grew dandelions or were sold as building sites. When the BBC announced it was taking the jaded radio programme, 'Top of the Form', off the air, right-wingers refused to believe that the decision had anything to do with programming. It was axed, they said, either because the competition was too cut-throat for pinko BBC tastes, or because children were now too ill-educated to answer the questions. The satirical radio show, 'Week Ending,' had a mock contest between Che Guevara's and St Mugabe's comprehensives in which everyone won, regardless of whether they knew the answers.

'How the dream of comprehensives turned into a nightmare,' I read in the *Daily Express*. 'Twenty years on, the chickens are coming home to roost ... a growing number of parents, politicians, academics and pundits are passing judgment on the all-in system ... and they are finding that it has failed.' The *Sun*, determined to promote sound cultural values amongst its readers, complained: 'Britain's comprehensives are coming out bottom of the class.' These perceived failures lay, according to such papers, at the heart of many of our national ills. The *Sun* (in an article on education) had discovered 'the emergence of a new breed of young thug seemingly unaware of the difference between right and wrong'. (The old breed presumably knew, but ignored, the difference.) A Government minister said in the aftermath of one soccer riot: 'Our teachers have much to answer for.' Even the Education *Guardian* ran an article under the subsidiary headline: 'Whenever I hear of a criminal brought to justice I always feel the real criminals go free.' The 'real criminals' were, of course, the teachers.

My own first dealings with the school to which our children would be going were dispiriting. In America our eldest son had been in classes with children eighteen months older than himself. Back in London, he faced repeating a year of schooling. Accustomed to American flexibility – there was often a three-year age span in classes – we challenged this ruling in order to prevent him losing momentum. The school claimed it hadn't the authority for such a decision, thereby illustrating why fee-paying schools have been able to pinch the word 'independent' to describe themselves. (A senior teacher told me that the education authority made no exceptions, and would even separate into different years identical twins born a few minutes either side of midnight on 31 August, the crucial cut-off date. It was so clearly untrue, and implied such a contempt for parental rights and concerns, that I have never been able to take that particular teacher seriously again.) I next had an interview with two borough officials, a young assistant director who appeared to agree with much of what I had to say, and an older woman. Each time the young man got close to conceding a point, his companion would intervene sharply, like a sheepdog attending to a straying lamb. 'Mr "X" has not been with the authority long enough to interpret our policies,' she ruled, her mouth snapping shut with a determination that eventually silenced us both. Although she would not move my son, she would, she said, inform the school of his academic standard – which obviously I had already done – so that he could be placed in suitable subject sets. Nothing happened. He spent the next eight weeks tediously working his way through the system, before arriving, somewhat disenchanted, in his final groups.

A year later my second son, in the company of a lively bunch of children from his primary school, entered the same comprehensive, borne along by a sense of excitement and curiosity that was, if anything, heightened in his first few weeks. He would come home bubbling with enthusiasm for what he had been doing, shoving his exercise books under my nose before I could get my coat off. The phone became a hotline as his friends exchanged notes on homework. He auditioned for *Oliver*, and got a place in the chorus, was selected for his year's soccer team, and embarked on community projects. I could not have imagined anyone making a more positive start in any school.

However, in our London borough 28 per cent of children do not go to local authority schools. In our street the figure is far higher: each morning the Volvos – yes, they usually are – sweep up and remove the neighbourhood children, some of them tiny things in elaborately striped blazers, caps and ties. Of course, those parents have the right to pay school fees, but how many of them give the alternative any thought? The head of a prep school in a town near Knutsford, who had himself sent a daughter – now at university – to his local comprehensive, told me: 'Many parents have made up their minds. They do not realistically assess what the comprehensive might offer. They don't even go and take a look.' Then he added with a smile that, since his livelihood depended on their business, he wasn't complaining. But I do. Every time a child is withdrawn from the State system, that diminishes the national drive to have the best. It is death by a thousand drop-outs.

Paying school fees assuages the consciences of the very busy. A friend, a television news correspondent and a workaholic, whose wife also works, decided that they couldn't give their children the additional support that he believed State education would require. Although he is such a strong Labour backer that I once suspected a future Labour Government might elevate him to the House of Lords and make him a minister, he felt none the less it would be unfair for his children not to be at the sort of school that – as he perceived it – took care of all their needs. He certainly escaped the agonizing over whether to speak up when things go wrong that similar people who do choose State schools often go through. These are the solid citizens who devote an immense amount of time to their schools – dispensing wine and cheese and organizing the annual fête – yet do not have the impact on what takes place inside the school to which their commitment should entitle them. They suffer from English reticence, but also enter a subconscious conspiracy not to draw attention to things that go wrong. They have a doubly vested interest in the school's reputation, which they fear will be damaged if unpleasant truths are aired. Their child is at the school, and their judgment is on the line. They do not wish to give succour to those who might say 'I told you so.' But their inhibitions deny them any real say in how the school is run. In the United States there is no invisible line on the ground beyond which parents may not step; Parent–Teacher Associations are formidable bodies whose function is not simply to raise funds for mini-buses. British teachers like to talk of 'partnership' – they reject the concept of parents being 'consumers' of education, because that relationship presumes rights which most teachers would not be prepared to concede. But the present partnership is chronically unequal.

A few days before John Rae retired as headmaster of Westminster School, I talked to him about the introduction of the General Certificate of Secondary Education (GCSE). Dr Rae, now director of the Laura Ashley Foundation, which gives grants to educational causes, was almost apocalyptic in his perception of what's happening to our State schooling. 'We are in danger,' he said, 'of getting a larger and larger semi-educated mass, while economic prospects grow worse. The fabric of social life is beginning to crack.' He added: 'Not enough State schools are well run, work smoothly or have good teaching. They go on about new exams, but the reality, for God's sake, is that the teacher doesn't keep order. Teachers are badly paid and under-respected, déclassé . . . pseudo-intellectuals. Too many have a chip on their shoulder and see parents as a threat.' When reported in the *Observer*, these remarks provoked the predictable wrath of teachers. But the poor morale of teachers is a consequence rather than a cause of the chronic unhappiness within British schools. Dr Rae asked: 'Are the British at heart afraid of releasing the potential of all their children? I think they are. We are still essentially rather aristocratic in our concept of society. We still don't believe in the great mass of what we used to call working-class people having the talent or ability to do anything other than unskilled jobs or play football. We fear a society in which we tap the talent of this great mass, because it is going to threaten our secure middle-class set-up, and it might threaten our rather cosy cultural elitism as well.'

Historically, schooling was rationed in Britain: so many first-rate educations for our leaders and colonial administrators, a few more second-rate for our managers and business people and fifth-rate for the rest. Anything better for the masses might create discontent or even political instability. Why clutter with dangerous nonsense the head of a man whose allotted role in life will be to dig ditches? ('Education,' declared a nineteenth-century MP, 'would enable [the poor] to read seditious pamphlets . . . and render them insolent against their superiors . . .')

Now we have potential instability for the opposite reason. Not enough Britons are adequately educated to fulfil their own aspirations or the necessary tasks of a high-tech society. Our rivals streak ahead because they do not suffer from damaging inhibitions about the potential of people. The Japanese will produce 400,000 more qualified engineers than Britain in the next five years. A Japanese engineer/craftsman is likely to start work at twenty-one rather than at sixteen. In West Germany, shop-floor engineers are considered 'professionals'. Many British children who do get a good education get the wrong one – too narrow and academic; but the broad majority leave school with stunted imaginations about their own possibilities, bound for an uncomplaining, but often unfulfilled, existence. A small minority – the notorious 'yobs' – emerge unscathed by learning, hostile and aggressive.

In his book, *The Challenge for the Comprehensive School*, David Hargreaves, chief inspector for ILEA (Inner London Education Authority), conjures up a telling image of what goes on in the back rows of our worst classrooms. Through the eyes of two average girl students, lessons are like 'very dull television programmes, which could not be switched off'. Occasionally the programme was interesting or loud enough to catch their attention, but never for sufficiently long for them to grasp the essential elements of the plot. 'The girls had lost track of the story long ago . . . they talked through the broadcast whenever they could ... the easiest form of resistance was to treat the lessons as background noise which from time to time interrupted their utterly absorbing sisterly gossip.' Mr Hargreaves concludes his apposite metaphor: 'In many respects it is a marvellous anticipation of their adult roles, where features of school will be replaced by the noise of a factory, the intrusions of the supervisor's exhortations, the monotony of unwanted routine jobs.' It is not surprising that attempts to converse with them are doomed. The majority of American school-leavers are, by comparison, stimulated rather than daunted by school – most of them having survived and thrived until they are eighteen.

The educations Mr Hargreaves wrote about are an assault on the self-respect of children. He added: 'In response [to this assault], the pupils set up an *alternative* means of achieving dignity and status by turning the school's dignity system upside down.' Hence yobbism. Dr Rae ended with the words: 'Do we have to believe in some racial theory whereby the Japanese are born better at maths? It is a well-worn cliché that the most vital national resource is the people. In practice, it's a fraudulent claim. If we pursued our latent human talent with the drive and energy with which we pursue North Sea oil, wow, think of it! Then you really could say "the British are coming".'

Another fraudulent concept is 'choice' as a remedy for poor standards. Further choice, as outlined in the 1987 Conservative manifesto proposal to allow schools to 'opt out' of local education authorities – giving mobility to the already mobile – would lead to greater polarization between the best and the worst in the schools. Those who could 'work' the system would do so, adding another tier of opting-out parents to the six per cent who now pay: the children of those who couldn't exercise that 'right' would be more thoroughly segregated in sink schools. Choice, said Mrs Joan Sallis, the national organizer of the Campaign for the Advancement of State Education, means that he with the longest arm reaches the highest shelf. 'It is a nice word for a nasty process.' A few parents are candid enough to admit that choice is about advantage – the right school tie, influential friends, an acceptable accent – as well as about a decent education. Put crudely, people pay school fees to get their children ahead in the rat-race. A stockbroker, responding to a survey, was honest: 'Everything is at the margin. I believe that the school will give my son a 5 per cent better chance, and he may just need that 5 per cent.'

Mrs Sallis, a ruddy-cheeked woman who looks like a farmer's wife, is a beacon for parents who are privately concerned that the stockbroker may have got it right. She stomps the country encouraging parents to start support groups for State education, and fires them with her own example – all three of her children, products of State education, have succeeded in markedly different ways – one as a high-powered mathematician, one as a garden designer, and one as a personnel officer in the NHS. Mrs Sallis comes from aspiring working-class Welsh stock; her father was a coalface worker for forty years. Education for her was the route to better things. There were always two fires lit in her home – one for the family and one for the children doing homework.

She became a civil servant and was bound for the top when she decided that raising children is a full-time pursuit. 'I wanted to deliver every spoonful of egg myself.' When her children were still young, she moved to an affluent London suburb, and was 'morally shocked' to find that local schools were 'a soup-kitchen service' in comparison with the fine parks, public buildings and lavish private homes. 'The attitude was that people who used the schools presumably couldn't afford anything better, and therefore ought to be grateful. "If you can't afford private schooling, don't grumble. If you can, you opt out." As a well-dressed, well-spoken, caring mother, I was regarded as a lunatic to be using the local schools,' she said. Mrs Sallis possesses a determined Welsh egalitarian spirit, which makes her hostile to the privileges and snobbery that are inextricable from private education. 'There is no more class-ridden country than ours,' she said, 'and no other country has such prestigious private schools: they provide not just an education, but a passport to a way of life. We grovel before people who are meant to be socially OK.' (An American friend living in London said: 'A sixty-year-old gets an important new job, and the first thing the papers mention, for God's sake, is what school he went to.)

Mrs Sallis also objects to fee-paying schools on educational grounds because many of them work on the principle that 'academic success is the only sort worth having.' In 1986 the historian Corelli Barnett, who argues that public schools – by creating an out-of-date elite with a soul above industry and commerce – are responsible for our industrial decline, told members of the Headmasters' Conference (the body that represents public-school headmasters): 'For bring Britain down as a trading nation.'

more than a century, your schools have done much to bring Britain down as a trading nation.'

Certainly when I was at such a school, only those who 'failed' academically entered industry. One boy, interviewed by a small family firm, was asked almost exclusively about his golf. The owner wanted a congenial companion, not a whizz kid. The business went bust a few years later. Middle-class parents are still gravely embarrassed by children who 'fail' in the conventional sense. How often you get, as Mrs Sallis said, 'a long spiel' why Sarah is a hairdresser or Charles a decorator. No other country has these hang-ups: Americans would expect such children to win out in their chosen careers, and become millionaire hairdressers or decorators.

Recently, I met a middle-aged architect, who in the fifties had been a pupil at Tulse Hill in south London, one of the first comprehensives. He was transferred there from a technical school and, in his own opinion, would today be a carpenter but for the stroke of luck of Tulse Hill opening on his doorstep. 'For the first time,' he says, 'I was trusted with control over the design of what I was doing.' That trust opened a new world to him. Thirty years later, we still agonize whether comprehensives can bring the best out of bright children. Now that 90 per cent of secondary-school children attend such schools, surely it is time to be positive. Even the few who are educated elsewhere must live amongst a majority who will go to comprehensives: private school alumni don't travel in separate compartments on the Underground. Barbara Simons, a deputy head at Knutsford, said: 'Every child has a birthright to go to a "good" school. If your child doesn't feel it is a good school, you have taken that right away from him.'

People who are sensible in all other respects fall prey to the endless propaganda pumped out about comprehensives. A well-spoken woman at a local action meeting on State education could hardly contain herself. 'What does one do?' she asked desperately, 'with that amount of panic and fear? What does one say to the people who are not here, who are sending their children to private schools?' A 'Good Schools Guide', published by *Harpers and Queen*, caught the tone of the social forces at work. 'State school pupils are sloppy, spotty and *louche*,' while 'in private schools, manners are good and the pupils are clean and polite.' Almost every action taken by Mrs Thatcher's Government, from the assisted-places scheme – which, even if one believed in its validity, would, in Dr Rae's words, be like 'trying to cure a famine by taking a few children to lunch at the Ritz' – to the proposed Crown Technology Colleges, has been an assault on the resources and self-esteem of the comprehensive system.

The head of an academically successful comprehensive was told by Sir Keith Joseph, then Education Secretary, that it was necessary to have 'centres of excellence'. 'Did he not realize that we're sending scientists to Oxbridge? What happens to our standards? Didn't he know of the academic achievements of comprehensives?' the head asked in despair. He added: 'The Government indulges in massive bloodletting, and then expresses surprise that the patient is anaemic and lacking his usual energy.' Measurable standards – passes at O and A Level, for example – have risen gently, but consistently, since comprehensives were introduced. The total of successful Oxford candidates from State schools in absolute terms now matches that from independent private schools.

Political pressures on what goes on in the classroom receive a massive amount of media space. In a minority of areas these pressures are real enough. One head teacher, who asked to remain anonymous so as to avoid retribution, told me: 'I am attacked because I have a "grammar school" ethos, whatever that means. Is it because I fight to prevent standards collapsing? There is now an inverted value system. Anything that corresponds to what successful schools used to do must be bad. "Standards" are the encrusted imposition of bourgeois values, and we who pursue them are assailed for "betraying the system". We are expected to apologize for pupils who do unusually well.' He had even been attacked because his school was praised in print for standards of behaviour that might be found in a public school. His was not an area where one would have expected a political assault on good schools. (Another head – responding to, rather than resisting, such pressures, but otherwise apparently sane – told me that he never advertised Oxbridge successes to the rest of his school, 'lest we seem to value that student more than, say, the capable musician'.)

The besieged head continued: 'Ideologues love to see things in confrontational terms, as if high standards for some impoverish the rest. It is a dangerous notion that the English don't need to compete and defeatist to think we should simply aim to be at peace with our own social engineering consciences. It is no good fudging the issue. Everyone has to know that he will only succeed the hard way, by being

genuinely competitive. Precision is necessary to be a surgeon, a manufacturer of engineering equipment or a sports star. Alternative
attitudes are a sad reflection on beliefs in the potential attainments of
comprehensive children.' The several heads of comprehensives and the
educationalists I met – perhaps because not protected by anonymity –
were not so forthright, but they subscribed to the same philosophy.
The unnamed head always teaches at least one bottom ability group
himself, and savours achievements like getting a semi-autistic child
through one CSE. Education, he said, is bedevilled by having to fight
the battles of twenty-five years ago. Parents, politicians, administrators look back to when they were at school, which was either a
golden age, and therefore to be restored, or a nightmare, the last ves-
tiges of which should be destroyed. Many of our most influential
citizens were the successful products of grammar schools. Often they
forget the failings of yesterday's system – the high drop-out rate at
sixteen of working-class pupils, the misery of the eleven-plus, the
appalling provision for those who failed it. Even exam results were less
shining than we remember: in 1960 research by the National Union
of Teachers found that 25 per cent of grammar school pupils left
with fewer than two O levels, and 50 per cent left with only four – yet
these were the 'selected' academically bright children.

A Knutsford parent from a small Welsh town recalled grammar
school boys fighting secondary-modern boys on the common that
divided their two schools. Each regarded the other group as foreign
and hostile – as green men from another planet. The eleven-plus institutionalized two societies, separating children inefficiently and divi-
sively at the age of eleven. The comprehensive pioneers rejected such
divisions. Professor Tomlinson, of Warwick University, said: 'If you
mix people thoroughly, you will introduce the bright not only to an
understanding of practical problem-solving, but also to appreciate
that people who operate in that way make just as effective a contribution to society.' His vision is of a better society: 'The ideal is to
develop people to the maximum of their capacities, and prepare them
for a diverse culture in which all are valued and give service. "I am an
individual with a personality and skills to develop, so are you." So
relationships are built on negotiation, not on power and aggression.
Successful economies grow in societies with strong social cohesion,
where management and shop-floor are not at one another's throats.
We do not have a generous view of each other. We believe in limited
potential, especially of those who do not dress or speak well.' I dis-

covered a Japanese saying when I visited Japanese factories in Scotland: 'It is better for one hundred men to take one step, than for one man to take a hundred.' The English have long worked on the opposite thesis.

Even the word 'comprehensive' is a liability, conjuring up a largely discredited era – tower blocks, Harold Wilson, new towns, plate-glass town halls and 'white hot' technology. To the British, 'equality' instinctively means levelling down; the creation of a grey, uniform society along East German lines, not the dynamic release of potential, which American equality strives towards. Belatedly, we have tried to undo the terminological damage. Local authorities call their systems 'all ability' or 'secondary', and individual schools replace the word 'comprehensive' with 'high'. If we had only called them 'high schools' from the beginning, maybe the name would have assuaged British snobbery, and we might have had a fighting chance to create community schools like those of our democratic rivals.

We forget now, so extreme is the debate over comprehensives, that they were created to cater for enhanced public expectations, rather than to satisfy the whims of left-wing Utopians. George Walker, the head of The Cavendish School, Hemel Hempstead, and formerly a moving spirit behind the York-based Centre for the Study of Comprehensive Schools, is also one of twelve State heads co-opted to the Headmasters' Conference. He said: 'Twenty years ago people had colour televisions and enjoyed foreign holidays. The expectation of a better school went with that. It was unacceptable to have all that material advance, and still get a letter saying that your youngster was going to the secondary-modern down the road.' The first stage, reorganizing schools, was widely accepted. In the play *Gotcha*, one part of the trilogy *Gimme Shelter*, written in 1976 by Barrie Keeffe, the anti-hero, a yob about to leave school with such an undistinguished record that not a single teacher appears to know his name, complains bitterly about 'this lovely comprehensive', where the head speaks Latin to the sixth-formers. 'Great school – great school,' reflects one character, 'going around talking in Latin all day. Great – that's the way to get your head smashed in in the factory.' For those who could make it, unlike Keeffe's 'Kid', it was a more optimistic age: pop stars, sports players, television personalities were creating a new breed outside conventional class divisions. Comprehensives were part of this break with the past. State education, the faithful believed, would become so good that virtually everyone would opt for it.

Wilson borrowed Hugh Gaitskell's phrase 'grammar schools for all', which offended educationalists trying to create a new type of school, but reassured the middle classes. It was Mrs Thatcher, when Education Secretary, not the much reviled Shirley Williams, who signed the most comprehensive reorganization orders. In those early years, schools were trying to teach children of all abilities according to a syllabus created for the top 25 per cent. Schools within schools developed. The urgent need was to devise curricula to cope with schools that contained future Oxbridge scholars at the next desk to children destined for Youth Training Schemes. The best State schools began to move from the world of pure scholarship to one of democratic citizenship. Parents – and editorial writers – who had themselves been to selective schools became alarmed. Their children did not know who the Younger Pitt was, so they shot off to school meetings to find out what was going on. There they were assailed by jargon from teachers who seemed reluctant to let them get too close to the school. All professions, as Shaw said, are indeed a conspiracy against the laity. A second suspicion was added: not only had standards collapsed, but some form of unacceptable ideological manipulation was taking place. The system, it appeared, had been hijacked.

This was the agonized scene to which we returned from the United States – a lot of very concerned people fed nothing more solid than scraps of local gossip and blatantly prejudiced newspaper headlines. George Walker complained of the 'lack of serious intellectual discussion' about comprehensives, and that there had never been a Dimbleby or Reith Lecture on the subject, for example. The *schools* never won the hearts and minds of the people, and the *concept* never caught the imagination of the intellectuals.

My visit to Knutsford was an attempt to give classroom reality to some of these concerns. I was at the school for a week, far longer than any parent would be before making up his mind about whether to send a child, but not long enough fully to penetrate the hidden agenda that tells you what an institution is really like. The school fosters an obvious *esprit de corps*. Staff and pupils are proud and offer a visitor a positive image. (I was very aware of the dangers of misreading the school: a former teacher had told me how his very poor school had always successfully closed ranks when an inspection was due.) If any teachers, mainly themselves the products of grammar schools, had doubts about the practicality of the comprehensive ideal, they

hid them. Many had experience in other forms of school – grammar
and fee-paying – yet said persuasively they were totally convinced by
the strengths of comprehensive teaching. Frank Walmsley, the senior
deputy head, said: 'Comprehensives are vastly superior for most, if
not all, pupils. I am very clear about it. The more able are not at a dis-
advantage: they do as well, if not better, as in grammar schools. The
world has changed. A good comprehensive will broaden their horizons and widen their later opportunities.'

Knutsford teachers were cautious about trumpeting the school's
academic record, though most acknowledged that 'unfortunately' the
school's reputation was largely based on university and A Level successes. Seventy per cent of the children leave with at least one O
Level, 46 per cent achieve four or more, and 17 per cent – of the
original 'mixed ability' intake – leave with three or more A Levels.
The school has 165 in its sixth form, 135 of whom are studying A
Levels. Each year it sends a handful to Oxbridge.

I met a group of six sixth-formers – four girls, two boys – three of
whom were to try for Oxbridge. They were articulate, self-confident,
ambitious. The school, they said, mixed well socially, though there
was some bullying in the early days. They claimed they had more
confidence than if they had gone to private schools. One said she
might be a teacher because of the inspiration of her English teacher,
which made the others laugh. Most had concrete career plans – one
to be an economic geographer at the United Nations. A teacher told
me later that the sixth was very left-wing – much as his contemporaries had been in the late sixties – but the pupils claimed to be a mixed
bunch. One did say: 'They just sit there groaning about Mrs
Thatcher: it's really boring.'

They were egalitarian in their own behaviour, rejecting the notion
of prefects, for example. At a parents' evening there was voluble concern at this lack of pupil structures. (Many thought prefects could
supervise lunch hours and cut down on litter and smoking. Feelings
grew heated. The cry 'why can't they be like we were' was taken up enthusiastically.) The sixth-formers were aware of the shortage of
resources –'outdated history books with pages missing,' said one – and
argued that the Government ought to reorder its priorities: money for
schools, not defence. They were also censorious of their less diligent
contemporaries – 'some go through the school wasting their own and
their teachers' time and the taxpayers' money: it makes you mad.'

'Carol', a problem child, never made the sixth: in her early days at

Knutsford she was frequently truant. Her father (Manchester over-spill) draws a disability pension, and hasn't worked for many years. When I visited the family, he was stripped to the waist, exhibiting a fine torso and some elaborate tattoos. Occasionally, he was shaken by paroxyms of coughing. His wife said she missed the cosiness of inner Manchester, but he was all for the wide open spaces. If he could, he said somewhat unconvincingly, he'd be a sheep-farmer in the Falklands. 'Teachers are not old enough, and there's not enough corporal punishment,' was his view of Britain's educational ills. Carol twice tried to kill herself. In her fourth year she was enrolled in a school programme known as the Knutsford Community Certificate, which involves attending college half a day a week and working in the community. She blossomed, taking a responsible role on a residential week away from school – younger children thanked her for her help, the first time she had been thanked for an achievement in her life, working hard for six months at a local hotel, and qualifying for a three-year catering course. She knew what she wanted to do – work for an airline – and, against considerable odds, looked set fair.

The next night I met 'John's' mother in her modern 'executive-style' house. She and her husband are both graduates who went to private/public schools, and sent their children to Knutsford with some trepidation. John left with four good A Levels to spend a year in industry sponsored by a multinational corporation before university. A primary-school friend of John's – said to have been of equal ability – who went to a local fee-paying secondary school with a strong academic record, dropped out of the sixth form after one year and took a non-degree course at a college. 'I haven't heard of anyone at a private school who did better than John,' said his mother, whose daughter got three A Levels at Knutsford and also went to university. 'I would tell anyone to use that school. If I had another child and could afford fees, I'd still send him there.'

How can one school get the best out of both Carol and John? Are they exceptions? Do pupils in the middle without any obvious special needs get equally stretched? Is there a trick to teaching 'mixed ability' classes, which, if only those educated in narrow peer groups could understand it, would set the national mind at rest over comprehensive schooling? I spent much of my time at Knutsford trying to find answers to these questions, sitting in on 'mixed ability' classes and talking with teachers. The aim is clear and laudable, and the problem simply stated. At one end of the ability range is the stock

English figure of the professor who cannot change a light bulb: at the other, thousands of children leave school branded as 'failures' because the traditional academic courses offer them nothing. Michael Duffy, head of King Edward VI School, Morpeth, and a former president of the Secondary Heads' Association, told me: 'By being taught in the same environment, children have equality of esteem, opportunity and provision. It is not a question of levelling down: clever children are entitled to good teachers, but so are the others. By teaching high flyers and low attainers in the same context, we are equipping them for adult life in all its dimensions. Within the school walls we are hard-headed and realistic about different children's abilities to learn. The key is the right lesson correctly delivered.'

Looking back on a 'traditional' education, it is clear that, as well as much first-rate teaching, there was a great deal of boredom involved in learning things that were either rapidly forgotten – whither has fled all that maths and Latin? – or redundant. Most of us also had hidden experience of 'mixed ability' teaching in such subjects as woodwork. I was extremely bad at it, and chiselled away hamfistedly while some others turned perfect lamp standards on lathes. It never occurred to any of us that we were suffering because of the wide range of abilities in that group. So long as the instructor had time to get round us all, and attend to our needs, we were learning. Recently, I coached a 'mixed ability' soccer team, whose players ranged from kids who could kick the ball into the net with either foot from the edge of the penalty area to those born with the proverbial two left feet. It was fun, watching the children develop week by week, with no obvious disadvantages to either extreme.

At Knutsford all children start in the first year in totally mixed classes, gradually being 'set' in ability groups according to the nature of the subject. I attended a first-year French lesson. It was the last period of the day, the sun was shining, and rugby was being played outside the window. The teacher, Gary Frost, engaged the children individually, prowling the classroom. '*Tu habites une ville? Oui ou non?*' This darting technique kept everyone's attention, even those I had marked down as reluctant scholars. Everyone made a stab at one or two answers, or read words in French. The written exercise was to copy some statements – one girl had finished while a boy was painfully writing the first sentence – and then to use the same phrases to write about their own families. No one noticeably flagged. It would obviously become harder to give everyone the sense of being in the same race as the year progressed, and the bright began to accumulate knowledge. But French is one subject that is set by the second year according to ability. I would not have been unhappy to have my child start in that class. In fact, one was then in a similar group in his own school.

History is cited as a subject in which new teaching methods allow pupils not only to go at their own pace, but also to learn techniques of far greater value than the 'Plato to Nato' string of dates. The aim is to teach children to handle evidence – primary and secondary – and to apply that skill in, for example, testing the accuracy of what they read in the newspapers. John Cloake, a history teacher about to take a class of fourteen-year-old GCSE students, said: 'Our greatest asset is a child's natural curiosity. So much of education works against that. We are not here to provide the answers. If I did, they would simply be chasing my version of the right answer.' In his lesson, the children were studying the development of medicine. He wrote an open chart on the board, with spaces for explaining who treated illness, by what methods and why, in prehistoric, Egyptian and Greek times. The children were encouraged to relate those developments to what was going on in the wider contemporary societies. There were again painful discrepancies between the speeds (and neatness) of the pupils.

Later, Mr Cloake filled out the blackboard charts, drawing the answers from the children themselves. For homework – and I was told that these fourteen-year-olds would be expected to do about an hour and a half each night – they were to compare two contemporary Greek accounts of severe illness, and assess their reliability, accuracy and usefulness. 'I am not looking for a lot of writing; I am looking for a lot of thoughts,' Mr Cloake told the departing scholars. Again I had a son who was at the same stage on the same course. From what I saw and from what he told me, these lessons are a success.

Knutsford insisted that all pupils take one subject at GCSE that is not purely academic, which is a problem with many parents. Mr Walmsley, the deputy head, had a queue outside his office every 'options' night of parents needing to be convinced that their children can 'spare' the time from purely academic subjects. The school was strong in design and art – encouraged obviously by a head who was trained as a potter. They have had artists in residence; the spirit of one, said Jeff Teasdale, the head of the department and himself an artist, 'still walks in the department.'

It is the boast of comprehensives that they are better prepared than are many private schools for the 'new' teaching ushered in by the General Certificate of Secondary Education, the sixteen-plus exam, which is based on the skills of learning rather than knowledge – what you can do, not what you know. 'The pinnacle,' said Mike Oliver, a deputy head, 'is more demanding than O Level.' Teachers I met gloated over the difficulties they expect some private schools to have. One said: 'Their teachers are actually going to have to talk to children, not sweep in, deliver a lecture, and sweep out.' The gloating, however, ceased when the conversation turned to resources. GCSE is posited on an extraordinarily generous ratio of teachers, and in some subjects is inescapably demanding of equipment. Mr Valleley, Knutsford's head, told of an instructional video showing a geography field trip, in which four pupils are being assessed by two or three teachers. 'If we matched that ratio, we'd have to turn out the whole staff to assess our geographers,' he said. Every teacher had a version of that truth. GCSE is judged by continuous assessment. Who teaches the children while that goes on? Class sizes have been growing. Steve Ings, a young science teacher, spoke of the difficulty of getting round twenty-eight children in one lesson instead of the twenty-one he used to instruct. Mr Valleley said the school would get £8,500 over two and a half years for new books and equipment – sufficient for the school's bread and butter – instead of the £15,000 he would like. That shortfall is common to most schools. The PTA meeting that I attended was so concerned with this topic, which boiled down to the provision of books, that the chairman had to guillotine the discussion. A teacher crystallized the dilemma: 'What is the good of, say, a video camera, if you haven't got a spare body to take off a group of five or six to work with it?'

Knutsford had a first-rate teaching staff, young and enthusiastic – 'I thought,' said one, 'that I could do a better job than my teachers did for me' – quite happy, for example, to stay after school for a curriculum development discussion. (Mr Teasdale attended one two days after his wife had had a baby.) But the teachers were frustrated by limited resources and poor staffing levels. Several have compensated for the fact that nationally falling school rolls have meant fewer promotion opportunities by writing text books. Although many insisted that concern about money came after professional considerations, most obviously felt underpaid, and wondered where the next generation of teachers was to come from. Some complained that the children were spoilt. 'Left to themselves, some of these children wouldn't have the wits to live in a shed,' said one. He added: 'Teachers are not appreciated. The public thinks that we come out of university with our heads full of stuff that will last us for forty years. Parents want a lot for nothing.'

Mr Ings, whose two younger brothers – one an army sergeant – earned more than he did, said: 'I am worried that I am going to burn myself out. I get emotionally tired, absolutely exhausted. But we've all invested so much time in teaching, we can't afford pessimism.' Several said they were hurt by society's stereotyped view of teachers. Maggie Jones, the head of business studies, said: 'People make bland statements that teachers get thirteen weeks' holiday and finish work each day at half-past three. Nobody sees what it's like – the piles of marking that you're still poring over at half-past nine. It gets on your brain, and you don't switch off. I get into all sorts of arguments. We get blamed for so many things. Surely there must be blame for everyone.'

Miss Jones was one of several who did not resume taking sports sessions after the original teachers' dispute. Plenty of sports were taking place, but a widespread staff attitude seemed to be that if something was worth doing it was worth being paid for. Another teacher said that if parents wanted their children to play cricket, they should enrol them in a club, and not expect the school to provide teachers and facilities. The experience of the Thatcher years had turned them vehemently against the Conservative Government. 'The school isn't full of left-wing, radical Trotskyists, but you won't find anyone prepared to be an apologist for Mrs Thatcher,' said one senior teacher. A colleague said: 'The mandarin class is totally indifferent to the State system.' He suggested that instead of spouting 'unthinking nonsense', critics should come into school for a week. 'That would dispel their worries.' If we are to get good teachers, we will have to cosset them. A head said to me: 'If you had an eighteen-year-old, bright in maths, physics, computing or technology, would you encourage him to go into teaching? My God, no. You could probably count the number of physics teachers in training on the fingers of two or three pairs of hands.' Teachers no longer enjoy the status of revered community figures, equal in esteem to the vicar and the doctor. My grandfather, a Midlands grammar school head in the early part of the twentieth century, had enjoyed that kind of respect in his town. School then was still the source of all learning: now children enjoy positive influences like foreign holidays, but teachers also have to contend with the sad fact that many of their charges spend more time in front of television than in the classroom. A teacher wrote to me that the 'lack of social status' was as bitter as the 'constant denigration' in the press and the poor pay.

An educationalist told me that her 26-year-old mathematician son was already earning four times as much as he would have been getting as a teacher. The daughter of one of the senior women staff at Knutsford was paid as much as her teacher father within a couple of years of starting as a financial analyst. Joan Gregory of the Centre for the Study of Comprehensive Schools said: 'Those in the schools are the only teachers we've got, and if we don't pick them up and dust them down, then we've got troubles.'

No school can turn every sow's ear into a silk purse: there must have been 'Carols' at Knutsford who have fallen by the wayside, and 'Johns' who failed to fulfil their potential. I was constructively taken to task by an *Observer* reader after the paper ran a feature based on my Knutsford visit. She described herself as 'an old enthusiastic teacher', and accused me of writing a 'panegyric'. She pointed out that there was no side-stepping the hard work that was associated with academic success in selective schools. 'Everything will be boring for adults who, when young, were conditioned to be entertained without effort or concentration,' she wrote. 'The satisfaction derived from learning by rote your multiplication tables, or three theorems or King Harry's speech before Harfleur – and fearing the consequences of not having learned them – would, if still present in our comprehensive classrooms, just tip the balance in the matter of their survival.' But I can see very few people as thoroughly exposed as I was – whatever their prejudices – coming away from Knutsford or a similarly well-run school without believing that such schools *can* work. With more resources, greater public and political support, and a full range of children, they might do magnificently. As a nation, we cannot afford for them to do otherwise.

❧ 10 ❧

'A PLASTIC LOLLIPOP'

'K D' Patel sat in a red leather armchair with his feet tucked beneath him. The undone buttons at the neck of his white shirt revealed an enamel medallion on a gold chain. His toes peeped from the slip-on white sandals he wore beneath tropical slacks. His wife, Lata, petite and pretty in pullover, jeans and boots, served tea. She was, I was amazed to learn, a Labour member of Brent Council, which seemed about as probable as Sue Ellen being a waterfront organizer for the Teamsters. Her real-life presence was difficult to reconcile with the image of a demure, sari-clad woman, smiling from her election leaflets. We sat in one corner of a large, ornate room, in which the furniture had been pushed against the red walls, as it might be in the waiting room for a doctor who offered exotic cures for the illnesses of affluence. There were marble-topped tables, and peacock feathers in vases, pistols and swords on the walls, and a bright, floral carpet under foot. Occasionally K D burped loudly.

Everything about the house and the man was unashamedly ostentatious: lions rampant on the suburban Wembley walls outside, palms each side of the front door, two Mercedes in the driveway, a vast enclosed swimming pool and disco area at the end of the garden. The property was a statement: 'I have arrived. I have succeeded. You take me on my terms.' Facing the swimming pool there was a 'guest' house, a three-storey town house. The whole property, said K D, was worth £850,000: I would have put it higher. The garden was ornate, with, I read in a self-publicity brochure that K D handed me, 'symmetry reminiscent of Mogul Gardens'. Three Alsatian puppies romped between the white statues and the ponds. Mrs Patel's colleagues on Brent Council met beside the pool to plan a socialist nirvana for their electors. 'Wasn't this just a little lavish for the home of a Labour councillor?' I asked Lata. She laughed: 'I started on the petrol pumps: I am as socialist as any of them.'

KD's professionally printed biography, written by 'a freelance journalist based in London', was entitled, 'KD PATEL: A Flair for Fortune.' It opened: 'Businessman, philanthropist and patriot, Kantilal Dahyabhai Patel . . . a neat, unassuming man, clearly at peace with himself without appearing complacent.' Walter Mitty could not have commissioned a more pleasing work of self-aggrandizement. But the achievements it reported in such gaudy prose were real enough. From a cotton mill in Gujerat at the age of sixteen, via ruination at Idi Amin's hands, to a millionaire in London, with little but his native wits to propel him. His father had died in Uganda when he was a baby, and his illiterate mother had returned to her village in India. KD's first capitalist venture had been a sweet stall, then a wholesale business that had gone bust: he re-emigrated to Uganda in his early twenties, still with considerable debts to settle in India.

While I had been in America, Britain's high streets were galvanized by a group of Asian immigrants – many, but not all, from East Africa – who were behaving much as immigrants to the United States have always behaved. With vigour, enterprise and courage, people like KD, many of whom had arrived penniless little more than the day before yesterday, were revitalizing corners of the British economy. They did it at best in an atmosphere of complacent patronage – CBEs and unwinnable parliamentary seats for acceptable Conservatives; at worst against violence and prejudice that make life for a person with a brown skin in certain parts of Britain an inconceivable agony.

In 1972 I had covered the arrival of one identifiable group of these immigrants, the 27,000 Ugandan Asian sent packing overnight as the result of a dream by a bloodthirsty madman, whom the British never took seriously because he was large, roly-poly, awarded himself ridiculous medals, and who had served as a sergeant in the King's African Rifles. They were received here in a spirit of official pessimism. These people represented a 'problem': they would need housing, welfare, schools, they would form ghettos. The anti-immigrant poison spread by Enoch Powell coursed in the public veins. Edward Heath's Government was unequivocal in accepting its responsibilities, but politically no one dare embrace these new Britons too fondly for fear of a backlash at the polls.

There was no welcome for them to match that on offer to newcomers to the United States, where football stadia full of new citizens of every colour and belief are sworn to the allegiance of their adopted country amidst patriotic razzmatazz. American immigrants are wrapped in an emotional welcome that declares a new beginning, not just for them but for the society they have joined. 'I am the son of an immigrant,' boasts Mario Cuomo, governor of New York, from the public platform. We demand 'Where do you come from?' of people who were born here.

Those who already knew the character and achievements of the Ugandan Asians forecast that the newcomers would rapidly buy their own houses; would start businesses; and would ensure that their children were well enough educated to become major contributors – doctors, engineers, accountants, business people – to the society they were joining. Those who didn't know them, like myself, but who met them at the RAF camps where they were housed, were struck by the improbable optimism of refugees who, in many cases, owned no more than the clothes they wore.

Most people, plucked from their homes, jobs and businesses and dumped summarily thousands of miles away in a strange, cold, indifferent land, without fluency in the local language, would have been utterly demoralized. Yet some of the younger Ugandan Asians appeared then to be crazily excited. This was the land on which they had set their hearts; and, although they arrived in appallingly adverse circumstances, they were determined to succeed. A young man, wearing an open-necked shirt and two rows of cowrie shells, in Britain only ten days, said: 'We were told there were not enough jobs to go round in England. In fact there are. The English just won't do them.' One brother already had a job in Dorset, and another a college place. That day one thousand supporters of the 'British Campaign to Stop Immigration' marched in Bradford, and a further one thousand took to the streets of Birmingham. According to a spokesman: 'We are not being racialist – if fifty thousand Eskimos came to this country, we could not take them.'

There were also older Asians, with poor English and no skills. They kept to their rooms in the camps, lacklustre and apprehensive. Their subsequent achievements were a greater triumph for human tenacity and the extended Asian family than even the business fortunes made by some younger people. Within ten years of their arrival, all 5,600 families who had been expelled by Amin had re-established themselves. A leading member of the community said: 'The people forty-five years plus had trouble – language, jobs, even the weather – but eventually they found work, often in department stores. They learned the ropes, got to know how business worked, and then started on their own.'

KD, who had friends in London, had bypassed the camps. (At first he had not believed he would be expelled, but rapidly changed his mind after soldiers had twice demanded the contents of his safe at gunpoint.) Leaving behind four businesses, including a car rental company, a travel agency – through which he issued himself and his family getaway tickets – and several petrol stations, he arrived in Britain with £1,500 and a few suitcases of clothes. He had been stripped of property worth £200,000 – enough in 1972 to buy three or four houses in Chelsea. He first worked as a manager for the Heron chain of petrol stations, clocking up overtime to make the money to start on his own, establishing contacts and learning the tricks of the trade as he went. By 1977 he was earning between £20,000 and £25,000 a year. When he did launch his own business, he worked, he told me, an 86-hour week. (His profile claimed it was a 110-hour week!) 'We didn't watch TV or have lunch breaks. By working hard, you can learn fast. If I had worked a forty-hour week, it would have taken twenty-five years to get where I am now.'

He said that a great crisis was required to bring the best out of the indigenous British. 'Faced with disaster,' and he cited the examples of Napoleon and the Second World War, 'they prove they are the best.' (I am writing this during the 'great freeze' of 1987, when the papers are full of British plumbers charging pensioners £160 for mending a burst pipe, and spivs demanding £1.80 for a bottle of milk and £1.00 for a loaf of bread. The Dunkirk spirit, invoked *ad nauseum* in the post-war years, was, whatever its original proof, somewhat less potent by 1987 than it had been in 1940. We had uncorked it like drunkards to cope with economic calamity, three-day weeks, the Argentinians, industrial anarchy and the cold.) KD's business is selling petrol and repairing cars. He employs mainly Asians. The English, he said, finish on the dot, or before. They start washing at five o'clock for a six o'clock getaway. They do not respond to an emergency (short presumably of the Second World War) – like getting a job promised for that day finished before they go home. This is largely why, he said, Asians employ other Asians.

Why, I asked, should a capitalist, who had been a vice-chairman of the Anglo-Asian Conservative Association, now support a wife as a member of a council that had become the national symbol of the 'loony left'? He was, he said, disillusioned with Mrs Thatcher, not because of her lukewarm enthusiasm towards the aspirations of brown-skinned Britons, but because she had not done enough for small businesses. 'In the beginning she was all right, but after four or five years I expected something substantial to happen, but it didn't.' Millions of pounds, he said, are pumped into British Coal and Austin-Rover, yet there is no encouragement for the entrepreneur. It is the enterprising businessman, as in the United States, who creates new jobs. KD felt there was little scope for further expansion in Britain. 'I am at a crossroads; I'm not satisfied.' He might, he said, try to start a new enterprise in the States. But he added: 'I am grateful to the British in every respect from the day I landed. I do feel at home, but in the US my progress would have been much faster.' It was a self-assessment I was to hear from other Asians.

Asians, who outnumber West Indians two to one in Britain, are lumped together as one cohesive people in the undiscriminating native mind, yet they are as varied in their backgrounds, cultures and languages as are western Europeans. Imagine the response of the British skinheads who harass Asians if they were to be abused as 'Eyetyes' when they travelled abroad on their beer-sodden package tours. A banker, who first came to Britain in 1933 to study for the bar, was later a chief minister in a princely state, then a judge and diplomat in independent India before returning to this country, is abused on Underground platforms as a 'Paki', and told to 'go home'. A former Conservative parliamentary candidate said: 'Once every Indian in Britain was treated like a maharajah; now even maharajahs are treated like uneducated immigrants.' An activist in the Federation of Bengali Youth Organizations told a woman who gratuitously called him a 'Paki' in an Oxford Street store: 'You wouldn't know a Paki, madam, if you fell over one.'

I write in chapter 11 about outright violence and intimidation, but even rich and successful Asians, living in what are known as 'safe' areas, are affected by attitudes that prevent the British moving towards a genuinely multi-cultural society. To the British psyche, fashioned by years of empire, black or brown means inferior. A well-educated Bengali said: 'A lot of people still expect you to speak with a Peter Sellers accent, and stare in amazement when you don't. Eventually they accept you, you're OK. It is just the "others". You're an exception to the stereotype, but the stereotype never gets altered.'

I had first read KD's story in a tabloid newspaper, under the headline 'YOU CAN STILL MAKE A MILLION FROM NOTHING!' and written, predictably, by an Asian journalist. Such reporting (and use of coloured reporters to do it) is part of the stereotyping: it is short-hand for 'anyone who really tries can make it in British society, so don't start whingeing about prejudice and unequal opportunity'. It is also part of a patronizing attitude: haven't *they* done wonderfully well? But the East African and other successful Asians are excep-tional. Brown and black British as a whole are twice as likely to be unemployed as white, and those whose families came from Pakistan and Bangladesh are three times as likely. In 1985 16 per cent of white young people between the ages of sixteen and twenty-four were out of work, while the figure for those of Bangladeshi and Pakistani ori-gin was 48 per cent. Of the ethnic groups, the Indians were the most successful, with 24 per cent of their young people without jobs, yet even this figure was half as many again as whites. (The survey that produced these statistics showed there were 2,400,000 members of ethnic minorities in Britain – 4·4 per cent of the population. Asians, accounting for over one million, formed by far the largest group.)

The reality of the problems facing ethnic minorities is illustrated by the slow progress made by the Vietnamese 'boat people'. A Home Office research group reported: 'It is difficult to identify any other refugee group arriving in any other Western country which has fared as badly.' While the Vietnamese elsewhere have prospered far beyond expectations, many in Britain live isolated, frightened lives – attacked even in Shropshire – without jobs, English or hope. Some families live in bed and breakfast hotels, a way of life that threatens the prospects for children born here. The only skill they have acquired after years in Britain is to operate the social-security system. Physics teachers, who 'topped up' with British qualifications, are doing manual jobs.

In America, Asians are already outperforming whites in schools and universities – 94 per cent of children whose families come from the Indian sub-continent graduate from high school, compared to 87 per cent of whites. Other Asian groups – Chinese, Japanese, Vietna-mese – have comparable success rates. Ivy League universities are so alarmed by the imbalance caused by Asian achievements – especially in certain maths and science courses – that they appear to discrimi-nating in favour of other groups. Siblings of Asians who came to Britain tend to do better in the United States. (Gujeratis have been concentrating on the hotel trade: the *Washington Post* ran a business-page story under the headline 'MOTELS, HOTELS AND PATELS'.)

In Britain the Coronary Prevention Group (CPG) reported in 1986 that Asians had a higher rate of heart disease than the national average, which is itself one of the highest in the world. Racism, low incomes, poor housing, unemployment and poor working conditions all take their toll. For most new immigrants, moving to Britain was as stressful as bereavement. They were isolated and helpless in the face of language problems and hostility or, at best, indifference from the host community. The CPG concluded there was 'urgent need' for research into the effects of discrimination on the health of Asians. This is the adverse context in which the success of men like K D Patel must be judged. It was easy, sitting in comfortable and substantial homes in Wembley or Harrow, to forget what odds Asians face in Britain.

G. S. Bakshi, a Sikh from the Punjab, lives in a mock Tudor home with a small swimming pool and a large rabbit hutch in the garden. Across open fields one can see Harrow School from his lead-paned front windows. At his side lay a portable car phone, brought in from his Mercedes: normally at that time he would have been on the road pursuing his property development business. A graduate in political science, economics and English from Punjab University, he arrived in Britain in 1965 at the age of twenty-seven. He had intended continuing his education, but first had to earn a living. He quickly discovered that his Indian degree was useless. 'I was hardly treated as a school-leaver.' He worked first in a Birmingham factory, and then in the Post Office, where, through massive overtime, he saved enough to buy his first shop. This was run by his wife, who had joined him in 1967, while he continued as a postman. The only white-collar job he was offered, as a clerk in the DHSS, paid less than the Post Office.

Looking back, Mr Bakshi smiled at the memory of attitudes that had angered him then, like that of the fellow postman, who had left school at fifteen and who wondered aloud whether Mr Bakshi – a graduate – had ever worn shoes before he came to Britain; and like that of the colleague who told him that it was all right for a white man to swear at a brown one, but not for the brown to swear back. But prejudice was Mr Bakshi's springboard. Had his degree been recognized, he would probably be working his way though the middle-management ranks of a large company instead of making a great deal more money running his own small one. For many, the corner shop is an escape from both the discrimination of the British workplace – in 1987 British Telecom were ordered to pay £1,500 compensation to three Asians, who had been abused by their superior as 'lazy Pakis', 'useless Pakis', and as 'coolieboys' who should be in a gas chamber' – and the restraint on earnings imposed by unions. If you work for yourself, the harder you work, the better you do. Thirty-seven per cent of Asian small shopkeepers have degrees, which is a telling measure of how inhospitable even educated Asians find the British Commercial environment.

Mr Bakshi's analysis of why white Britons are not as entrepreneurial as some brown Britons drew two themes together. Prejudice against coloured people and lack of enterprise were, he believed, intricately linked in the conditioning of the British working class. At home, in the days of empire, they were treated as 'white coolies', much as black natives in the colonies. They were kept ignorant, not encouraged to be either constructive or creative, trapped by economic necessity. What the factory owners required were human machines who would go to the factory in the morning, and be content with the pub in the evening. A class was created which was almost without initiative.

But in the human pecking order there was still one inferior being – the coloured man. Mr Bakshi said: 'The English suffer from a superiority complex – in working class, middle class and upper class – a belief that the British are the superior nation in the world. The media brainwash them. They will eventually have to come to their senses and realize that the Raj is over, and with it British domination in the world.' The empire, he said, also fatally encouraged industrial inefficiency in Britain. 'Forty years ago it didn't matter what the cost was. Goods could be dumped on the colonies. Now Britain is overmanned and undermodernized,' said Mr Bakshi. He argued that the British will to work is sapped by the welfare state, though he was also critical of Mrs Thatcher, whose monetarism, he felt, had been too radical. She should, he said, have diverted funds used to support the unemployed in order to modernize industry.

The self-made Asians I met all had remarkable stories of fortitude and determination to tell. Seen from their perspective, their sometimes punitive attitudes towards the unemployed – very different from those of the liberal English for whom life has been tolerably easy – are at least understandable. Ram Bedi, a Hindu, born in what is now Pakistan, had, as a teenager, to flee his home in his pyjamas at the time of partition. He travelled a thousand miles across India to a state where he didn't speak the language to get a job as a railway clerk in the fifties, with three pounds in his pocket, he went to join relatives in Northern Ireland, where he sold clothes from a van to remote farmers. Later he opened a wholesale warehouse in Cookstown, working from 8.00 a.m. to 11.00 p.m. Three times his premises were damaged by IRA bombs. In 1978, he prudently retreated to England, and started a business manufacturing wire hangers for dry-cleaners. When I met him, his small company was producing sixty million hangers a year, exporting almost half, and had an annual turnover of nearly one million pounds: he was a Fellow of the Institute of Directors, lived in a large house overlooking Windsor Castle, drove a Mercedes with a personalized number plate, and was the first Asian president of the Slough Rotarians. He took me to the weekly Rotary Club luncheon, proudly wearing the chain of office that bore the names of fifty-four past presidents.

As we drove to lunch, he showed me a large clothes shop run by Asians, who had been working out of their homes five years before. There is no mystery about the Asian success: it is achieved by hard work, sustained by strong families. Ram Bedi employs ten people and is still expanding. An energetic man, with gold-rimmed glasses, who was going grey at the temples, he tapped the table from time to time, the gesture of a man who gets things done. He had invited me to lunch on the very day I rang, a contrast to the delaying layers of public relations that so often cocoon large firms – 'frightfully busy time of year, old boy. Let's see. How about early, no, better make that later, next month. After we've had a chat perhaps we could pop you in to see the chairman. He might be able to squeeze in half an hour.' The chairman is usually delighted to see one, and the problem is getting away.

'I want,' said Mr Bedi, 'willing people who will work, not take Saturdays off. They need to want to make money and be happy. I don't mind working long hours. I couldn't stop at five o'clock and sit in the pub. If I had no job, I'd clean windows – you can make £400 a week, or £200 a week as a gardener. It's up to the people.' He amused leading local business people by rounding on Nigel Lawson when, as Chancellor of the Exchequer, Mr Lawson visited a local lunch club. 'I told him "there is so much unemployement, yet I can't get people for my factory. You pay them fifty to sixty pounds a week, so they are not interested in jobs at seventy-five pounds. They have no incentive. They should be sent to us first before they get the dole." People should be protected, but they should have some incentive to work.'

Ramniklal Solanki came to Britain from India in 1964 as correspondent for an Indian group of papers. Shortly afterwards, because of an Indian currency crisis, his salary was frozen in India, and he was forced to take a job as an assistant timekeeper at an engineering firm at twelve pounds a week. The then Indian High Commissioner suggested he should start a paper for the growing Gujerati community. There were no Gujerati typesetting machines, so Mr Solanki wrote the paper by hand. On Friday nights he would board a long-distance coach for a provincial city, and, over the weekend, furnished with a list of local Gujeratis, would call door-to-door selling subscriptions. The initial circulation was 1,500. His wife by this time had arrived in England, and supported them both on a nine pounds a week job.

The paper received a significant boost with the arrival of the Ugandan Asians, most of whom were Gujeratis. Mr Solanki distributed it free in the resettlement camps. 'People needed advice, how to live in this country, what to do, even – for those from remote villages – how to use toilets and baths.' Today that paper – Garavi Gujarat ('Pride of Gujerat') – sells 41,000 copies weekly. In 1985 Mr Solanki launched a sister magazine, Asian Trader, aimed at the burgeoning Asian business community: 'Our people were going into business and wanted advice,' he said. An Economist Intelligence Unit report in 1986 found that the decline in independent grocers had been halted by Asian shopkeepers, who by then comprised half the nation's total. In London the figure was 70 per cent.

Mr Solanki employs thirty-five people, including ten journalists, operates his papers from his own plant off the Blackfriars Road in south London, and is in Who's Who. He is a short, rotund man, who slips in and out of his cluttered office with bewildering frequency, introducing a visitor to other members of his busy newspaper community – many of whom belong to his family. His wife, clad in a sari, does layouts; one son, Kalpesh, sells advertising space (from an office even more cluttered than his father's, in which pride of place belonged to a trouser press, on which rested a cake of soap and a shoehorn); and a second son, Shailesh, on vacation from University College, London, was writing for Asian Trader.

The Solankis exemplified the strength of the Asian family unit, the cornerstone of Asian success in Britain. (West Indians, with their high number of single parent families, often don't have sufficient support to see them through the inevitable crises of immigrant life.) Mr Solanki had involved in his business, or helped, not just his immediate family, but his father, three brothers and two sisters. Kalpesh had read law at university and been called to the bar: Shailesh was reading economics and wanted to be a journalist. The business, they said, was in the blood: they had learned it at their father's knee.

Before Mr Solanki could afford machinery the family had to collate by hand each copy of the paper. Inspired by their father, they had worked hard – in Harrow public library after school and on Saturday mornings. (Everyone else studying at those times would be Asian, they said.) With great pride, they showed me the complicated computers required to set Gujerati type. They were learning from the British all the time. (And the Japanese were learning from them. The Solankis had recently been visited by a group of Japanese business school professors, curious about the minor economic miracle achieved by British Asians. No similar group of British professors, or British anybody elses, had called, though they did get an occasional letter from schoolchildren and students asking about Asian business success. Deep in the jungle something stirs.) Kalpesh in particular, visiting companies to sell advertising, was widening his horizons. What he learned is passed on to the community through *Asian Trader*. Asian firms, he said, would have to start taking a longer view, investing more in customer relations.

Solicitor Ramesh Vala, who came to Britain from Kenya to read law at the London School of Economics in 1973, made the same point more bluntly. Although we met when the City was being shaken by scandals like the Guinness affair, he felt vehemently that Asians had to learn from the British tradition of fair dealing, and that they too often cut corners in pursuit of quick profits. 'In the long term, it is more important to be honest and make a name for yourself. Ethics,' he said, 'are paramount to the English professional. An Asian too often says: "I'll do it because it makes money." If you are patient, hang on for two years, you will be more successful. I have nothing but contempt for Asians who make money, but contribute nothing back to society.'

Mr Vala was then one of only two Asian partners in the top hundred solicitors' firms in London. He had become a partner in his twenties, and – in his immaculate grey suit, white shirt and heavy-rimmed glasses – looked the part. (His partnership – in Harley Street – was even more immaculate. A vistor waits in what appears to be a boudoir, adorned with reproduction French empire furniture, leather-clad phones, chandeliers, and a Grecian urn, filled, even in mid-winter, with carnations, lilies, and chrysanthemums. I was offered tea, coffee or Perrier water.) The young Solanki brothers had said that, because of prejudice, it was prudent for an Asian to go it alone: 'The English are not used to seeing a brown face in a position of authority.' Mr Vala was sterner: he criticized Asians for opting out when the going got tough and starting their own businesses, rather than striving to succeed inside big firms. This practice had, however, been to his advantage, since the new, smaller partnerships couldn't handle big deals, and Indian clients, who like when possible to do business with one of their own, were making a beeline to his firm.

'My fear,' he said, 'is that unless Asians show a social conscience, in two or three years' time they will be disliked even more than they are now. People see us as milking society, taking all the cream.' He cited various scandals involving Asians from the Johnson Matthey affair to doctors making amorous advances on patients. Practices once almost taboo to Asians – divorce and sending old people to homes – were losing their stigma.

Asians, he said, tended also to opt out in their personal lives. Their response to a poor school was not to join the PTA but to remove their child. 'In East Africa they never participated in politics, concentrating instead on carving out a niche for themselves. They ignored the host community, and failed to see the dangers until it was too late. Unfortunately the same may be happening here,' he said. He suggested that communities should make gestures like raising five pounds from each person to donate to the local hospital, adding pragmatically that they should make sure the gift was reported in the local papers. Asians in Britain need to protect themselves from British racial and social prejudice by entering visibly and energetically into public life. He was particularly concerned that there should be Asian members of parliament, contrasting the influence and weight of the forty or more Jewish MPs with the impotence many leading Asians feel.

Kanti Nagda, who runs the Sangat Community Centre in Harrow, and founded an Anglo-Indian Art Circle, devotes his life to trying to ensure that what happened to Asians in Uganda will never happen in Britain. 'Asians must get into the corridors of power, have their voices heard and be part of the decision-making process. If you are there, you will be heard; if you are not, you will be ignored,' he said. In Uganda, Asians had got on with making money, leaving politics first to the Europeans and then to the Africans. There were only two or three Asian MPs: Asians could have been the ruling group in several cities. 'Politicians only understand one language – the cross on the ballot paper.' Mr Nagda identifies parliamentary constituencies where the immigrant vote could swing the seat; tests candidates' views on issues relevant to ethnic minorities; and makes Asians and Afro-Caribbeans conscious of the issues so that they reflect their own interests in the way they vote. At the borough level, these tactics, he said, are paying off. Not only are black and brown councillors now senior figures, but translation units have been set up, cultural centres – like the one he runs – established, vegetarian meals on wheels offered, and special health services provided.

Six years after arriving in Britain, Mr Nagda was in *Who's Who*. In Uganda he had taught history and Gujerati – and written a novel. He was in his early twenties when Amin expelled the Asians, and came to Britain with only fifty pounds in September 1972. Within three days he had a job as an accounts clerk with an American firm, and owned a house within two months. 'There's no point in worrying over what you've left behind,' he said. 'Forget it.' A slim, wiry man, with a goatee beard, and a touch of white at the front of his dark hair, he brings the energy to his educating mission that his fellow refugees have put into business. His upbringing had been utterly conventional by Ugandan Asian standards. His father owned a general store, and when friends came, discussed business *ad infinitum*. 'It was a heritage for us. That gets to you. But I wanted to make Asians aware of the mistakes they made in East Africa.' He feared that militant anti-racism would backfire. He cited the hounding of Maureen McGoldrick, who had been suspended as headmistress of a Brent primary school because she was reported to have said she didn't want more black teachers in her school. (Miss McGoldrick, shown nightly on television being embraced and kissed by Asian mothers and children in her school playground, was everyone's idea of the perfect head teacher. She clearly loved her job and her children, and her strong face told of her determination. As public opinion swung behind her, the councillors, black and white, who were trying to sack her, appeared increasingly out of touch with public sentiment.)

Mr Nagda had little time for the far left: 'We have to live with the majority, and to live peaceably we have to come to terms with them. We must accept for the present that we are in a "foreign" country. I'm not saying we will accept abuse and discrimination, but a minority cannot fight the majority. It will be a long time before Britain is a genuinely multi-cultural society.'

His headquarters, tucked away behind rows of suburban homes, with bottleglass windows in replacement, mock-Victorian doors, and privet hedges, was symbolic of those patient compromises and unheralded advances that will be necessary for years if Britain is ever to be a multi-racial country. It is a start that Pooter now lives next door to Patel: up to 35,000 people in Harrow are Asian, the vast majority from Uganda. Harassment there is not unknown, but at least in owner-occupier areas it is not an open sore. As I left, Asian women in saris, clutching plastic bags, strolled towards the community centre in disconnected pairs for a session with the chiropodist.

One Asian was elected – for Leicester East – in 1987. However, if Asians were proportionately represented in parliament, there would be twenty-four Asian MPs. (There had been three previously, but they were all in 'pre-immigration' times – two in the late nineteenth century, and one in the twenties. A Bombay-born barristers actually sat for Bethnal Green as a Conservative for eleven years from 1895, a combination that in the modern context would boggle the mind.) Several Afro-Caribbeans – including Bernie Grant and Diane Abbott – also won seats for Labour in the 1987 election, and Asians fear privately that, despite their own single representative, these Afro-Caribbeans – mainly on the hard left – will be seen to speak for all minorities. Successful, entrepreneurial Asians ought to be more at home with the Conservative Party than with Labour. But history – in the form of the post-war Labour Government that saw India to Independence in the teeth of opposition from Winston Churchill – helps Labour. Several Asians said they felt Conservatives to be less welcoming than Labour Party members. 'Conservatives are very nationalist-minded people. They don't spell it out, but I sense that they feel we are different,' said one.

Major Narindar Saroop fought Greenwich for the Conservatives in the 1979 general election. He is a caricature of the anglophile Indian, and, as such, falls uneasily into a no man's land between the white British and the new generation of Asians. We met at one of his clubs, the Cavalry and Guards on Piccadilly, the lobby a bustle of tall men in pin-striped suits, some young and loud, some somewhat doddery, most unmistakable members of the British upper classes of the country home and a 'spot of lunch in town' variety. Their black well-worn shoes sparkled as if batmen still dutifully polished then each morning. A tiny Scottish porter – who probably *had* been a batman – darted in and out from behind a huge Victorian reception desk. There were occasional cries from a major-domo of 'My dear general ...' and 'Brigadier, I'll be right there, Sir ...' A very elderly party was on a phone trying to reach a woman who had clearly been an early flame – Poona 28? 'I'm up in London for a dinner, and wondered whether I could give you some lunch. Must warn you though; I've got to catch the 2.44 from Euston. Not much time for sitting in a comfortable chair drinking coffee.' He emerged from the phone, with grey moustache and gold-rimmed glasses, looking as pleased as if, as a young subaltern, he had landed his first date.

Major Saroop was at home in this environment. Neatly swept back grey hair, pin-striped suit, yellow striped shirt, infinitely courteous. His *Who's Who* entry lists his recreations as: 'keeping fools, boredom and socialism at bay'. 'Randal, my dear fellow,' he cried to an elderly man, with swollen arthritic hands, who was tottering past and who turned out to be the Irish poet/peer, Lord Dunsany. They traded nicknames and anecdotes happily inquiring after each other's nearest and dearest. 'I am the only man ever to have been ordered to fight to the last cartridge twice, and survived,' said Dunsany, pausing an instant before adding 'never actually fired a shot.' Arrangements were made for the two men to meet the following day with Kenneth Rose, 'Albany' of the *Sunday Telegraph*. It was a cosy world, and it was attractive no doubt to belong, but we were a very long way from either Wembley and Harrow or London's east end.

Major Saroop seemed but remotely connected to the experiences of his fellow Asians, but he had some shrewd opinions. The world of the Cavalry and Guards Club was under siege, as much from the Thatcherites as from the left. He spoke of a 'communications trap', by which he meant poor English, and said that Asian-run corner shops were 'quite popular from all I hear.' He told me that a Conservative Government was in the interests of British Asians, because they would prosper best in a country that was strong both internally and externally. When a country is weak, there is a tendency to turn on minorities. Asians are natural patriots, he said, but they should also vote Conservative out of self-interest.

Looking ahead, the major was fearful. 'The next generation,' he said, 'will be more under stress, without the emotional or spiritual comfort their elders had.' This will be partially compensated for by fluent English. He added, however: 'It is in the British psyche to feel superior to coloured people, and prejudice is more prevalent amongst the working classes. Everyone likes to look down on someone. It is hard for the British to come to terms with the overturning of this order of things when, for example, Asian children do better than their own at school.'

Major Saroop had once been complacent about race relations – 'the incidence of racial prejudice is far less than imagined, but more than can be identified' – but he appeared to be changing his tune. Thatcherism, with its abrasive intolerances, had led to a general hardening of attitudes; the British were becoming less easy-going. It was sad, he said, because for two centuries the British had been a gentle and civilized people. But manners were deteriorating, even courtesy on the pavement: people were less tolerant of things to which they didn't subscribe – like smoking. Mrs Thatcher, he complained, 'lets the walking wounded take care of themselves.' It was Tory 'wet' talk from a disillusioned man. As we parted he asked me what I thought of proportional representation, which, after having been rebuffed for safe Conservative seats, he obviously thought was the only way an Asian such as he was going to get into Westminster.

Mr Vala's chosen Asian parliamentary candidate was Mrs Zerbanoo Gifford, then the Liberal candidate for Harrow East. He and some other young professionals had formed a small group to advance her campaign. Mrs Gifford is scarcely the typical 'immigrant' – perhaps less so even than Major Saroop. She is, for a start, a Zoroastrian Parsee – her father is president of the world Zoroastrian movement. She was brought up largely in English hotels owned by her father –'a good preparation for public life: you're on duty twenty-four hours a day when you live in a hotel. I didn't feel I had a private life' – was educated at Roedean and Watford Technical College, which, she said, immediately confuses the class-conscious English, and is married to an English solicitor. She is what the Americans call 'feisty', full of spirit and fire, without modesty, false or otherwise. When she talks about being prime minister one day, it's hard to tell whether she's joking. She is irrepressible and self-confident in the way Edwina Currie appears to be.

For three years she was subjected to racial harassment that would have driven someone less resolute from public life. It began during the 1983 general election campaign when she was standing against Cecil Parkinson – she polled 14,000 votes, the highest of any ethnic candidate. She was alone in the house, taking a bath when the telephone rang. An anonymous caller said: 'We know you are alone. We are not going to let blacks run this country. We are coming to get you right now, and we are coming through the greenhouse.' The caller must have been watching the house and have known the layout. Later calls were both racist and sexual, and one was a threat to kidnap her two small boys. Mrs Gifford was convinced that these were not 'yobbo' calls, as most of the callers spoke quietly and did not swear. A man slashed the front door with a knife; someone tried to drive her off the road. After she had been adopted for Harrow East as a candidate for the 1987 election, the local paper was told in another anonymous call that the intimidation would continue.

Mrs Gifford eventually responded by telling the full story to a right-wing Sunday paper, which she felt would be a more effective way of rallying support than going to the liberal press. A report there, alongside the Thatcherite editorials and tittle-tattle about the aristocracy, would bring home to the comfortable suburban reader that racial harassment was not suffered only by illiterate Bengali peasants in Brick Lane, but also by well-spoken, well-educated, public-spirited members of the middle classes. A similar prominent feature in the 'bleeding heart' press would have had a fraction of the impact.

When I lunched with her, she was nervous whenever she had to go to the front door, although the house was by then well protected by alarms. She exudes enormous energy, keeping a conversation going over her shoulder even when she leaves the room to attend to domestic concerns. She told me that a few days earlier at the Oxford Union she had rounded on misguided leftists who had been denouncing members of the ethnic minorities who joined the Conservative Party. 'I had to attack their closed minds, explain to them the nature of democracy.' She told also of a clash she had had with Roy Hattersley, when he dismissed the validity of her perspective because she was not like 'my Asians' – i.e. those who live in Hattersley's Birmingham constituency. Both the lefties and Hattersley surely knew they had been in a fight. Mrs Gifford can take a tough line with the far left without being denounced as a race collaborator, because her well-publicized harassment gave her unimpeachable battle honours.

The Gifford home was furnished and decorated in upper middle-class English taste, restrained and understated where KD Patel's had been brash and exuberant. Mrs Gifford was a little alarmed that I had been to see KD, though she hastily added 'of course, you did have to see him.' His style was not one she wished to be associated with, nor did she want KD held out before native English eyes as an example of the 'success' to which other British Asians aspired: the names she gave me of people to see were of upper-class, cultured Indians, members of London clubs and old families.

Mrs Gifford had just taken part in a Liberal Party inquiry into the immigrant experience, and said she found most members of ethnic minorities were crying out for some sign of welcome. What really struck her was that, despite the talents and education of British Asians, nowhere have they made a real breakthrough – not in the City, the armed forces, academia, the professions. She was amazed how slow the British have been to make a virtue of minority communities. Brown Britons, she said, should be encouraged to be bilingual – not for any ideological 'mother tongue' reason – but so they could open up Far Eastern markets. India, after all, is the second largest potential market in the world. Society suffers, she said, if a minority feel like outsiders. 'It would help the economy to grow if we were encouraged.' Prominent Asians in British society could assist the country's image abroad. 'What wonderful P R I'd be,' she added with one of her ambiguous laughs.

Bestriding two worlds – the brown and the white – Mrs Gifford is able to test British attitudes in subtle ways. If she phones someone, and – in her best Roedean voice – leaves the name 'Mrs Gifford', she is invariably called back; if she leaves her maiden name 'Zerbanoo Irani', the odds against the call being returned lengthen considerably. There is a similar difference in reaction from, for example, the police, depending on whether she is wearing western clothes or a sari. 'People even speak more slowly when I wear a sari.' She wears Indian costume, 'when I want to look pretty' and on public platforms, because she feels that visible gestures from public figures give moral support to the tens of thousands of Indian women who wear a sari all the time. She told of the snobbery she meets: for example, the subtle change of attitude when visiting a British embassy when she lets drop she was at Roedean. Abroad you see Britain as others see it, she said. 'The first thing I am asked on foreign soil is "Aren't the British racist? How can you hope to be elected to parliament?" I find myself having to defend Britain, act as P R for my country once I am past the white cliffs of Dover.' She dismissed Mrs Thatcher as insular and mean-minded. Like other Asians, she finds the Napoleonic gibe that the English are a nation of shopkeepers ridiculous. If they were, how would the Asians have established themselves here? 'More closed shop, than shopkeepers,' said Mrs Gifford.

A steel, she said, had entered her soul as a result of the intimidation she suffered. 'Nothing now knocks me off balance. If your life has been in danger, it makes you aware of the importance of doing something with it. My father said: "If you don't carry on, they will have won, and you'll never be able to do anything."' If she gets to Westminster, her presence in itself will be a significant statement. But she knows what she is up against. How long, she wondered, will it be before it is a political plus to have been an immigrant or the child of immigrants? 'My father sacrificed for us. We now have the right to fulfil the dreams he had for us.'

One of Mrs Gifford's suggested contacts was J. K. Gohel, who first came to Britain in 1933, when all Indians were still 'Maharajahs'. 'If I saw an Indian then, I'd run half a mile to shake him by the hand.' He had stayed here until the early years of the war, qualifying as a barrister. We were, apparently, no less ignorant then of foreign ways than we are now. A fellow student wondered what Mr Gohel would do with his law degree when he returned to India: the idea of brown people having courts and justice hadn't occurred to her. Mr Gohel had been in Britain during Dunkirk, and remained impressed nearly half a century later. 'The British are best when the chips are down. It is a different cup of tea when they are faced with an emergency.' After a distinguished public career in India, he returned to Britain in 1960 in time to catch another chapter he admires in British history – decolonialization. 'Only the British had the guts, the sense and the wisdom to withdraw with grace,' he said. He lamented American leadership in world affairs, likening the United States to a wrestler – too much brawn and sadly not enough brain. They've no idea of history or how the world works. Britain, which really knows better, has become 'a cheerleader for American policies, whether it agrees with them or not.'

We met at the private bank where he worked, a discreet place of business near the Inns of Court, which was not, I was informed sternly, to be mentioned by name in any writing. Mr Gohel wore an Oxford blue turban, slightly lop-sidedly, and a pin-striped suit, cut in the Nehru jacket style. His fifty-plus years of watching Asians in Britain gave him a balanced view. When the first post-war immigrants returned to visit their villages, they seemed like millionaires, so brothers and cousins were encouraged to come. It was a 'gold rush': better housing, better clothes, free health, free education, the dole if needed. East African Asians were already on the second rung of the ladder, established shopkeepers. There was no mystery about their success – 'hard work and economical living'. It's in their blood, traders for a thousand years. They were helped by 'the comparatively easy-going English. *They* don't feel the world owes them a living. If you want something, you must earn it, and earn it the hard way. What incentive do you have if you are not driven hard?' That, he said, was the deficit side of the welfare state. A family with several children was better off on benefit: what incentive did they have left?

He gave Asian characteristics – culture, religion, family solidarity – a longer lifespan in the British environment than did Major Saroop – three or four generations, an estimate that was supported by a survey carried out for *New Society* amongst young Asians in 1985. The Asians interviewed said that English young people had too much freedom, did not care enough about their education and were workshy. An eighteen-year-old Sikh girl said: 'It is not good to have that much. The girls think it is a good thing to go out with a different boy each week. They have no self-respect ... Then you see them pushing prams along, and most of them aren't married.' A Muslim father said: 'A culture in which parents are left in old people's homes and old people are beaten to death or beaten up for the sake of a few pounds, such people are not fit to be human beings.' A Hindu father complained: 'The English are not really bothered. Education is free. They don't really appreciate the ample opportunity to educate themselves. They concentrate on meeting people. Pubs. Skinheads. Punks.' But I suspect that the attitudes defined in that survey are eroding faster than Mr Gohel would wish. Young Asians I met spoke about smoking, drinking and eating taboo meats. 'How,' asked one, 'can you live in this country and not eat at McDonalds's?'

Why, I asked Mr Gohel, are the British prejudiced? The colonial powers, he said, had to argue that they travelled halfway round the world to conquer other people's countries for the good of the natives. They had the guns, so we didn't argue. A picture was painted of a barbarous people, who had to be civilized by the British, of a nation of snakes and elephants, with people living in trees. The legacy is the deep-seated belief that coloured people are inferior. Most people don't know any better.

Mr Gohel is a lifelong Conservative. 'Asians have everything in common with the Tories – a belief in family and God, in property-owning, in the creation of wealth, and' – this with a smile – 'in paying as few taxes as possible. Labour's historic moment – child labour, long hours, exploitation – is past. The unions are no longer the defenders of the people, but their masters. They harass the general public.' A Labour Government, he said, would be a tragedy. 'The nation will revert to less work for more pay. The Government will place its own 'isms' before the welfare of the country. The economy will suffer, and we will be the scapegoats – "Pakis go home".' Labour makes smiles and promises when in opposition, he said. In office, the smiles remain, but the promises are like 'a plastic lollipop'. It seemed an apt image for much of immigrant experience in Britain.

This elderly, distinguished man had had his own brush with skin-heads. Leaving a cocktail party east of the City, he had been unable to find a cab, and had gone to an Underground station. He was sur-rounded by five or six youths who started abusing him. He tried to ignore them, but the abuse and jostling got worse. A train came just in the nick of time. 'I try to be discreet, avoid the area of pubs at clos-ing time. In the thirties, when I was a student, we would go anywhere at any time. The bobby on the corner was a reassuring figure. We dress differently, and have different customs, but we can smile and cry like the rest of humanity. The British working man in his ignor-ance thinks of us all as coolies.' However, he added, there is not a single Asian who has not got a friend or two, whom he meets over 'a cup of tea, a pint, or a tandoori chicken.'

Across the world Asians put their trust in education: when they do well in business, they like to advertise their success with worldly goods, like expensive motor cars. These aspirations come together in Britain in the large number of Asian children who are being educated privately. Fee-paying is both an investment and a status symbol. Ram Bedi, the coathanger manufacturer, said: 'I paid for the best education for my four children.' He was clearly satisfied with the return. His eldest daughter was fluent in four languages, his second daughter had a degree in computing, and his third was studying to become a chartered accountant; a son was still at school. Another Asian said that British State schools were just not good enough.

Mr Nagda, of the Sangat Community Centre in Harrow, said: 'Asians put education top of the shopping list. Asian children take up more than 50 per cent of the places at Wembley and Harrow private schools. If the children are in State schools, parents make sure they spend time on their homework. If children are not highly educated, it is difficult for them to get good jobs and survive in this country: they have to be better educated than white people.' His own children were at a comprehensive: 'If my children are clever, no matter what school they are at, they will study hard and be at the top of the class.' In the United States the 1986 Westinghouse Science Talent Search, open to all American high school students, was totally dominated by Asian pupils: the organizers reported that in each case the pupil had had the strongest possible support from parents throughout his school career.

If a good education is one form of insurance against prejudice, preparing a bolt-hole is another. The Indian Government has recently opened the way for investment in India by Indians living abroad. Praful Patel, a former member of the Ugandan Resettlement Board and a Labour parliamentary candidate, was engaged in late 1986 in promoting such investment, and reported a strong response. Of course, by no means all investors were thinking in 'bolt-hole' terms, but few Asians, however successful, escape moments of pessimism about life in Britain. 'I have given up,' said Ramesh Vala, the Kenyan solicitor, 'on the media ever making a positive effort to educate the British that, beneath the colour of our skin, we are all the same people.'

In 1986 Prafulla Mohanti, an Indian painter and writer, who had come to Britain in 1960, produced a chillingly sad autobiography. For twenty-five years he had closely observed a decline in British decency and tolerance; at the same time, on visits to India, he found himself an increasingly alien figure, aghast at the corruption, nepotism and bureaucracy he found. His expatriate experience was tragic. When he arrived as a young architect, he had thought 'of England as a land of daffodils ... men wore bowler hats ... there was no poverty and people were honest and fair.' The immigration officer greeted him with the words: 'I hope you will be as happy in my country as I was in yours,' a welcome that became increasingly ironic.

Before his story ends, he had been driven from his home in London's east end, attacked in parks, spat upon by skinheads, and demeaned by the police. He had a dream that he would one day return to his native village armed with the technology and money to cure its Third World, primitive ills. His tragedy became the impossibility of marrying the strong spiritual values and simple, unstressful human relationships he brought with him from the East to the greater practical knowledge he discovered in the West. He grew ever more isolated between two incompatible worlds.

It is that bleakness that men like Major Narindar Saroop fear may lie in ambush for coming generations of British Asians – whatever their material success.

$\mathbb{E}$(11)$\mathbb{E}$

'WE ARE HERE TO PROTECT OUR OWN'

It was the coldest night for twenty years. London was immobilized by snow that had crippled railways, closed schools and blocked roads. 'TODAY IS CANCELLED' read the headline in the London *Standard*. The east end was quiet and beautiful, its grime invisible beneath three inches of soft snow, which shone like phosphorus, catching and reflecting the light trapped in the city sky. I had walked a mile or so, entranced by the peace. The only people on the back streets were children, throwing snowballs and shouting. A gaunt Victorian school looked romantic against the white backdrop; the hulking tower blocks became architectural. They may have affronted the humanity of the thousands of families stacked up inside them, but in the fresh, lucent snow, they rose like brooding cliffs from the Victorian terraces below.

Outside one row of homes, Asian girls in saris were throwing snowballs, shrieking in sharp east London voices: 'Quick, 'ere she comes. Duck.' A snowball flew past my head, and we all laughed. At the street corner, light shone from a small sweet shop: inside, through the steamed-up window, I saw a boy on tiptoe pointing to something in a large glass jar. My feet were so cold that each step was an agony, but I felt deeply contented, as if the years had rolled away and I, and everyone trapped in this overcrowded, dirty corner of London, could make a fresh start. The snow was a fond beguiler, wrapping the world on which it fell with innocence.

An hour later I sat in a miserable upstairs room, where the wind cut through the window frames, piercing even outdoor clothing with sharp draughts, and stirring the soiled, floral curtains. Gas and electric fires blazed futilely, the hot air seeping through the poorly built walls. Someone had begun to fix the room – unpainted wood supported a newly made archway to the back of the house – but had abandoned the endeavour. There were piles of discarded brochures and magazines dumped on the floor, and a sit-up-and-beg typewriter lay beneath unattended business bumph. It was the room of a man who had given up; a set for Pinter's *The Caretaker*. Through the archway in a 'kitchen', unwashed mugs were stacked alongside throwaway, but not thrown away, paper cups. The water supply to the sink had frozen.

From time to time there was a raucous, challenging shout from the street, and my companion, a slim Asian wearing several sweaters, an ancient grey leather jacket and an incongruous pair of heavy, black working-man's boots, leapt to the window, and peered round the curtains, keeping to one side so that he couldn't be seen from below. 'Did you hear that? "Bang, bang, bang." It's them again.' Four or five white youths loafed along the otherwise deserted road. Seeing them through my companion's eyes, I felt the menace they represented: arrogant, hostile, unafraid, masters in this benighted tract of Canning Town of all they surveyed. The shabby room was bleaker yet when we resumed our seats.

Ezaz 'Terry' Hayat had a story to tell that would have been sad enough if it had been the isolated case of one good man's ambitions destroyed by thuggery and official indifference. But it was by no means isolated. Within a few miles of where we talked, thousands of other brown-skinned Britons cowered in similar beleaguered rooms. By day the streets of the east end of London teem with Asians, women in saris, men in turbans and Muslim caps, children in school uniforms. By night, on the roads round the estates in which they are packed, there is scarcely a brown face to be seen.

Like most people who live removed from direct experience of racialism, I knew that Asians are frequently discriminated against and abused in Britain's inner cities. They are, the Home Office has reported, fifty times more likely to be victims of racial attacks than are whites. Responsible papers run regular features, especially after such outrages as the arson murders of women and children – the most horrifying of these racial attacks. But few, I suspect, have an inkling of the ubiquitous nature of racial harassment, which is a deep stain on the national reputation for tolerance. Shortly after my return to Britain, I read of a Pakistani girl who lived in the east end and worked as a secretary in the City, who had to wash her hair almost every night. During an average day, someone – from a balcony overhead,

on an Underground platform, on the street, from the stairs of a bus –
spat at her. Such assaults do not show up in police files, nor are they
reported to neighbourhood monitoring units. But they are part and
parcel of a systematic humiliation, which becomes, like the weather,
accepted by Asians as inescapable and therefore scarcely worth commenting upon. I had to jog people's minds before they bothered to
recount such incidents. Several Asians said they were never abused.
'Not even called "Paki bastards" in the street? Spat at, or told to "go
home"?' I asked. 'Oh that. Yes, of course. We don't take any notice
of that: that's part of everyday life.' A girl, born to Pakistani parents
in the east end, said: 'I have had abuse all my life. I'm used to it. I
don't take any notice of what they say.'

Mr Hayat, who came to England from Kenya when he was twelve,
had schooled himself in similar stoicism. He had studied electronics,
but, like most East African Asians, had set his heart on running his
own business. He joined the family leather concern – manufacturing
and selling: at one time they owned four shops – but, through a series
of disasters, the enterprise collapsed. A strike cost the family a substantial contract with C & A; they were twice robbed of uninsured
goods. One by one the shops went, and finally the business folded.
Mr Hayat set about rebuilding his fortunes by training as a motor
mechanic. For seven years he was employed by the Post Office,
worked as much overtime as he could, and bought a house, while he
dreamed his independent dreams. A year before we met he had sold
his home, borrowed from bank and friends, moved his family into
rented property, and bought a derelict shop in Barking Road, Canning Town, in the heart of London's old docklands. He negotiated a
franchise with Southern Fried Chicken, and converted the shop himself. 'I tried to make it as nice as I could. I thought people would be
pleased that there was something decent coming to their area,' he
said. One evening, as he worked, some children threw stones at glass
he was about to put in the windows. He shouted at them, and they
vanished. The incident seemed no more than a tiny cloud in a sunny
sky. When he opened early in 1986, business was brisk enough for Mr
Hayat to believe he would prosper.

However, after a few weeks a gang of local youths began coming
to the shop. They called Mr Hayat and his black assistant names –
'nigger', 'Pakis', 'black bastards': they shouted contradictory orders,
stole the ketchup and anything else they could lay their hands on,
asked in leering tones for 'white' not 'black chicken' – 'know what I

mean, nigger?' – wheedled or conned their way out of paying, blew smoke round the serving area. The abuse got worse day by day. Police who bought food in the shop said they would speak to the 'boys'. Mr Hayat said: 'They told me, "We know them all. We've warned them – blah, blah, blah" – but it made no difference.' The youths started to threaten violence. 'I'd really like to get you outside and smash your face in, nigger,' the ringleader said to the black assistant. The gang occasionally produced knives and other weapons.

Mr Hayat had been trained in professional self-control. 'Ignore the customers' insults, and don't start anything unless they jump the counter. Let them say what they want. If anyone comes in and "mouths" it, let him. Don't lose your temper.' He paused, and added in a quiet voice: 'Apparently it doesn't work like that in this area. You've got to stand up for yourself.' The plate-glass window was smashed, catapults fired at the shop. Every time there was an incident, the shop lost more custom: 'decent people', as his assistant put it, stayed away. Mr Hayat installed closed-circuit television, and placed a pickaxe handle amongst the sauce bottles and paper napkins beneath the counter.

His assistant, Dalton Macauley, was a large, cheerful and very black youth of eighteen, with a curious ancestry. He had been born in Washington, DC, to an American father and British mother; the family moved to Sierra Leone when he was two, and he had finally come to London when he left school. He was something of all three countries, sitting at the back of the shop on a steel table next to the 'Henny Penny Fryer', swinging his feet in their Hi-Tec basketball boots. I half expected him to say 'Have a nice day,' but his accent was a hard to comprehend mixture of black America, West Africa and the east end. He lived close to the shop, and one night one of the white youths tried to run him down as he crossed the road. At midnight, when he closed the shop and put the bins out, they'd walk by taunting 'nigger, nigger'.

Inevitably Dalton lost his patience, once vaulting the counter to get at his tormentors, who kicked in the shop window and ran into the street. Mr Hayat was approached three times by men who suggested life might be more comfortable if he paid protection money. He refused. A ringleader said: 'This is a white man's area. We're going to shoot you. Burn the place down with petrol bombs.' A few nights later two petrol bombs were thrown at the shop. By then Mr Hayat was calling the police three or four times a week. But the soft soap continued. Dalton said: 'We'd be told, "They've been taken care of, they'll never come close to the shop. Don't worry, they'll never do this, they'll never do that." They'd be back again straight away.' Mr Hayat asked the police to spare one man for one day to protect the shop and watch what was going on. 'They refused. Told me that if I was scared I should "go home". I don't know which "home" they meant.'

He was trapped. Fighting back wasn't worth it because it drove away customers. 'You don't,' as Dalton put it, 'open a shop to make a fighting place, but to make a living.' Appeasement was almost as bad. The youths sensed that the two men were scared, and played cat and mouse with them. They would stay away from the shop for a few days or weeks, allowing custom to seep back. Then they'd stage another confrontation. 'My business,' said Mr Hayat, 'was going completely dead.' One night, fearing an attack, he assembled some friends in the back of the shop, reasoning: 'If there were more of us, we'd have a better chance of survival.' That evening the police *did* come, accused Mr Hayat and his friends of plotting criminal mischief, and threatened to prosecute them for gang warfare.

The health of both men began to suffer. Dalton said: 'I can't take the pressure, no more. So much headaches. I can't sleep, man. Headaches, can't sleep. I want to leave the shop. But I won't run. They'll only chase me to my home.' (He did, in fact, later leave, opting for unemployment rather than the intolerable pressures of the shop.) Mr Hayat passed through that phase. He abandoned his hope of moving his family into the upstairs flat, which was why the conversion was unfinished. He couldn't place them in an environment in which they would be insulted daily and possibly in mortal danger from arsonists as they slept. He himself battled on hoping for a 'miracle'.

What actually happened was the bloodiest fight yet. At about ten o'clock one winter's evening, his brother-in-law, Mike Lone, originally from what was Tanganyika, with Mr Lone's son, Naeem, and a cousin were leaving the shop after a visit. One of Mr Hayat's persistent persecutors was on the pavement with a glass of beer in his hand. As the Lones left, he started his familiar abuse, calling Mr Lone a 'Paki bastard'. Mr Lone told his son and nephew to ignore the man, and made a sign with his finger to his head, as if to say 'he's mad'. The youth threw his beer over Mr Lone, followed by the glass, which narrowly missed his head and smashed against the car. He ran to a pub opposite, and seconds later rushed back out with a mob of about fifteen young whites at his heels. 'They were coming out of the pub like flies,' said Mr Hayat. The gang pitched into the Lones, with four or five youths on Mr Lone and another four or five on his son. Sticks, knives, bottles, scaffolding poles were used. A girl joined in with her high-heeled shoes. Traffic halted as fighting spilled across the road.

When it was over, Mr Lone had to have seven stitches in a jagged wound below his right ear – two inches further down and his neck would have been slashed open – and three stitches in a head wound. His back also was badly hurt. His son had broken his hand, and had to have stitches in a face wound. Two of the assailants were arrested in the pub, where they had returned to continue drinking, and two others were charged later. (As I write, their trial is yet to be held.)

The affray ruined two lives. Mr Hayat's business virtually ceased. The night I was there the shop door only opened when the wind blew it. 'Crack' it would go every five minutes as a fierce gust swirled down Barking Road, deceiving the listener upstairs that business was being done below. Dalton took a total of £35 in twelve hours on that day. Mr Hayat said: 'The publicity from this case has ruined my business right to the ground. I've tried selling, but nobody wants to know. I can't shut because I can't pay off my debts. I have lost everything. Sooner or later the shop will have to go. When it does, I'll never be able to stand up again and do anything positive.' (Later he was negotiating with a potential buyer, but at a price that would leave him with nothing with which to start again or to buy another home.)

Without the thuggish assaults, with decent police protection, he would have had a comfortably expanding business, a home for his family and the beginnings of a secure future. The casual destruction of his life by a band of teenage racists left him with mixed emotions, and fantasies of a Government-stimulated conspiracy to drive immigrants out of the country. He has white friends, and has lived happily in many parts of Britain outside London's east end, but his bitterness was winning out. 'If a white man goes to Africa or India, believe me, they give him so much respect. I have been here twenty years. Is it my fault that the economy's in trouble? What are we? Are we really second-class citizens? If we are, they should come out and tell us, then at least, like in South Africa, we'd know where we are and what to expect.

'The way this country is going with all this racialism in the hearts of people, it is not worth living here. I've had enough, not because I'm scared, but because I've lost heart and interest in the shop. Made me hard now. I've stopped being a nervous wreck. Trouble doesn't really bother me any more. I'm not scared of these boys.' He was, however, strangely frightened of being arrested for a revenge attack, and going to prison, a disgrace he felt he couldn't survive, but a danger he thought was real enough. 'Coloured people are arrested these days if they fight back, even if they are innocent,' he said, and told the story of a friend who had been chased in his car by white youths who appeared determined to drive him off the road. Knowing that such things happen – pursuing skinheads forced a car driven by Asians to crash in a Thames Valley chase in the autumn of 1986 – he sped away, finally having to stop at a zebra crossing. The youths jumped out, and one punched him in the face. A passing police car stopped. The youths claimed they were restraining the Asian because he had been driving recklessly. The Asian gave his version, but was promptly charged with dangerous driving. The case was eventually dropped after his father took it up with his MP. The police told the young Asian that, if he had a complaint, he would have to take private proceedings against the white youths.

I heard many similar stories. One of the most extraordinary was the November 1986 attack on the Markazi Mosque in Christian Street, Tower Hamlets. Fifty youths stoned the mosque. Police arrived as the worshippers came out to defend the building, and, although the attackers were within sight and could be identified, the only people arrested were three of the congregation.

'The police,' said Mr Hayat, 'are the biggest gang. I am sure the Government is encouraging them to ignore white hooligans.' A few nights before I visited, another, more serious, affray had taken place a few yards from the Southern Fried Chicken shop. White youths attending a party had, it was said by black youths at another party, been squirting tear gas through the letter-box where the black gathering was being held. Three blacks went to remonstrate, and one was slashed in the face with a broken bottle, losing, so it proved, the sight of one eye. (Two months later the police appealed for witnesses on BBC's 'Crimewatch', but received the smallest number of responses ever to a national television appeal.) 'It's boiling here, man, boiling,' said Dalton Macauley, 'someone is going to get killed.' As I left, two white men in their late twenties emerged from a housing estate near Mr Hayat's shop. They were built like bulls, wore rolled jeans, denim jackets, bovver boots, woollen caps above shaven heads, and each had a powerful dog on a lead. Whatever business they were about that cold night, they were not vigilantes protecting Asian shop-keepers.

The next day I went to see Mr Lone in an Essex suburb. Londoners were still being advised to stay at home; British Rail was in disarray. But the odd tube, damp and cold, juddered its way through the east end, past a landscape of gas works, terraced homes, small factories and high-rise flats that had assumed the unreal, romantic aspect of a Lowry painting. Then the pebble dash terraces, with snow-bound vegetable patches and potting sheds, and finally ribbon development along arterial roads, from where bank clerks, book-keepers and office girls commute into London. The elderly ticket clerk smiled hugely: 'Taxis. No. No rank here. No phone either. You'll have to go to the hospital and ring from there.' It might have been the Scottish Highlands, rather than a station less than twenty miles from Throg-morton Street.

At the time of the attack, Mr Lone was forty-six. He had come to Britain in 1965 with high expectations. The British he had known in Africa had been professional people, 'gentlemen'. Here he was shocked by the difference. He met prejudice in the soccer team he joined – players refused to recognize him on the street, especially 'if they were with their mother, girlfriend or sister'; prejudice at work – a foreman who held back his application for promotion, a worker who wouldn't have a coloured man as a 'mate'. There were compen-sations: another foreman protected him, a fellow player urged the manager to play Mr Lone in the first team.

He had had another traumatic experience ten years earlier. He had been driving on a summer's day with his young family when a pair of motorcyclists had spat at them, their spit flying through the window and hitting his eight-year-old son in the face. The boy started crying, and Mr Lone turned the car round and caught up with the youths. They jumped from their bikes, shouting: 'Get out, you Paki bastard,' and hit him across the head with a heavy piece of wood. Police were passing, and took Mr Lone to hospital, where he was detained for three days with concussion, yet they refused to prosecute, saying it was a civil matter. (Mr Lone learned later that the same youths *were* prosecuted for a similar assault on a white victim.) When Mr Lone recovered – he was off work for several weeks – he wrote to the Metro-politan Police Commissioner. 'What protection does a citizen get for defending himself against hooligans?' he asked, adding ironically: 'Will it be in order for me to hit someone with a similar piece of wood?' To me he said: 'The law and the police are very soft. If an Englishman is attacked by a black man, it is a big issue. If a black man is attacked, it is of no importance unless someone is killed.'

Nothing, however, had prepared Mr Lone for the ferocity and unexpectedness of the attack outside Mr Hayat's shop. 'For a few minutes I thought the world was turned over,' he said. I met him two months after the assault: he pulled up his trouser legs, and his knees were still black with bruises, his facial scar was livid. But, worst of all, his back injury – he thinks he was hit by a lump of wood – had become progressively worse. He found it hard to stand for long, and had been forbidden to lift anything. His business – repairing domestic appliances from his own shop – had ceased. 'I had always been concerned about the future, but this made me wonder. You plan for things, and then something like this happens and everything stops,' he said, adding 'except the bills.' The local authority small business adviser suggested he should sell or let his shop so that he had an income. His life, like his brother-in-law's, had been destroyed by the yobs of Canning Town.

Mr Lone lost a stone in weight, and didn't feel like eating. He had been a keen sportsman, who before the attack jogged each night, played badminton and table tennis. Those activities had, of course, also stopped. There was about him a similar lacklustre air of fatalism to that about Mr Hayat. He was too dejected to make plans, though he talked enviously of brothers in Canada. 'They don't have these kinds of attacks there. In Germany, when a Turkish *gastarbeiter* was murdered, the Government made a major outcry. This country is not improving. Racial discrimination is against the law, but apparently it is not illegal to attack someone because of the colour of his skin.' Of the attack on his son and himself, he said: 'It is unbelievable that this is happening in England. It is very hard to interest the papers: only the Asian ones take any notice. If this had happened to whites, it would have been all over television, everywhere.'

It is hard to disagree with that judgment. Imagine a white-owned shop in the middle of an area almost exclusively inhabited by West Indians. Every day a gang of young West Indians enters that shop, hurling racist abuse at the owner, stealing, fighting and smashing things. Respectable customers stay away and the business begins to collapse. The police say they will have 'a few words' with the black yobs, then visit and warn the white shopkeeper that he will be 'done for gang warfare' if he has friends round for solidarity and protection.

How long would such a story stay off the front pages of the popular tabloids? MPs would bob up and down, 'Any Questions' would work itself into a lather of self-righteous indignation, and Enoch Powell would be trundled out to say 'I told you so.'

Seen through Asian eyes, the police, for all their protestations – to which I will come – are a highly partial force. Mr Lone, who is, colour apart, a model industrious, self-employed citizen of Mrs Thatcher's Britain, had recently been stopped by police. He and his son were ordered out of their van and separated, and the van searched. 'What are you looking for?' asked Mr Lone. 'We'll tell you when we find it,' replied the police, who were rude and casual. When they had found nothing, it emerged that they had been searching for drugs. How many white service engineers going about their business get stopped and frisked on such suspicions? 'They push you around, ask unfair questions, say "Hey blackie, come here,"' said Mr Lone. Conservative, middle-aged citizens like him are beginning to approve of the tougher attitudes inevitably being adopted by younger Asians. After the Canning Town attack, a group of friends met to discuss what they should do. After listening to his elders, a younger man burst out: 'This is all talk, all bullshit.' In the minds of a rapidly swelling number of Asians, the time for 'bullshit' has passed.

That night, after leaving Mr Lone, I travelled to another world. The address I had been given in West Ham appeared at first to be an abandoned property. What had once been a shop window was crudely boarded with corrugated iron. The battered blue door, with its letterbox above the height of a man's head, looked as if it had not been opened in months. Eventually a glimmer showed in the half-light above the door, and first barking and then shuffling could be heard. A Pakistani woman, a scarf wrapped around her head, signalled me in. Her face was tired and lined, and the hair beneath the scarf was grey. I took her to be in her sixties, and was very surprised to learn later she was only forty-nine.

She led me into a small back room which was a tailor's den: a middle-aged man in a woollen hat and a thick, rollneck pullover sat at one of two Singer sewing machines. Paper patterns hung from the blue panelled walls, and pieces of cut material cluttered every surface. A young woman, dressed in baggy pink trousers, embroidered slippers, and a green cardigan, was on the phone. The room was a tiny sweatshop: looking at the two treadle machines, I sensed the hours of toil that had been passed there, and the solitary drudgery that went to make a subsistence living. Neither of the older people spoke good English, though the man, who had arrived in Britain in 1961, tried with a loud, insistent voice, adding from time to time 'You understand' in such an imploring manner that it was impossible not to say 'Yes.' His wife had only joined him in 1967. Such separations, and the loneliness they bring, are suffered by many immigrants.

This was a family under siege. Cocooned in their workshop, barricaded behind the corrugated iron, and warmed by a gas fire and whirring electric blower, they were safe for a while from an outside world of sustained hatred which, by then, had trapped them in that hole for four years. On the floor lay a large, nondescript dog, defiantly named 'Soldier', their ultimate deterrent. Nasreen, the daughter on the phone, nineteen and employed as a clerk by the council, fiercely bright and voluble in the consonant-swallowing manner of the east end, had, I discovered, been conducting a campaign to free her family from their misery that had reached as far as Mrs Thatcher herself.

She had become something of a media-freak, producing dog-eared *Daily Mirror* cuttings, and a large blue file of correspondence. Life had been, she said, repeating a phrase that had pleased John Pilger of the *Daily Mirror*, 'sort of like living beneath a table'. Pilger had gone one better, dubbing her 'Anne Frank With a Telephone.' Her *pièce de résistance* was a dog-eared, red diary, in which she had recorded her family's persecution. It was monotonous stuff – a catalogue of harassment: windows being smashed; stones thrown – Nasreen's father was nearly hit by a rock; the door kicked in; rubbish tipped on the step – 'it's good for you,' one of their persecutors had said; excrement dumped at the door – once, at least, a whole bucketful; urine seeping into the hall; graffiti spray-painted on their walls; and endless, endless name-calling. 'Paki' must punctuate yob talk as regularly as 'fuck'.

Her mother was a nervous wreck, worn down by years of sitting through the night, watching into the street in case the house should be attacked. The police had either lost interest or were indifferent. The one time the family brought a private prosecution against assailants – the recommended procedure for common assault – the magistrates bound over both the family and their tormentor, making a mockery of justice. Nasreen's father – like Terry Hayat – had seen his dreams destroyed by harassment. He had for years run a market stall in Petticoat Lane, and had bought the house with the shop in order to move up in the world. In the event, he lost even the stall. Louts attacked his van; finally, it was stolen together, says Nasreen's father, with £33,000 worth of leather jackets. With those jackets went the stall, and the tailor now sits at his treadle producing garments on piecework for a local manufacturer.

What especially bewilders the family is that they had lived in the east end without persecution for fifteen years. Their MP told them to cut their losses, and move into council accommodation, but the family refused. Said Nasreen: '*They'll* think they've won, and that we just gave up.' Occasionally, there is a break in the harassment, but it always starts again. The tensions in the home become intolerable. Nasreen's father is blamed for buying the house; her mother, a sufferer from acute asthma, is on permanent medication, including tranquillizers and sleeping pills. The stale, trapped air in that back room hits the visitor as he comes through the door: 'We have no relatives in this country, so we don't go anywhere,' said Nasreen bleakly.

Her father, who had been silent for some time, nodding encouragement to his forceful daughter, boomed into life again, contrasting how kind the English had been a quarter of a century ago with his treatment today. Then if you were lost, he said, or on the wrong bus, someone would patiently help you. Today, they say, 'if you can't speak the language, why don't you go home, Paki?' He added: 'I cannot believe what is happening. How it has changed. The police used to help, but the world's changed so much. When there's trouble, they tell us to get inside, and say they'll deal with it. But we don't feel they do anything.' Nasreen added: 'We're all human beings. All it is, we are a different colour and wear different clothes.'

It is easy to assume that purgatory of this nature is suffered by immigrants only when they and their white neighbours live in conditions of overcrowding, poverty and unemployment. But there have been a growing number of serious attacks in suburban areas, such as petrol being poured through the letter-box and set alight while a family sleeps. I stumbled across an example of what it can be like to be brown in Britain in the remote Durham village of Easington Colliery.

While I was researching the north–south divide, a story broke about an Indian shopkeeper, who, driven mad by eight years of persecution from local youths, had snapped, and attacked two teenagers with a metal bar. He was charged with wounding the youths. Although the judge sentenced the Indian to a suspended nine-month prison term, he directed his judicial strictures almost entirely at the village, and bound over the victims of the shopkeeper's assault. The judge said: 'If there is any more harassment of this family, the magistrates should send the culprits to this court. With any luck I will be able to deal with them.' The story ran across the front page of the *Northern Echo* under the headline 'JUDGE SLAMS RACE-HATE VILLAGE.'

The shopkeeper, Harbnajan Bhondi, was a chubby, friendly man of thirty-six – though he looked considerably older – who ran a sweet shop cum general store halfway down Easington Colliery's steep main street. He was by no means a bloated capitalist – even by Easington standards. His shop was one of many in the large village, and business, because of local prejudice, was poor. 'When I first came here I was taking five hundred pounds a day. But now I am lucky if I take a hundred, which is a hell of a difference. Instead of going up, I am going down.' During the miners' strike Mr Bhondi had given nearly eight hundred pounds to NUM funds.

He led me upstairs to his sitting room, another of those beleaguered rooms with drawn curtains to which I became accustomed. One of his sons pulled back the orange drapes to show three or four airgun pellet holes in the ugly reinforced glass. The back bedroom windows were boarded. Downstairs, the shop window was covered with a grille that might have deterred the Great Train Robbers. Mr Bhondi had just been released from hospital, where he had been treated for a nervous disorder. 'I was,' he said, 'shaking like a jellyfish.' His children had been removed from a local school because of bullying. Once more, immigrant hopes had been destroyed by racial violence and prejudice. Yet the people of Easington Colliery regarded themselves as the salt of the earth, far superior in their tolerance and lack of snobbery to southerners.

Mr Bhondi came to England with his father when he was twelve. His ambition had been to be a doctor, but poor English restricted his education. He trained as a welder and mechanic, and worked for nearly eight years at Ford's Dagenham plant at the same time driving a minicab, putting in long hours to amass some modest capital. In 1978 a friend in Newcastle saw an advertisement for the Easington shop, and the Bhondis came north. 'We had the impression it was nice and quiet here, but that only lasted a few weeks,' said Mr Bhondi. In the first year, the shop window was smashed fourteen times. Such attacks became so frequent that, by the time of the court case, the family no longer got up in the night if they heard a crash.

Daily they were insulted in the shop and on the street – 'black bastards' and 'nig-nogs'. Their intimidators rattled the metal grilles at all hours. The children never left home on their own except to visit specific friends, or to go to their new school, where the headmaster kept a tight eye on bullies. Mr Bhondi worked from 9.00 a.m. to 9.00 p.m., only leaving to buy supplies, or visit friends and relatives in other parts of the north-east. If he left his car on the street, it would be vandalized.

For years, the police were inert. 'You'd call them, and they'd come and take the brick away,' said Mr Bhondi. Eventually, the Bhondis themselves obtained the names and addresses of their assailants by paying village informers. After Mr Bhondi had involved his MP, the police became more supportive, and a police constable had recently spent a week in the shop in an effort to deter further attacks. Mr Bhondi said with gratitude: 'They are the only reason we are alive.' His instinct was to face his persecutors out: 'If I leave, they'll think I'm running. There'll be a few like them in the next place. It will start all over again, just like the westerns. I don't want to be a fugitive.'

The Bhondis were no threat to anyone in Easington Colliery – they had been, when they arrived, the only Asian family. A social worker neighbour said: 'Mr Bhondi's friendly and generous. I don't think I'd be like that if what has happened to him and his family had happened to me.' I talked to several people about the family's ordeal; most said that it was clearly a bad business, but they had been unaware of it, which, in such a small community, seemed inconceivable. I heard about it on my first day there – before the court case. A local councillor was honest, if not very courageous. 'I am aware of it. But I've never kept up with it. I would have to delve into it before I could answer any questions.'

She spoke, I felt, for the rest of us, particularly the national leaders. Intellectually, we know what goes on: we can scarcely avoid it if we take a serious newspaper. In 1986 wide coverage was given to a report of the House of Commons Home Affairs Committee, which opened with the words: 'The most shameful and dispiriting aspect of race relations in Britain is the incidence of racial attacks and harassment . . . the problem is especially serious in a few boroughs . . . and is particularly directed at those of Asian origin.' The MPs cited a Greater London Council catalogue of reported abuse; 'racist name-calling, rubbish, rotten eggs, rotten tomatoes, excreta, etc., dumped in front of the victims' doors, urinating through the letter-boxes of the victims, fireworks, burning materials and excreta pushed through letter-boxes, door-knocking, cutting telephone wires, kicking, punching, spitting at victims, serious physical assault, damage to property, e.g. windows being broken, doors smashed, racist graffiti daubed on door or wall. Dogs, cars, motorcycles are still being used to frighten black people. Shotguns and knives have also been used.'

They quoted evidence from the Manchester Council for Community Relations, which stressed the need to remember: 'the reality which lies behind all of these cases – an individual or family living in fear, subject to humiliation, stress and physical danger, frequently too terrified for their safety to allow children to play outside, driven to tranquillizers and sleeping pills, constantly on the alert wondering whether tonight will bring a brick through the window, or tomorrow morning the words "NF – Pakis go home!" on their front door. Family life is destroyed as the parents and children, almost invariably, show their frustration, anger and fear to each other. What was a home becomes a prison.' The MPs commented: 'The harm caused by racial incidents is not simply the injury and damage they impose directly, but the fear and the blighted lives to which they give rise.' They also were struck by the degradation caused by spitting, and quoted a Bangladeshi who told them: 'The daily walk to and from work and school becomes a never-ending nightmare.'

The committee stated the crux of the problem: 'It is difficult for a white person to imagine the constant fear and the experience of attacks and harassment upon one's self, one's children and one's home motivated solely by racial hatred.' The MPs added: 'This lack of awareness goes far to explain why policies and measures to counter racial attacks have developed only slowly and on an *ad hoc* basis.'

John Tufail-Ali is a member of the management committee of the Community Alliance for Police Accountability (CAPA) based in Tower Hamlets. The day I went to see him in one of those all-purpose protest buildings – 'Self-defence for Unemployed Women' was being advertised in the lobby, and free newspapers for Gays were on display – Sir Kenneth Newman, the former Metropolitan Police Commissioner, launched an initiative against racial harassment. In a radio interview Sir Kenneth lambasted organizations like CAPA: 'These so-called monitoring groups operate from an ideological stance and are very clearly anti-police . . . they have this long history of tendentious commentary.' Which, though often true, is a useful sleight of hand for dismissing the allegations that monitoring groups bring to public attention.

Mr Tufail-Ali is an unusual man. He appears to be a Yorkshireman, with sandy, curly hair and an instantly recognizable accent. But, he told me, his mother had been a Pakistani – a Pathan from Lahore – from whom he had taken his name, and he had been brought up in Dorset. His father was a soldier, and at fifteen he also had joined up. In the army he found himself a part of what he called 'virulent racism'. Like the police force, he said, the army envelops its men in 'a hermetic existence, which sees itself as separate from civilians. This creates an elitist ethos, and is rigidly hierarchical. If you are at the bottom of such a system, you have to find someone who is inferior to you. That's why racism is prevalent in uniformed ranks.' He said his father had brought him up to feel superior to his mother on two counts; because she was coloured and because she was a woman. In his twenties he had had a crisis of remorse – that's when he'd taken his mother's name – resigned from the army, gone to university and been radicalized.

I started to talk about the prevalence of petty racism, like spitting. Before I could continue, he – clearly believing I was ignorant of more serious assaults – cried 'Can I disabuse you?', and from the top of his desk picked up and brandished a thick wodge of documents, which were a record of racial incidents for the first nine months of 1986 in the Tower Hamlets police division. I later saw the entries for one month, in which most of the victims had been Asian. The incidents included:

VICTIM: Asian male, aged thirty-two years.
INCIDENT: Assault.
REMARKS: One of two white males aged twenty to twenty-five slashed victim in the face, inflicting a wound requiring nineteen stitches in an unprovoked attack.

VICTIMS: Three Asian boys, aged eight, nine and eleven.
INCIDENT: Assault, Abuse, Threats.
REMARKS: Victims were walking back to their school with a teacher when two white boys aged about thirteen years abused and threatened them. One of the victims was hit and another was kicked. The boys had previously verbally abused the victims.

VICTIMS: Asian male, aged thirty-eight years.
INCIDENT: Criminal Damage.

REMARKS: A male suspect attempted to smash the window of an un-occupied Indian restaurant with an iron bar and failed. The suspect ran off leaving a bottle containing petrol and a piece of rag outside the premises at 2.45 a.m.'

Those incidents are taken at random: the list continued in similar vein for many pages. The most dispiriting reading was the column marked 'Results'. The only 'solution' recorded was when a white man drew a knife and threatened an Asian in the presence of a police officer, 'refused to desist and was arrested'. Typical comments were: 'Local inquiries made with no useful information being obtained' (entered many times), and 'Area searched with victim with no trace of suspects.'

These bald reports say nothing as to the diligence of the police. Mr Tufail-Ali said: 'There seems a marked reluctance by significant sections of the police to pursue racial abuse effectively. Black people lose faith because they get no positive support. By complaining they lay themselves open to reprisals. Eventually this produces emotional paralysis.' Sir Kenneth Newman would disagree entirely, but, after meeting many victims, I had to side with Mr Tufail-Ali.

Sir Kenneth had said in his radio interview: 'What is important is that the official policy of the force is definitely against any form of racism, and that policy is clearly located in written instructions. We are an equal opportunities employer, and have adopted the code on that subject, so institutionally we are definitely not a racist organization.' Nothing in that statement could be faulted, except its spirit, which reflects the complacent attitude of the British Establishment on this issue. 'Official policy ... written instructions ... code ... institutionally ...' They all miss the point. Only the looniest of the left would actually accuse Scotland Yard of having an officially institutionalized racialist policy. What would cut ice would be if the police showed more enthusiasm for tackling racial intimidation, if a few of the 'rotten apples', on whom all malpractice in police forces is blamed, were detected and thrown out of the barrel, and if the rest of the force kept its racial opinions to itself.

When Mike Lone reported a break-in near his shop, the police came within three minutes; when he and his son were in danger of their lives, the attack was over before the police appeared. When white youths stoned an east end mosque and the police arrived only in time to arrest three worshippers, a senior officer was widely quoted as having said: 'We are British police, and we are here to protect our own people.' Monitoring groups accuse officers of 'harassing and intimidating victims'. One organizer said: 'They ask questions like "How did you provoke this?" and "Did you do anything to provoke this?" They also ask about the immigration status of victims. Our experience shows that the police are racist and blatantly so, using words like "wogs" and "niggers" in front of witnesses.' An Asian whose house was destroyed by an arsonist during a spate of such attacks in the summer of 1985 said: 'I can't believe that white families would get taken to the police station and be questioned for eight hours if their house had been burned down.'

Monitoring groups are magnets for bright young Asians with a commitment to their communities. Nishit Kanwar's family were Hindu Punjabis, and he came to England from Kenya in 1972 at the age of ten. He is a handsome, articulate young man, who went to grammar school and then to Keele University, where he read international relations. (He laughed when I asked whether that qualification might have helped him towards a 'conventional' career.) He was, he said, politically conscious from a young age. He works for the Newham Monitoring Project in the borough that recorded the highest National Front vote in Britain in the 1979 and 1983 general elections. East enders, he said, tended to regard their patch as 'white by right', and added, 'in this area a lot of people expect abuse: it is part and parcel of the price they pay for living here. These conditions drive people to extremes: the environment fosters a physical response. People are imprisoned by the fear of going outside. When you visit, it all comes pouring out.' He estimated that 60 per cent of school-leavers from ethnic minorities in the borough were out of work. 'When the docks thrived, the east end was the bread basket of London, now it is the dumping-ground,' he said.

Although there was a 'thriving local fascist community', he estimated that no more than 5 per cent of attacks are by members of the National Front. 'It is much more likely to be the next-door neighbour.' The monitoring group, which gets three hundred emergency calls for help a year – the majority reporting racial attacks, but a substantial number complaining of police harassment, knows most local extremists and where they operate, and can therefore make accurate assessments. His own car had been vandalized a few nights earlier; the project office had been attacked with a pickaxe handle; he showed me the enclosed steel letter-box, installed to prevent arsonists pouring petrol into the hall and setting fire to the building. The police, he said, 'were as much part of the problem as the attackers.' He claimed that the group's phones were tapped. 'We cannot conduct a phone call because of the crackling: it's a joke.'

The violence and the police indifference, he said, were breeding a tough generation. 'Asians are no longer prepared to accept the stereotype of passive victims. They are fighting back.' Ninety-six per cent of blacks under eighteen had been born in Britain. 'They are much more militant. They have nowhere else they can call home, but they are still referred to as "immigrants". They are going to respond increasingly violently.' He cited the well-publicized cases of the 'Newham 7' and 'Newham 8', in which young Asians were charged with offences involved in fighting back. The police, he said, were now trying to 'criminalize' Asians as they had done West Indians, accusing them of involvement in gang warfare. In 1986 a Scotland Yard report was 'leaked' to crime correspondents, which alleged the 'rapid rise of violent, military-style Asian gangs in organized crime in Britain.' Such leaks are taken at face value by papers like the *Daily Mail*, which reported beneath the headline 'NEW GANG MENACE AS ASIAN "ARMIES" MOVE IN. The gangs are suspected of involvement in drug trafficking; armed robbery; prostitution; protection rackets; and ritual rape. One police raid recently uncovered an arsenal of weapons, including guns, sledgehammers, machetes, swords, an axe and daggers.' *That* puts racial harassment in its place.

Courts, however, will accept that defensive violence makes for *bona fide* mitigation. The Newham defendants were acquitted of the more serious charges brought against them; Mr Bhondi from Easington found a sympathetic judge; and others have not been jailed as they might have expected had they not been seeking to defend or avenge themselves. Some Asians who have attacked the wrong targets, as one group did who jumped out of a car and beat up two passing whites, have been leniently treated. One of that group told the court: 'When we go anywhere, there's always racialist abuse, racist remarks about us. It's about time the Asians started doing something. When I got beaten up, nobody helped: people just walked by ignoring it. If you go to the police, they just write it down and do nothing. It's something that doesn't just happen to you one day; it's every day of your life.'

Few mainstream newspapers cover the harassment of Asians in depth or with much enthusiasm. Research is mainly carried out by monitoring and academic groups, and detailed reports appear in ethnic minority papers like *New Life*. C. B. Patel, *New Life*'s founder, emigrated from India to the former British colony of Tanganyika as a young man, moving to Britain to study law when his job was Africanized. He sold insurance to support himself, and rapidly built a small empire of shops. With capital behind him, he fulfilled an ambition he had cherished since his African days to establish an English-language paper for Asians. He first bought an ailing Gujerati paper in London, *Gujerat Samachar* ('Gujerat News'), and ten years ago started *New Life*, which now sells 25,000 copies.

The paper concentrates on Asian affairs, but also covers other ethnic communities. After an over-lavish launch, Mr Patel ran the paper on a shoestring, printing it from his basement and doing much of the distribution himself. The paper is now published near Hoxton Market in east London, and Mr Patel is still a hands-on 'editor-in-chief' and proprietor. When I went to see him, I was told he was out: in fact he was asleep, having been up all night ensuring that the paper was distributed despite the heavy snow. He meticulously cleared his desk of the disorganized clutter of journalism, swiftly changing from editor to proprietor. He was in his late forties, with thinning hair, an open-necked shirt, and checked jacket and trousers that didn't match. He half-smoked gold-banded cigarettes.

Some Asians accuse *New Life* of concentrating too much on negative aspects of immigrant life, a criticism anticipated by Mr Patel before I could raise it. The paper's most notable feature is a weekly 'Score of Shame', a report of racialist attacks throughout Britain. A typical week included: arson in Wakefield; a restaurant smashed up in Bolton; a shop window destroyed in Windsor; an old woman terrorized by a gang in her Bradford home; taxi drivers in the same town subjected to a series of assaults. 'We would like,' said Mr Patel, 'to bring out more positive aspects of life, but the reality of the attacks is hard to avoid: we learn of eighty to eighty-five a week.' I thought I'd misheard him. 'No,' he repeated, 'that's right – four thousand plus attacks a year that we get to know about.'

Having lived in both India and Africa, Mr Patel is not blind to racial, religious, and caste hatreds to be found elsewhere in far more widespread and virulent form than in Britain. 'This country is as civilized as any in the world. I have tremendous respect for the tolerance of the British. I do not say that most police are racist. The British bobby is a good institution. But there are black sheep, and there is a lack of resolution in stamping intimidation out. The law is made an ass, and law and order not meaningfully established.' He added: 'In

Britain the colour of skin is a uniform. Unlike previous immigrants, we won't be able to discard that uniform.' The intimidation stunts the natural dispersal of successful immigrants into the wider society. 'It creates a siege mentality; coloured immigrants will stick together in ghettos,' said Mr Patel.

I told him how President Reagan – whose record on racial issues is patchy – had gone to a black family's suburban home at which the Ku Klux Klan had ignited a burning cross on the front lawn. It was an immediate, emotional and effective gesture of society's atonement. The Reagans drank coffee with the family and embraced them on the spot where the cross had burned. Asians I met frequently complained of the lack of equivalent, visible leadership in Britain. Mr Patel asked: 'When was the last time that Mrs Thatcher went on national media, and gave a bold, brave stand, accepting full-heartedly that Britain is now a multi-cultural society and denouncing the attacks?' It was, of course, a rhetorical question. He contrasted Mrs Thatcher's low profile on the issue with the Queen's clear commitment to a multi-racial Commonwealth. Pandering to racism would, he said, create 'a Frankenstein, a monster.' He added: 'The Government can stop racial harassment any time they want. It requires leadership. They have the resources if the leadership is there. Asians are a docile community, who want to get on and establish financial security. They will not seek confrontation or fight their white neighbours.'

He said that certain east end pubs are known hotbeds of racism, yet the police do nothing about them. 'You can bet they would soon smash a kebab house run by Indians from where racial attacks were being launched. The British are not racist. They do not open their papers and say "I am glad to see Patel's shop was burned down." People think I am a "wet" when I talk like this, but things could be very different if the prime minister gave a lead. Increased racism will create a lot of pain, and everyone – not just immigrants – will suffer.' Mr Patel took me to the stairs as I left. 'Had I seen the graffiti on the building?' he asked. They had trouble, he said. People kicked and rattled on the door. They were close to a National Front office. Outside on the white walls I read the tediously familiar 'NF', 'Blacks out' and 'Pakis go home'.

The Asians who suffer most from deprivation and harassment are Bengalis in London's east end, most of whom came from the Sylhet province of Bangladesh. In January 1987 a House of Commons subcommittee reported that it was an 'educational and social disaster' that 74 per cent of Bangladeshis in their last year at school cannot speak English fluently. On top of appalling overcrowding – three families sometimes in a two-bedroomed flat, parents and small children sharing beds, older children on sofas; in private accommodation perhaps seven families cooking on one stove – this poor English, said the committee, restricts Bangladeshis' access 'to health and social services, and they appear to be disproportionately affected by racial violence'. The Bangladeshis have lower average earnings than any other ethnic group, have exceptionally high unemployment, and their children do badly at school. In one school in Tower Hamlets, 84 per cent of the pupils are Bengali. A community leader said: 'They are so very, very poor in Bangladesh that here they are in heaven. But that does not justify putting them in ghettos.' It was a view with which the Commons sub-committee agreed.

Brick Lane, with its sari shops, leather clothing manufacturers and Indian restaurants, is the heart of the community. Through upper windows, partially covered with newspapers and ragged curtains, a passer-by can glimpse the sweatshops. 'Shirts, blouses, dresses, trousers', read the signs. Jewish names are still painted above some shops now owned by Bengalis. The men wear thin, flapping trousers, and the women in winter look pinched and cold. The people peering from the balconies of the council estates behind Brick Lane and the children on the playgrounds are all brown. It was here in July 1987 that Prince Charles paid a visit, expressing dismay that the Bengalis were living in conditions that matched those of the Indian sub-continent.

The Federation of Bangladeshi Youth Organizations (FBYO) had a room in a former school that is now a community resource centre. Abdus Shukur, an FBYO volunteer, *had* overcome the disadvantages on which the Commons sub-committee reported. He arrived in 1968 at the age of twelve, had been ignored by his teachers because of his bad English, and had dropped out of school. Failure had been a shock, because in Bangladesh he had been one of the brightest in his school. Here he was considered a 'dimbo'. He said: 'The teachers' attitude was "don't worry about him; he can't do anything." I just wanted to get out, without O Levels or anything, because the school system held no charms for me. When I did get out, I found that, as a black person, I couldn't move, only do manual jobs.' When I met him, he was reading for a degree in order to become a teacher. 'The thing is that I am a survivor, but very few can come through because the odds stacked against them are so high,' he said.

Most Bangladeshis work, he said, for fellow Bangladeshis because to get other employment 'you have to be twice as highly qualified as a white contemporary. You have to be damn good. As a white, you're OK if you're mediocre.' He estimated that one or two members of every Bangladeshi family in Tower Hamlets were subjected to either racial abuse or suffered prejudice in the course of each year. It might be overt on the street, or covert in the DHSS office. His father, a businessman, returned to Bangladesh on retirement. 'He asked: "Why should I have to put up with this on a daily basis?" But my generation is trapped. We have been to school here, have our friends here, we cannot "go back". I have three kids, all born here. They know nothing different apart from a four-week holiday to Bangladesh. My four-year-old came back from school, and asked "What's a Paki?" Try explaining the connotations of that word to a four-year-old.'

Brown and black Britons desperately need an identity rooted in their parents' culture to serve as an anchor in a turbulent world, according to Mr Shukur. White immigrants can shed their antecedents and, within a generation, be assimilated, but 'the one thing we can never give up' – and he touched the back of his brown hand – 'is the colour of our skin. This is the one thing that still divides. Children are at a crisis; they have nothing to cling on to. They are looking for an identity that parents have too often stripped from them.' The English have remained monocultural, he said, very self-centred and arrogant. 'The "Great" in Great Britain is no longer accurate. Some people still fantasize on how it used to be and blame their altered condition on blacks. We're not the people to blame because we're at the bottom of the shitpile anyway. Most of us dream of returning "home". But where is home? We came in search of prosperity and a better education. As time went on, that dream was shattered. It's very difficult to make it here. Right at the bottom it's very difficult to scrape a living.'

Mr Shukur handed me a copy of *Jubo Barta*, the 'National Journal of Bengali Youth', which led its front page with a bitter attack on the popular press coverage of race. The reporting complained of was specifically about the 1986 imposition of visas for visitors from the Indian sub-continent and two West African countries, but immigrant groups are consistently unhappy with Fleet Street. On this occasion, there appeared to be a direct link between inflammatory press coverage and intimidation on the ground. Headlines from one paper were daubed on an Asian-owned Tower Hamlets newsagent's shop.

The story was the flavour of the week in mid-October 1986. The headlines cited by *Jubo Barta* included: 'THEY'RE STILL FLOOD-ING IN' – London *Standard*; '3,000 ASIANS FLOOD BRITAIN' – the *Sun*; 'IMMIGRANTS PARALYSE HEATHROW' – *Daily Mail*; 'ASIANS START HOUSING CRISIS' – *Daily Mail*. The *Star* commented: 'Britain finally began to drop the portcullis and raise the drawbridge against the alien hordes.' The *Sun*, under the banner headline 'THE LIARS', reported 'the 1,001 lies used by immigrants to cheat their way into Britain'. One pop paper wrote: 'Remember too that every male immigrant to this country represents either an addition to the dole queues, or a job lost to a native Briton, or both. We can afford neither . . . Some of their customs – child brides, arranged marriages, marriage to first cousins – are repugnant to Western minds. Many of them refuse to conform to our way of life, our laws and our customs . . . Nothing the Tories have belatedly done will solve any of these problems, but at least they will not be aggravated by more brown tidal waves.' Letters to the Director of Public Prosecutions, point-ing out that this article seemed a prima facie case of incitement to racial hatred, and therefore an offence, went unanswered.

A cartoon in the *Daily Mail* showed an immigrant arriving at Heathrow. He was depicted wearing a turban (the immigrants con-cerned were Bengalis, who do not wear turbans) and carrying a bed-roll; the caricature was clearly designed to make absolutely sure that the dimmest reader realized this person was both alien and destitute. The cartoon was divided into four pictures. In the first the immigrant is saying: 'Well, here I am arriving penniless at Heathrow.' In the second: 'Ooh look! £50 of taxpayers' money to stay at a posh hotel for my first night.' In the third: 'So this wonderful reputation the British have got themselves thoughout the world is true – they are . . .' In the fourth: 'stupid'. Almost nothing in that cartoon was factually accurate, and every pen stroke was suffused with malice. It is not sur-prising that people who read such cartoons daub racial insults on Asians' homes, make jungle noises at black footballers, or that their children run into corner shops, and shout 'Paki bastard.' The press is also guilty of omission. Mr Tufail-Ali showed me stories in ethnic minority papers, which had not been reported nationally, that – had they involved white people – would, without doubt, have made big news. Concern for ethnic minorities is known as 'bleeding hearts' journalism, and it is not popular in these swashbuckling days of young fogies, the new right, and newspaper editors of the Tebbit tendency. *Laissez-faire* race relations may have an intellectual appeal to those who espouse *laissez-faire* economics, but they can be, literally, deadly.

The most poignant experience I heard of was that of Mr Tahir Khan-Lodhi, who arrived in Britain from Kenya in 1964 with twenty-five pounds in his pocket. Twenty-one years later he bought for £10,400 – from the Queen's cousin, the Earl of Lichfield – the lordship of the manor of Bentley in Staffordshire. A banker with a house in Kent and a flat in the west end of London, he seemed to have fulfilled the immigrant dream. The title, of course, was mere flummery, but it had long and romantic historical associations. It was the daughter of a lord of the manor of Bentley who, in 1651, smuggled Charles II to safety after his concealment in the oak tree.

When Mr Khan-Lodhi obtained the title, he said: 'I read in the papers that it was for sale, and, as you are aware, there is much romance in owning a manorial lordship for sentimental reasons. For me it was just a beautiful dream. The title has been held for centuries by the same group, and it was a rare opportunity for me to enter that sort of landed family.' A year later when I contacted him, he was bitter and disillusioned, comparing the resentment his success had stirred up in Britain with the encouragement he imagined he would have received in the United States. The British, he said, were both lazy and keen to run down other people's triumphs. There was so much jealousy he was even considering re-emigrating.

The edition of *New Life* published the week I went to see C. B. Patel made sad reading. The front-page lead story began: 'It's only the third week of 1987, but it seems some things don't change. Racism is alive and well.' It told the story of the young man blinded in one eye by the gang of whites who had been tear-gassing a black party. Inside, an editorial commented on a report by British Euro-MPs that there is a racial attack in Britain every twenty-six minutes: 'Our community now instinctively avoids dark or lonely places, or certain areas or certain housing estates ... Police, apparently sympathetic, mysteriously seem to lack the power to stop the nightly attacks by known youths.' The article ended: 'It is also worth remembering that the vast majority of the white population are on our side too.' The tragedy of the immigrant experience is that the positive dimension has been squandered. Where, I was asked by the successful and the abused Asian alike, is the will to make us welcome?

⅔(12)⅔

DAMN YANKS

Shortly after my return from America I was invited for a drink to the home of a liberal acquaintance. He was a thoroughly decent man, impulsive in his gestures of kindness to others; I had never heard him speak ill of anyone. I started enthusing gently about life in the United States. Suddenly he rounded on me quite vehemently. 'I have never been to America, and I never wish to. If someone gave me a free ticket tomorrow, I wouldn't go.' A few months later I wrote an article in the *Observer* about Americans living in Britain in which I commended Americans for their generosity, their achievement in creating a vibrant, exciting, harmonious nation out of so many disparate people, and praising them for their assistance during the war. I pointed out that the British are deeply influenced by American culture and style. I concluded: 'This is not an occupied country. Without the Americans, it might have become one.' That single sentence did it. People wrote to say they would never buy the *Observer* again. I was abused across the length and breadth of the country.

A man from Welling wrote that the 'nearest approximation [to the occupation of Britain] is the current one of American penetration of the economic and military front, supported politically by some of our own "Quislings".' A London woman commented: 'Cultured people in this country do not consider that much of value . . . has ever percolated through from America to us. Noisy, pushy and ignorant American tourists are here on sufferance.' (What, I wondered, would a Spaniard conclude about the character of the British if he took as his crucial evidence the behaviour of British holidaymakers in the Mediterranean?) A London man wrote: 'I find Americans . . . intolerant, ignorant, bullying and small-minded.' Many correspondents argued that Washington and Moscow were twin sources of evil, with Washington, if anything, the more dangerous (this view is also frequently recorded by opinion pollsters from people who simultaneously say that Britain ought to keep her own nuclear weapons). Russia's contribution to winning the Second World War was lauded, and America's denigrated – 'Americans lost one in 325 of their population', wrote a man from Essex, 'the Russians one in eight', as if, somehow, service to a cause could be counted by wounds. The United States was castigated for historical sins – genocide of native Americans, slavery; for social ills – crime, racism, handguns; for imperialism – Nicaragua, South Korea, Thailand (!), El Salvador, Grenada and elsewhere.

None of these letters mentioned the 1939 Soviet–Nazi pact, the subjugation of eastern Europe, Stalin and the gulags, dissidents or secret police, Hungary 1956 or Czechoslovakia 1968, or Afghanistan. None of the writers troubled to recall the few blemishes in the British historical record – feudalism, the thumb screw, colonialism, child labour, transportation, and one or two we have in common with the Americans, like the slave trade and the treatment of indigenous peoples around the world. One writer summed up his feelings: 'Any impartial observer of world history in the last century should conclude that, next to fascism, the single most murderous influence on a global scale is clear: the domination of America.'

The central thrust of many of these letters was that the sins of the United States were so great that it was unacceptable to have to read anything in praise of any aspect of American life. To enjoy Disney World was to excuse slavery; to praise American generosity was to condone the murderous slaughter of the inner cities; to laud the opportunities available to the vast majority of Americans was to be callous towards the sufferings of the very poor. The United States was a seamless web of evil. (Eventually, when I thought that post on the subject was exhausted, there came just one letter saying kind things about Americans – from a retired squadron leader, living in Botswana, who as a young pilot officer had watched formations of B-17s taking off each morning from British soil. 'Five hours later I would see them limping back, fewer in number . . . great holes in wings and fuselages, Very lights looping off them to indicate burns and bodies aboard.')

I was reminded by these diatribes of reading an account of an anti-imperialist seminar in Mexico City. A left-wing French intellectual was holding forth about the evils of Uncle Sam; one of his audience, having heard it before, wandered to the back of the room and looked through the window. Below in the street was a great throng. 'Who are those people, and what are they doing in the street?' he asked a

Mexican standing by. 'Oh,' came the reply, 'there's always a crowd there. The American Embassy is round the corner. Those people are queuing for visas.' There may not be similar crowds in Grosvenor Square, but more British emigrate to the United States than the combined total from other western European countries: were it not for Green Card restrictions, the annual migration across the Atlantic would amount to a haemorrhage of Britain's most ambitious and enterprising countrymen. The man in the street likes the idea of a society that educates all of its children adequately; where the wrong accent is not an instant barrier; where effort will bring decent rewards; and in which open government rather than secrecy is a national presumption.

Taking stock eighteen months after my return, I found myself inevitably making comparisons between Britain and the United States. There are, of course, aspects of both countries that a wise man would incorporate in his blueprint for a decent society. (Like many who have lived on both sides of the Atlantic, I had fantasies of the perfect nation rising, like Atlantis, in the middle of the ocean.) But, as it is Britain I have come back to and where my children are growing up, it is Britain I am concerned with. The United States, still growing and brimful of self-confidence, will go on making the brash mistakes that some Englishmen find so distasteful. But America will also develop and mature, creating new opportunities for its people, and needs no one to fear for it. But Britain, staid in her ways, slapping preservation orders on outmoded ways of thought and action, needs taking by the shoulders and shaking. Coming back aross the Atlantic was like leaving a stiff, invigorating breeze to plunge into a stuffy, smoke-filled back room. Anti-Americanism is often the old codger in the corner's objection to having the window opened an inch to let in fresh air.

'Enterprise' has become a loaded word in Britain, almost interchangeable with Thatcherism. Enterprise is part of Thatcherism, certainly, but Thatcherism is an ideology which has been applied to matters that ought to lie outside the market-place, like university research and race relations. It has an intellectual purity which offends common sense. Many who 'fail' are not equipped to compete, and their failure is not due to some deep moral flaw or inadequacy which is susceptible to exhortation or bullying. That most over-borrowed of Hamlet's notions is perfectly applicable to Mrs Thatcher – there *are* more things in heaven and earth than are dreamed of in her philosophy. Where she is hated – as in Skelmersdale and Easington – it is not for her advocacy of enterprise, but for the limitations to her compassion and for her hectoring style. The tilt of her head, the glint in her eye, the tone of her voice unite to tell those who dare quibble with even the small print of her beliefs, 'Nonsense, you have got it quite wrong.' By being such a person, she damages the cause she espouses, like the dogmatic, self-righteous schoolteacher, whose pupils instinctively reject his lessons, valuable though they might be. Among the lasting consequences of Thatcherism will be harsh divisions between the uncaring and the uncared-for classes.

The Revd Deryk Evans told one of his congregation in Skelmersdale to stop taking her spiritual temperature all the time – 'You only take your temperature when you are ill.' If that is an accurate perception, Britain indeed is ill. By early 1987 taking the national temperature, addressing what the Victorians called the 'condition of England' question, had become an obsession. 'HOW FAR HAVE WE SUNK?' asked the *Spectator*. In the *Daily Telegraph*, Lord [Jo] Grimond wrote: 'Creeping disillusion rises like mist from the stagnant waters that surround us. Drugs and violence are spawned by vexation, boredom and disappointment.' The Conservative editor of the *Sunday Telegraph*, Peregrine Worsthorne, wrote of 'the country's frightening collapse into barbarism', and suggested that, outside economics, Thatcherism may be a cause rather than a cure of our national ills. Whatever your politics, there was plenty of saloon-bar evidence by the beginning of Mrs Thatcher's third term that things weren't what they used to be. A health administrator said to me: 'The last eight years represent an abrupt turn in British social history. We have run out of steam in a process that began in the early nineteenth century – the drive to improve public health, education and housing.' He added: 'A country can thrive either on its natural resources, which we have been squandering, or by selling things abroad. We are fast becoming a nation of bric-à-brac dealers who live by selling our junk to one another.'

People who wrote to me at the *Observer* after a series of articles I had written on aspects of Britain tended to an elegiac tone, decrying what they saw as an erosion in national decency and personal standards, and looking back wistfully to a vanished era of higher personal and moral standards and greater social cohesion. Their targets were various: a GP was disgusted by patients who skived off work; a Ford export manager had watched the disintegration of the car industry 'with a growing state of despair as we tore our industries apart via industrial anarchy'; the many correspondents who saw the 'yob' as a menacing symbol of national decline. Each age has looked back with nostalgia. In 1802 Wordsworth wanted to turn the clock back 150 years:

> Milton! thou shouldst be living at this hour:
> England hath need of thee; she is a fen
> Of stagnant waters.

Milton himself had feared that 'an age too late' might 'dampen my intended wing'. We as Britons believe instinctively that there has been an erosion in human stature: our politicians are not what they were; our policemen are more corrupt; there are not so many of 'the old school' about; those who teach our children are puny mortals set alongside the characters we remember from the classroom. Even where there has been a measurable improvement, as in sport, we still contend yesterday's men were giants: can there be a modern soccer player to compare with Stanley Matthews?

That said, there is no doubt that, despite B M Ws and the wine bars, Britain is suffering from a national malaise. Most people, like my letter-writers, know this, and deplore whatever facet of the malaise that affects them most. Britain did lose an empire, and did fail to find a role, but yearning to go backwards is fruitless. When Harold Macmillan died in December 1986, the period of his premiership was cast as a golden age, but at the time many who were idealistic had demonstrated against the 'Supermac' era as the hated culmination of 'thirteen years of Tory misrule'. What we do need is an injection of the values that have been branded as 'wet' by those – like City sharks – who find them inconvenient. I returned to a country devoid of moral political leadership. Ancient Lord Hailsham, dressed up like something from Gilbert and Sullivan's HMS Pinafore, occasionally sounded the alarm – 'We have betrayed the young because we have not taught them spiritually. We have left them with nothing to believe in, nothing to be proud of, nothing to hope for, nothing to seek.' The Church of England, no longer the Conservative Party at prayer, discovered the deep despair of the inner city, and, to the fury of the Government, broadcast the reality. On Merseyside and Wearside, people who had not darkened the door of a church in years turned to bishops David Sheppard and David Jenkins – castigated on the right as meddling clerics – for leadership. The politicians responded with their own moralizing. It is cheaper, of course, to throw morality at a problem than money.

I suspect that many decent people are opting out of the moral struggle. They may have given up their personal ambitions because the price was too high but still feel powerless to assert publicly the principles they believe in against the prevailing climate. The British reward system has perverted values – the 25-year-old money trader earning his tens of thousands knows deep down that he is not 'worth' that money – and the media propagate a spurious reality which washes like a rolling tide through the minds of readers and viewers. The real sins of television are not the current affairs programmes that embarrass the Government – the song and dance about these in a land where free speech is supposed to prevail is nauseous – but in the mind-numbing game shows and the escapism of the soap operas. The glossy American ones – 'Dallas', 'Dynasty', *et al.* – reduce life to a progression of snakes and ladders. In one episode a character loses a wife or a deal: two episodes later he'll win a better wife and a better deal. Our home-grown 'EastEnders' is a catalogue of verbal violence and hatred. Whenever I have watched it, I have never seen anything other than people snarling at one another – lovers, spouses, fellow drinkers, business partners – or actually fighting. Mary Whitehouse monitored two 'EastEnders' episodes and found four assaults or attacks and the entire cast involved in continuous bitter argument. 'All this made absolute nonsense of the codes of family and children's viewing which the BBC has published,' she said. For once I must agree with Mrs W!

Is it surprising that – two generations after the 1944 Education Act – the *Sun* sells over four million copies a day? Its essence was succinctly encapsulated by the *New Statesman* – 'big breasts, "Britain is best" and "Bully bites head off budgie".' The real gap between the two Britains could perhaps be most accurately arrived at by separating those who read the *Sun* from those who deplore its existence. The *New Statesman* concluded its analysis: '[the *Sun*] is the profane and bitter anger of the working class against those who set themselves up to tell them what to think and what to do'. The extension of middle-class values – which post-war liberals expected would happen by example and osmosis – was aborted by the 'them' and 'us' gulf that runs through the heart of these divided islands.

The right, being so in the ascendancy, has grown arrogant in its haste to pooh-pooh uncomfortable facts, like the deep inequalities of health between rich and poor, which time, nutrition and medicine have done little to erode. (A *Daily Telegraph* reader, applauding the demise of the Health Education Council, wrote: 'Surely we do not need an expensive report to tell us that the poor, with their likely disadvantages of inferior diet, housing and general discomforts are more likely to die earlier and contract diseases than those who are better off? [Assertions] that this situation is unacceptable in a democracy are difficult to understand.' The poor, as ever, are always with us.) At best, commentators do not believe the facts, dismissing them as the twisted work of the derided servants of the 'nanny state', like social workers: at worst, they don't care. In a society of 'haves', the 'have-nots' can rapidly become objects of derision, taunted for their poverty and inadequacies. Writers on the new right are witty and plausible, and they undoubtedly hold the high ground, but their logic often does not stand scrutiny.

I have before me an article in the *Daily Telegraph* by Norman Stone, Professor of Modern History at Oxford University, which argues that the crisis in British science will not be cured by money. It carries a characteristically new rightist headline – 'BRAINLESS TALK ABOUT THE BRAIN DRAIN' – with its ill-concealed sneer at anyone 'wet' enough to worry about the issue. Professor Stone uses three of his four columns to provide an entertaining account of how James Watt, Thomas Arkwright and Jethro Tull made their contributions to society without the first notion of what pure science was about, how the Cavendish Laboratory scraped by, and how the only general benefit from the American space programme has been the non-stick saucepan. Having put whingeing scientists thoroughly in their place, confirmed the prejudices of his £75,000-a-year City readers, and made it intellectually respectable not to care that British science is being driven into the ground, with one sentence he throws his argument into reverse: 'We must accept nowadays that science is much more complicated than in the past and requires money.' With one bound, our hero is free. Real life is not so easy.

One doesn't have to swallow all (or even most) tenets of Thatcherism to advocate capitalist enterprise as the most efficient engine to drive society and create the surpluses needed for collective action and for protecting the unfortunate. The records of nationalized industries and the attitude of State and local government bureaucrats demonstrate the inefficient way forward offered by the alternatives. But how do we translate that realism into action? Enterprise is bred into Americans: the kid brown-bagging groceries in a supermarket on a Saturday morning may well be the son of successful, rich parents.

How many privileged youths in Britain learn the fundamentals of enterprise from the bottom up? Young Americans working their way through college see nothing wrong in service, be it ever so humble. It gives them a grounding in the creation of wealth and close contact with less privileged or less gifted citizens, which stands them in good stead both in their careers and in everyday life. The director of a British enterprise trust said that when he visited schools he asked pupils if they had ever done anything 'enterprising', like repairing bicycles for money or selling home-made cakes. It was rare if more than one in twenty put up a hand. In an American school there was only one kid who *didn't* shoot up his arm.

In Britain, we have instilled in us the notion that enterprise is exploitive: one man's profit is made at another man's expense. The idea that it might create another man's opportunity didn't occur to me for many years. When John Bloom, the one-time washing-machine tycoon and pre-Thatcher Thatcherite, was a national serviceman at a remote R A F base, he chartered buses to take his fellow erks for Saturday nights out. What appalled me then was that, instead of splitting the cost amongst his comrades at arms, Mr Bloom made a profit on the deal. But, if he had not had that motive, a large number of bored teenagers might have spent Saturday cooped up in the Naafi drinking tea. And, although there are people who would have arranged the bus for nothing (and even borne the loss if someone had failed to pay up), there are, sadly, not enough such citizens to go round.

During the 1987 election campaign, we were constantly told that Britain was top of this or that league table for productivity, growth in employment and industrial efficiency. With three million unemployed, sixteen million in 'poverty', with the run-down, filthy inner cities, the lengthening hospital waiting lists, the physically depressing schools, the manufacturing output still below the level of eight years earlier, the rapidly widening balance of trade deficit on manufactured goods, common sense should indicate that the statistics, if not entirely a sham, are widely misleading. An understanding of the fundamentals of commerce and manufacture is growing; a schoolchild is more likely now than twenty years ago to be taught something of the economy of his own country; the concept that work has an objective – usually the satisfaction of a customer – beyond a wage for the worker is gaining ground; more people are breaking free of large, stultifying employers and doing something for themselves. But it will take a yet greater change in outlook and effort before the British society and economy will be regenerated in the manner in which Americans daily make things happen by responding urgently and automatically to necessity and opportunity. 'If you mention an idea at a dinner party,' said one former British diplomat in Washington, 'by noon the next day three of your fellow guests will have done something about it.'

In September 1986, the city of Southampton organized a reunion for GI brides who had sailed for a new life in the United States forty years before. Most had been very young, working class, and many had not known their husbands more than a few weeks or months. The women knew that it would be many years before they saw Britain again. 'You'll be sorry. You'll be back,' the dockers had shouted as they boarded their ships. 'We left under a cloud,' said one. 'In 1946 marrying a Yank was selling out to silk stockings and Hershey bars.' I met them at Broadlands, the late Lord Mountbatten's home, where they had been invited to a garden party: I was curious to know how different their lives had been in the States from those of siblings and friends whom they had left behind. The Solent Silver Band played wartime melodies, and in a corner of a marquee Patience Strong, wearing two strings of pearls and a hat that made her look like a straw lady, read from her poems:

> Behind the prison bars of Europe,
> men are listening in the dark . . .

The brides sat on red plush chairs swapping reminiscences of Tidworth camp, where they had been waited on by German POWs, processed and deloused. Having found one another again, they were determined to hold on. 'Just remember, if you ever get to California . . .'

A woman originally from Wales had been shocked to find her nephews and nieces on the dole: 'I didn't realize how hard it was for those who are out of work,' she said. Of a group of four sisters present, three had married blue-collar Americans, but nevertheless had enjoyed a life – cars, detached homes, kitchen gadgets, holidays – that it took the sister who stayed behind and married a builder thirty years to catch up on. An exuberant woman from Florida in a wild pink dress burst out: 'Like Martina Navratilova, I was born to be an American.' Even in her sixties, life was still very much a ball – 'parties, travel, dances, bridge.' A woman who had married a farmer in the middle of Alabama said she felt that it was only in the last ten to fifteen years that working people in Britain had been allowed a decent education. Both her sons had graduated. 'Here I am sure they would have been just labourers,' she said. Her nephews and nieces in Britain had left school at fifteen. She herself had studied for a degree: 'I would never have made it in England.'

They were frank about the disadvantages of American life. Several spoke of the financial disaster that could overwhelm a family if someone suffered a long, terminal illness. One woman, who had broken several bones in an accident, had been pitched out of hospital the day her insurance ran out, although she was only half mended. A retired couple were paying $2,400 a year on health insurance. I joined a jokey group. 'You ask me what would have happened if I'd stayed. Well, I'm old and grey now, and I would have been old and grey if I'd stayed,' said one in answer to the inescapable question. A woman started to talk about her brother. Her parents in Britain had died when he was fourteen, and he had been sent to join her in Florida. He had been a bright, ambitious boy, an honours student at college, and before long was running his own building business – the American dream personified. One day a gunman walked into his site hut and shot him dead. No one was ever arrested and no motive ever deduced.

While I have been writing this book, one vital section of British society has been voting with its feet. By 1987 the quantity and quality of the 'brain drain' was threatening the intellectual and economic future of Britain. *The Times*, normally as close to Mrs Thatcher as a coat of paint, suggested that the exodus of scientists was paving the way for Britain's 'exclusion from the twenty-first century': one thousand scientists a year were crossing the Atlantic. In March 1987 scientific and engineering research was halted for the rest of the year. Professors were forced to 'mothball' departments because of lack of chemicals; the breakdown of vital pieces of equipment like lasers threatened others. Scientists cancelled or postponed research they had spent months setting up.

The immediate crisis was caused by a pay rise for university workers which the Government awarded but refused to fund, throwing the burden on the fully stretched Science and Engineering Research Council (SERC). The amount of money involved was a derisory fifteen million pounds out of a total of £660 million. Scientists at all levels and in most disciplines were being offered jobs in the United States at upwards of three times their British salaries; across the Atlantic newly graduated British PhDs were paid more than their erstwhile professors. The Government responded to its critics by claiming that tax cuts would create a climate in which research could thrive – as if a few hundred pounds on a salary would compensate for the collapse of scientific departments. Scientists were particularly bitter because the SERC crisis coincided with the 1987 pre-election budget in which Chancellor Nigel Lawson disposed of nearly five billion pounds of public money in various giveaways.

The Government's fundamental misunderstanding of why scientists were leaving made campaigners like Denis Noble, Professor of Cardiovascular Physiology at Oxford University and a founder of the Save British Science Society, almost laugh in their anguish. Scientists were concerned with the destruction of everything they had worked for, and the government offered them peanuts. A physiologist already in the States said of his British experience: 'I even collected dole for two weeks. I will not go back on the dole, or to an emasculated research career.' In many subjects like inorganic chemistry and molecular biology a vital proportion of the best and brightest had already left Britain, creating a siphon effect that was rapidly sucking further talent across the Atlantic. A House of Lords Select Committee on Science and Technology reported: 'the overall picture conveys an impression of turmoil and frustration'.

It was not just scientists who were feeling they could no longer do their best work in Britain. Philosophers and historians were also departing. Philosopher Bernard Williams, Provost of King's College, Cambridge, himself about to depart, said: 'Today's problem is not fundamentally about salaries. Cuts in Government support, a lack of job opportunities and new requirements encouraging early retirement have led to a very high degree of demoralization.' He also claimed that the United States had become a more stimulating environment for philosophy; key issues are pitched into the public arena by the American legal system and Supreme Court. He told the *Sunday Telegraph* that, when he left, he would have 'the feeling of leaving behind a place in decline . . . you don't have to be a rat to leave a sinking ship. The passengers may also have to leave. So many people in England feel it is going downhill. You get tired of people – including oneself – saying it. I don't think it is as nice a place as it used to be.' As a reporter in Washington D C, I had felt something of the intellectual stimulation described by Professor Williams. It was not simply that I was writing about bigger events than I would have been in London, but that important ideas were chased about in public.

Few anti-Americans take the trouble to understand the positive side of American life. They watch 'Cagney and Lacey' and 'Miami Vice', see news extracts of Reagan bumbling his way through a press conference, and run into camera-festooned mid-westerners blocking Underground escalators, and persuade themselves that is all there is to America. They turn their faces from the unpalatable truth that the United States is the intellectual, literary, philosophic and academic heart of the English-speaking world. Britain has pockets of excellence, like the theatre and television (up to a point), and has civilized, literate men of affairs like Roy Jenkins and Michael Foot, but such achievements and people should not be mistaken for general superiority. It is not materialism that attracts the likes of Professor Williams and the annual average of a thousand 'brain-drainers' to leave for America, and, inasmuch as anti-Americans believe that it is, they delude themselves.

I met Professor Denis Noble, of the Save British Science Society, in an eyrie at the top of an office block near London's Victoria station. There was nothing on the door to indicate the presence of the Society, and the young woman who helped me find the rooms said she thought something 'secret' went on inside, which sounded unlikely. But it turned out that SBSS shared its accommodation with an organization that might be a target for the animal liberationists. Professor Noble sat at a leather-topped table writing an article in pencil: he had become more of a polemicist than a physiologist in recent months. He was a gentle, patient man, with longish, floppy hair and a cardigan, but he had been made angry enough by the paucity of Government funding for universities and science to tear himself away from all but general supervision of his life's work into the rhythms of the heart to fight the cause of science in public. We met on the day that SERC had announced the freezing of all research, and colleagues occasionally thrust their heads round the door when news organizations rang for comment.

Professor Noble had launched SBSS eighteen months earlier over dinner at his Oxford college, Balliol. The diners agreed that the traditional British way of lobbying, softly behind closed doors, was doing science a disservice. Their dilemma was: 'How does a profession that normally trusts in quiet discussions between distinguished people respond when the system totally breaks down?' They planned a once only 'SOS', placing an advertisement in *The Times*, expecting two hundred responses and sufficient contributions to pay for the ad. They received two thousand more or less anguished replies, and SBSS was founded. The media response had been overwhelming: the SBSS cause had been in the press virtually every day, and several television programmes were in the making. Polls showed widespread public support for the campaign. The Government's attitude, according to Professor Noble, was that British scientists were not hard-headed enough – one junior minister had accused them of being 'just as happy to work on a white elephant as on a winner' – and that they lacked public support, a notion retained apparently from the 1968–72 days of student unrest and the general feeling against the universities.

The scientists answered that all manner of American companies were beating a path to their laboratories. Professor Noble's own research, which he described as 'very fundamental', was exciting interest from US drug companies: there is a huge potential world market for successful heart drugs. Had he himself been offered jobs abroad? 'Yes, of course, anyone in my position has been.' Two or three years earlier he had made a decision to stay, but added: 'If the situation does collapse entirely, I might – for the sake of my research – have to say that I would be better off abroad under reasonably calm conditions.' The Government told SBSS to go to industry, and industry sent them back to the Government, claiming that it needed improved tax incentives for research and development before it could justify the expenditure to its shareholders.

I asked whether it helped that Mrs Thatcher had been a scientist. Professor Noble laughed: 'Just because she had a little bit of science in her background, people believe she understands. It's not true.' There was not, he said, a single scientist in the Cabinet, and precious few in the top echelons of industry. The reason was no longer principally the amateurism of British industry, but the subject specialization at sixteen which removed budding scientists from the world of value judgments. Scientists therefore enter industry ill-equipped to argue their point of view against professional managers. 'We are told that quite frankly not many scientists are up to it,' said the professor. Being an advocate required very different skills from those of the laboratory scientist, who had to lay out all his doubts on the bench.

Professor Noble, a fluent French speaker, supported the idea of an exam like the baccalaureate, with its compulsory breadth of subjects.

He argued that British science was a victim of the Government's ideology. Science, according to ministers he had dealt with, should be out in the market-place. But, he argued, they overlooked such foreign practices as massive Federal funding in the United States and 150 per cent research and development tax breaks in Australia. Sir Keith Joseph, when Secretary of State for Education and Science, had told an Oxford audience of scientists – worth, according to Professor Noble, thirty million pounds of public investment – that, since the Government could not possibly afford what they wanted, they should go abroad. Colleagues who did not attend the meeting anxiously phoned those who had, asking, 'Is the outlook that bad?' Sir Keith had shattered the morale of several hundred scientists in one speech.

Professor Noble said: 'Sir Keith said we couldn't afford more for science. He's an honest man, and I am sure he believed it. But there are right-wing governments in most industrialized countries, and they are affording it.' President Reagan had doubled the budget for the National Science Foundation shortly before SERC halted British research. Commenting on President Reagan's move, the American magazine *Science* said: 'The nation's science and engineering enterprise must have the financial resources to do two things: remain at the leading edge of discoveries and produce the technical personnel that the country needs. Both are essential to our economic competitiveness and must be done even in times of fiscal stringency . . . where we have a clear lead, we must preserve it; where we are lagging, we must catch up.'

Egged on by campus journals, American universities and research institutes that had once restricted their raids on British academics to second-tier people, were, by the spring of 1987, going for the very best. One head-hunter from California's Silicon Valley said that he had once enjoyed rounding up British computer scientists, but he had become frightened by his success and that of others. 'When I recruit in Britain, I am worried I am consuming the seed corn.' More than ten professorial chairs in computer science at British universities were already vacant, and Oxford, having failed to find a suitable candidate for its chair, had readvertised. Traditional, conservative Oxford's refusal to give Mrs Thatcher an honorary doctorate should, said Professor Noble, have posted the danger signals to the Government.

The despair felt by young scientists was captured in a letter to Professor Noble from a young woman who had just obtained her PhD. She had an impressive academic track record, and several publications, but was being forced to work as an 'academic visitor' without pay. 'I accept the lack of pay and proper position because I passionately believe in what I am doing, and am holding on to a lifelong dream – although I realize I could become a tax inspector and earn £9,000 p.a. (as often advertised in the *New Scientist*!).' She had been, when she wrote the letter, shortlisted for a job in North Carolina. Such was her frustration that she added: 'I feel I would be foolish to turn the job down if offered it – even if accepting it would mean leaving my husband, family, friends and the England I love.' (She also commented that she felt discriminated against in Britain because she was a woman and married – 'every application I have completed here asks for my marital status whereas *none* of those for the US and Canada even ask!') The sheaf of letters sent to SBSS included dozens of examples of wasted opportunities at the highest levels. A Cambridge scientist had arrived home from an international symposium in Japan, where she had been the key speaker, to find a grant rejection from SERC in the post. She wrote: 'An area of basic and applied research, where Britain has been pre-eminent and indeed where we are also very successful commercially, is being allowed to collapse in a disorganized, unplanned way. Should I continue to seek funds in this area? Is the expenditure of time and effort worth it? I am seized by a great weariness.'

An area of science in which Britain has a lead at least in Europe is 'artificial intelligence', the programming of computers for uses beyond sophisticated number-crunching to simulate higher mental processes, like reasoning, problem-solving and understanding language. The acknowledged academic centre for this endeavour is Edinburgh University, and one of its bright stars was Peter Jackson, who headed the 'Experts' Systems Group', which is developing computer programs that can tackle real problems, using the kind of knowledge that a doctor or geologist, for example, calls on when making decisions. It is very much 'new frontier' stuff.

Dr Jackson had had, in his own word, a 'chequered' career, starting, but not completing, an English degree, working in London as a social worker, taking a first-class degree in psychology, moving to computers and artificial intelligence in his late twenties. In the spring of 1987 he was plotting his departure to the United States. It was hard to find brain-drainers in the act of stealing away who were prepared to talk, and even Dr Jackson was anxious about the reaction of colleagues and superiors when the news leaked out. The crucial elements of his story, I suspect, would have applied to the hundreds of our brightest and best motivated research scientists who were then exploring American possibilities.

The day before we met, news was released that one of Britain's academic stars, Professor Colin Blakemore, Oxford University's youngest ever professor of physiology and a former Reith Lecturer, was in Los Angeles exploring openings for himself and his entire twenty-strong team. 'I don't want to leave England, but I might have to,' he said.

Dr Jackson had reached the point at which he wanted to go, come what may. He was thirty-eight, and the struggle to get where he was had been intense. At a time when his contemporaries were already well-launched on their careers, he had been struggling through his PhD on £2,500 a year at a university where he had almost no intellectual support, teaching himself advanced computer languages – including L I S P, the language of artificial intelligence – and competing for use of the department's one computer with large numbers of undergraduates. 'If I had not been highly motivated, I would have quit after a year,' he said. His marriage did collapse. He had been qualified a year, when, in 1983, the 'New Blood' lectureship scheme was launched to create more posts in Information Technology. He applied and got his Edinburgh job, and at the same time the Government 'Alvey' initiative, designed to forge a partnership between industry and university research, pumped a great deal more money into research and development. Through 'Alvey' he was instrumental in raising £3,500,000 for his project, and created five new posts. After the years of sacrifice, extreme hard work and achievement, he was paid under £15,000 a year.

By 1987 Dr Jackson was faced with the break-up of his group: much of his energy was exhausted on 'loony people in industry' – his Alvey partners – who often had no technical background, were 'parasitic on our intellectual contribution', but still wanted equal rights and say. The result, he felt, given the university's narrow skill base and slender resources, had been wastefully overambitious projects. Alvey funds, he suggested, could have been better spent on training fresh people in the basic skills of artificial intelligence. The time and energy he had to put into raising money and administering his team left him with insufficient to satisfactorily pursue his own research into 'introspective systems capable of reasoning about their own knowledge and belief'. His workload also cut deeply into his private life. Financially, he survived only by outside work, including writing a book, *An Introduction to Expert Systems*, published in both Britain and the United States, for which he had just received a royalties cheque for four thousand pounds – 'it went just like that,' he said, clicking his fingers, 'on debts, credit card bills and overdrafts.'

His prospects in Britain were poor: in due course promotion to 'senior' lecturer, worth another three or four thousand pounds a year. 'My salary is a joke and an insult. I feel very personal about it. I've given up years of income, and want something back. There's a feeling around that we're in this business for our health. I have not had the personal fulfilment, nor the financial rewards, so why am I doing this at all other than the fact that it is a job and is keeping me alive?' In the United States, where he went for six or eight weeks every year to keep in touch, he was expecting between $50,000 and $100,000 a year.

'What about British industry?' I asked. Dr Jackson laughed sourly. After his Alvey experience he told his head of department that he would not work with British industry again. Even collaborating, he had had 'terrific rows'. He said: 'The idea of working for them would be just a joke. I wouldn't last five minutes. The managers are yes men and office boys.' He was particularly scathing about the big companies, which he described as 'deadheads'. At Edinburgh University his head of department had nothing he could tempt him with to stay. A professor at another university offered to put together a tailor-made 'package' for him, but no British university could match what was on offer in America.

Professor Noble had fed me one of those nuggets of information that are sufficiently startling to stick in the mind, popping out occasionally when one is thinking of something altogether different. It was that Bulgaria, alone in Europe, had a lower proportion of graduates entering first jobs than Britain had. One of the most overworked British clichés is 'our well-educated workforce'. It is a consoling phrase, but it is sadly untrue and part of the myth with which we cocoon ourselves. The elitist nature of British education, the early specialization, the poor quality of many of our teachers, our historic hang-ups about the potential of the broad mass of children, the low targets we set children, all conspire against producing sufficient trained workers for the needs of a high-tech society.

Howard Thompson of the British Council was the British 'education attaché' in Washington DC in the early eighties, and has worked closely with the World Bank. According to him, a World Bank mission arriving to sort out Britain's economy would find the prescription very easy – 'a massive expansion of post-secondary school education.' No country, he argued, can have a thriving economy without educating a critical mass of its people to a decent level. In the United States, where 87 per cent of children stay in school until they are eighteen, where 40 per cent go to college, companies spend more on internal training than Federal, State and local governments together spend on public education. Although a few days after I met Mr Thompson, the Government announced plans to create a further fifty thousand higher education places, Britain still loses out both ways: our educational system rejects 80 per cent as unfit for further formal learning after sixteen, while industry spends derisory sums on training. The Manpower Services Commission attempts to fill the gap, but the number of worthwhile YTS schemes can only touch on the problem. When my family came back from Washington, I met a primary school head teacher in a middle-class district of London, who appeared to assume that it was unusual for a child to stay in full-time education after the age of sixteen: in the States in a similar area the child who is not expecting to go to college would be the exception.

Mr Thompson said: 'American education aims to get the best out of the greatest number. We are trying to educate the very best to the highest level. We ignore a large percentage of those who could be stretched much further.' Americans, he added, are thought of as 'natural' democrats, but actually they work hard at it through mechanisms designed to release potential. It is easy to sneer at degrees in hairdressing, but people who take them are going to have a better shot at business than the youth who leaves school at sixteen. Widely available higher education, giving the greatest number of people the greatest chance, is closely related to an adult democratic society. The British, said Mr Thompson, are full of good intentions, but bad at carrying them into effect. 'The Government has not seen the centrality of education to economic development.'

Mr Thompson spent considerable time on World Bank related business in China. He had seen there opportunities for the export of British scientific and educational equipment, and had first lectured to an appropriate British trade organization about the Chinese potential in 1983. But four years later nothing had been done; people were still talking. 'Foreigners want to buy certain things that we make, but our manufacturers are not geared up to explore the markets. I was rocked on my heels when I got home from the States by the reluctance of our salesmen to get on a plane and export,' he said. The lack of enterprise amongst the best educated British was even illustrated, he argued, by the hostility of students to a system of repayable loans rather than grants. 'What can possess these intelligent kids to think they have a right to a free university education? They will benefit with enhanced salaries for the rest of their lives, yet they resist loans even when resources are so scarce that university places are being closed down.'

It is the British rather than the Americans who really compete with one another, often – in world markets – fratricidally, said Mr Thompson. For example, civil engineers seeking a contract in the Third World seldom get together behind the firm with the best chance, which would allow the local high commission or embassy to lobby on behalf of just one contender. British rivals never share information, and operate in units that are far too small.

The virulent rejection of anything to do with America by, on the one flank, left-wing intellectuals like E. P. Thompson, and, on the other, by saloon-bar populists whose prejudices can be traced back to the wartime complaints – 'overpaid, oversexed and over here' – compounded the claustrophobia that I felt on my return. The America they disliked was not the America I had found, and the Britain they inhabited was hardly the model society they apparently imagined it to be. If we, the British, were so damn superior and clever, why had we made such a mess of things? Why were more than three million people out of work? Why did we import millions of pounds' worth of the goods we had invented? Why was our environment so filthy that we needed a national clean-up campaign? Why were our soccer hooligans so vicious that English clubs were barred from Europe? Why were we offering free airline tickets to 5,600 despised Americans to come here and spend their dollars? Why did many elderly people and some Asians lock their doors at dusk? Which country, America or Britain, I wondered, would the notional visitor from outer space prefer? I have twice visited Vietnamese boat people awaiting resettlement in Hong Kong camps, and heard in no uncertain terms which destination they would choose.

We, the children of Kipling and Rhodes, find the nationalism of Ronald Reagan – 'America, the last best hope of man' – nauseous; we, the besotted celebrants of royal births and weddings, sneer at such beanfeasts as the centenary of the Statue of Liberty; we, who have almost no Afro-Caribbean middle class, castigate Americans for their racism. The list of such contradictions would be a long one, and there are many aspects of life in Britain that the judicious space traveller would embrace. But many Britons sincerely believe that their country is superior to other nations in areas in which we have long been overtaken. We will deny heatedly that the Italians are economically better off, or that the Taiwanese send a higher number of young people to university, as if such facts flew in the face of nature. The journalist Ian Jack reported in the *Sunday Times* on a peace mission made by Liverpool's civic leaders to Turin after the Heysel Stadium carnage. The Liverpudlians had no concept that life in Turin might be different from the life they knew; that shops might offer fresh fruits and mountains of cheeses rather than sliced white bread and tinned peas; that working people might earn middle-class salaries in enterprises like Fiat and Olivetti; that football could flourish outside a mean and deprived culture.

British civil servants, visiting Washington from London, often condescended towards their opposite numbers, smirking at what they perceived to be a lack of American sophistication: some embassy families, notably those of specialist officials seconded from other ministries, lived as if they were on a Third World posting, mixing exclusively amongst themselves, laughing at strange native habits, and counting the days until they returned to Surrey or Berkshire. An American Assistant Secretary asked me once why a British visitor was 'Sir' Edward. I explained the system and that promotion beyond a certain rank in the civil service triggered an automatic knighthood. 'You mean, the guy's a bureaucrat like me? I thought he was an aristocrat,' he expostulated. From the far side of the Atlantic, Britain often looks like Ruritania.

It also often looks politically and diplomatically insignificant. The 'special relationship', as Professor Sir Michael Howard has pointed out, was built around the personality of Winston Churchill. It was compensation for Britain's loss of power and prestige, posited on the fragile notion that we had historical wisdom in diplomacy to offer in return for American muscle. (Then we also had atomic scientists and a worldwide network of naval bases.) The majority of Americans now do not trace their ancestry back to these islands. Reporting on Anglo-American relations on the eve of a visit by Margaret Thatcher to Washington, I found foreign policy old-timers still prepared to use the word 'special', but to younger bureaucrats Britain was simply one of several western European countries lumped together in one basket. The State Department official I went to see had responsibility for six or seven countries, including the Benelux nations. When Americans read of British commentators and journals complaining that Britain is an 'occupied country', as *Time Out* did after the 1986 Libyan bombing raids – 'overarmed, overeager and over here' – they have to pinch themselves. The United States remains a deeply isolationist nation, the money spent on US forces in western Europe is resented, as is the country's role as a 'world policeman'. Contrary to liberal imaginings in Britain, there is no great imperialist head of steam in middle America. The most potent political rallying cry is 'bring the boys home', as President Reagan did quickly enough after the 1983 Beirut bombing that cost the lives of over two hundred US Marines. Populist enthusiasm at least to reduce American forces in western Europe is held in check with difficulty. Senior figures like Senator Sam Nunn, chairman of the Senate Armed Services Committee, and Zbigniew Brzezinski, Jimmy Carter's National Security Adviser, have advocated major cuts in troop levels. If the decision were left to a poll of the American people, the 'occupiers' would be home within weeks.

Anti-Americanism in Britain is based not only on a misunderstanding of America's foreign policy aspirations, but also – as the US ambassador to London, Charles Price, pointed out in March 1987 – on an image of the United States that is as much at variance with reality as would be a picture of Britain as a land of Henley and Wimbledon and inner city riots. Much of the distorted image, it is fair to say, is propagated by Americans themselves, through television and films, showing violence, materialism, and an infatuation with physical attributes like beauty and toughness. Mr Price complained that this created a biased picture which was seized on by those in Europe who, for political or philosophical reasons, disliked the United States. 'America the violent, America the crass, America the inept have all become everyday images in Europe. Meanwhile, America the steadfast ally, America the generous and America of the many Novel laureates get short shrift or lost entirely,' he said.

A liberal/left solicitor said: 'I have travelled a great deal and have come across nothing that can match the quality of small town England, no culture that is superior. We are tolerant, have a strong sense of community, and value eccentricity. Village England is alive and kicking, and carries the genes of the British genius for good living, for whole living. If I am told that the price for keeping up is to become a mobile, materialistic, enterprise society, I would rather settle for a lower standard of living.' Such a choice is, of course, a luxury for the few. Anti-materialism is relative. To E. P. Thompson it is, no doubt, embodied in a familiar tweed jacket and a book-lined study. To young people in the inner city, it is embodied in a bleak life in filthy, drab surroundings. The solicitor added that he thought that materialistic societies would come tremendous croppers, victims of social dislocation and cultural shallowness. 'Once you are wrapped up in status symbols, you're finished. Life becomes a series of Pavlovian reactions.'

That may provide comfort for people who believe they have souls and a way of life superior to what they perceive to be basically American values. But we are too far down the materialistic road to turn back. The real pressure is going to come on the cohesion not of those societies that create material aspirations, because that is now true of all advanced countries including those in the eastern bloc, but of those that are unable to satisfy them – or, in our case, to satisfy even the basic needs of a significant minority. When the poor were required for their labour, they could derive dignity and solidarity from the knowledge that the whole national edifice rested on their abused shoulders; now that they are required only for their consumption, they are as valued as their paltry spending power.

If imperialism and materialism are the chief charges against the United States, the British left also confuses the States and the American people with what it dislikes about American politics. Accustomed to exerting ideological hegemony over its own followers, the left does not understand the pluralistic nature of American democracy. It perceives a winner-take-all society, 235 million humans fighting to the top of a massive greasy pole, with destitution awaiting those who lose their grip. In fact, the American education system is far more 'socialist' than anything we have managed to devise, children compete with a standard and not with each other, and there are prizes for all. Schools are programmed to get the best out of everyone. At home we have a shelf groaning with sports trophies. Visitors are deeply impressed. 'Your children must be great athletes,' they say. The truth is that in the leagues in which our children played, every child was awarded a trophy.

American democracy is also more devolved than the British variety. Tiny communities call themselves 'cities' or 'towns', run their own police forces – maybe a couple of sheriffs, enact their own 'laws' and elect a school board. An elected representative – even in Congress – is free to follow the dictates of his conscience (and of less noble motivations like 'pork barrel' enticements); it is not heresy to depart from the small print of your party's manifesto. As a human (rather than political) symbol, Reagan's achievements say a great deal about American democracy. He was born in Tampico, Illinois, to a rolling-stone father who sold shoes intermittently and struggled with a drink problem. (Reagan, rather uncharitably, in his autobiography described finding his father dead drunk on the porch one afternoon.) The family moved many times following the ups and (more usually) the downs of Jack Reagan's career: Ronald was pulled in and out of various schools. We know the future president was not blessed with great intellectual powers, but he gained a place at a local college and was awarded a degree. He went forth to earn his living – at first as a radio sports commentator – and the world was truly his oyster; and that was two generations ago. If Reagan had been born in Britain in 1911 in similar social, geographic and economic circumstances, I doubt he would have had the opportunity to make a significant mark.

Before I left America, I sought Britons who had settled there to discover what had drawn them across the Atlantic and what they missed about Britain. Later I interviewed expatriate Americans living in London to ask them the reverse questions.

I stumbled upon my American Brits by being asked to join the British Embassy cricket XI, which was to play two games in Philadelphia. I had supposed that both the local teams would be comprised of Americans, but natives provided only a small minority of one team and were not represented on the other. (Cricket, being almost entirely defensive – *not* getting out is the foundation of batting success – is not a game to which Americans take easily; bowling with a straight elbow, they find technically agonizing.) But what surprised me more were the differences between the two teams – one blazers and pink gins, the other bucolic and beer – and the social range of expatriates they included. Here on two foreign fields we had a complete cross-section of the old country, divided Britain in the old sense – public school types and the rest. They had exported their social class with them. One ex-public school boy said that he would not mix with someone with a broad Brummie accent – 'we would have nothing in common.' But among Americans he (and the others) behaved as an American might, moving easily between economic and social groups. They had become bi-cultural.

The first game was at the Merion Cricket Club (founded 1865) on Philadelphia's upper crust 'Main Line'. The grass was unnaturally green, and certainly springier than cricket turf ought to be. In the middle the most ferocious fast-bowler could only get the ball to sit up gently on the matting strip; the grandeur of the dark red, Victorian Gothic pavilion dwarfed the mediocre standard of play. At the end of the nineteenth century, ten thousand would turn out to watch such matches as the Gentlemen of Philadelphia v Mr Warner's English XI. The club had survived by turning itself over to tennis: in the days when the American Open was played on grass, the principal warm-up tournament was staged at Merion. But, with fifteen thousand British in and around Philadelphia, cricket was making a comeback. While the few American spectators peered at their notes – 'How to watch a cricket match' – a cross-section of the English upper middle classes – including a professor of material sciences, a research doctor, a banker and a lawyer – padded up. The players' ambiguous loyalties were symbolized by the union flag and the Stars and Stripes flying one each side of the scorer. Tea was duly served, but it was poured from coffee urns.

A few miles away beside a much less well-kempt field, a very different bunch of Englishmen had just finished another cricket game. A barrel of Whitbread's bitter on the verandah of the battered white pavilion drew appreciative drinkers, and a Yorkshireman in a flat cap called out, ''Ow's it going, Norman?' If you'd shut your eyes, you could have been in Barnsley. That night, these expatriates – heat conservation engineers, a fork-lift truck repairer, a textile salesman, a cost accountant, and the rep for a small manufacturer from Lancashire – ate fish 'n' chips, and drank more British beer in the Dickens Inn, an 'English pub' near the river in old Philadelphia. In and around the city, the expatriates have a choice not only of two cricket teams, but also of a variety of other societies such as the Daughters of the British Empire, the English Speaking Union, the Royal British Legion, a British Officers' Club, St George's and St Andrew's societies and a Pickwick Club.

Most of the newly arrived Britons were workaday people seeking a prosperous and congenial environment in which to advance careers well launched before they arrived. The paradox was that, despite their high-profile imported habits, they had embraced essential American values. In Britain they had despaired of ever being part of a vibrant, entrepreneurial society. They embodied the spirit of get-up-and-go invoked by Mrs Thatcher, only – sadly for her and for the prosperity of Britain – they had indeed got up and gone. Their common observation about the States was: 'If you put some effort in, you'll get something back. You can achieve very quickly.'

Dudley Pugh, a cost accountant from Derby, who had arrived in 1971 at the age of twenty-three, said: 'I was living at home and going nowhere. By the time I had paid my parents board, the bills on my car and gone out twice a week, there was nothing over.' To many, America was an escape from the frustrations imposed on them in Britain by education, class or simply the philosophy that, on the whole, problems outweigh possibilities.

Val Sauri, a dentist who had been in the United States since 1961, all his working life, said: 'I thoroughly enjoy going back, but, by the end of a visit I'm frustrated. The attitude is "You can't do it".'

Richard Stephens, a hotel concierge, said: 'I went home for a week and stayed three days. People were sitting in the same chairs as they were ten years ago, and carrying on the same conversations.'

Mary Griffiths had been in America fifteen years, her husband having been recruited when there was demand for skilled British labour. In Philadelphia she had founded and was running *UK Magazine*, a bi-monthly publication which carried useful information, such as details of cheap charter flights, and relayed gossip about Britain. She had missed these things herself, and thought, 'Don't complain; do something about it.' Had she stayed in her native Coventry, she believed she would have remained a secretary. 'It's a man's world in Britain: I still feel it when I go back,' she said.

The expatriates' view of Britain tended to be locked into the era when they left home. Peter Stone, a steel company executive and linchpin of the Merion Cricket Club – he kept the score wearing the full club regalia – left Sheffield when Harold Wilson renationalized steel. An ex-army officer, he dressed whenever the occasion arose in the ceremonial kilted uniform of the Queen's Own Highlanders. He revelled in what he called British 'bullshit', and 'putting on a damn good show'. He recounted with gusto stories of fierce verbal clashes with Philadelphia's well-organized Irish community. He said: 'My loyalties are to Britain, but I couldn't stand the unprofessional way of carrying on business. That's why Sheffield went downhill. The MD would wander in at 9.30, coffee at 11.00. In Detroit he's in at 7.30, and lunch is a quick hamburger. Sheffield did nothing to develop the product and was weak on marketing. A son of the company without much to offer might say, "I think I might do a little bit of selling." It was the old boy net, what bed you were born in.'

John Knowles, an architect, said he had been depressed on a recent visit home to find how downcast young people were: 'England is still class-conscious and doesn't offer the opportunities it should. On a train to Liverpool I met five young men who had just been interviewed for a job and had all been turned down. They blamed their failure on not having the right accent.'

John McNamara, a Londoner in his early fifties, lived in a log cabin beside a dark creek, from which the 'plop' of jumping fish occasionally broke the silence. I visited him at dogwood and azalea time, when the gardens and woods were bright splashes of red and orange, pink and white. Mr McNamara had been living in London, married to an American. When they decided to move to the States, he wrote to eight hundred British companies, seeking to represent them, received seven hundred replies, and one hundred interview invitations: he saw forty firms, negotiated ten agencies, and, in the end, made his living out of one. That went broke, and he switched to represent R. J. Draper, who make sheepskin-lined slippers in Glastonbury. Three years later the firm – having won the Queen's Award for Exports – and Mr McNamara were doing very well indeed. 'I get across to Americans because of my accent, which hasn't changed, thank God. I get to people who normally would be difficult to see. I try to appear in some senses as if I had just got off the plane,' he said. He was divorced soon after his arrival, but had remarried. 'I live here much as I would in England – dinner with friends, squash, general socializing.' He took me to the Philadelphia Racquet Club (founded 1889) to watch two of his friends play real tennis. Old retainers laid out the players' clothes, and took them away after the game. It could have been Victorian London.

James Batt, in his early thirties, was manager of a major Philadelphia Hotel, the Plaza. He had worked in Saudi Arabia, Dallas and

Miami, and 'liked the egalitarian nature of American society, and the idea that success buys privilege.' People who came to charity balls at the hotel were a 'good cross-section, not all Hooray Henrys as they would have been in London.' Americans trusted him to understand about protocol, and the hotel regularly put up celebrities. His ambition was to build a track record on which he could borrow the money to start a similar hotel of his own. He found it much easier to cross social barriers than he had in Britain, and he admired the way ordinary people worked. Many of his staff had two jobs: the night bellman drove a school bus, and the garage attendant played in a band. 'To them, it is perfectly normal to work that hard, and they live well as a result,' he said.

I met Peter Leigh in London. An Oxford graduate, then in his early forties, he had first fallen for the United States when taking a vacation job. Back at Oxford in the early sixties he had found it highly suspect to be enthusiastic about America. 'There was a noticeable streak of resentment against Americans. The leadership class in Britain had not got over the fact that their country was not Number One any more. The rules had been changed without their permission, and they were still sulking. Coming to terms with no longer being top dog implies that the system will be different in future, something they were reluctant to take on board.' He had returned to the Harvard Business School, and now worked as 'corporate controller' for a Californian biological research and genetic engineering company.

He was in Britain to supervise the takeover of a small high-tech company at Abingdon, Oxfordshire, which had been developing an innovative idea, but had spread its energies too thinly. He was struck, as he always was in London, by the capital's inefficiencies. He was staying in a major hotel, which was apparently incapable of taking decent messages. An assistant manager had told him that they had been waiting three months for message pads – 'as if he were helpless, like a victim.' Messages were therefore on scraps of paper that would 'be understandable if taken by Aunt Millie who had flour all over her hands when the phone rang.' People in the front line just hadn't been trained.

But he was more struck by the rigidities of class. 'Too few people here believe they can make a difference. There is a kind of caste system, with expectations set very early in life. In the States most people believe most of the time that tomorrow will be better, and that they can contribute: here it is enough if tomorrow is no worse,' he said. In the States people are valued more highly. He had had two months on the dole shortly after his arrival, and 'I was still treated like a human being, and not as an agent of a communicable disease.' He had recently visited a vice-president of a large paper-making company. As they were touring the works, a man covered in grease had made bowling gestures to the vice-president. It turned out that the two men were members of the same club, and were going tenpin bowling that night. There was probably a gap of $100,000 between their salaries. The night before we met, Mr Leigh had been having a drink in a Covent Garden bar where he fell into conversation with two stone-masons. When they learned that he had emigrated to the States, one said with genuine bewilderment: 'You speak all right; why did you have to go?'

Many Americans who live in Britain like the feeling of being wrapped in a cloak of known history. They enjoy walking on streets where men who spoke their language have trod for several centuries. The continuity gives their inherited cultures a framework. Opera singer La Verne Williams said: 'You're closeted in the States. In London you feel more the pulse of the world. Once you have the taste, you really don't want to lose it. You can reach out and touch the great people, and, if you are lucky, work with them.'

Expatriate Americans also like the small scale of Britain. Choreo-grapher Robert Cohan, a director of the London Contemporary Dance Theatre who came to London from New York nearly twenty years ago, said: 'London is like a small town: everything seems to move in slow motion. You get a great deal done until your speed slows down.' A journalist friend said he was amazed that he could not get Britons to meet him for breakfast, or, if he could, that they would suggest a 10.30 meeting, and eat their way through bacon and eggs. Working lunches were also inflated meals, stretching into the afternoon with puddings and brandies.

Bing Taylor, a founder of the *Good Book Guide*, who has lived in London for nearly twenty years, said he admired the freedom from conformity in Britain, but he was, none the less, contemplating going home for the sake of his children, who, he believed, were being dragged down by English schooling. 'Children want to be stretched, to be curious, to learn,' he said, and he contrasted the negative attitude his children were beginning to adopt with the 'brightness and enthusiasm' of their American-raised cousins. He thought Britain needed an imaginative leader like John F. Kennedy, and was appalled by the staying power and destructiveness of the class system. 'It is so divisive. It is frightening that people cannot find a way to rid themselves of these attitudes,' he said, observing that the British adapt even the minutiae of life – vocabulary, topics, attitudes – to the perceived class of the person to whom they are talking.

Americans often arrive with the romantic notions about Britain that are still cherished by many British, and they, naturally, resent change. They also usually are comfortably off. Stanley Olson, biographer of the painter John Singer Sargent, who has an English accent, wears suits lined with red silk and affects a languid air, said he found it ludicrous to seek to impose American solutions on English problems, as he suspected Mrs Thatcher was trying to do. 'To look up from a computer to see the Irish State coach pass by is high comedy,' he said.

Anti-Americanism is, as Mr Leigh observed at Oxford a quarter of a century ago, evidence of Britain's relative political and economic decline. The Labour front-bench spokesman, Michael Meacher, suggested to his constituents in the spring of 1987 that the issue of sovereignty was the most important one facing the electorate – 'the right of the British people to run their own affairs in their own way, which is now being massively encroached upon by American interests and power ... Mrs Thatcher is the leading protagonist of the American hegemony. She has been a willing, even a deliberate, conduit of American colonial power.' He added: 'Not for centuries have British interests been so humiliatingly subordinated to a foreign power.'

We are, it is true, inextricably linked to the United States, occasionally in ways that are unacceptable – like the US extra-territorial laws cited by Mr Meacher. But for most Britons, access to American ideas and aspirations (and I'm not talking about politics) has a liberating influence. Go to Gatwick Airport, and talk to people returning from short American vacations, and you will find them to be charged up and alive from their experiences. No leading post-war American politician would have dreamed of saying of his people, as Ernest Bevin said of his, that they 'had been crucified on the poverty of their own desires'. Forty years on the persistence of two Britains remains a bleak indictment of that poverty.

AFTERWORD: MOANING MINNIES AND MONTRACHET

A few days after I had finished the hardback version of *The Return of a Native Reporter*, Mrs Thatcher called the 1987 General Election. It was both a defiant and an arrogant gesture, summoning the people to the polls a year before she was required to when she enjoyed a Commons majority of 136. She was saying to her disorganized and demoralized opponents, 'Put up or shut up,' knowing full well that the arithmetic of British politics then would give her a comfortable 'mandate' on the basis of a minority vote. As we know, she got her vote – the lowest proportion of those cast for a winning Prime Minister since the Second World War – and claimed her mandate. Thatcherism, having won the economic arguments, was ready to sweep on to the commanding heights of the social agenda. The shift in ideology that had been so apparent since my return was about to be translated into concrete political terms.

Ten years before, at the tired tail end of the last Labour Government, Lord Hailsham warned of the fundamental dangers to democracy of an 'elective dictatorship' – that is, a government that uses its Commons majority to steamroll into law dogmatic and narrowly supported policies. As the *Guardian* pointed out at the end of 1987, we did not hear much from his Lordship on this topic during his years on the Woolsack. But by early 1988 Mrs Thatcher had expunged all but nominal opposition in her own ranks; had down-graded the Cabinet; had abolished tiers of government – such as the metropolitan councils – that harboured opposition; had persistently misused instruments of government like the Official Secrets Act for political advantage; had presided approvingly over a growth in inequalities in such basic areas as health and education. She seemed content to use her minority support at the polls to ride roughshod over the wishes of the dissenting majority. The 'mandate' was to bring us the universally disliked 'poll' tax, Kenneth Baker's education 'reforms', which will place unprecedented powers in the hands of the Secretary of State, the abolition of the University Grants Committee, and the untrammelled growth of executive power, as the House of Commons struggled under the heaviest legislative programme since the war. Fleet Street, which would have blown a tempest had a left-wing Labour Government sought to embrace similar authoritarian powers, was vocal only when the lash of Mrs Thatcher's authority fell across its own buttocks. The one consolation for Mrs Thatcher's critics, noted a wag, was that the last attempt – in 1380 – to impose a flat-rate poll tax was followed a year later by the Peasants' Revolt.

The self-proclaimed task for Thatcher's third term was to roll back the welfare state; the beleaguered and the broken – some of those people I had been meeting when I was writing this book – were to have the drip-feed of dependency ripped from their arms. John Moore, the Social Services Secretary, articulated the upbeat message of the hour in a speech that was widely interpreted as setting the tone for the brave new world into which – willy-nilly – we were to be led. 'Dependence on welfare benefits can corrupt the human spirit,' he said, advocating 'the sheer delight of personal achievement instead of the sullen apathy of dependence'.

What could be privatized would be; schools with articulate, socially competent parents were to be encouraged to 'opt out' of local authority control, threatening to create three tiers of education – the private, the directly funded and 'sink' schools for children of the impoverished; prudent citizens would be well advised to take out private health insurance. *Sauve qui peut* became the watchword of the hour. For a few summer months we lived in Panglossic times: unemployment came down; the Stock Exchange indices soared beyond man's most avaricious yearnings; production improved. A City merchant banker, dealing in Japanese shares, was revealed to be earning £2.5 million a year – or over £10,000 for each working day. To those who had it all already, the perks flowed ever more generously – a top-of-the-range company car was said to be worth £29,000-a-year. Mrs Thatcher lectured the Americans on their economic management.

I have not argued in this book that economic Thatcherism has been wholly bad for Britain. I endorse the virtues she preaches – hard work, enterprise, self-sufficiency (where possible) – and salute many of her achievements, such as the far greater control over inflation. We had grown slack; too many people believed that they had a right to do well out of life without requiring the skill or effort to put anything back in. We had long suffered from a football-pool mentality; we believed that the way to get rich was to put crosses on a piece of paper and sit back. But, despite the greater realism of many, after eight years of Thatcherite governance the reward system seemed just as perverse and to have little to do with knowledge or culture. Why struggle through nightschool to become a teacher when your native wits might be worth six figures dealing/speculating in foreign currency? Affluence had become all and, with it, a coarsening of national sensibilities. The sixteen million on or near the poverty line should look to their bootstraps and not to the rest of us for succour.

The political disaster is that there is no one to gainsay Mrs Thatcher. I had spent much of the election campaign wandering the remoter regions of the nation in the front of the yellow 'battle buses' chosen by the Alliance to convey its twin leaders on their futile missions. The question I struggled with as I bumped through the West Country or twisted down narrow roads in the Scottish Borders was why it was apparently so difficult to sell a moderate and reasonable package to a people who – for all the intolerance at either extreme of British politics – themselves remain centrist and balanced. I knew from writing this book that there was in the country a fatigue with the old, polarized ways; the common sense of the Alliance was very much the common sense of middle England. But what the people I had met also wanted in public life was passion and vision. Where Mrs Thatcher proclaimed her programme for the millennium, the two Davids offered six-point plans. The dual leadership with its incompatibilities was a disaster. David Steel's capacity for self-destruction was apparent from the moment he volunteered to me the phrase 'Tweedledum and Tweedledee' as we lurched through his constituency one Saturday morning. He was a man, in any case, for the margins. When he joined the Liberal Party, it commanded just 2.5 per cent of the popular vote; his expectation was of a lifetime in guerrilla politics. Had his instinct been for the centre-stage, he would have chosen a different political vehicle.

David Owen had a stubborn streak. Although he was in the American sense the most packageable of British politicians, he eschewed his own potential. He told me he was not an admirer of Jack Kennedy, who had been far more 'style than substance', and that he disdained the cheapening of complex issues. Like Coriolanus, he would not – as he would see it– pander to the public appetite for meretricious campaigning. The passion that his cause – and his despairing supporters – so badly needed was a private virtue. 'When you are a doctor, you have to learn to control your tears, your grief,' he said. Without passion the political centre could not – and did not – hold.

On the Saturday after the election I was in Edinburgh to hear Neil Kinnock address the Scottish Miners' Gala. Having until then only seen gobbets of his speeches on television, I had not realized quite how devoid of content they were. The empty phrases rolled round the interior of a damp marquee. His audience, which had been warmed up by some formidable old-timers like Mick McGahey of the National Union of Mineworkers, was in nostalgic mood. Being there was like stepping back three decades in British political life. This was unreconstructed cloth-cap Britain. Outside in the drizzle, families huddled over picnics; inside, Mr Kinnock invoked a world of 'them and us' in a setting that had already been a caricature when Peter Sellers starred in *I'm All Right, Jack*. Could, I wondered as I sprinted up an Edinburgh hill in search of a working phone box, this ramshackle party ever be modernized? What, anyway, did party functionaries like Brian Gould mean by 'modernization?' Show or substance? Was the fragrance of a million red roses all that that wet tent needed? It seemed unlikely. What – aside from her own arrogance – was left to unseat Thatcher now? Her dreams of the year 2000 did not seem so fanciful in the soft rain of that Scottish afternoon.

In the now two years since my return from the United States I have not been able to divorce Britain's social, economic and political problems from its class structure. The radical right likes to have it both ways. It pooh-poohs the notion that we are a class-ridden society; yet it remains intrinsically snobby, while continuing to take full advantage of the privileges that our caste system affords those at the top. It is fashionable to accuse liberals of hypocrisy and of oppression – the imposition, that is, of their liberal views on those who are not liberal. John Rae, the former headmaster of Westminster, in an article in *The Times*, characterized the contemporary liberal as 'an upper-class twit with his heart on his sleeve and his stomach replete with roast pheasant'. In my experience, the pheasant, the claret and all the other goodies were far more likely to be in the bellies of

the Thatcherites, who had the further advantage of being able to
enjoy them without being overly troubled by conscience. In the
meantime, class divisions continue to bedevil Britain. The young
people of a middle-class, suburban area, such as the one I live in,
are segregated into two camps from the minute their parents decide
which form of education they should have. Within a very short
time, formerly best friends with a great deal in common walk meta-
phorically and literally on opposite sides of the street. The division
is a tragic microcosm of the geological fault that runs through British
society.

The Royal Family remains a national obsession, its younger
members clammering for incessant attention. They also want it both
ways; they succumbed to the fallacious yuppy idea that 'you can
have it all', revelling in the publicity their antics attract, yet complaining of intrusion when those antics stimulate inevitable press
curiosity. Too late they discovered that those who mount tigers
seldom can dismount. Right-wing commentators suggested that the
Press was bringing disrepute on its own head by the activities of the
royal 'rat pack', but there was at least as much evidence that the
young royals themselves were losing respect. A survey of young
people elicited the following comments: 'They're on a cushy number.
All that money just for shaking hands and cutting pieces of string,'
and 'They live off us. Big cars, big houses and loads of horses.' The
royals reached a nadir at which even royalists cried, 'Enough,' when
several of them made fools of themselves by appearing in a special
staging of *It's a Knockout* – the perfect game for a nation that
scoffs at intellectuals. In the same idiom an army captain shot a
champagne cork 109 feet 6 inches and had a major colour supplement feature devoted to his achievement. The ultimate accolade
in Mrs Thatcher's new Britain was, it seemed, to gain an entry in
The Guinness Book of Records – preferably for something entirely
trivial. (Class tentacles reach even here; had the record breaker been
a corporal rather than a captain, his achievement would have had
something to do with beer.) It was not necessary (and perhaps even
dangerous) to worry our heads about more important matters: those
could safely be left to our benign leader.

This was the prevailing mood in which this book was first published in September 1987. On the right it had, therefore, a gloomily
predictable reception, which reinforced much of what I had been
trying to say about the polarized nature of the country I came home

to. I was struck again by the closed minds we bring to arguments or analysis with which we do not automatically agree – the left, of course, is equally guilty. In the aftermath of the General Election, it was tantamount to a lack of patriotism to pick holes in the grand Thatcherite design of things. Any suggestion that the ice was beginning to crack beneath our feet was rejected out of hand. Under the headline 'Britain's Breed Apart', The *Sunday Times* attacked the notion that there was anything left to criticize. 'Britain's intelligentsia has become the lost tribe of the 1980s . . . so it has retreated to its own left-wing laager, where erudite moaning is taken for wise critique . . . Rarely have the ideals of the country's intellectual elite been so out of kilter with the aspirations of plain folk.'

This was the unvarnished advocacy of populism. I was flattered that this book was linked in that leading article to other such apparently misguided works as the film *My Beautiful Laundrette* and Ian McEwan's novel *The Child in Time*. We stood accused of being 'smugly negative', and gathering at 'favourite watering holes, where (even in such supposedly hard times) the Montrachet flows freely'. An accusation of being 'smug' is a difficult one to repudiate without appearing to justify the adjective. But what the writer – and those unswerving Thatcherites he stood for – appeared to be saying was that in these stirring times those who were not whole-heartedly for us (by which he meant the dominant political philosophy) were against us. He was seeking to create a national mood music familiar to all who have lived under authoritarian governments of both right and left. It was not what we have been accustomed to in Britain. Mrs Thatcher was already assaulting the last redoubts from which effective opposition could be deployed – education authorities and turbulent councils; now her acolytes were turning on even the freedom to think differently. Although celebrated as the advocate of such individual liberties as the right to buy shares (and to drink in pubs all day), Mrs Thatcher was proving reluctant to tolerate the bedrock freedom – the right to oppose.

She did manage to unite virtually the whole media by her obsessive pursuit of the former MI5 man Peter Wright's memoir *Spycatcher*. Even after over a million copies of the book had been sold worldwide, and all its chief allegations had been aired in Britain, the Government was still seeking blanket injunctions to prevent anybody from saying anything about the principles or practice of national security. The reporting of Parliament and the courts was restricted in a manner unknown in peacetime, and editors and broadcasters were not sure whether they could even mention the wretched Wright's name. Two or three quite separate issues were cynically rolled into one in order to suppress both public knowledge and discussion of general topics, such as the power and account-ability of the security services, and specific allegations, such as whether Roger Hollis, the former head of MI5, had been a spy and whether elements within MI5 had tried to destabilize Harold Wil-son's Government. Robert Armstrong, the Cabinet Secretary (inevit-ably ennobled the moment he stepped from office), trotted round the world being 'economical with the truth'. What the *Spycatcher* affair did – and continues to do as I write in the early days of 1988 – was strip bare the Prime Minister's intolerant way with opposition. Her attitudes to *Spycatcher*, the Zircon affair – when the BBC's Glasgow offices were raided – and the suppressed radio programme *Defence of the Realm* are all of a piece and illustrative of her character.

As I write this, Mrs Thatcher is passing Herbert Asquith's record as the longest-serving Prime Minister this century: 'She has raised this country from its knees,' opined The *Daily Telegraph*. As she becomes more millennial in her utterances – we shall go 'on and on and on' – and more clearly determined to stamp Thatcherism indelibly on the nation she leads, commentators are already looking to the year 2000, in which she would – if she survived that long – overtake Robert Walpole as the longest serving premier of all. She would then still be considerably younger than Gladstone was when he formed his third administration, and younger than Ronald Reagan is today.

But even as she has been sketching her grandiose vision, the foundations of both her economic and her political security have been shaken. The notion that in the City money could make money indefinitely – breeding incestuously like gerbils – almost without regard for whether it was helping to make anything else of a more useful nature was severely dented by the stock market crash of 19 October 1987 that came to be dubbed 'Black Monday'. The Government had to pull the BP privatization flotation, and millions of new capitalists woke up to the truth that share-buying is not a game in which investors inevitably get something for nothing. (Some were so besotted by the incessant propaganda of the previous years that they still queued on the deadline morning to pay way over the odds for heavily devalued shares.)

As the pillars of the temple of Mammon came tumbling down, it was (inevitably) the small man who got most hurt. (The spectacular small victims included a 23-year-old trainee accountant who lost £1 million gambling with other people's money, and a schoolboy, whose £20,000 deficit on dealings put his family's home in jeopardy.) Despite its technology, 'Big Bang' failed to keep pace with itself, and a massive backlog of settlements accumulated. Few stockbrokers – even those who advertised their services to the small investor – could any longer be bothered with tiny deals; corporate raiders ignored the petty capitalist, who therefore could not take advantage when prices were momentarily forced up. Within a few weeks the prospects for a widely based share-owning democracy were set back years.

The Thatcherite ideal – thrift, hard work, responsibility – had somehow been perverted by the mood music that played a tune of greed. Two Tory MPs fell from grace and Parliament (one of them briefly into gaol) for making illegal multiple applications for privatized shares. Mrs Thatcher may have conducted the national budget according to the principles of Mr Micawber, but the ethos of her me-first philosophy encouraged the people who elected her to go on a staggering binge. As the *Guardian* commented: 'Just why Mrs Thatcher should think it is economically sound to allow people to borrow at penal rates of interest . . . to purchase (say) depreciating Japanese videos, while unsound to allow the public sector to borrow at barely half the rate to finance profitable capital projects is a mystery . . .' Between 1979 and 1987 consumer credit climbed by 300 per cent, much of it at interest rates so exorbitant that the lenders were clearly as callous as they were greedy. The very poor were borrowing in order to repay borrowings, accumulating interest that they were forced to bear like millstones round their necks. By the end of 1987 homes were being repossessed at an unprecedented level – 2,900 owner-occupier families were evicted between July and September, the majority for debts incurred on second mortgages and credit cards. Homelessness consequently stood at dire levels.

On the day that Mrs Thatcher set her longevity record, promising that she would turn her attention to such issues as 'fairness, honesty and courtesy to others', a report from the Family Policy Centre revealed that during the first six years of Thatcherism the income of the poorest fifth of the country fell by 6 per cent, while that of the richest fifth rose by 9 per cent. Within that poorest fifth, specific groups like one-parent families had fared even worse – their average net income had fallen by 11 per cent. The centre – the chairman of which was Sir Campbell Adamson, a former director-general of the CBI and the chairman of the Abbey National Building Society – commented that this disadvantaged 20 per cent had been 'left behind in a pool of poverty which is getting wider and deeper'.

Those who pointed to these contradictions and their devastating consequences – often clergymen – continued to be branded 'moaning minnies' by true Thatcherites. The journalist Paul Johnson in one of his off-the-cuff diatribes against compassion wrote: 'It says much for the intellectual bankruptcy of the Church of England that, at such time of crisis ['Black Monday'], the best its senior primate could do was to encourage the destructive British vice of envy ... envy is very dear to bishops. It is the dynamic of their economic theology.' What the much abused Dr Robert Runcie had done was to suggest that City salaries were too high, a judgement rapidly backed by City firms themselves as they slashed wages and laid off staff. Even as the November 1987 unemployment figures showed a drop of 50,000, a leading City analyst forecast that financial institutions would have to shed 50,000 workers as a consequence of the Crash.

Unrepentant, the clerics stuck to their guns. The then Dean of St Paul's in London told of a reduction of 1,726 hostel beds in the capital at a time when homelessness was rising fast, and related the story of an acquaintance who had had to give up his bed for a 75-year-old woman whose electricity had been cut off. He added crisply: 'No doubt those who were reported as speaking of "state junkies" at a recent conference are not aware of the deterioration of services and the suffering of so many in our great cities ... It is tragic that when there are many of us whose standard of living is secure ... the community, as represented by the Government, cannot achieve a more warm-hearted approach to the unfortunates.' The Bishop of Durham said the Crash had exposed the 'increasingly dangerous near-nonsense of what are called the global financial services industries'.

The Church itself was making news at the time, with the suicide of the cloistered canon who penned an anonymous attack in *Crockford's* accusing the Archbishop of Canterbury of being a wimp. Thanks to this and a passionate debate about whether active gays should be clergymen, little notice was taken of its leaders'

pronouncements on other matters. But there were surprising noises
from different quarters – not least mumblings from the Foreign Secretary, dogged, dependable Geoffrey Howe, in the form of a letter to
his constituents. He stressed the 'social and moral' context within
which market forces should operate. He wrote: 'We have come a
long way over the last eight years, but we still have a long way to
go in tackling social tensions, tensions caused by generation gaps,
racial differences, class and regional differences.' This was widely
interpreted as muted criticism of Mrs Thatcher – a 'gentle rebuke',
commented the *Guardian*. Under the headline 'Not too much social
Darwinism in 1988, please', a leader in the final *Sunday Telegraph*
of 1987 stated: 'Encouraging the unambitious to struggle is a good
thing; but if the ambition is already there, too much encouragement
may push it into selfish and anti-social ruthlessness.' At the top end
of society, readers were told, unbridled self-interest 'has begun to
have positively nasty results'. One had to look at the masthead to
check which paper one was reading.

The consequences of the narrow pursuit of self-interest – largely
in financial terms – continued to exaccerbate the already critical
situations I report on in this book. At the end of 1987, Sir George
Porter, the president of the Royal Society, warned that Britain was
doomed to join the 'third world of science'. Sir George, who won
the Nobel Prize for Chemistry in 1967, said, 'The time has come to
hold the line somewhere, before individual creative science is lost
altogether,' adding that the existing loss of young scientists through
lack of opportunity was 'the saddest and most deplorable result of
the philosophy of the present time'. The director-general of the
Engineering Council asserted that Britain was in danger of running
out of qualified engineers. British universities continued to suffer
through cuts.

At the same time there were daily stories of crisis in the National
Health Service – children dying because of postponed operations;
hospital wards being closed down; nurses striking. Notable doctors
who had supported Mrs Thatcher as recently as the General Election
presented a petition to Downing Street. The heart of the problem
was poor staffing levels caused by inadequate wages. Measures were
proposed to give health workers and other essential professionals,
like teachers, preferential mortgages so that at least some of them
could afford to live in the south-east, where the Crash did nothing
to steady the nonsensical rise in house prices.

By the end of 1987 the gap between housing costs in the south and the north was wider than ever. The average semi-detached house in an inner-London borough reached £105,950, while in Doncaster it was £22,850 and Birmingham £32,900. London overtook Paris as the most expensive city in Europe for new flats, with prices ranging from £4,178 to £4,873 per square metre: this meant that London had become more costly than traditional high-price cities such as Geneva and Stockholm. Commercial enterprises – unlike public ones – saw the sense and necessity of subsidizing their workers; building societies and banks, for example, paid substantial London bonuses. The National Provincial Building Society added £3,450 to the salaries of staff with five years' service.

If one overlooked the 20 per cent stuck to the bottom, the measurable affluence of the British people was increasing. In 1987 it took a man on the average industrial wage a mere 6.2 minutes of work to earn the price of a loaf of bread compared with 7.4 minutes five years earlier. We were catching up with the French and even the Germans, though our incomes were still massively below those of Americans. But there was a paradox to this wealth. As increasing numbers afforded video-recorders and Greek holidays, so increasing numbers could not afford a decent first home, and at the margins thousands more were crammed into rotting 'B & B' hotels, their children growing up with the deprivations of rootlessness more common to Third World cities.

Were even those who undeniably were better off spending their money more wisely? Were we raising our sights? Was it becoming a greater pleasure to live in Britain than in (say) France or Italy? Had the British people's aspirations increased in line with their incomes? Did more money mean wholemeal bread and lean meat, or did it mean more white bread and sausages? Breathless reporters, usually of right-wing persuasion, scurried to such temples of contemporary affluence as the MetroCentre at Gateshead, where the supposedly impoverished citizens of the north-east spent money like Americans on a binge in Las Vegas. They filed awestruck dispatches. Of course, they had not seen the people who could not afford to be there, nor, I suspect, did they stop long enough to examine what the money was actually being spent on. We aspire low; seeking the mediocre, we are so easily sold tat: never mind the quality, feel the width. Crucially, were we better off in those aspects of life that could not be measured by market forces? Were we becoming more or less the law-abiding, tolerant and peaceful society that Sir Geoffrey Howe, at least, hankered after in his epistle to his electors?

The superficial evidence was not encouraging. Towards the end of 1987 the *Daily Mail* surveyed young people and found that their attitudes were both punitive and selfish. Child molesters' cell doors should be left open so that other prisoners could 'kick hell out of 'em. That'd learn 'em,' said a 15-year-old Yorkshire girl. A 14-year-old Glaswegian, asked about famine relief in Africa, said: 'A lot of it is their own fault. If we don't interfere, it'll be a good way of cutting the population.' The French and Belgian police were admired because 'they go straight in with truncheons and don't mess around.' The *Mail*'s writer commented that if these attitudes held up into adult life, we 'can expect a Britain many of whose citizens have precious little time for liberal, free-spending sentiments'.

The series made bleak reading. However, my many conversations with adults had left me more optimistic. The majority of Britons remain more decent and altruistic than the survey would suggest. They believe there *is* a better way – a potential marriage between market economics and social responsibility; they reject the argument that freedom inescapably means destitution for those at the bottom. The tragedy of the 1987 General Election was that this yearning was not translated into political action. The absence of leadership for these widely shared aspirations has many millions resigned to settling for second- or even third-best. Our education, our housing, our nutrition, our health, our safety are neither what they could be nor what they ought to be. If this lament falls under the eye of a *Sunday Times* leader writer, will he or she please note that my plea is for something *better*, a raising of expectations, not a levelling down? We did need economic realism and more self-discipline; Mrs Thatcher gave them. We need now to ensure the preservation of such qualities as tolerance, mutual respect, the championing of reason over might, the concern for the less fortunate and the observance of the law that have made Britain a country worth living in. It is not in Mrs Thatcher's character to be a woman for all seasons. It sounds corny perhaps in these triumphal times, but a nation is a family; beyond the responsibility to ourselves we have a responsibility to others less fortunate. If not the mother, Mrs Thatcher is at least the house mother of our family, elected not simply to chide and discipline but also to care and aid. The real danger of unbridled Thatcherism, as I report in this book, is that its legacy may prove to be a harshly divided society, with detrimental consequences that in the end destroy even the most positive benefits of her long period in government.

FOR THE BEST IN PAPERBACKS, LOOK FOR THE

In every corner of the world, on every subject under the sun, Penguin represents quality and variety – the very best in publishing today.

For complete information about books available from Penguin – including Pelicans, Puffins, Peregrines and Penguin Classics – and how to order them, write to us at the appropriate address below. Please note that for copyright reasons the selection of books varies from country to country.

In the United Kingdom: For a complete list of books available from Penguin in the U.K., please write to *Dept E.P., Penguin Books Ltd, Harmondsworth, Middlesex, UB7 0DA*

In the United States: For a complete list of books available from Penguin in the U.S., please write to *Dept BA, Penguin, 299 Murray Hill Parkway, East Rutherford, New Jersey 07073*

In Canada: For a complete list of books available from Penguin in Canada, please write to *Penguin Books Canada Ltd, 2801 John Street, Markham, Ontario L3R 1B4*

In Australia: For a complete list of books available from Penguin in Australia, please write to the *Marketing Department, Penguin Books Australia Ltd, P.O. Box 257, Ringwood, Victoria 3134*

In New Zealand: For a complete list of books available from Penguin in New Zealand, please write to the *Marketing Department, Penguin Books (NZ) Ltd, Private Bag, Takapuna, Auckland 9*

In India: For a complete list of books available from Penguin, please write to *Penguin Overseas Ltd, 706 Eros Apartments, 56 Nehru Place, New Delhi, 110019*

In Holland: For a complete list of books available from Penguin in Holland, please write to *Penguin Books Nederland B.V., Postbus 195, NL–1380AD Weesp, Netherlands*

In Germany: For a complete list of books available from Penguin, please write to *Penguin Books Ltd, Friedrichstrasse 10 – 12, D–6000 Frankfurt Main 1, Federal Republic of Germany*

In Spain: For a complete list of books available from Penguin in Spain, please write to *Longman Penguin España, Calle San Nicolas 15, E–28013 Madrid, Spain*

A CHOICE OF PENGUINS AND PELICANS

The French Revolution   Christopher Hibbert

'One of the best accounts of the Revolution that I know . . . Mr Hibbert is outstanding' – J. H. Plumb in the *Sunday Telegraph*

The Germans   Gordon A. Craig

An intimate study of a complex and fascinating nation by 'one of the ablest and most distinguished American historians of modern Germany' – Hugh Trevor-Roper

Ireland: A Positive Proposal   Kevin Boyle and Tom Hadden

A timely and realistic book on Northern Ireland which explains the historical context – and offers a practical and coherent set of proposals which could actually work.

A History of Venice   John Julius Norwich

'Lord Norwich has loved and understood Venice as well as any other Englishman has ever done' – Peter Levi in the *Sunday Times*

Montaillou: Cathars and Catholics in a French Village 1294–1324
Emmanuel Le Roy Ladurie

'A classic adventure in eavesdropping across time' – Michael Ratcliffe in *The Times*

Star Wars   E. P. Thompson and others

Is Star Wars a serious defence strategy or just a science fiction fantasy? This major book sets out all the arguments and makes an unanswerable case *against* Star Wars.